USING RAPIDFILE™

USING RAPIDFILE™

Edward Jones

Osborne **McGraw-Hill**
Berkeley, California

Osborne **McGraw-Hill**
2600 Tenth Street
Berkeley, California 94710
U.S.A.

For information on translations and book distributors outside of the U.S.A., please write to Osborne **McGraw-Hill** at the above address.
A complete list of trademarks appears on page 399.

Using RapidFile™

1234567890 DODO 89876

ISBN 0-07-881014-0

To Dad

Contents

Acknowledgments

This book evolved with the help of a number of people whom I would like to thank. At Osborne/McGraw-Hill, I want to thank Cynthia Hudson, who conceived of the project and contributed greatly to its development; also Nancy Carlston and Lindy Michel, whose careful editing resulted in a first-class product. At Ashton-Tate, a big note of thanks to Catherine Mone, whose technical assistance was invaluable, and additional thanks to Steve Allin and Michael Arrigo for helpful comments and direction. I would also like to thank Jan Statler at Wilmer, Cutler & Pickering, for providing an objective user's view.

Introduction

Welcome to the world of RapidFile, a database manager for the IBM PC and IBM compatibles. Software of this nature had been around for some time prior to the introduction of RapidFile; even before personal computers were available, mainframe computers offered database managers under a plethora of strange-sounding names. When the task of filing and managing information moved over to personal computers, one not-so-pleasant characteristic of mainframes moved along with the task: user unfriendliness. Like database managers for mainframes, database managers for PCs required the use of obscure commands resembling a foreign language. Ashton-Tate's dBASE II was the most popular package of this type during the early days of PCs. PC users needed the power of a sophisticated database manager, so thousands of users put up with the odd language to handle necessary tasks. Later releases of dBASE and similar software from competing firms have done much toward making PC-based database management a less arduous task. But many PC users do not need the complexity of a relational database manager; they desire power and ease of use in a single software package. It is for those PC users that RapidFile exists, and it is for those users that this book was written.

What is in this text? Chapter 1 provides an introduction to RapidFile by displaying ways in which the product can be used and by describing the data-sharing capabilities of the product. Chapter 2 provides hints on the importance of database design and offers a brief introduction to the concepts used in all computer databases.

Coverage of specific use of RapidFile begins in Chapter 3, which details how to install and start the program, how to create a database, and how to add records to a database. Chapter 4 further explores the concepts of managing your data in RapidFile by detailing how you can find desired data, select only records that meet a specified criteria, sort files in different orders, remove unwanted records, and change the appearance of records.Chapter 5 covers the use of layouts, a powerful RapidFile feature that permits the saving and recall of file characteristics (such as the order in which a file is sorted, the way records are displayed, and any unique record selection criteria).

The primary objective of any database manager is to provide useful reports based on the data in the database. Chapter 6 delves into this topic in detail by covering RapidFile's Quick Report and label-generating features and by showing how selective data and numeric totals and subtotals can be included in a report.

Chapter 7 covers the area of file management by showing how the design of a database can be modified and how to perform helpful DOS functions—such as erasing and renaming files and using DOS commands directly—from within RapidFile. Chapter 8 introduces the memo writer, RapidFile's integrated word processing program. The chapter shows how the memo writer can be used to edit and print documents and to build form letters that automatically include data from a database file.

Chapter 9 continues the coverage of RapidFile's report-generating capability by showing how to design and use Custom Reports. Thischapter also details the use of Report fields, a way of providing various types of calculated data within a report. Chapter 10 covers the use of numbers that must be calculated within fields and the use of numbers within numeric expressions.

Chapter 11 provides instruction on more advanced uses of the memo writer, including the search-and-replace options, the use of headers and footers, and the use of varied printing options to change the appearance of your documents.

In a business world crowded with software packages, the ability to transfer data can be critical. This text provides extensive treatment of this area—Chapters 12 and 13 discuss data transfer between Lotus 1-2-3 or Symphony and RapidFile. These chapters go farther than simply explaining how to transfer data from one package to the other; they also provide important hints on how to best prepare your files to minimize cleanup once the data has been transferred.

Chapter 14 covers data transfer between RapidFile and dBASE II, dBASE III, or dBASE III PLUS. This chapter also provides important hints about dealing with limitations of such transfers, including limitations imposed by dBASE II's capabilities and dealing with memo fields within dBASE III or dBASE III PLUS. Chapter 15 details how data can be exchanged with pfs:FILE and its near-twin, IBM Filing Assistant. As in prior chapters on data exchange, hints help the reader to minimize the limitations of pfs:FILE data which is used within RapidFile. Chapter 16 concludes coverage of data-sharing by showing how to exchange data between RapidFile and other software, such as R:Base 5000, PC-File III, and most word processors.

Chapter 17 highlights how to use RapidFile's built-in macro capability to automate often used procedures. Chapter 18 provides examples of how RapidFile can be used to manage typical applications, such as sales or personnel management. Chapter 19 details how you can customize RapidFile so that various settings within the program—such as margins, menu styles, and screen colors—are to your liking.

The style of the text encourages learning by doing, so you will get the best results if you have your PC and your copy of RapidFile and follow along with the exercises. Ample illustrations have been provided, so if you do not have a PC and Rapid-

File, you can still become familiar with RapidFile's use just by reading. Try the exercises, and try building your own applications with RapidFile. After putting RapidFile to work, you will probably find the task of database management to be simple, which is what computer owners have wanted all along.

Introduction to RapidFile

Chapter 1

RapidFile is a database manager for use with the IBM PC, XT, AT, and other computers compatible with these systems. RapidFile provides database file management, report capabilities, word processing, and form-letter capabilities within a single package. RapidFile uses a series of menus to provide simple, direct access to various features of the program.

You can use RapidFile to create database files containing necessary categories (fields), and you can display information in the format that best suits your needs by using the forms-design capabilities of RapidFile. Selected information can be printed in a number of ways. Figure 1-1 shows just one example. RapidFile also contains memo writer, a powerful word processor that can be used alone or with RapidFile to store large amounts of textual information. RapidFile's abilities to process words and to examine and show information in different ways make it one of the most flexible database managers in its class.

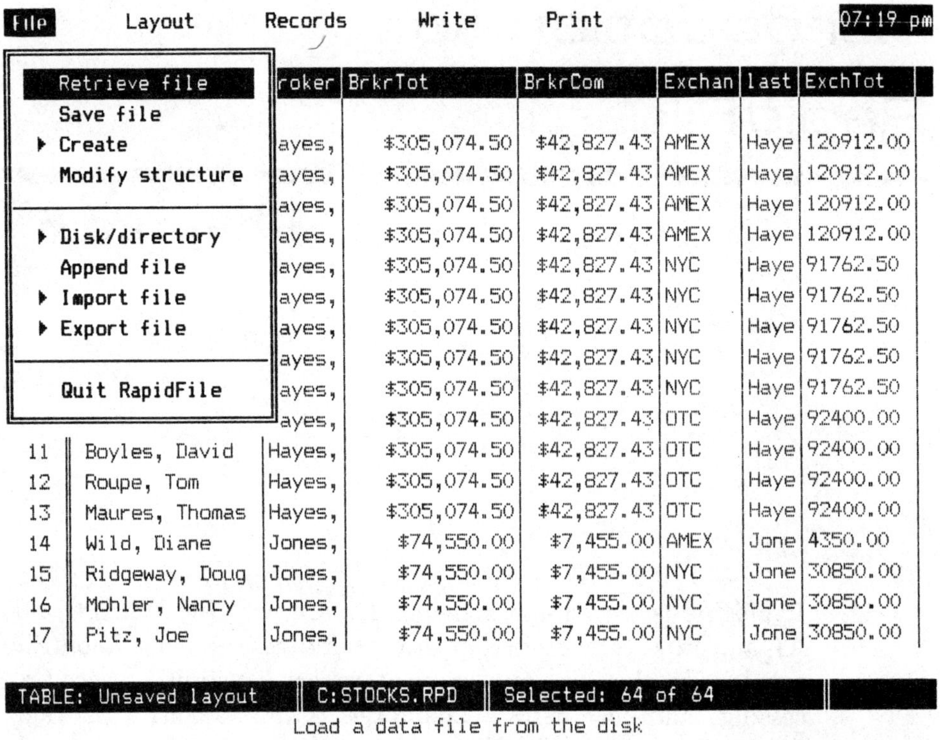

Figure 1-1. RapidFile in use

WHAT IS A DATABASE?

Although the term *database management* is usually used in reference to computers, it also applies to any system in which information is catalogued, stored, and used. At the center of any information management system is a *database,* which is collection of related information grouped as a single item. Figure 1-2 is a database. Metal filing cabinets with customer records, a card file of names and phone numbers, and a notebook with a penciled listing of a store inventory are all databases. The physical objects—the filing cabinet and the notebook, for example—are not databases; the way information is organized makes a database. Objects like cabinets and notebooks only aid in organizing information. RapidFile is one such aid.

Information in a database is usually organized and stored in a table by rows and columns. Figure 1-2, for example, is a mailing list in database form. Each row contains a name, an address, a phone number, and a customer number. Each row is related to the others because they all contain the same types of information. Because the mailing list is a collection of information arranged in a specific order—a column of names, a column of addresses, a column of customer numbers—it is a database.

Name	Address	City	State	ZIP	Phone No.	Cust. No.
J. Billings	2323 State St.	Bertram	CA	91113	234-8980	0005
R. Foster	Rt. 1 Box 52	Frink	CA	93336	245-4312	0001
L. Miller	P.O. Box 345	Dagget	CA	94567	484-9966	0002
B. O'Neill	21 Way St. Apt. C	Hotlum	CA	92346	555-1032	0004
C. Roberts	1914 19th St.	Bodie	CA	97665	525-4494	0006
A. Wilson	27 Haven Way	Weed	CA	90004	566-7823	0003

Figure 1-2. A simple database

Rows in a database file are called *records*, and columns are called *fields*. Figure 1-3 illustrates this idea with a comparison of a database file to an address filing system kept on 3×5 file cards.

Each card in the box is a single record, and each category of information on a card is a field. Fields can contain any type of information that can be categorized. In the card box each record contains six fields: name, address, city, state, ZIP code, and phone number. Since every card in the box contains the same type of information, the information in the card box is a database file. Figure 1-4 identifies a record and a field in the mailing list database.

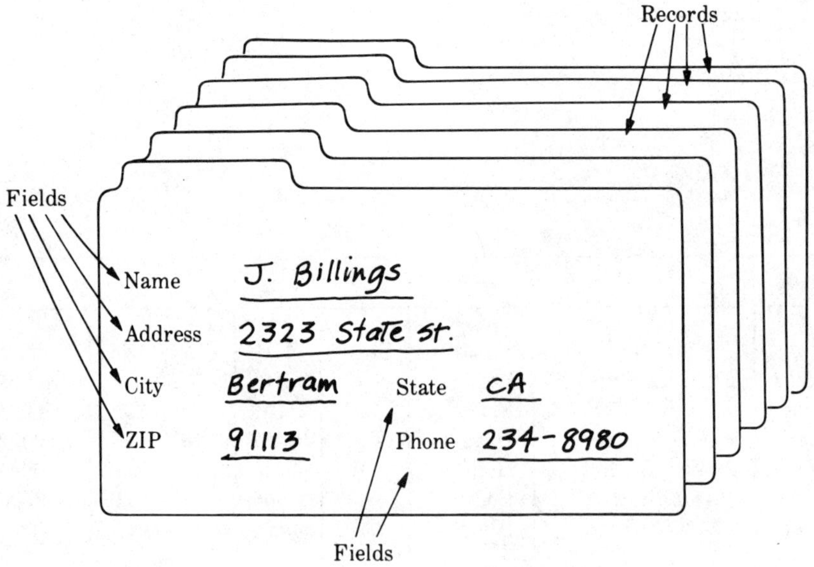

Figure 1-3. Each card represents a record; information is separated into fields.

Field

Name	Address	City	State	ZIP	Phone No.	Cust. No.
J. Billings	2323 State St.	Bertram	CA	91113	234-8980	0005
R. Foster	Rt. 1 Box 52	Frink	CA	93336	245-4312	0001
L. Miller	P.O. Box 345	Dagget	CA	94567	484-9966	0002
B. O'Neill	21 Way St. Apt. C	Hotlum	CA	92346	555-1032	0004
C. Roberts	1914 19th St.	Bodie	CA	97665	525-4494	0006
A. Wilson	27 Haven Way	Weed	CA	90004	566-7823	0003

Record

Figure 1-4. A record and a field of a database

USING A DATABASE

In theory any database is arranged in such a way that information is easy to find. In Figure 1-4, for example, names are arranged alphabetically. If you want to find the phone number of a customer, simply locate the name and read across to the corresponding phone number.

You are already interested in how a computerized filing system (a database) can make information storage and retrieval more efficient than a traditional filing system, and you will find that RapidFile offers many advantages. A telephone book, for example, is fine for finding a specific person's telephone number. But if all you have is the address and not the name of the person who lives there, the telephone directory becomes almost useless for finding that person's telephone number.

A similar problem plagues conventional office filing systems. If the information is organized by name and you want to find all the clients located in a particular area, you could be in for a tedious search. In addition, organizing massive amounts of information into written directories and filing cabinets could consume a great deal of space. A manual database can also be difficult to modify. For example, adding a new phone number to the listing may mean rearranging the list. If the phone company were to assign a new area code, someone would have to search for all phone numbers having the old area code and replace it with the new one.

When a database is teamed with a computer, many of these problems are eliminated. A computerized database is fast—finding a phone number from among a thousand entries or putting the file in alphabetical order takes just a short time with RapidFile. A computerized database is compact—a database with up to a thousand records can be stored on a single floppy disk. A computerized database is flexible—it has the ability to examine information from a number of angles, so you could, for example, search for a phone number by name or by address.

Tasks that would be time-consuming to accomplish manually are more practical with the aid of a computer. In principle a database in a computer is not different from a database recorded on paper and filed in cabinets. But a computer does the tedious work of maintaining and accessing a database, and it does it quickly. A computerized database that can do all of this is known as a database management system, or *DBMS* for short.

HOW RAPIDFILE MEASURES UP

Database managers for personal computers fall into two main categories: *file managers* and *relational database managers.* File managers are designed to work with one file at a time and tend to be easy to use. RapidFile falls into the file manager category. Other products classified as file managers include pfs:FILE by Software Publishing, PC-File III by ButtonWare, Microsoft File by Microsoft, and Reflex by Borland International. Relational database managers are designed to work with multiple files simultaneously and are usually more difficult to master than the file managers. Products in this category include Ashton-Tate's dBASE III PLUS and R:base 5000 by Microrim.

As a product, RapidFile appeals to PC users who must manage straightforward files of information: customer and client lists, lists of sales, inventory information, and so on. Unlike many popular file managers currently on the market, RapidFile is a very visual package, which makes it easier to learn to use effectively. The learning curve is further reduced with aids like the disk-based tutorial provided with the package and by the product's design, which makes heavy use of detailed menus.

One major advantage offered by RapidFile is hinted at in the name of the product. RapidFile is fast in retrieving and sorting your data. You can sort files in any desired order and on a combination of fields. You can select groups of records to work with, filtering from view all records that do not meet certain conditions. Because RapidFile has such a variety of capabilities, you can use the product in many different ways. Some of those ways are described in the following sections.

As an Enhancement to Spreadsheet Programs

RapidFile can exchange data directly with both versions of Lotus 1-2-3. Many other spreadsheets are file-compatible with 1-2-3 Version 1.1, and such spreadsheets can also be used with RapidFile. Simple database management can be done with 1-2-3 and Symphony, another Lotus product. However, both these packages are limited in terms of the size of database they can handle. Because RapidFile can store up to 65,000 records, you can use it to manage a database that grows too cumbersome to keep in a spreadsheet. You can select a specific group of records in a large RapidFile database, easily copy those records in 1-2-3 file format, and use those records in the spreadsheet to take advantage of the math capabilities of 1-2-3 (see Figure 1-5).

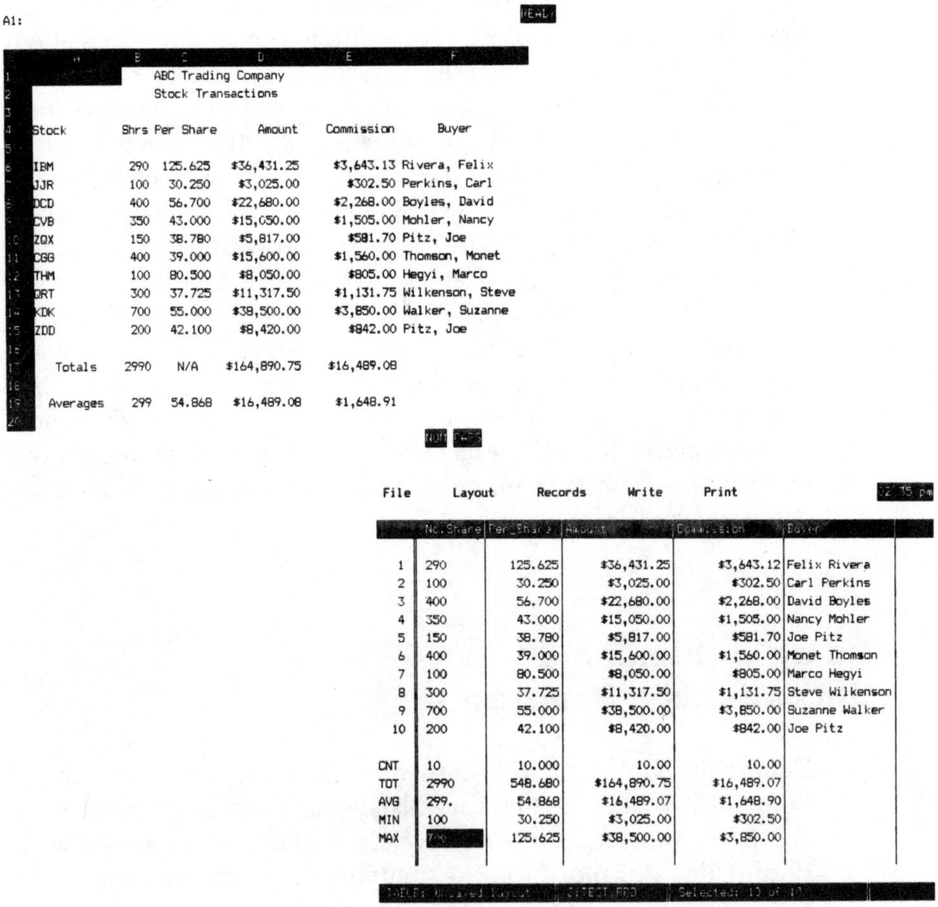

A1: READY

ABC Trading Company
Stock Transactions

Stock	Shrs	Per Share	Amount	Commission	Buyer
IBM	290	125.625	$36,431.25	$3,643.13	Rivera, Felix
JJR	100	30.250	$3,025.00	$302.50	Perkins, Carl
DCD	400	56.700	$22,680.00	$2,268.00	Boyles, David
CVB	350	43.000	$15,050.00	$1,505.00	Mohler, Nancy
ZQX	150	38.780	$5,817.00	$581.70	Pitz, Joe
CGG	400	39.000	$15,600.00	$1,560.00	Thomson, Monet
THM	100	80.500	$8,050.00	$805.00	Hegyi, Marco
QRT	300	37.725	$11,317.50	$1,131.75	Wilkenson, Steve
KDK	700	55.000	$38,500.00	$3,850.00	Walker, Suzanne
ZDD	200	42.100	$8,420.00	$842.00	Pitz, Joe
Totals	2990	N/A	$164,890.75	$16,489.08	
Averages	299	54.868	$16,489.08	$1,648.91	

File Layout Records Write Print

	No.Share	Per_Share	Amount	Commission	Buyer
1	290	125.625	$36,431.25	$3,643.12	Felix Rivera
2	100	30.250	$3,025.00	$302.50	Carl Perkins
3	400	56.700	$22,680.00	$2,268.00	David Boyles
4	350	43.000	$15,050.00	$1,505.00	Nancy Mohler
5	150	38.780	$5,817.00	$581.70	Joe Pitz
6	400	39.000	$15,600.00	$1,560.00	Monet Thomson
7	100	80.500	$8,050.00	$805.00	Marco Hegyi
8	300	37.725	$11,317.50	$1,131.75	Steve Wilkenson
9	700	55.000	$38,500.00	$3,850.00	Suzanne Walker
10	200	42.100	$8,420.00	$842.00	Joe Pitz
CNT	10	10.000	10.00	10.00	
TOT	2990	548.680	$164,890.75	$16,489.07	
AVG	299.	54.868	$16,489.07	$1,648.90	
MIN	100	30.250	$3,025.00	$302.50	
MAX	700	125.625	$38,500.00	$3,850.00	

Figure 1-5. Sharing data with 1-2-3 by Lotus

As a Replacement for a Word Processor with Merge Features

Many word processors have a mailing list function that allows you to create two documents: one with a list of names, addresses, and other pertinent information; and the other with a form letter (boilerplate). The word processor merges the two documents, creating a personalized letter for each name and address in the file containing the list of names. WordStar, with its MailMerge option, is probably the best-known product of this type. Microsoft Word, MultiMate, and WordPerfect also provide this capability. But in all cases you are limited to using the list of names as little more than a word processing document. With most word processors you cannot, for example, sort the names. And you cannot tell your word processor to display only last names between A and E with ZIP codes of 90000 or greater. RapidFile can perform such tasks and provide complete form-letter capability (see Figure 1-6).

As a File Manager

RapidFile offers enhancements over similar products. If you are currently using (or considering) a file manager like pfs:FILE, you will find RapidFile's ability to examine data through various standard and customized layouts to be a plus. RapidFile offers six standard ways to examine data; pfs:FILE offers two. One of the six layouts, shown in Figure 1-7, highlights RapidFile's ability to show data in Table (tabular) and Form layouts at the same time. RapidFile can also handle twice the number of records that pfs:FILE or Reflex can handle. As of this writing, the only file manager commonly available that offers similar capabilities for viewing a database in different ways is

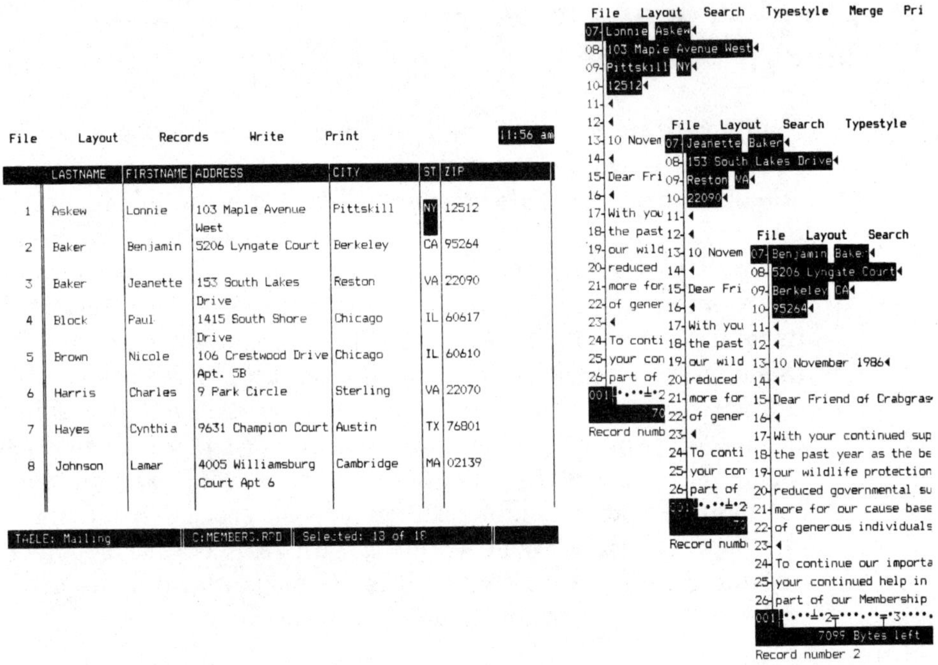

Figure 1-6. Merging database records with form letters

Reflex. Reflex is limited, however, in terms of the maximum number of records it can handle. (The theoretical maximum for Reflex is around 32,000, but in practice the maximum is

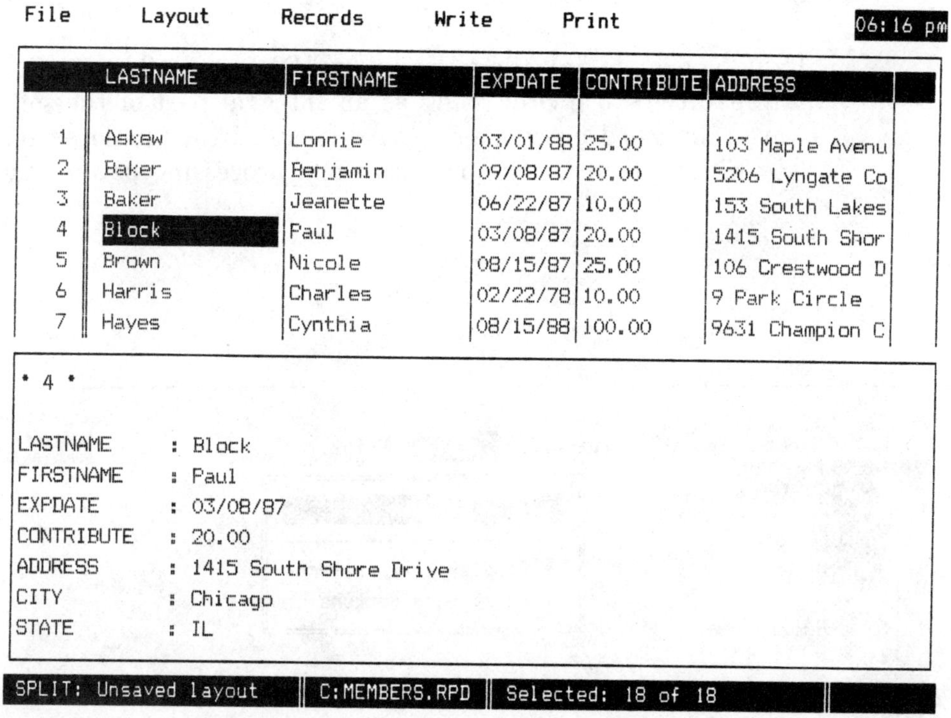

Figure 1-7. Split Table/Form view of a RapidFile database

usually lower and varies with the amount of RAM present in the computer.) RapidFile uses virtual memory techniques to store large files on disk, so you can manage much larger databases than would be possible with Reflex.

As a Word Processor

RapidFile is the first file manager for IBM compatibles to offer full-featured word processing as an integral part of the software. The word processing feature is called the memo writer (see Figure 1-8), and it provides word processing power that

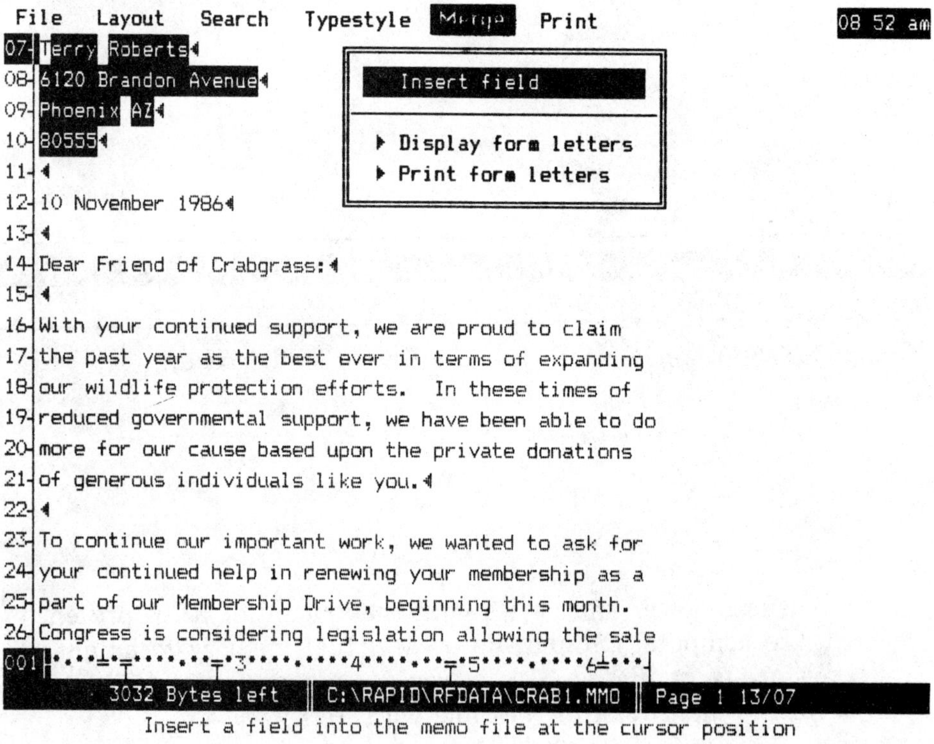

Figure 1-8. An example of memo writer

matches or exceeds that of most low-end word processors. Word processing features provided by the memo writer include full control of margins and tabs; centering and left and right justification; page numbers; headers and footers; search and replace; and a variety of type styles and character options, including bold, italic, superscript, and subscript. The memo writer can be loaded alone or with the file manager portion of RapidFile. The maximum size of a memo writer document is 64K (K equals 1000 bytes, about 32 pages of single-spaced text).

Some combinations of word processors and file managers can duplicate the performance of RapidFile when purchased together. However, transfer of data between such products is often cumbersome. And you will usually pay more for the word processing software and the file manager together than you would pay for RapidFile.

THE LIMITATIONS OF RAPIDFILE

Although RapidFile is an excellent package, it does have its limits (as all software packages do). The math capabilities are not as powerful as those found in low-end spreadsheets. RapidFile also lacks the capability to display data in graphic form, such as in a bar or pie chart. These limitations can be overcome by using RapidFile along with 1-2-3 or with another spreadsheet that is file-compatible with 1-2-3, such as Twin by Mosaic Software or VP Planner by Paperback Software.

RapidFile also lacks the ability to handle multiple files simultaneously, a limitation shared by all file managers. Most users of relational database managers rarely use the relational capabilities of such products in their applications. If your application truly requires the power of a relational database, you should probably be looking at a product like dBASE III PLUS. In addition, RapidFile lacks a built-in programming language like that offered by dBASE III PLUS.

SYSTEM REQUIREMENTS

To use RapidFile, you will need a 16-bit microcomputer using PC-DOS—the IBM PC, XT, or AT; the COMPAQ Portable or Deskpro; a model in the Tandy 1000, 2000, or 3000 series; an Epson computer; a Leading Edge computer; or an AT&T PC. Any microcomputer that is fully software-compatible with the IBM PC should be able to use RapidFile. Your computer must have a minimum of 256K of memory. You must be using DOS version 2.0 or a newer version. Your system should have two floppy-disk drives or one floppy- and one hard-disk drive. (Because of the size of the files on the RapidFile System disk and Help disk, it is impractical to use RapidFile on a system with only one floppy-disk drive.) RapidFile can be used with a monochrome or color monitor and with any printer that can print at least 80 columns of text.

SPECIFICATIONS

Specifications for the file manager include the following:

Maximum database size:	16 megabytes
Maximum number of records:	65,000
Maximum record size:	8000 characters
Maximum field size:	254 characters (larger with memo writer)
Maximum fields per record:	250
Maximum sort keys:	15
Maximum matching conditions:	7

Specifications for the memo writer include the following:

Maximum file size:	64,000 characters
Minimum document width:	20 characters
Maximum document width:	255 characters
Maximum page length:	255 lines
Maximum fields in merge:	255
Maximum header/footer size:	80 characters
Maximum search/replace string size:	24 characters
Maximum printed copies per document:	999

Database Design

Chapter 2

At this point you're probably eager to load RapidFile into your computer and begin using the program. There's an excellent reason for not doing that just yet. Planning is vital to effective database management. Database design requires that you think about how the data should be stored and how you and others will ask for data from the database file. During this process your problem (which RapidFile was purchased to help solve) will be outlined on paper. Just as you would not haphazardly toss files into a filing cabinet without designing some type of filing system, you cannot place information into a database file without first designing the database. As you do so, you must define the kinds of information that should be stored in the database.

ABOUT DATA AND ATTRIBUTES

Data and *attributes* are two important terms in database design. Data is the information that goes into your database. Attributes are the types of data that make up the database. A person's last name is data. An attribute is another name for a field, so an entire group of names is considered to be an attribute. Names, phone numbers, customer numbers, descriptions, locations, and stock numbers are common attributes that your database file might contain.

In addition to thinking about what kinds of information will go into the database, you must give careful consideration to the ways in which information will come out of the database. Information comes from a database in the form of a *report.* When you ask the computer for a list of all homes in the area priced between $100,000 and $150,000 or for a list of employees earning less than $15 per hour, you are asking for a report. When you ask for John Smith's address, you are also asking for a report. A report is a summary of information. Whether the computer displays a few lines on the screen or hundreds of lines on a stack of paper, it is providing a report based on the data contained within the database file.

To practice the techniques of database design, you will design a database using a hypothetical example. National Friends of Crabgrass is a Washington-based nonprofit association. Like many Washington-based associations, Friends of Crabgrass depends on contributions from the public to stay in existence. The salaries of the staff, the rent, the phone and utility bills, and the payments on that PC with 256K RAM and the letter-quality printer are all paid with contributions from the 3000-plus members of the association. The association solicits different types of members (student, regular, charter, and lifetime), and the membership type is, for the most part, based on the generosity of the person contributing to the cause. Until the purchase of the PC, the association was tracking member names, addresses, and contributions with a bulky (and often out-of-date) 3 × 5 card system. A small surplus in the budget allowed the association to purchase the PC to better handle the member list. The association wants to track member address changes and contributions as well as have the ability to solicit funds through mass mailings to members.

Being a small, nonprofit group, Friends of Crabgrass did not have hundreds of dollars to pay a PC consultant to come in and write a fancy program using a high-priced database manager. Instead, the staff decided to find a program that all staff members could use without special training or a degree in computer science, and RapidFile seemed to fit the bill. Successive chapters of this text will show how the staff at Friends of Crabgrass successfully used RapidFile to manage information. By following these examples, you will learn how to put RapidFile to work for you.

STEPS IN DATABASE DESIGN

Designing a database file, whether it is for the National Friends of Crabgrass or for your own purposes, involves two major steps:

1. Data definition (an analysis of existing data)
2. Data refinement (refining necessary data).

Data Definition

During the first phase, data definition, you must make a list on a piece of paper of all the important attributes involved in your application. To do this, you must examine your needs in detail to determine exactly what kinds of information must be stored in the database.

In discussing the design for the database, the staff at Friends of Crabgrass determined the need to store and access specific information about each member: the name of the member, the date that the member's membership expires, the size of the last contribution, the address of the member, and the type of membership. The resulting list of attributes is shown in Figure 2-1.

An important point to remember is that during this phase of database design you should list all the possible attributes of your database. You may list more attributes than are actually needed by your particular application, but this is not a problem; you will eliminate unnecessary attributes during the data refinement stage.

1. Member name
2. Membership expiration date
3. Amount of last contribution
4. Member address
5. Type of membership

Figure 2-1. Initial list of attributes

Data Refinement

During this phase you will refine the list of attributes on your initial list so that the attributes form an accurate description of the types of data that will be needed in the database. At this stage it is vital to include suggestions from as many other users of the database as possible. The people who use the database are likely to know what kinds of information they will need to get from it.

When the staff of Friends of Crabgrass took a close look at their initial list of attributes, they realized that most of the refinements were obvious. The address attribute, for example, needed to be divided into street address, city, state, and ZIP code. In your own case some refinements may quickly become evident, and others may not be as evident. Going over your written list of attributes will help make necessary refinements more obvious. For example, when the staff of Friends of Crabgrass examined the initial attribute list, they realized that the index card system of members contained multiple occurrences of members with the same last name. To avoid confusion, the name attribute was further divided into last name and first name. Figure 2-2 shows the refined list of attributes.

During the design phases it is important that potential users be consulted to determine what kinds of information they will expect the database to supply. Just what kinds of reports will they want from the database? What kinds of queries will users make? Asking these types of questions should help you determine what is important and what is unimportant in terms of your database.

You may have noticed that throughout the entire process, the specific data—such as members' names, addresses, and so forth—has not been discussed. It is unnecessary to identify any specific data at this point; only the attributes need to be defined.

1. Member last name
2. Member first name
3. Membership expiration date
4. Amount of last contribution
5. Street address
6. City
7. State
8. ZIP Code
9. Type of membership

Figure 2-2. Refined list of attributes

Keep in mind that even after the database design phases, the design of the database file is not graven in stone. Changes to the design of a database file can be made later if necessary. But if you follow this systematic approach to database design for your specific application, the chances are better that you won't create a database that fails to provide the information you need, and you will avoid extensive redesign.

RapidFile allows you to change the design of a file at any time, although such changes are often inconvenient to make once the database is designed. Here is an example: If you were to use RapidFile to create a database to handle a customer mailing list, you might include attributes for names, addresses, cities, states, and ZIP codes. At first glance this might seem sufficient. You could then begin entering customer information into the database and gradually build a sizable mailing list. But if your company later decides to begin telemarketing using the same mailing list, you may suddenly realize that you have not included an attribute for telephone numbers. Using RapidFile you easily could change the design to include the needed attribute. But you would still face the possibly mammoth task of adding a telephone number for every name. If this information had been added as you developed the mailing list, you would not face the inconvenience of having to enter the phone numbers as a separate operation. Careful planning and time spent during the database design process can help avoid such pitfalls.

Getting Started

Chapter 3

RapidFile consists of four disks and documentation. The disks are the System disk, the Help disk, the Tutorial disk, and the Sample Data/Utility disk. Before using RapidFile, make backup copies of all four—the disks are not copy-protected, so you can do so. Use the copies as working copies, and store the original RapidFile disks in a safe place. If a copy is damaged or erased, you can make a replacement easily.

Before making a backup copy of the RapidFile System disk, you must run an identification procedure, to prepare the disk for use. Until the identification procedure is completed, the program on the RapidFile System disk cannot be used. Start your computer in the normal manner, and if you are using a hard disk, switch to drive A (the DOS prompt should be on your screen).

Jot down the serial number listed on your RapidFile System disk, then insert the System disk in drive A. Type the following:

```
ID
```

and press RETURN. You will see a screen similar to the one shown in Figure 3-1.

```
═══════════════ RapidFile Version 1.0 ═══════════════

Before starting RapidFile, you must enter information that
identifies you as the licensee.  This permanent information
will be redisplayed every time you start RapidFile.

For each of the three items below, type your entry and press ↵

    User Name:              _________________________

    Company Name:           _________________________

    Your Serial Number:     __________
     The serial number is on the System Disk #1 label.

Review the information you've entered.  If you want to make any
changes, press Esc to start over.  If you're satisfied with your
entries, reinsert System Disk #1 in drive A: and press ↵ to
record them permanently.
```

Figure 3-1. The Identification screen

The Identification screen requests you to enter your name, the name of your company (if any), and the serial number of your RapidFile package. Once entered, this information will be stored in the program, and will be displayed each time you begin using RapidFile.

Fill in each blank line with the appropriate information, pressing RETURN as each is completed. If you don't want to enter your own or your company's name, type any two letters on that line. If you make an error, you can press ESC to start over.

Once you have entered all the information requested, a prompt will appear at the bottom of the screen: **Check over your responses. Would you like to re-edit them? (Y/N)** If no changes are needed, enter N for "No." You will be prompted to check that the System disk is in drive A. With the disk still in drive A, press any key, and the Identification program will store the registration information in your RapidFile program. When the process is complete, the DOS prompt will reappear, and you can proceed to make backup copies of your disks.

COPYING RAPIDFILE

To create a copy of the RapidFile disks using a computer with two floppy-disk drives, use the operating system as follows:

1. Format five floppy disks with the operating system's FORMAT command. The extra disk will be used as a working disk to store the files you create with RapidFile. (If you are using a hard disk, an extra disk is unnecessary.)
2. Use the COPY or DISKCOPY command to copy all the files on the System disk, Help disk, Tutorial disk, and Sample Data/Utility disk from the original to a backup disk. Do this by placing the original RapidFile disk in drive A and the formatted, blank disk in drive B and entering

   COPY A:*.* B:
3. Label the disks appropriately, and store the original RapidFile disks in a separate place.

If you are using an IBM PC XT, an IBM PC AT, or an IBM compatible equipped with a hard disk, copy all the files from the RapidFile disks onto your hard disk. An installation program provided on the RapidFile System disk will automatically create individual subdirectories for storage of the Rapid-

File programs and the data files you will create. Make sure that you are using drive A by entering

A:

Press RETURN, place the RapidFile System disk in drive A, and—assuming that your hard disk is drive C—enter

INSTALL C:

If your hard disk is a drive letter other than C, use that letter in place of the letter C.

A message indicating that RapidFile will be copied onto your hard disk will appear. Press any key and the copying process will begin. After the files have been copied from the System disk, you will be prompted to insert the Help disk, and then the Sample Data/Utility disk. Once all the files have been copied onto your hard disk by the Install program, you can use RapidFile without loading the System disk.

MAKING THE RAPIDFILE SYSTEM DISK SELF-BOOTING

If you are using a floppy disk-based system, you can make the RapidFile System disk self-booting (it will then have the ability to start your computer). To do this, you must add the operating system (DOS) to the disk. Perform the following steps:

1. Place the DOS disk in drive A and turn the power switch of your computer to On.
2. After DOS has loaded remove the DOS disk and place the original RapidFile System disk in drive A.
3. From the DOS prompt type

   INSTALL A:

   and press RETURN

4. Follow the instructions on the RapidFile DOS Installation screen, and then press any key to continue. Follow the instructions on the second screen of installation information, and then press any key.
5. Now that DOS is installed on your System disk, remove the System disk from drive A and insert the Help disk.

Your System disk can now be used to start your computer. Use the DOS command DISKCOPY (not the COPY command) to copy the contents of the original System disk and Help disk to the backup System disk and Help disk. By using DISKCOPY instead of COPY, you will make the backup copy of the System disk self-booting. To do this, perform the following steps:

1. Place your DOS disk in drive A.

2. From the DOS prompt enter

   DISKCOPY A: B:

   and press RETURN.

3. When the PC prompts you to insert the source and destination disks, remove the DOS disk from drive A. Insert the original System disk in drive A, and insert the backup copy System disk in drive B. Then press any key to start the copying process.

4. When the prompt **Copy another?** appears, enter Y. Insert the original Help disk in drive A, and insert the backup copy Help disk in drive B. Then press any key to start the copying process.

When the DOS prompt returns, you can put away the original RapidFile disks. The backup copy can now be used to start your computer. See your DOS manual, if necessary, for more details on the use of the COPY and DISKCOPY commands.

LOADING RAPIDFILE

To begin using RapidFile, insert your copy of the System disk in drive A (hard-disk users can ignore this step). If you are using a hard-disk subdirectory, switch to that subdirectory with the DOS CD\ command. From the DOS prompt enter the command

RF

After you have started RapidFile, you will see a sign-on notice and a copyright message. At the bottom of the message, you will see this: **Press RETURN to assent to the License Agreement and begin.**

Press RETURN, and the message will be replaced by the Welcome screen, which instructs the users of two floppy-disk drives to remove the System disk and insert the Help disk. (If you are using a hard disk, this message does not appear because Help is already available.) After inserting the Help disk, press RETURN and the File menu for RapidFile will appear (see Figure 3-2).

Much of the ease of use RapidFile offers stems from the menus the program provides. Five menus are available when RapidFile is loaded. They are the File menu, Layout menu, Records menu, Write menu, and Print menu. Using the various menus, you can save and retrieve files, create new files, select, edit, and delete records, write memos and form letters, and print reports.

Only one of the five menus can be opened at one time. After you load RapidFile the File menu is open. When a menu is open, the appropriate menu choices appear in a rectangular box called a pull-down menu.

At the bottom of the screen is the message **Load a data file from the disk.** This message is an explanation of the option that is currently highlighted within the File menu. The explanations will change as different options are chosen.

Press the DOWN ARROW key once. You will see the highlighted bar move to the "Save file" option of the File menu. Continue

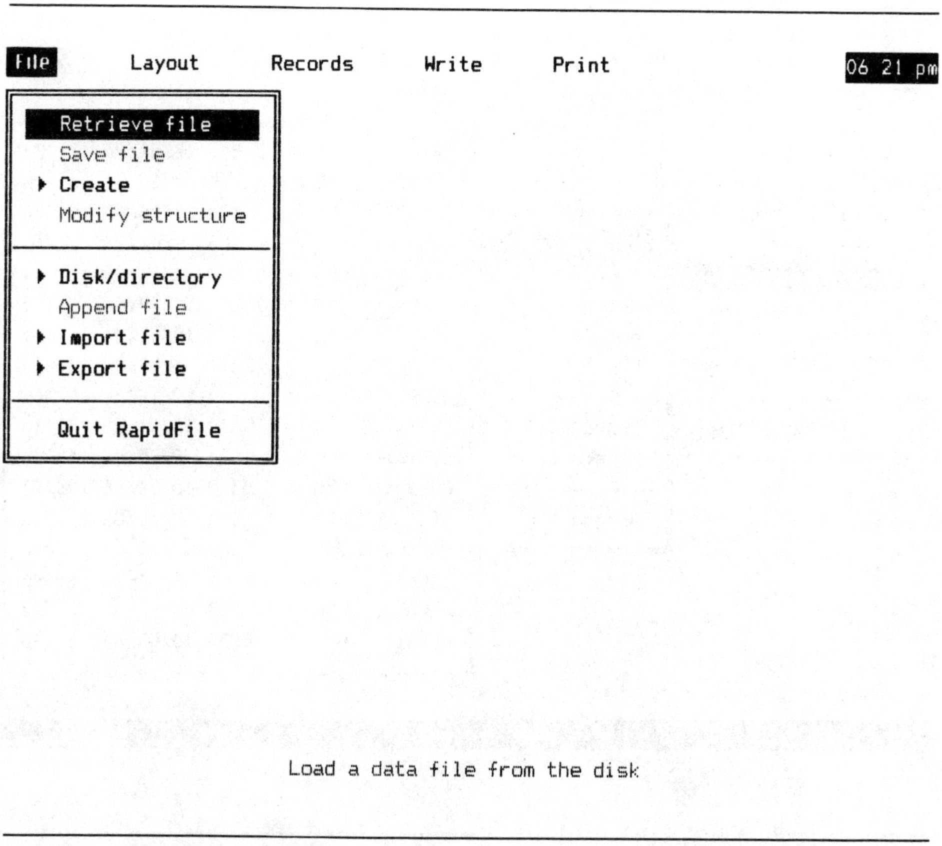

Figure 3-2. The File menu

pressing the DOWN ARROW, and note that the highlight can be moved to any menu option. Pressing RETURN selects the menu option that is highlighted.

An alternate (and faster) way to select any menu option is to press the first letter of the option. As an example, with the File menu still open, press D (for "Disk/directory"). The "Disk/directory" option will be selected, and a directory of all files on the disk will appear (see Figure 3-3).

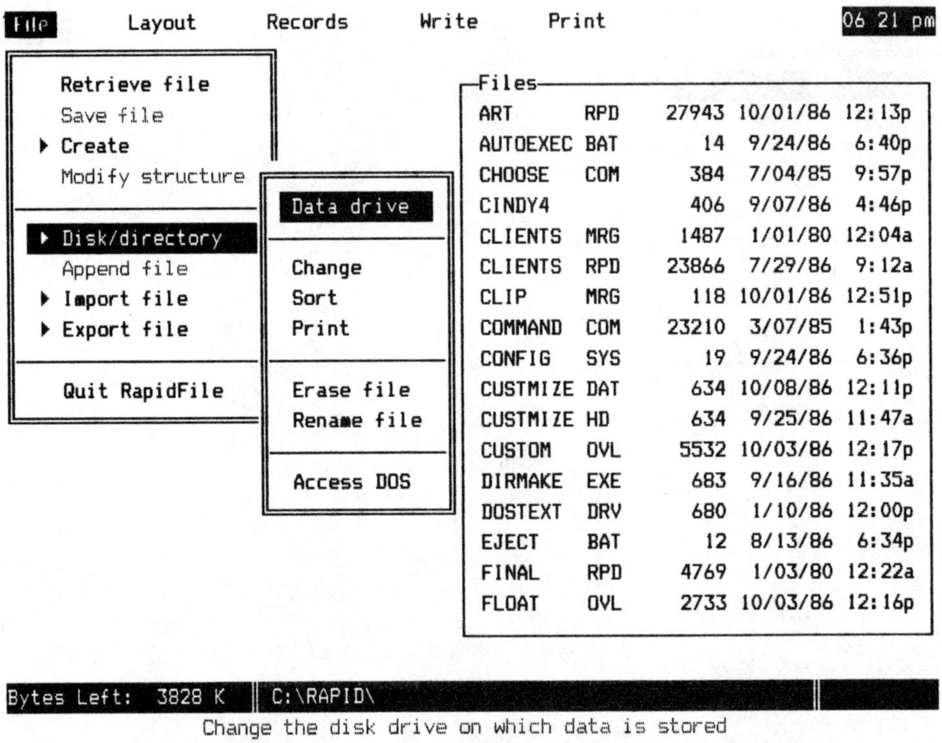

Figure 3-3. The disk directory

In addition to a window that displays the names of all files on the disk, a second window opens, providing additional options named “Data drive,” “Change,” “Sort,” “Print,” “Erase file,” “Rename file,” and “Access DOS.” The various selections within this submenu will be explained in detail in a later chapter. However, note that RapidFile often provides options in this manner. The submenus provide additional choices in response to a selection made from one of the main pull-down menus.

CANCELING A SELECTION

If you open a submenu and later decide that you do not wish to use any of the submenu selections, you can close the submenu with the ESC key. Press ESC now to close the submenu. The File menu will remain on your screen.

Try pressing LEFT ARROW or RIGHT ARROW successively. As you do so, the various menus (File, Layout, Records, Write, and Print) will open and close. By using the arrow keys you can access any choice on any RapidFile menu. To display the pull-down menu that was most recently opened, press F10 at any point in the program.

SHORTCUT KEYS

RapidFile allows you to open menus quickly by entering a combination of the CONTROL key and the first letter of any menu. As an example, try pressing CONTROL-P now. This will open the Print menu. CONTROL-L will open the Layout menu. This shortcut is often faster than using the arrow keys to move to the desired menu.

PARTS OF THE SCREEN

In addition to the menus, RapidFile displays other important information as shown in Figure 3-4. At the upper right corner of the screen is the time, which is provided for your convenience. Like most clock-related functions on the IBM and IBM compatibles, this clock will be accurate only if your PC's system clock is accurate. When a file is loaded for use within RapidFile, the bottom of the screen will display a highlighted Status Bar that displays the letter of the default drive, the name of the

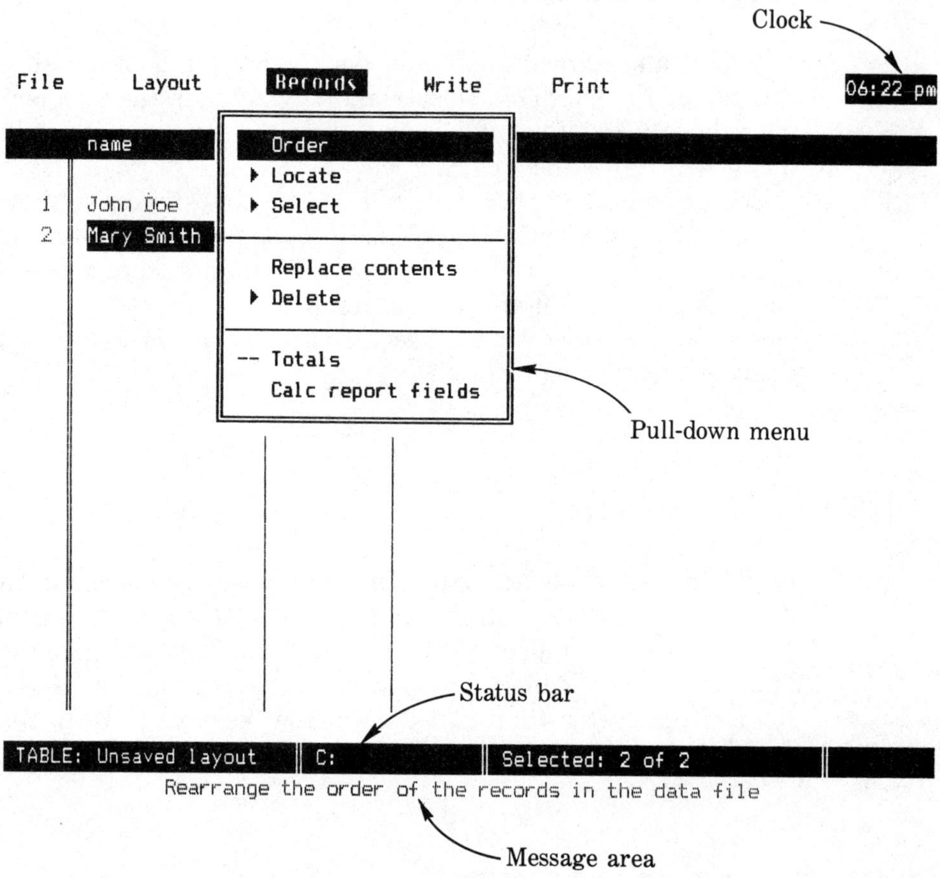

Figure 3-4. Parts of the screen

database file that is currently in use, and the number of records in the file that are selected—that is, available for use. Underneath the Status Bar is an area called the Message Area. This area will display various messages and prompts, depending on where you are within the program.

ABOUT THE MENUS

The File menu (Figure 3-5) provides choices that relate to retrieving (or loading) files, saving files, creating new files, changing the design of an existing file, and exiting the program. The File menu also offers the options "Import file" and "Export file," which are useful for transferring data between

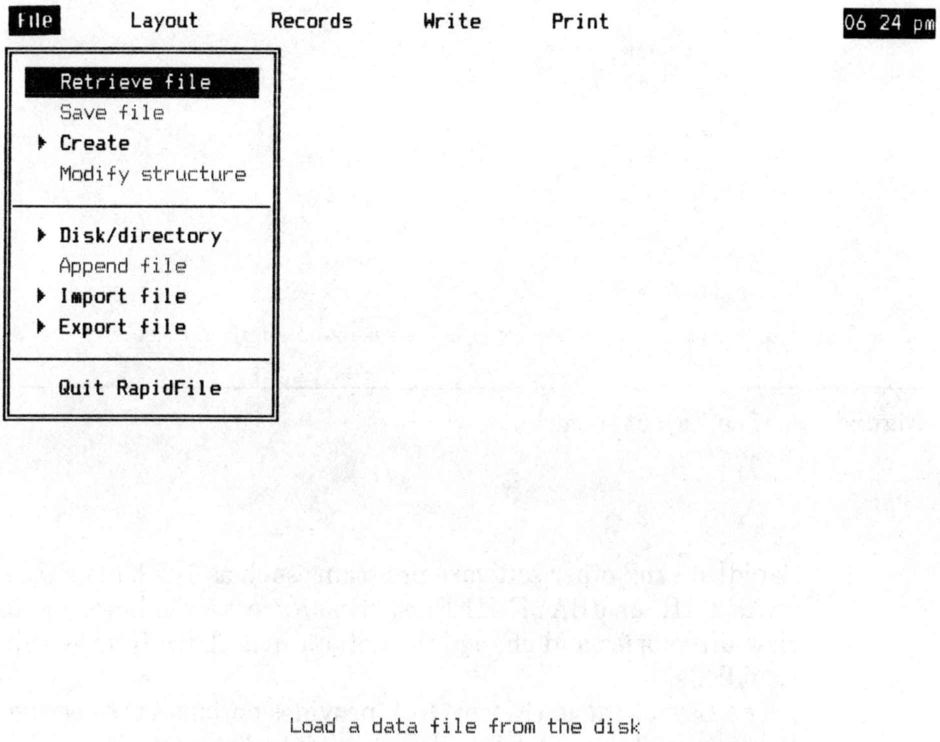

Figure 3-5. The File menu

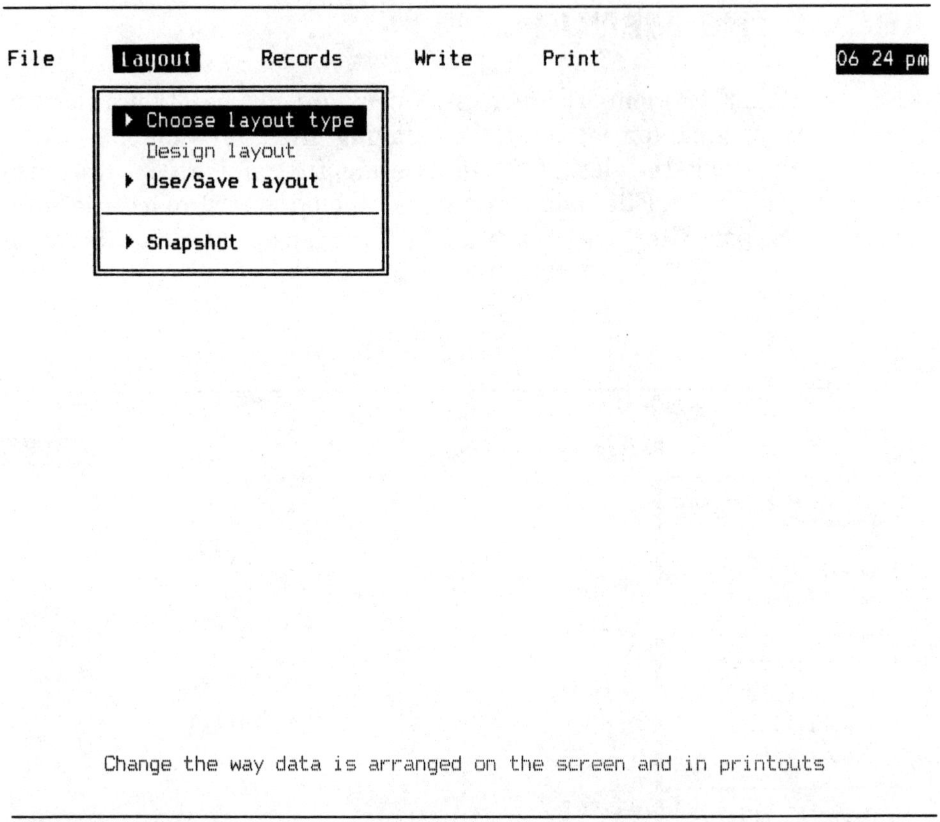

Figure 3-6. The Layout menu

RapidFile and other software programs such as 1-2-3, pfs:FILE, dBASE III, or dBASE III Plus. "Disk/directory" allows you to view directories and change the default disk drive from within RapidFile.

The Layout menu (Figure 3-6) provides options for selecting, creating, and using layouts. Layouts control the way RapidFile displays data, both on the screen and through various reports. The Layout menu also provides a "Snapshot" option. Snapshots

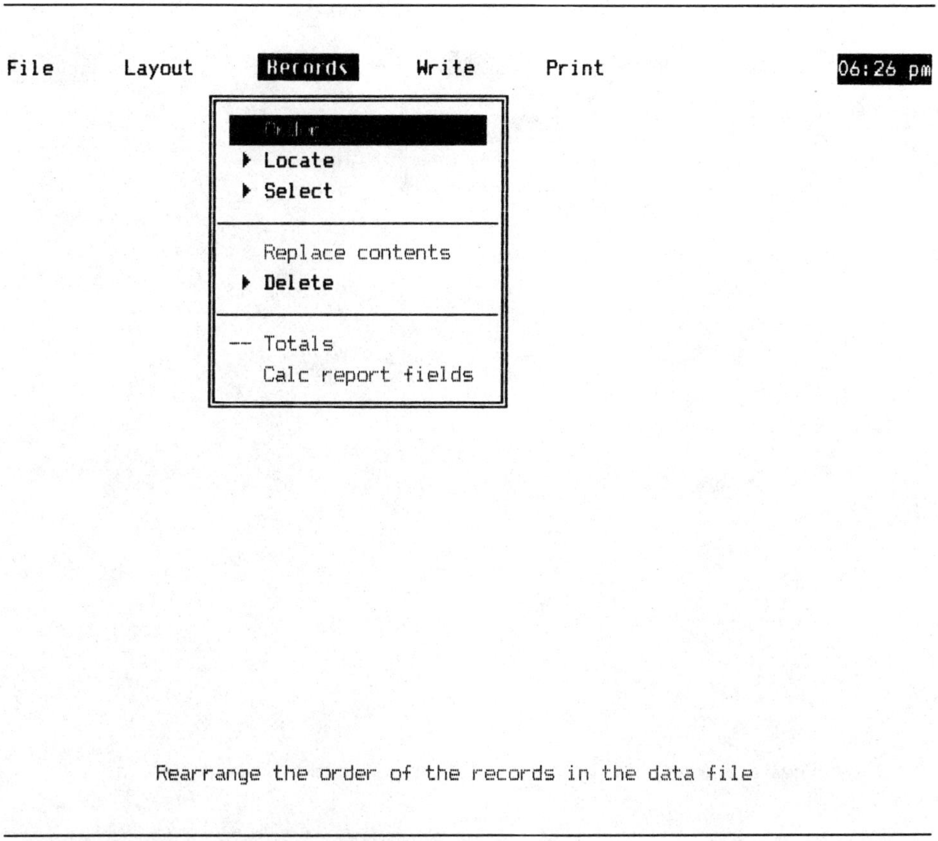

Figure 3-7. The Records menu

are used by RapidFile to save a record of the appearance of a RapidFile database so that reports based on that appearance can be reproduced later by recalling the snapshot.

The Records menu (Figure 3-7) offers options for changing the order of records, locating a specific record, selecting groups of records that meet certain criteria, and performing certain numeric operations on records.

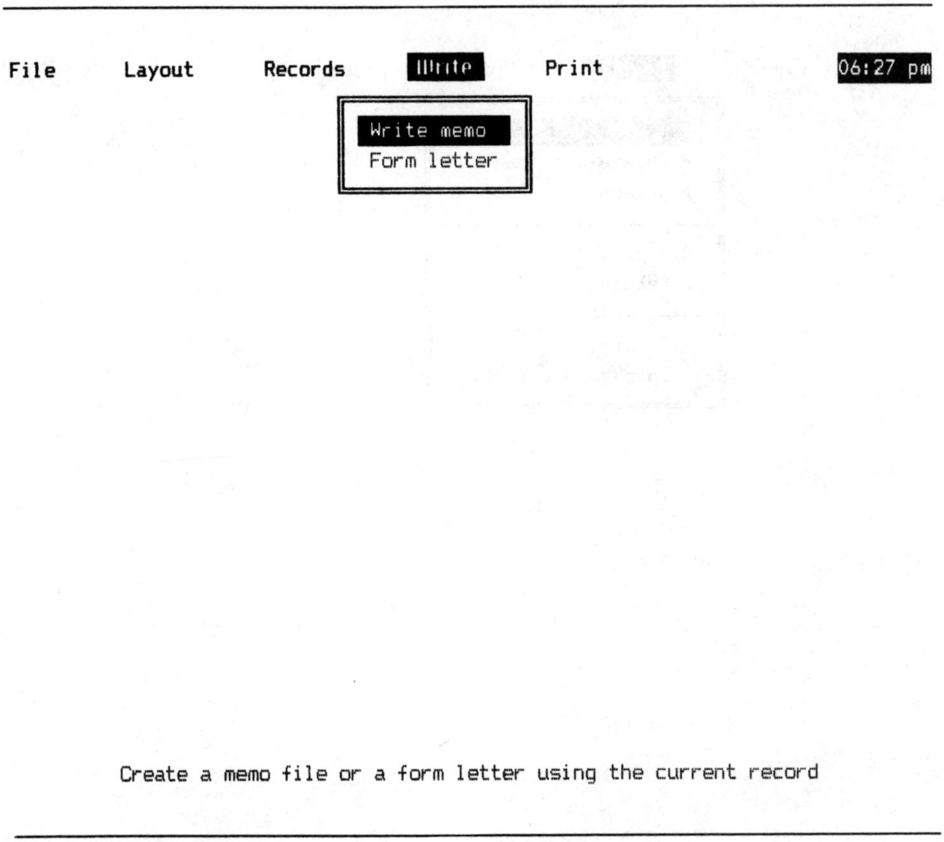

Figure 3-8. The Write menu

The Write menu (Figure 3-8) offers options for writing memos and for writing form letters for use with data stored in a file. The Write menu calls up a feature known as the memo writer, a powerful word processor that is an integral part of RapidFile.

The Print menu (Figure 3-9) provides choices for printing information stored by RapidFile. This information can be in

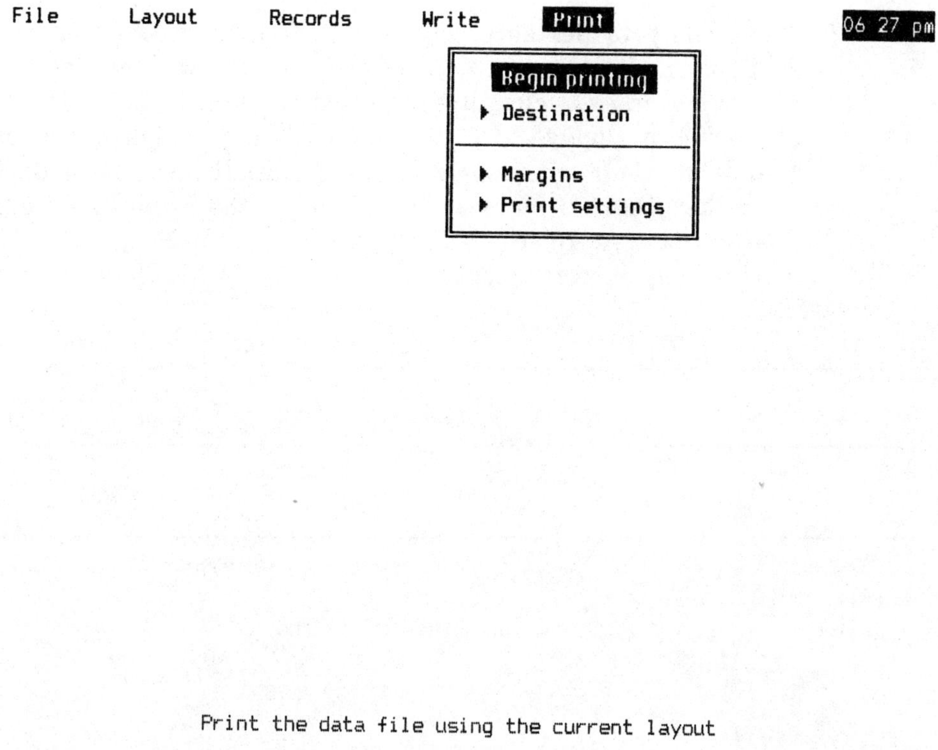

Figure 3-9. The Print menu

the form of records, it can be a form letter, or it can be a memo written with the memo writer. Various submenus accessed through the Print menu allow for margin setting, page numbering options, headers and footers, optional page titles, and specialized printer codes for such effects as compressed printing.

GETTING HELP

RapidFile provides an extensive set of Help screens that are available if desired. Again, floppy-disk users will receive the message to insert Help before they get to the File menu. If you are using a floppy-based system and plan to make use of RapidFile Help screens, remove the RapidFile System disk after the program has loaded and insert the RapidFile Help disk in drive A. To see the Help screens, press F1; you should see the Help screen shown in Figure 3-10. If the Help screens

```
RapidFile Help          Starting and Stopping Printing

START               From the Print Menu, perform these steps.
PRINTING
                      1.  Choose the print destination

                      2.  Set the margins and page length

                      3.  Set the print settings

                      4.  Choose Begin printing

PAUSE OR      Once printing begins, pause at any time by pressing ESC.
STOP          At the Cancel/Resume prompt, choose Cancel printing to abandon
PRINTING      printing and return to the file. If you choose Resume printing,
              the printer continues from the point at which it paused.

Previous Screen  Next Screen  Print Destination  Index  Exit
Use ← → to select an option, then press ↵.                 ESC to Exit
```

Figure 3-10. The Help screen for printing

are unavailable, a message at the bottom of the screen will remind you to insert the Help disk in drive A.

Pressing PGUP and PGDN will cause various Help screens to appear. You can also use the LEFT ARROW or RIGHT ARROW key to highlight the "Next Screen" option, the "Previous Screen" option, or the "Index" of Help screen topics. Pressing RETURN after choosing the screen option causes the screen of choice to appear. You can obtain information about any of the major RapidFile topics from the Help screens. After selecting the "Index" option, for example, you can use UP ARROW and DOWN ARROW to highlight any topic within the Index. Press RETURN to display the Help screen for that topic.

The Help screens are also *context sensitive*, meaning that RapidFile automatically examines where you are in the program and tries to display Help screens appropriate to that area. As an example, press ESC to exit the Help screens, and then enter CONTROL-L to open the Layout menu. Suppose, at this point, that you decide to ask for help. Press F1 to bring up the Help screens, and you will see a Help screen that deals specifically with layouts.

To gain familiarity, you may wish to take a few minutes to browse through the Help screens. When you are done viewing the screens, press ESC.

As mentioned, F1 is always used to display the Help screens. Uses for the other function keys will be discussed in detail later, but, in a nutshell, the remaining function keys perform the tasks shown in Table 3-1.

CREATING A FILE

The "Create" option of the File menu is used to create a new file. The "Create" option actually performs three tasks: It creates a file, allows you to define the structure (or design) of the file, and opens the file so that records can be added to the file.

Table 3-1. Function Keys and Associated Tasks

Key	Function
F2 (EDIT)	Opens Edit panel for making changes to data.
F3 (FLIP)	Switches between layouts, between filtered and full directories, and between data and field names when in form, label, or custom report layouts.
F4 (ZOOM)	Opens current cell into full view through the memo writer.
F5 (TAG)	Marks one or more records.
F6 (HIGHLIGHT)	Highlights the current record.
F7 (MOVE)	Moves highlighted data.
F8 (COPY)	Copies highlighted data.
F9 (IMPLEMENT)	Executes a chosen operation.
F10 (MENU)	Displays pull-down menus.

Let's create the file from the list of fields provided by our planning session in Chapter 2. Each attribute in the list outlined in Chapter 2 becomes a specific field within the file. Open the File menu with CONTROL-F, and enter C for "Create." A submenu will appear, asking if you wish to create a new file or an additional field for an existing file. Enter N for "New File," and the RapidFile File Creation screen will appear (Figure 3-11).

The File Creation screen usually lists each field as it is defined. Since no fields have been defined as of yet, the screen is empty. The message at the bottom of the screen says, **Type the field name, then press ↵**. When naming a field, use the name that best describes the contents of the field. Field names can be up to 13 characters long and can be made up of letters, numbers, and underscores. If spaces are used, RapidFile will automatically convert those spaces into underscores. So, a field

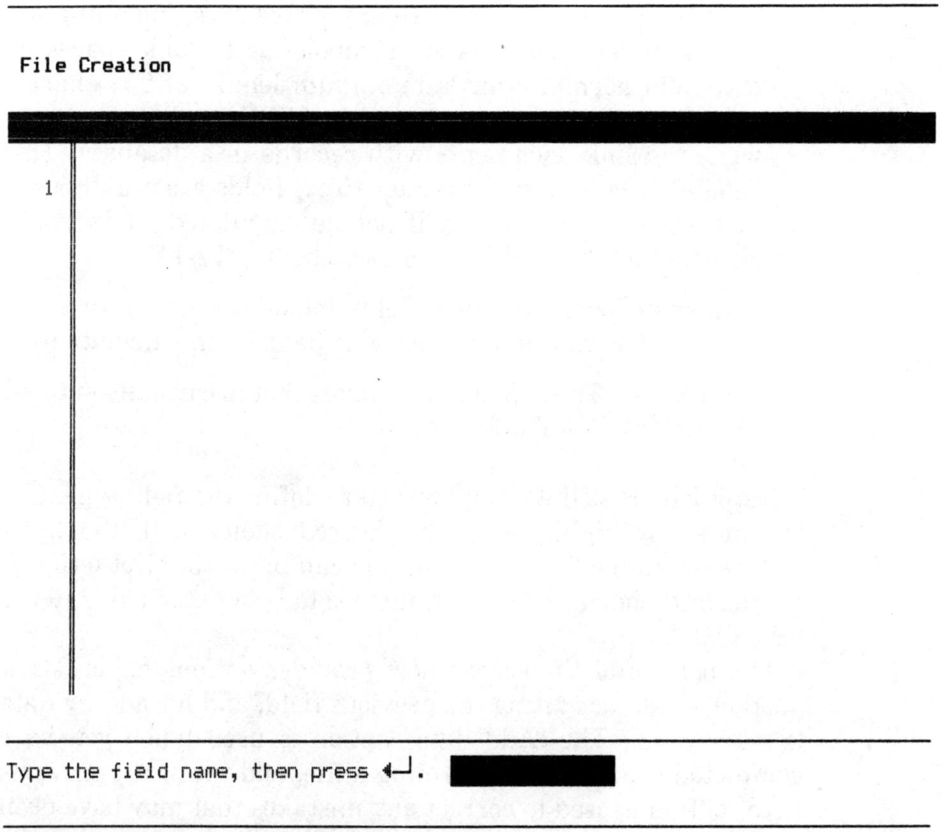

Figure 3-11. The File Creation screen

that you name My Parts will be stored by RapidFile as My_Parts.

Looking back at the list, the first field will be for the members' last names, so enter Lastname for the field name. Once you press the RETURN key, a message at the bottom of the screen will ask you to select a field type. RapidFile uses three types of fields. They are

- Text fields: Text fields store any characters, including letters, numbers, punctuation symbols, and blank spaces. A text field normally has a maximum length of 254 characters. (There are ways around this limit by using the memo writer to link documents with records in a database. This capability will be covered later.) Text fields are usually used to store numbers that will not be calculated. If in doubt about which type of field to use, choose "Text."
- Numeric fields: Numeric fields include numbers (with or without decimal places) that will be used in calculations.
- Date fields: These fields store dates that are usually entered in the MM/DD/YY format.

RapidFile is still waiting for you to define the field type. You can do so by highlighting the desired choice with the LEFT ARROW or RIGHT ARROW key, or you can press the first letter of the desired choice. Since Lastname is to be a text field, enter T for "Text."

The bottom of the screen now provides options for creating another field, for editing the previous field, and for adding data (Figure 3-12). The "Add data" option is used when you have completed the process of defining a file, and the "Edit previous field" option is used to correct any mistakes that may have been made in defining a previous field. In this case enter C for "Create another field."

For the field name, enter Firstname. After you have entered the field name, you will note that the bottom of the screen now provides five choices for type of field: text, numeric, date, calculated, and report. Calculated and report fields will be discussed in later chapters. The calculated fields provide calculations of other numeric fields in a file, and the report fields provide sophisticated options when producing reports.

Again enter T for "Text" to define the type of field. Enter C (for "Create another field"), and enter Expdate for the name of the field. This field is to represent the membership expiration

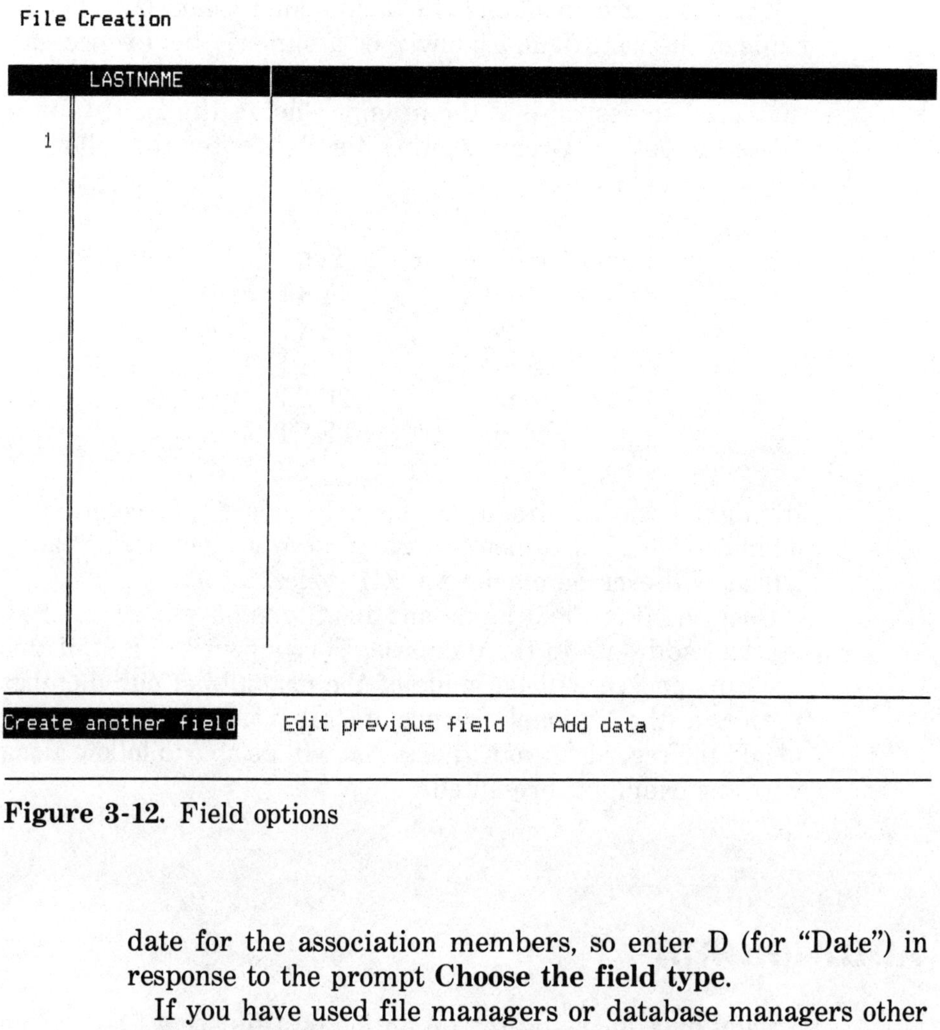

Figure 3-12. Field options

date for the association members, so enter D (for "Date") in response to the prompt **Choose the field type.**

If you have used file managers or database managers other than RapidFile, you may have already noticed a major difference between RapidFile and those programs. You have not needed to specify the width of any field, a task that must be done with most database managers. RapidFile uses *variable width fields,* which eliminate the need to specify field widths.

This results in less wasted space within your data files.

Enter C to create another field, and enter Contribute for the name of the next field. This will be a numeric field representing the amount contributed by the member, so enter N for "numeric" in response to the prompt **Choose the field type.**

Use the option "Create another field" to enter the following fields and field types:

Field Name	Type
Address	TEXT
City	TEXT
State	TEXT
Zip	TEXT
Type	TEXT

It might seem at first that the ZIP code field should be a numeric field. This is not necessary, however, because no calculations will ever be made with ZIP codes.

Once the final field name and field type have been entered, you can add data to the database. Throughout the rest of this book, much use will be made of the example of our member records at the National Friends of Crabgrass. It would be wise to add the records to your file, so you will be able to follow along with the examples presented.

ADDING DATA

To add data following the definition of a file, select the option "Add data," which is displayed at the bottom of the screen. Enter A for "Add data," and a table for the new file will appear (see Figure 3-13).

RapidFile can present data in one of two layouts: *table layout* or *form layout.* The form layout will be discussed shortly. What

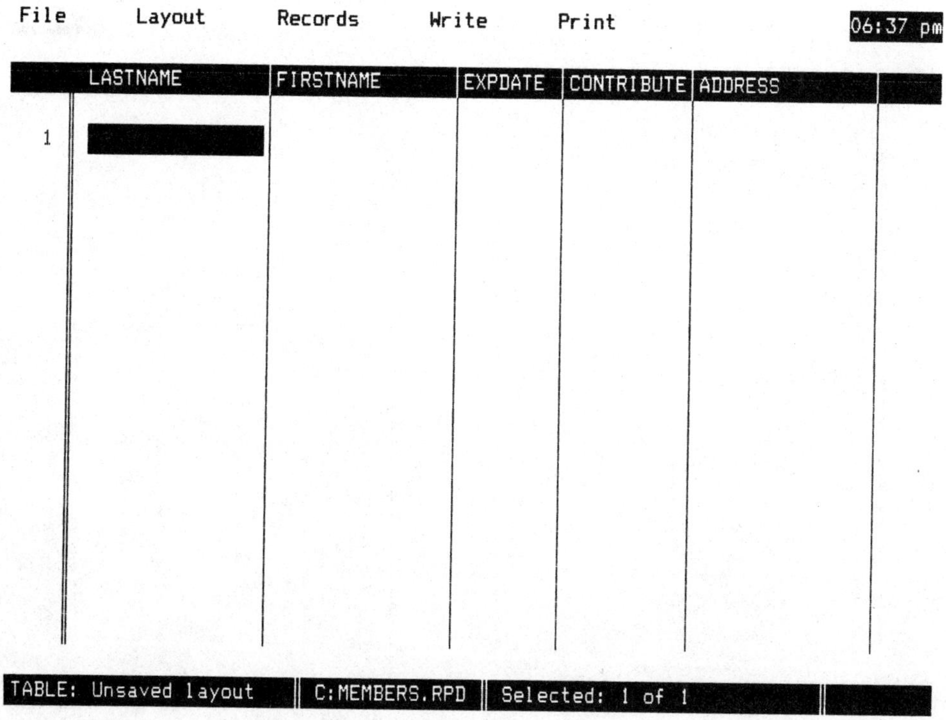

Figure 3-13. A file in table layout

you are looking at now is the table layout. A table layout presents records in a columnar (or tabular) format. You can add records by typing the data for each field and pressing RETURN to proceed to the next field.

Currently, the Lastname field is highlighted, awaiting the first entry for a member's last name. Enter Harris. When you press RETURN, the highlighted field will automatically move to the Firstname field.

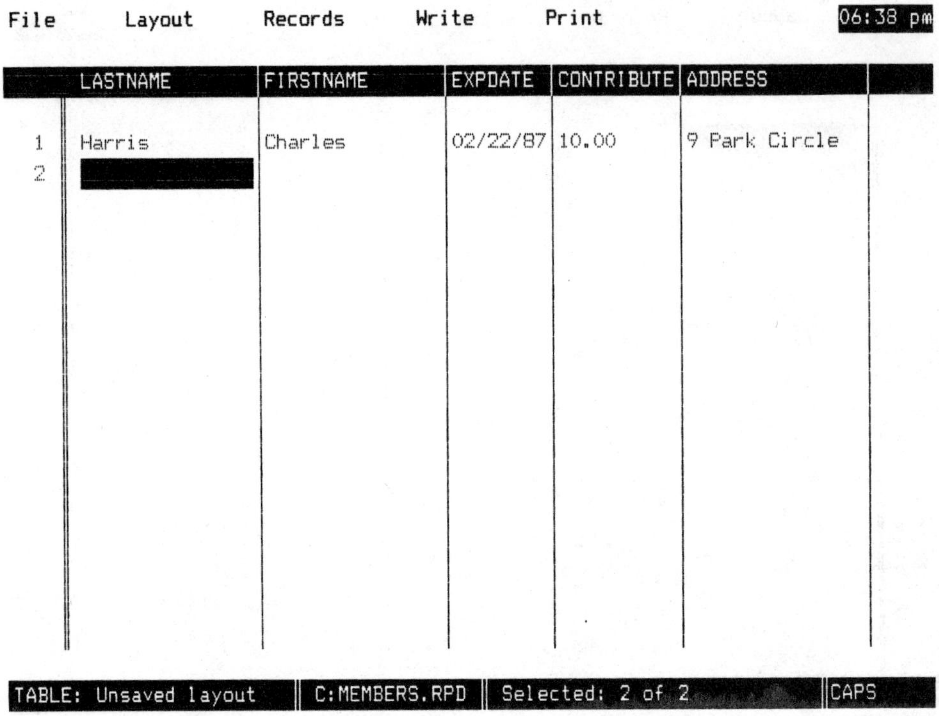

Figure 3-14. Table layout with first record entered

Enter Charles and press RETURN, and the highlighted field will move to the Expdate field.

For the Expdate field, enter 02/22/87 (and include the slashes). For Contribute, enter 10.00. For Address, enter 9 Park Circle. For City, enter Sterling; for State, enter VA; for Zip, enter 22070; and for Type, enter Student. When you press RETURN after the entry of the last field, the highlight will automatically move to the next blank record as shown in Figure 3-14.

Add the remaining association members as listed below.

Sloan
Wanda
10/15/86
25.00
2723 Hunters Woods Plaza
Reston VA 22091
REGULAR

Roberts
Norma
03/08/87
20.00
6120 Brandon Avenue
Phoenix AZ 80555
REGULAR

Askew
Lonnie
03/08/87
20.00
103 Maple Avenue West
Pittskill NY 12512
REGULAR

Jones
Renee
05/15/87
30.00
2508 Columbia Pike
Arlington TX 75780
REGULAR

Shaw
Michael
07/21/87
35.00
7105 Little River Lane
Annandale FL 30508
REGULAR

Baker
Jeanette
06/22/87
10.00
153 South Lakes Drive
Reston VA 22090
STUDENT

Baker
Benjamin
09/08/87
20.00
5206 Lyngate Court
Berkeley CA 95294
REGULAR

Hayes
Cynthia
08/15/88
100.00
9631 Champion Court
Austin TX 76801
CHARTER

Brown
Nicole
08/15/87
25.00
106 Crestwood Drive Apt 5B
Chicago IL 60610
REGULAR

Block
Paul
03/08/87
20.00
1415 South Shore Drive
Chicago IL 60617
REGULAR

Schultz
Bobby
11/17/87
10.00
1338 Redskin Drive
Herndon VA 22070
STUDENT

Smith
Larry
01/12/88
100.00
6505 Brandon Avenue
Los Angeles CA 90055
CHARTER

Mills
Ernest
04/30/87
20.00
500 Embarcadero Street
San Francisco CA 95002
REGULAR

Sand
Lucy
01/01/99
500.00
142 Haven Way
Annapolis MD 18955
LIFETIME

Johnson
Lamar
12/01/87
40.00
4005 Williamsburg Court Apt A
Cambridge MA 02139
REGULAR

Your completed database should resemble Figure 3-15.

File Layout Records Write Print 06 55 pm

	LASTNAME	FIRSTNAME	EXPDATE	CONTRIBUTE	ADDRESS
1	Harris	Charles	02/22/87	10.00	9 Park Circle
2	Sloan	Wanda	10/15/87	25.00	2723 Hunters Wo
3	Roberts	Norma	03/08/87	20.00	6120 Brandon Av
4	Askew	Lonnie	03/08/87	20.00	103 Maple Avenu
5	Jones	Renee	05/15/87	30.00	2508 Columbia P
6	Shaw	Michael	07/21/87	35.00	7105 Little Riv
7	Baker	Jeanette	06/22/87	10.00	153 South Lakes
8	Baker	Benjamin	09/08/87	20.00	5602 Lyngate Co
9	Hayes	Cynthia	08/15/88	100.00	9631 Champion C
10	Brown	Nicole	08/15/87	25.00	106 Crestwood D
11	Block	Paul	03/08/87	20.00	1415 South Shor
12	Schultz	Bobby	11/17/87	10.00	1338 Redskin Dr
13	Smith	Larry	01/12/88	100.00	6505 Brandon Av
14	Mills	Ernest	04/30/87	20.00	500 Embarcadero
15	Sand	Lucy	01/01/99	500.00	142 Haven Way
16	Johnson	Lamar	12/01/87	40.00	4005 Williamsbu
17					

TABLE: Unsaved layout | C:MEMBERS.RPD | Selected: 17 of 17

Figure 3-15. Table containing all records

SAVING A FILE

While you work with a file in RapidFile, that file exists primarily in the memory of your computer. RapidFile gets much of its speed from an efficient computer technique called *virtual memory,* whereby parts of the file are kept in your computer's random access memory (RAM) and parts of the file are kept on the disk. The file is not permanently saved to disk until you issue a command to save the file through the File menu. Once all the records have been entered, open the File menu by pressing CONTROL-F. Enter S for "Save file," and a window listing any existing files will appear at the right side of the screen. Note that the prompt at the bottom of the screen indicates that you can enter the name for the file.

RapidFile permits standard DOS filenames, which are a maximum of eight characters in length and must begin with a letter. In this case, we will use MEMBERS for the name of the file, so enter MEMBERS. RapidFile automatically assigns the extension .RPD to any database file that is saved. You do not need to specify this extension when saving files.

During the saving process a moving arrow appears at the bottom of the screen denoting the progress in saving the file. When the process is complete, a message appears at the bottom of the screen indicating that the file has been successfully saved. The message also indicates the remaining free space on the disk in the default drive.

TABLE LAYOUT VERSUS FORM LAYOUT

Until now you have been viewing the data within the database in one fashion—as a series of records, with one record occupying each row and the fields of each record occupying a column. Most users find it easiest to grasp the concept of a database when it is presented in this manner. It is easy to see a number of records, and the records and fields are clearly distinguished. However, there are also drawbacks to presenting a database in this manner. The most significant drawback is the inability to see more than a few fields at one time. For example, when viewing the members file, the staff at Friends of Crabgrass can see only the fields that cite last and first names, expiration date, contribution amount, and street address. To view the City, State, ZIP code, or Type fields requires the use of the arrow keys. To make matters worse, once these fields are brought into view, the name fields vanish from the left side of the screen. This makes it difficult to remember which line (record) containing the city, state, ZIP code, and type data corresponds to a particular member.

To get around this problem, some database managers display data as an on-screen form instead of in the format of a table. Such a form usually resembles a paper-based form like the 3 × 5 cards used by Friends of Crabgrass before the computer came along (see Figure 3-16). Two advantages to this method of

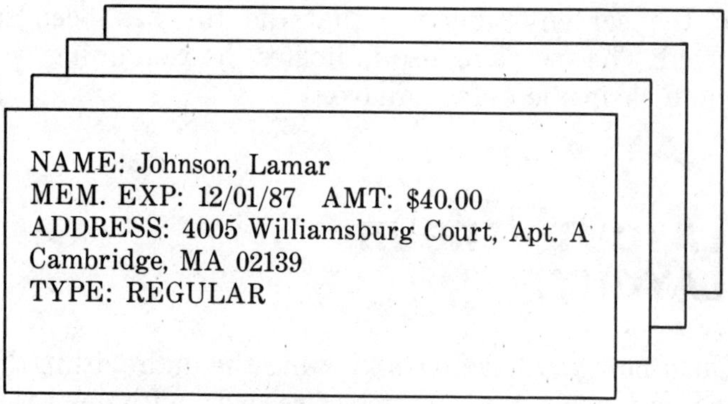

Figure 3-16. Example of a paper-based form

viewing data are that (1) people are often accustomed to working with a database in this format, particularly if they have just moved to a PC from 3 × 5 cards or a similar filing system, and (2) you can view more fields. RapidFile allows you to look at your database file in either manner. Figure 3-14 presented a database file in "Table" layout. RapidFile can also display the file in "Form" layout, which resembles a paper-based form that displays a single record at a time.

Press CONTROL-L to open the Layout menu shown in Figure 3-17. The Layout menu offers the following options: "Choose

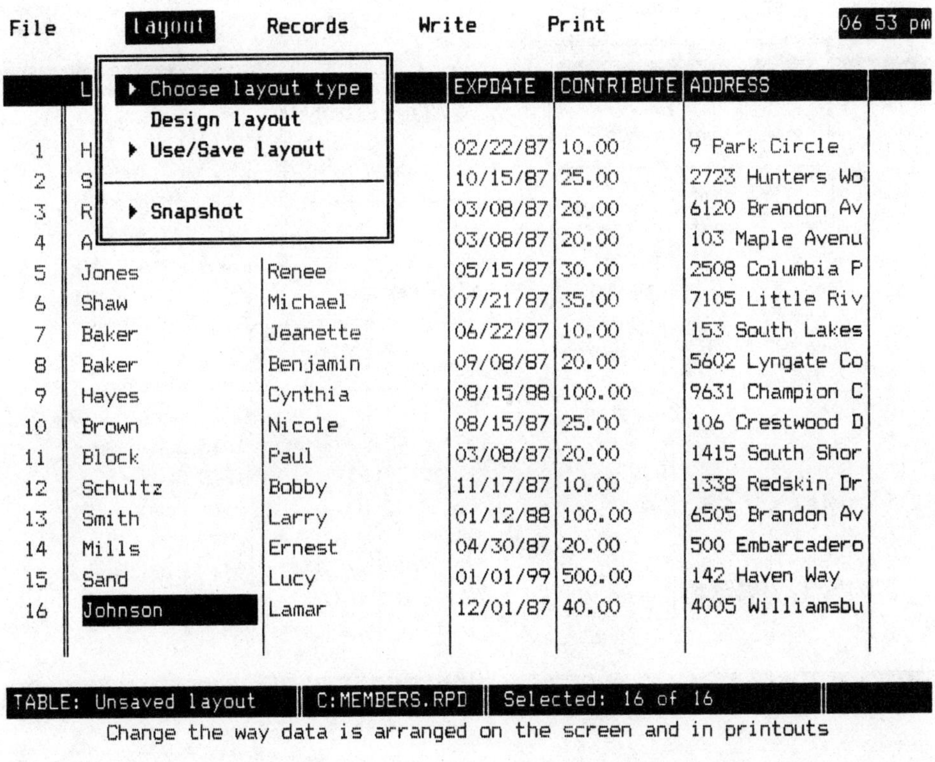

Figure 3-17. The Layout menu

layout type," "Design layout," "Use/Save layout," and "Snapshot." The "Design layout," "Use/Save layout," and "Snapshot" options apply to more sophisticated custom layouts that you can use to control how data is viewed or printed. These options will be covered in detail later. For now, choose a different layout by entering C for "Choose layout type."

A submenu opens (Figure 3-18), revealing six options: "Table," "Form," "Split table/form," "Label," "Quick Report," and "Custom Report."

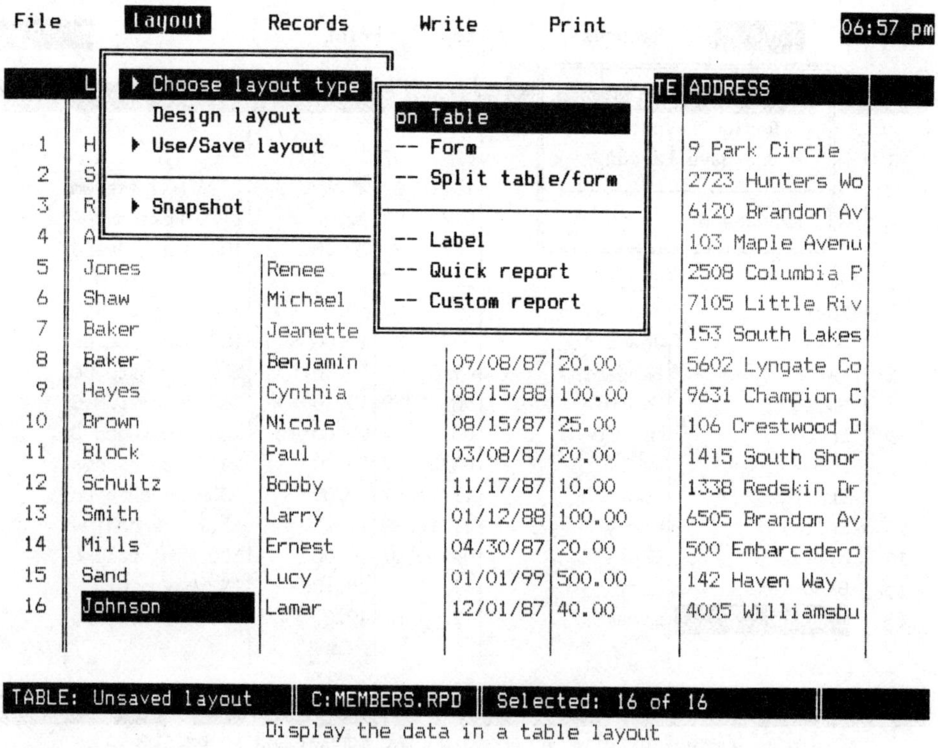

Figure 3-18. The submenu of the Layout menu

The "Table" option is currently on. By default RapidFile opens a file using "Table." You can change to forms by using the "Form" layout choice on the submenu. Enter F for "Form," and RapidFile will display a single record in a form layout (see Figure 3-19).

Moving around in the database is somewhat different when using "Form" layout than when using "Table" layout. Try PGUP and PGDN, and then try the UP ARROW and DOWN ARROW keys.

```
 File     Layout     Records     Write     Print                07 01 pm

* 16 *

LASTNAME       : Johnson
FIRSTNAME      : Lamar
EXPDATE        : 12/01/87
ADDRESS        : 4005 Williamsburg Court A
CITY           : Cambridge
STATE          : MA
ZIP            : 02139
TYPE           : REGULAR

FORM: Unsaved layout  | C:MEMBERS.RPD | Selected: 16 of 16 |
```

Figure 3-19. A form layout

Note that PGUP and PGDN now move from record to record; previously, in "Table" layout, they moved up and down by a whole screen of records. UP ARROW and DOWN ARROW, which in "Table" layout moved from one record to another, now move the cursor between fields of a single record. Navigate in "Form" layout mode with the keys shown here:

Key	Result
UP ARROW	To previous field
DOWN ARROW	To next field
HOME	Top of form
END	Bottom of form
PGUP	Previous record
PGDN	Next record

While viewing records in either "Table" layout or "Form" layout, the F3 (FLIP) key can be used to switch between the layouts. Try pressing F3 repeatedly, and note the result as RapidFile switches between the "Table" and "Form" options.

RapidFile also offers a split layout, which shows both layouts simultaneously. Press CONTROL-L to open the Layout menu, choose C for "Choose layout type," and choose S for "Split table/form." The screen will display two views of the database—a table layout on the left side of the screen and a form layout on the right side of the screen (Figure 3-20).

When you switch to the "Split table/form" layout, the cursor usually appears within the table layout portion of the screen. Try using the arrow keys, and note that the cursor moves within the table. As you move between records within the table, a complete view of the same record is presented within the form layout portion of the screen.

While in the "Split table/form" layout, F3 will switch the cursor between the layouts. Try pressing F3 repeatedly, and note that the cursor moves from the "Table" option to the "Form" option and back again.

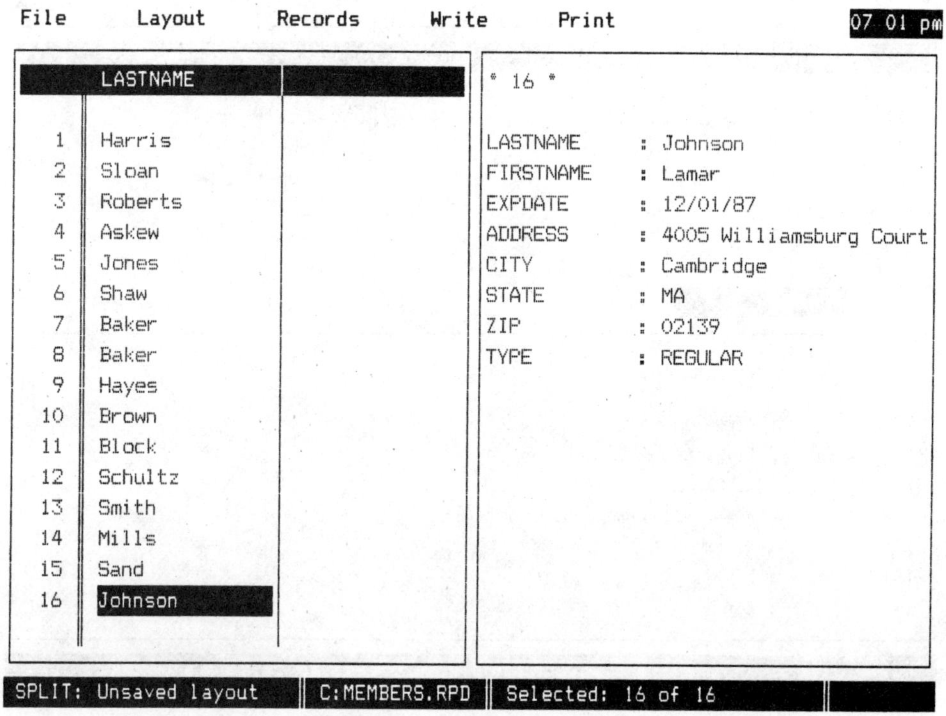

Figure 3-20. A split table/form layout

Three additional key combinations are helpful when you are viewing records using "Split table/form" layout. These combinations are CONTROL-V, CONTROL-grey+, and CONTROL-grey−. The CONTROL-V key combination alternates between a vertically oriented display and a horizontally oriented display. Try entering CONTROL-V now. What you will get is a display resembling Figure 3-21.

```
File        Layout        Records        Write        Print                 07:04 pm

     LASTNAME          FIRSTNAME          EXPDATE    ADDRESS

 10  Brown             Nicole             08/15/87   106 Crestwood D
 11  Block             Paul               03/08/87   1415 South Shor
 12  Schultz           Bobby              11/17/87   1338 Redskin Dr
 13  Smith             Larry              01/12/88   6505 Brandon Av
 14  Mills             Ernest             04/30/87   500 Embarcadero
 15  Sand              Lucy               01/01/99   142 Haven Way
 16  Johnson           Lamar              12/01/87   4005 Williamsbu

* 16 *

LASTNAME       : Johnson
FIRSTNAME      : Lamar
EXPDATE        : 12/01/87
ADDRESS        : 4005 Williamsburg Court A
CITY           : Cambridge
STATE          : MA
ZIP            : 02139

SPLIT: Unsaved layout  | C:MEMBERS.RPD | Selected: 16 of 16
```

Figure 3-21. Horizontal view using the "Split table/form" option

Enter CONTROL-V again, and the display returns to a vertical orientation. Also, try CONTROL-grey− and CONTROL-grey+ keys. (Use the + and − keys at the far right side of the keyboard, not the ones located above the equal sign and the underscore along the top row of the keyboard.) CONTROL-grey− will make the table layout smaller and increase the size of the form layout. CONTROL-grey+ will make the form layout smaller and increase the size of the table layout. The effects of these key combinations are shown in Figures 3-22 and 3-23.

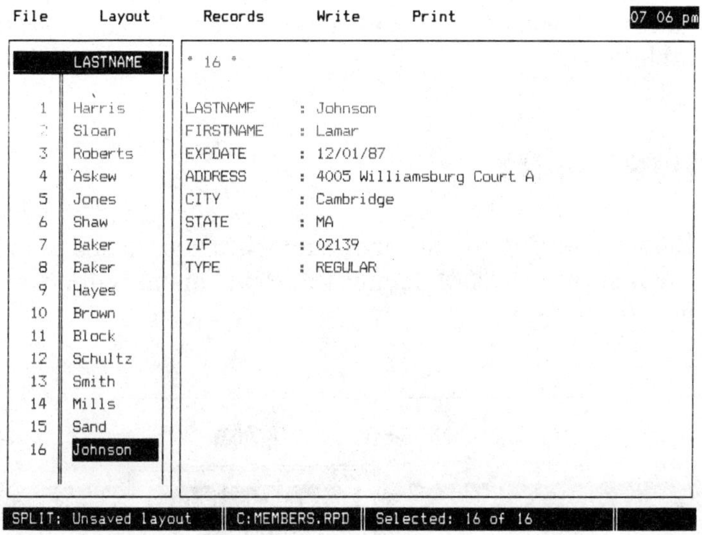

Figure 3-22. Results of repeated use of CONTROL-grey−

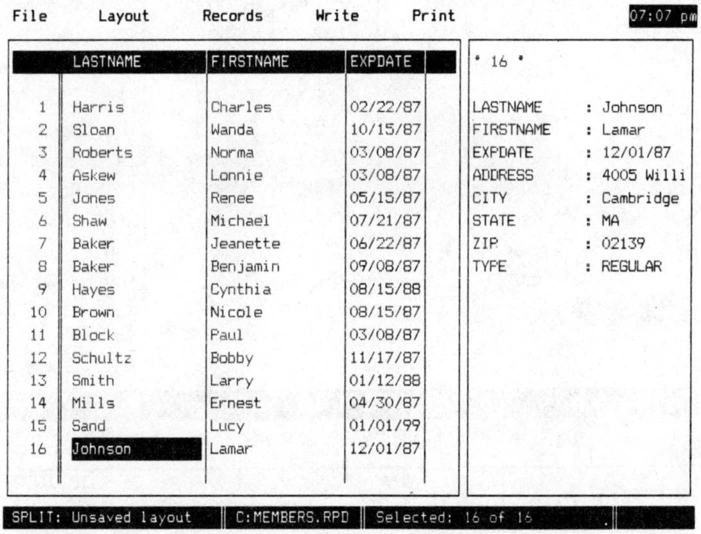

Figure 3-23. Results of repeated use of CONTROL-grey+

Enter CONTROL-L to open the Layout menu, enter C for "Choose layout type," and enter T for "Table" to return to a table layout.

PRINTING A FILE

Before printing make sure your printer is turned on and ready. Then enter CONTROL-P, and the Print menu will open (see Figure 3-24).

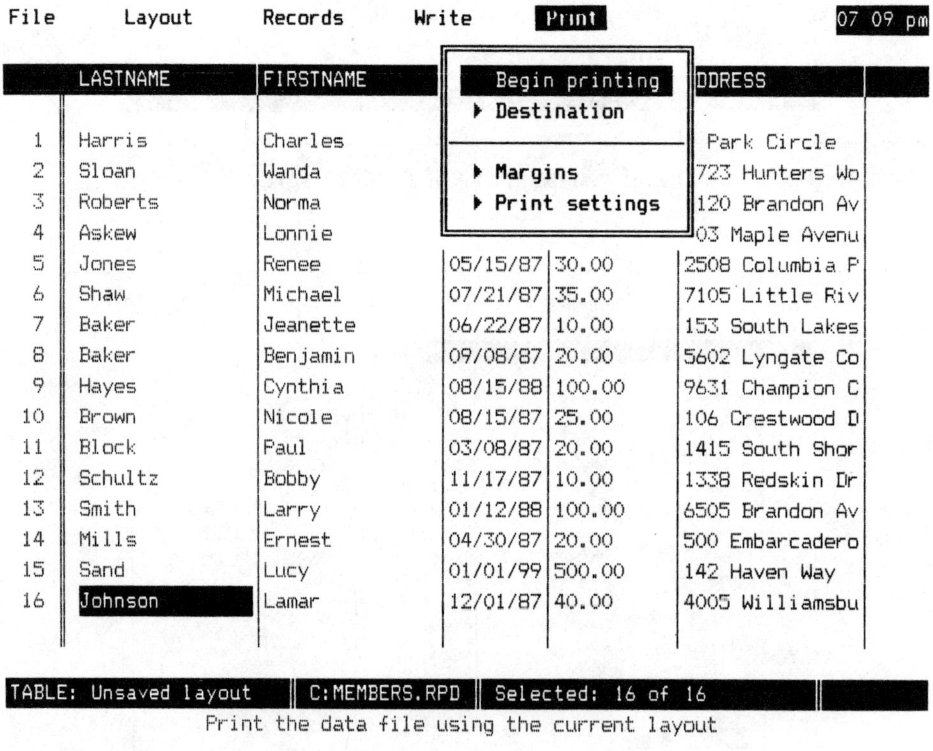

Figure 3-24. The Print menu

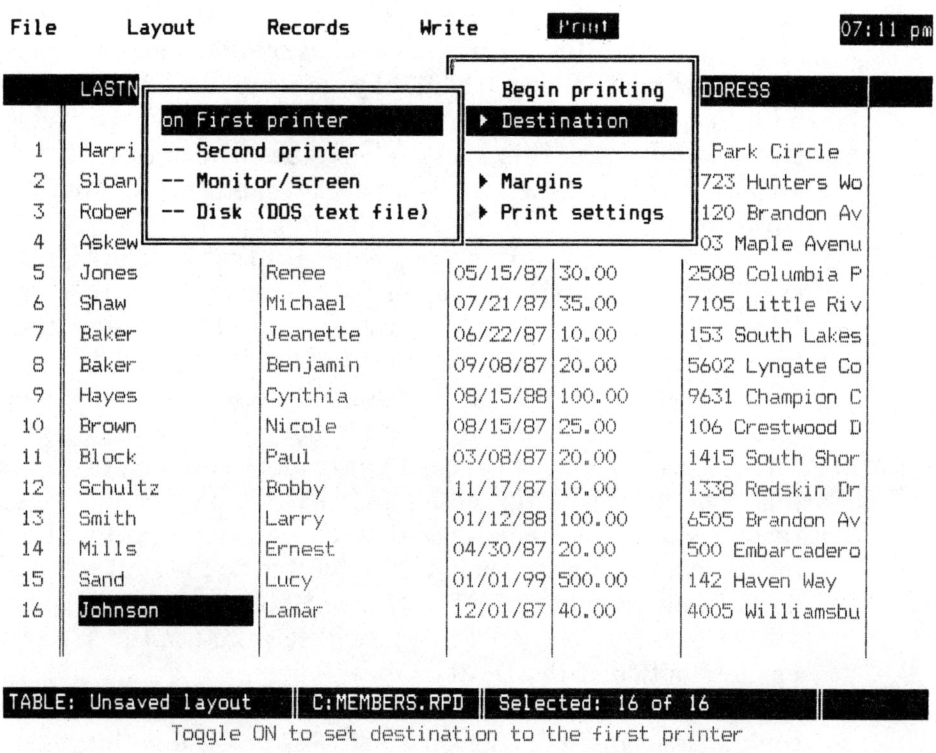

Figure 3-25. The Destination submenu

The Print menu contains four options: "Begin printing," "Destination," "Margins," and "Print settings." You will need to use the "Destination" option to tell RapidFile that the printed results are to be sent to your printer.

Enter D for "Destination," and the Destination submenu will appear (see Figure 3-25). The submenu gives you a choice of "First printer," "Second printer," "Monitor/screen," or "DISK" (a DOS text file stored on your disk). If your printer is connected in the way that most printers are, the "First printer" option will work fine. "First printer" causes the data to be sent to the first parallel port (LPT1) of your computer. This is where most PC printers are attached. You must customize your installation to tell RapidFile about other types of printers such as serial printers attached to COM ports; Chapter 18 will tell you how.

To send data to the first port, enter F to select "First printer." The word *on* will appear in the submenu, indicating that RapidFile will send the data to your printer. Press ESC to close the submenu.

Now enter B for "Begin printing." The printed file should resemble the one shown in Figure 3-26.

If you see a message saying **Printer not ready**, check to see that your printer is turned on and that the on-line switch, or ready switch, is in the on position. If the printer still will not print, find out if your printer is connected to the first parallel port of your computer (LPT1). If the printer is connected to the second parallel port (LPT2), you will have to use the "Second printer" option of the Destination submenu.

If the printer is a serial printer connected to one of your computer's communications ports (COM1 or COM2), things will get a little trickier. There are two ways to make your printer work with RapidFile. You can use the DOS MODE command to redirect the data usually sent to LPT1 to your serial printer instead (see your DOS manual for details). Or you can customize RapidFile so it uses the serial ports of your computer for printing (see Chapter 18 for more information on this topic).

If you continue to have printer problems, use the combination SHIFT-PRTSCR to test the printer. This combination should cause the contents of any screen to print (although solid lines will usually appear as rows of letters). If you cannot get your printer to print when you press SHIFT-PRTSCR, then you have a printer interfacing problem, and you will have trouble getting the printer to work with RapidFile. You must solve the interfacing problem before you can print.

Rec#	|Lastname	|Firstname	|Exp Date	|Contribute	|Address
1	|Harris	|Charles	|02/22/78	|10.00	|9 Park Circle
2	|Sloan	|Wanda	|10/15/86	|25.00	|2723 Hunters Wo
3	|Roberts	|Norma	|03/08/87	|20.00	|6120 Brandon Av
4	|Askew	|Lonnie	|03/08/87	|20.00	|103 Maple Avenu
5	|Jones	|Renee	|05/15/87	|30.00	|2508 Columbia P
6	|Shaw	|Michael	|07/21/87	|35.00	|7105 Little Riv
7	|Baker	|Jeanette	|06/22/87	|10.00	|153 South Lakes
8	|Baker	|Benjamin	|09/08/87	|20.00	|5206 Lyngate Co
9	|Hayes	|Cynthia	|08/15/88	|100.00	|9631 Champion C
10	|Brown	|Nicole	|08/15/87	|25.00	|106 Crestwood D
11	|Block	|Paul	|03/08/87	|20.00	|1415 South Shor
12	|Schultz	|Bobby	|11/17/87	|10.00	|1338 Redskin Dr
13	|Smith	|Larry	|01/12/88	|100.00	|6505 Brandon Av
14	|Mills	|Ernest	|04/30/87	|20.00	|500 Embarcadero
15	|Sand	|Lucy	|01/01/99	|500.00	|142 Haven Way
16	|Johnson	|Lamar	|12/01/87	|40.00	|4005 Williamsbu

Rec#	|City	|State	|Zip	|Type
1	|Sterling	|VA	|22070	|STUDENT
2	|Reston	|VA	|22091	|REGULAR
3	|Phoenix	|AZ	|80555	|REGULAR
4	|Pittskill	|NY	|12512	|REGULAR
5	|Arlington	|TX	|75780	|REGULAR
6	|Annandale	|FL	|30508	|REGULAR
7	|Reston	|VA	|22090	|STUDENT
8	|Berkeley	|CA	|95294	|REGULAR
9	|Austin	|TX	|76801	|CHARTER
10	|Chicago	|IL	|60610	|REGULAR
11	|Chicago	|IL	|60617	|REGULAR
12	|Herndon	|VA	|22070	|STUDENT
13	|Los Angeles	|CA	|90055	|CHARTER
14	|San Francisco	|CA	|95002	|REGULAR
15	|Annapolis	|MD	|18955	|LIFETIME
16	|Cambridge	|MA	|02139	|REGULAR

Figure 3-26. Printed file in table layout

-1-	
LASTNAME	: Harris
FIRSTNAME	: Charles
EXPDATE	: 02/22/78
CONTRIBUTE	: 10.00
ADDRESS	: 9 Park Circle
CITY	: Sterling
STATE	: VA
ZIP	: 22070
TYPE	: STUDENT
-2-	
LASTNAME	: Sloan
FIRSTNAME	: Wanda
EXPDATE	: 10/15/86
CONTRIBUTE	: 25.00
ADDRESS	: 2723 Hunters Woods Plaza
CITY	: Reston
STATE	: VA
ZIP	: 22091
TYPE	: REGULAR
-3-	
LASTNAME	: Roberts
FIRSTNAME	: Norma
EXPDATE	: 03/08/87
CONTRIBUTE	: 20.00
ADDRESS	: 6120 Brandon Avenue
CITY	: Phoenix
STATE	: AZ
ZIP	: 80555
TYPE	: REGULAR
-4-	
LASTNAME	: Askew
FIRSTNAME	: Lonnie
EXPDATE	: 03/08/87
CONTRIBUTE	: 20.00
ADDRESS	: 103 Maple Avenue West
CITY	: Pittskill
STATE	: NY
ZIP	: 12512
TYPE	: REGULAR

Figure 3-27. Printed file in form layout

Because you are in "Table" layout, the printed file resembles the file you see on the screen in "Table" layout. You have the option of printing a file that reflects the "Form" layout. Press F3 to change to "Form" layout. Then open the Print menu with CONTROL-P and enter B for "Begin printing." You will be prompted to define which records should be printed: all records, the current record (the one highlighted with the cursor), or the remaining records from the current record to the end of the file. Enter A for "All records."

The file will be printed, but this time the results will appear like those shown in Figure 3-27.

When the printer is finished, press CONTROL-P again to open the Print menu, and enter M for "Margins." The Margins submenu will appear (Figure 3-28).

You can change any of the options by highlighting the desired option and pressing RETURN. You will then be prompted at the bottom of the screen to enter a new value. Type the value, press RETURN again, and the change will take effect. As an example, if you want wide margins at the left side of the page, highlight the "Left margin" option and press RETURN. Then enter 10 and press RETURN again. This will reset the left margin to 10. If you have a wide printer you can change the right margin from the default setting of 80 to 132. This will take advantage of wide paper because more columns will be able to print on a single sheet when printing in "Table" layout mode.

The options "Top margin" and "Bottom margin" control the minimum space between the top and bottom margins, respectively, and these options are set in the same manner as the other margin options. "Page length" lets you change the page length from the standard setting of 66 lines per inch, which is just right for regular computer paper. But if you decide to use custom computer forms (such as preprinted checks or other small forms) you will need to change this value to get proper results when printing. Press ESC to close the Margins submenu, and enter P to open the Print settings submenu (see Figure 3-29).

This submenu is used to control special printer options—page numbering, whether record numbers will be printed, whether you desire borders between columns, and whether the

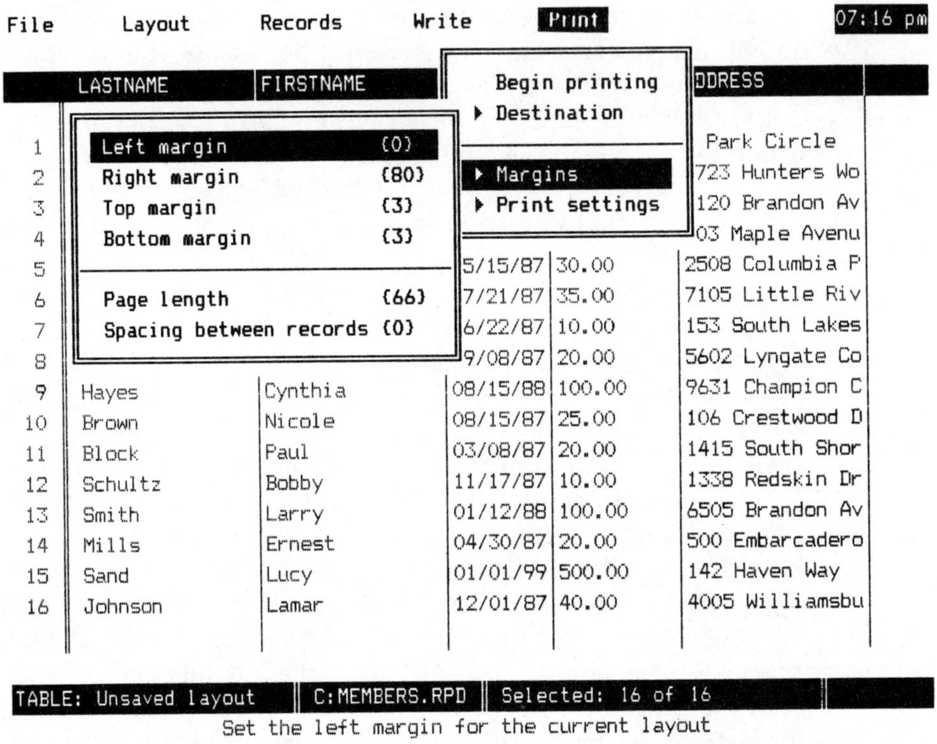

Figure 3-28. The Margins submenu

printer should stop after each page. When the option "Omit repeated data" is turned on, RapidFile will suppress the printing of repeated data in any field. These options will be covered in detail in a later chapter. For now, press ESC twice to close both menus.

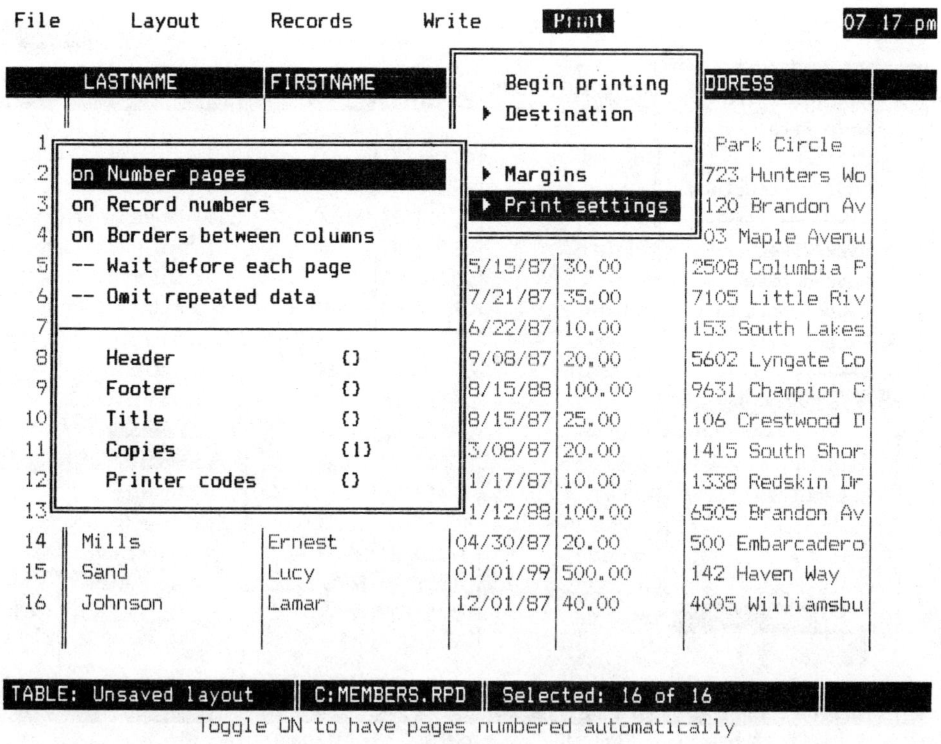

Figure 3-29. The Print Settings submenu

Use PGDN, if necessary, to get to the end of the database, and move the cursor until you are at the last name entry for the last record in the database (Johnson). Press F2 to edit this entry. Add a comma and Jr. to the end of the name, so that the entry reads "Johnson, Jr." and press RETURN.

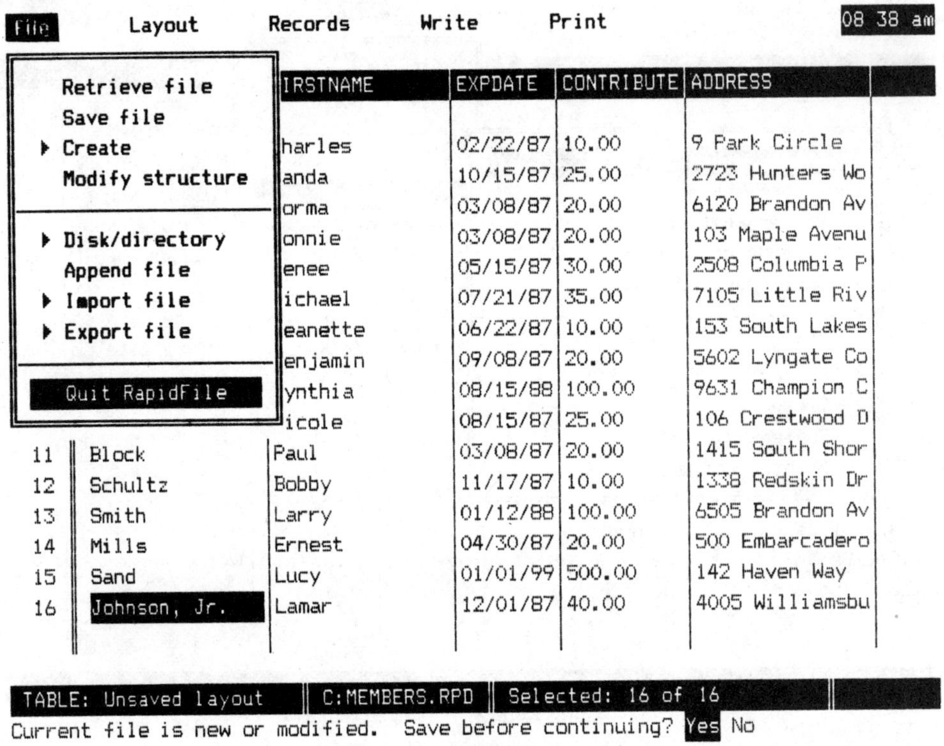

Figure 3-30. The File menu with save prompt

EXITING RAPIDFILE

Enter CONTROL-F to open the File menu, and enter Q for "Quit" to leave RapidFile.

Recall, however, that you made a change to Lamar Johnson's record and the change has not been saved. RapidFile reminds you of this by displaying the prompt **Current file is new or modified. Save before continuing?** (see Figure 3-30).

Enter Y (for "Yes") to request the save operation. Next you are prompted to enter a name for the file you want to save, and the previous name, MEMBERS, appears automatically. Just press RETURN to keep the previous name for the file.

RapidFile saves the revised version of the file; it replaces the previous MEMBERS file with the file containing the changes you made. The message that is now displayed says **Leave RapidFile? Yes No.** Enter Y for "Yes," and the DOS prompt will appear.

Managing Your Database

Chapter 4

As you work with your data in RapidFile, you will find that you spend much of your time adding new records, finding records, making changes, rearranging records in a desired order, and performing similar tasks that keep your database up-to-date. This chapter will detail how you can effectively perform these tasks.

First, load RapidFile by inserting the System disk in drive A or by switching to the hard-disk subdirectory that contains the program. Enter RF, and press RETURN twice to bypass the license agreement and Welcome screen. Within a moment the RapidFile File menu will appear.

RETRIEVING FILES

To load a file that was previously saved, use the option "Retrieve file" from the File menu. Press R for "Retrieve file," and select MEMBERS from the window of files that appears. In a moment the Friends of Crabgrass membership listing will appear.

ADDING RECORDS TO AN EXISTING FILE

To add a new record, you must get to the bottom of the database and move the cursor down by one record. Even if the database is large, you can do this quickly by entering CONTROL-END. Whether you are in "Table" layout or in "Form" layout, CONTROL-END will take you to the last record in the database.

Once you are at the last record in the file, press DOWN ARROW if you are in "Table" layout or PGDN if you are in "Form" layout. Then proceed to fill in each field as you did in Chapter 3. Press RETURN upon the completion of each entry.

In addition to adding records at the end of a database, RapidFile offers ways to add records at any location within a database. The combination CONTROL-A (for "Add") will insert a blank record below the present location of the cursor in "Table" layout (or below the current record in "Form" layout). CONTROL-INS will insert a blank record immediately above the present location of the cursor when in "Table" layout (or immediately above the current record when in "Form" layout).

EDITING RECORDS

Editing a record is basically the same whether you are in "Table" layout or in "Form" layout. Edit a record by positioning the cursor on the field you wish to edit, and then press F2 (EDIT). An area known as the Edit Panel will open at the bottom of the screen. The Edit Panel contains the current contents of the field. Using the arrow keys INS and DEL, you can make any desired changes to the data. Once the changes have been made, press RETURN, and the changes will take effect.

As an example, suppose that Lonnie Askew has just renewed membership in the association and made a contribution of $25. You want to update the database to reflect this change. Use

UP ARROW or DOWN ARROW to highlight the entry for Askew, and place the cursor in the Expdate field.

Press F2 and the Edit Panel will open, displaying the current expiration date (see Figure 4-1). Use DEL to remove the existing date. Enter 03/08/88 and press RETURN to make the change.

Move the cursor to the Contribute field and press F2. Change the amount to 25.00 and press RETURN. You have added the needed changes to your file.

File   Layout   Records   Write   Print   09 07 pm

	LASTNAME	FIRSTNAME	EXPDATE	CONTRIBUTE	ADDRESS
1	Harris	Charles	02/22/87	10.00	9 Park Circle
2	Sloan	Wanda	10/15/87	25.00	2723 Hunters Wo
3	Roberts	Norma	03/08/87	20.00	6120 Brandon Av
4	Askew	Lonnie	03/08/87	20.00	103 Maple Avenu
5	Jones	Renee	05/15/87	30.00	2508 Columbia P
6	Shaw	Michael	07/21/87	35.00	7105 Little Riv
7	Baker	Jeanette	06/22/87	10.00	153 South Lakes
8	Baker	Benjamin	09/08/87	20.00	5602 Lyngate Co
9	Hayes	Cynthia	08/15/88	100.00	9631 Champion C
10	Brown	Nicole	08/15/87	25.00	106 Crestwood D
11	Block	Paul	03/08/87	20.00	1415 South Shor
12	Schultz	Bobby	11/17/87	10.00	1338 Redskin Dr
13	Smith	Larry	01/12/88	100.00	6505 Brandon Av
14	Mills	Ernest	04/30/87	20.00	500 Embarcadero
15	Sand	Lucy	01/01/99	500.00	142 Haven Way
16	Johnson	Lamar	12/01/87	40.00	4005 Williamsbu

03/08/87

Figure 4-1. The Edit Panel

A SHORTCUT FOR SAVING

Whenever you are updating a file, it is always wise to save the file often so that unforeseen accidents (such as a power failure) will not cause the loss of work. RapidFile provides a handy shortcut for saving a file and for continuing to work with the same file afterward. The combination CONTROL-RETURN will save changes to a file and leave you in the same file.

Press CONTROL-RETURN now. The Message Area will display the message **Saving File**, and the changes will be stored on disk.

DUPLICATING DATA IN OTHER RECORDS

If you must enter the same data within a series of records, you can copy the data from one field (or from all fields) within a record to successive records. This saves time during data entry. As an example, suppose that Friends of Crabgrass received membership contributions from multiple members of the same family. It would be tedious to re-enter the same data for all fields except the field containing the first name. RapidFile offers two key combinations to copy data from one record to another: CONTROL-" will copy the entire record, and F8 (COPY) will copy one field within a record. If you highlight a record with F6 (HIGHLIGHT) before performing the copy, RapidFile will copy data from the highlighted record. If no record is highlighted, RapidFile will copy the data from the record immediately above the cursor.

Try copying the contents of a record. Move the cursor to the record for Norma Roberts. Assume that two more members of the Roberts household, James and Terry, have joined the organization. Since you want to copy the data from the record for

Norma Roberts, move the cursor to that record, and press F6 to highlight the record.

Next move the cursor until it is just below the last record in the file. Press F8 and Roberts will appear in the Edit Panel. Press RETURN to copy the name with no changes into the new record.

Move the cursor to the Address field of the new record. Since the record for Norma Roberts is still highlighted, a COPY command will cause the contents of the Address field to be filled with the contents of that same field for Norma Roberts. Press F8 and RETURN to copy the data.

Move to the City field and then press F8 and RETURN. Do the same with the State field, the Zip field, and the Type field. Now all that remains is to fill in the data that could not be copied because it differs from Norma Roberts's record. In the Firstname field for the new record, enter

James

In the Expdate field enter

05/06/87

and in the Contribute field enter

25.00

To copy an entire record, simply highlight the desired record, and then press CONTROL-". To try this, highlight the new record you just created by moving the cursor to that record and pressing F6. Then move the cursor to the end of the file and press CONTROL-". Another record for James Roberts will appear. Use F2 to change the entry in the Firstname field to Terry, and the additions to the file will be complete. Press F6 twice to remove the highlight from the record.

LOCATING RECORDS

Finding a record is of prime importance in most database applications. When the office manager asks you for "that person named Sand who lives in Maryland and gave us a lot of money last year," you want to be able to search quickly through your database and come up with the answer. For our sample file it may not be much of a problem because you can see all the records when in "Table" layout. With a membership roll of more than 3000 members, however, it would be unthinkable to search with PGUP and PGDN. RapidFile has the ability to do a fast search on any field in the database using the "Locate" option of the Records menu.

Locating a Record by Record Number

If you happen to know the record number of a given record, you can locate that record with a shortcut. The combination CONTROL-G is used for this task (it is easier to remember if you assume that G stands for Go To). Enter CONTROL-G now. RapidFile will prompt **Go to record number 1...18**, and the cursor will appear in an entry field that displays the current record number. Just type in the number of the record you want (try 12 in this case), and press RETURN. Once you have entered 12, the cursor will move to that record.

Locating a Record with a Search

Finding a record by the record number is fine if you happen to know the record number. With databases of any size, however, you will probably not know the number. To find a given record when you do not know the record number, enter CONTROL-R to open the Records menu (see Figure 4-2).

You will use the Records menu often throughout the next two chapters, so a few words about the options are appropriate here. The option "Order" is used to change the sort order of records in a file (such as whether the records are arranged in alphabetical order, or by date, or by amount contributed). "Locate" is

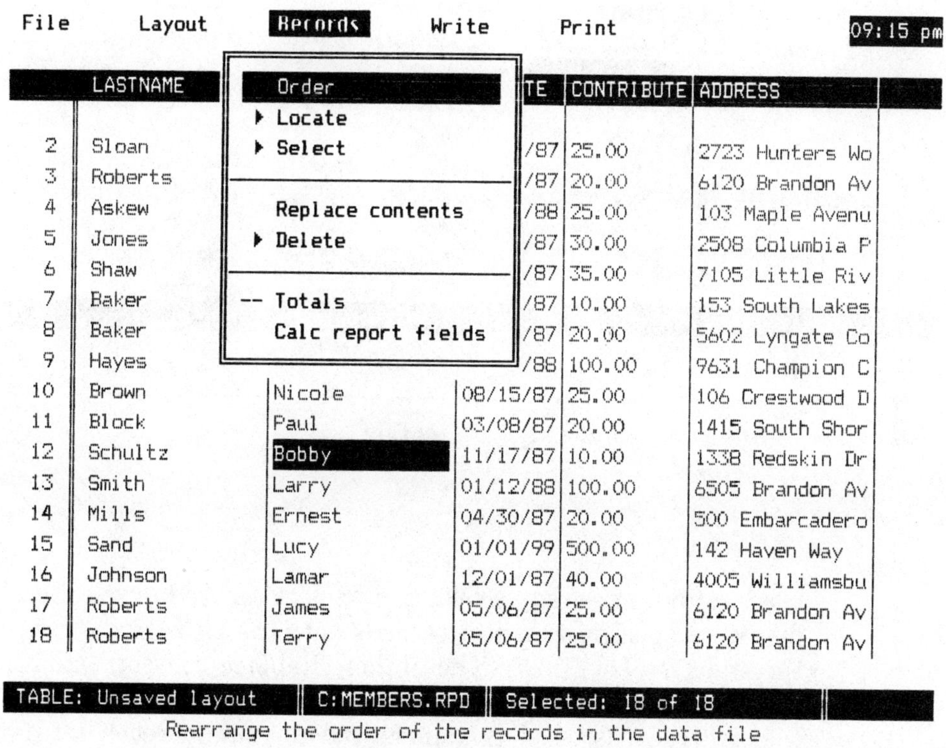

Figure 4-2. The Records menu

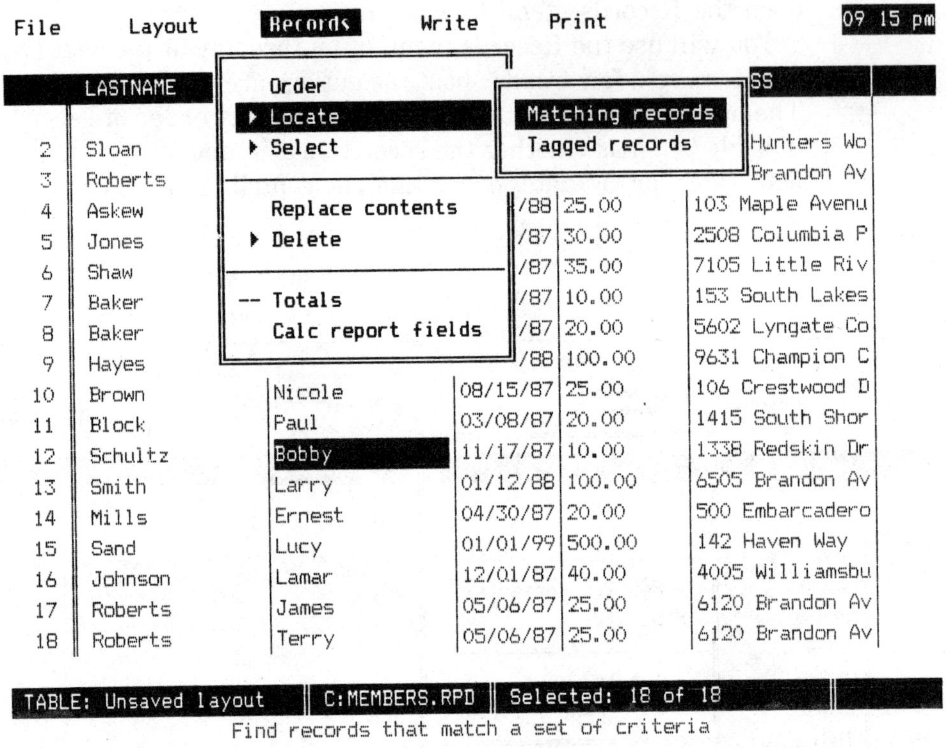

Figure 4-3. Submenu for the "Locate" option

used to find a desired record, and "Select" is used to select and display a specific group of records (such as all records where the state is New York). The option "Replace contents" allows you to change the contents of a given field for an entire group of selected records. "Delete" allows you to remove records from the database, and "Totals" adds numeric fields and provides totals for those fields. "Calc report fields" is used to provide calculations on special numeric fields within reports. This option will be covered in more detail in a later chapter.

Consider solving the problem of the office manager at Friends of Crabgrass. With the Records menu open, enter L for "Locate." A submenu will appear, giving you a choice of "Matching records" or "Tagged records" (Figure 4-3). The subject of tagged records will be discussed later. For now enter M for "Matching records." The table layout of the database will be replaced with a screen entitled Locate Matching Records (see Figure 4-4).

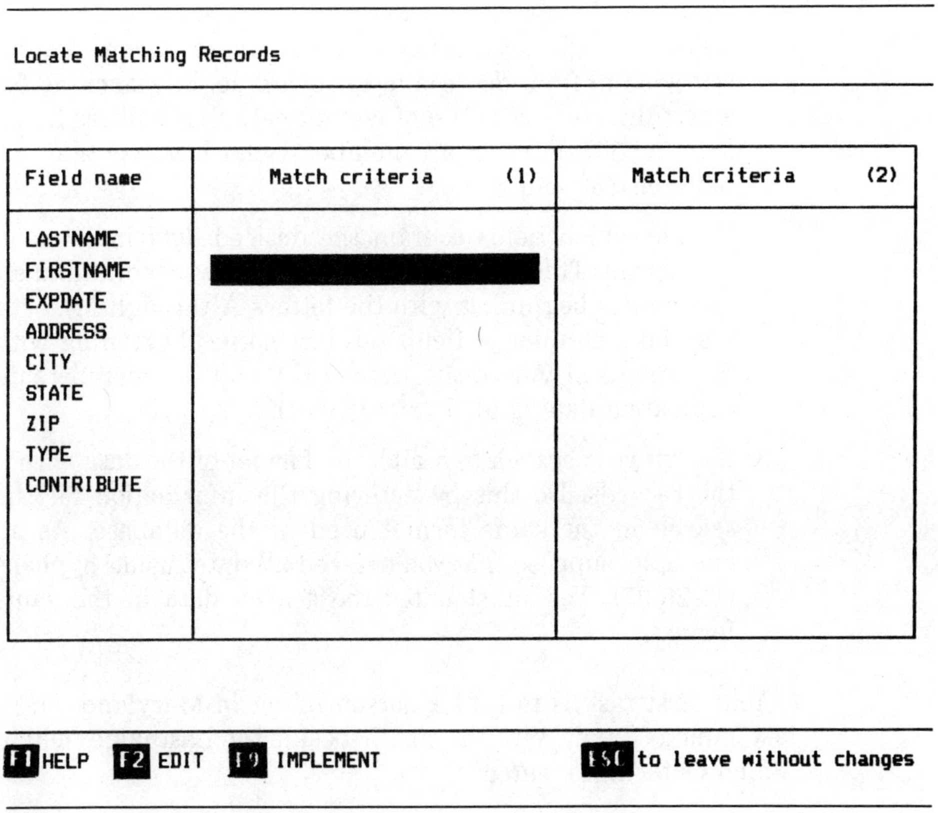

Figure 4-4. The Locate Matching Records screen

The Locate Matching Records screen allows you to enter matching criteria, or requirements, that a record must meet before it will be located. You can move the highlighted cursor around the columns using the arrow keys. The leftmost column of the screen will show the names of all fields in the database. To the immediate right of all field names are columns titled Match criteria (1) and Match criteria (2). To the right of Match criteria (2) are additional columns that are presently invisible. These columns come into view only if needed, as you will see shortly. Place the cursor next to the field you wish to search and then enter the information for the desired search.

Using a Criteria screen is a three-step process.

1. Determine the text, range of numbers, or range of dates you wish to find. You could, for example, be searching for a certain name, a group of last names, all members living in a certain city, or all members who have contributed between $50 and $100.
2. Decide which fields contain the desired data involved in the search. This may be one field (if you wanted to find all last names beginning with the letters A through M), or it may be a number of fields (all last names beginning with A through M where the state is CA and the membership expiration date is 01/01/88 or later).
3. Design your search to match the format of the data within the records. Do this by entering the information for the search in the same format used in the database. As an example, suppose that you entered all dates using hyphens (11-25-67). You must enter the search data in the same format.

Your first task is to find a person living in Maryland whose last name is Sand. With the cursor beside the Lastname field in Match criteria (1), enter

Sand

After entering the name, move the cursor down until it is beside the State field, and then press F2. Enter

MD

for Maryland. Your screen should resemble Figure 4-5.

Once you have entered the match criteria, you can find a desired record by pressing F9 (IMPLEMENT). Press F9 now and you will see the cursor move to the desired record in the database as shown in Figure 4-6.

Locate Matching Records

Field name	Match criteria (1)	Match criteria (2)
LASTNAME	SAND	
FIRSTNAME		
EXPDATE		
ADDRESS		
CITY		
STATE	MD	
ZIP		
TYPE		
CONTRIBUTE		

F1 HELP F2 EDIT F9 IMPLEMENT ESC to leave without changes

Figure 4-5. Entering match criteria

File Layout Records Write Print 09 22 pm

	LASTNAME	FIRSTNAME	EXPDATE	CONTRIBUTE	ADDRESS
2	Sloan	Wanda	10/15/87	25.00	2723 Hunters Wo
3	Roberts	Norma	03/08/87	20.00	6120 Brandon Av
4	Askew	Lonnie	03/08/88	25.00	103 Maple Avenu
5	Jones	Renee	05/15/87	30.00	2508 Columbia P
6	Shaw	Michael	07/21/87	35.00	7105 Little Riv
7	Baker	Jeanette	06/22/87	10.00	153 South Lakes
8	Baker	Benjamin	09/08/87	20.00	5602 Lyngate Co
9	Hayes	Cynthia	08/15/88	100.00	9631 Champion C
10	Brown	Nicole	08/15/87	25.00	106 Crestwood D
11	Block	Paul	03/08/87	20.00	1415 South Shor
12	Schultz	Bobby	11/17/87	10.00	1338 Redskin Dr
13	Smith	Larry	01/12/88	100.00	6505 Brandon Av
14	Mills	Ernest	04/30/87	20.00	500 Embarcadero
15	Sand	Lucy	01/01/99	500.00	142 Haven Way
16	Johnson	Lamar	12/01/87	40.00	4005 Williamsbu
17	Roberts	James	05/06/87	25.00	6120 Brandon Av
18	Roberts	Terry	05/06/87	25.00	6120 Brandon Av

TABLE: Unsaved layout ║ C:MEMBERS.RPD ║ Selected: 18 of 18

Use ↑ ↓ to locate previous/next record,
END to count, ESC to exit.

Figure 4-6. RapidFile highlights the located record

Notice that the Message Area contains the prompt **Use ↑↓ to locate previous/next record, END to count, ESC to exit.** In cases where multiple records meet the search criteria, you can move the cursor among those records with UP ARROW and DOWN ARROW. END will provide a count of the number of records meeting the criteria, and ESC will end the search.

Press ESC now to end the search. Unlike some file managers, RapidFile is not *case significant* in finding a record; in other words, you could search for Sand, sand, or SAND, and the desired record would be found.

Matching on Two or More Fields

To search for records that meet criteria in two or more fields, simply type in the information in the proper format next to each desired field. If, for example, you wish to find all members living in California who donated $20 during the last membership drive, you will need to place CA in the match criteria area next to the State field and 20.00 in the match criteria area next to the Contribute field.

To try this, enter CONTROL-R, and then enter L to select the "Locate" option of the Records menu. Enter M for "Matching records," and the Locate Matching Records screen will appear. Note that the screen contains the criteria used during the last search. You will need to delete the previous criteria to start a new search.

Place the cursor next to the Lastname field and press the DEL key to delete the name Sand. To enter the first field criteria, place the cursor next to the State field, and press DEL to delete MD. Enter the letters

CA

and then press RETURN.

To enter the second field criteria, place the cursor next to the Contribute field and enter

20.00

Your screen should resemble the one shown in Figure 4-7.

Locate Matching Records

Field name	Match criteria (1)	Match criteria (2)
LASTNAME		
FIRSTNAME		
EXPDATE		
ADDRESS		
CITY		
STATE	CA	
ZIP		
TYPE		
CONTRIBUTE	20.00	

F1 HELP F2 EDIT F9 IMPLEMENT ESC to leave without changes

Figure 4-7. A screen with match criteria for two fields

Press F9 to implement the search, and the cursor will move to the first desired record in the database that meets the search criteria (see Figure 4-8). Press DOWN ARROW once, and the cursor will move to the next record that meets the criteria. Press ESC to end the search.

File Layout Records Write Print 09:26 pm

	LASTNAME	FIRSTNAME	EXPDATE	CONTRIBUTE	ADDRESS
2	Sloan	Wanda	10/15/87	25.00	2723 Hunters Wo
3	Roberts	Norma	03/08/87	20.00	6120 Brandon Av
4	Askew	Lonnie	03/08/88	25.00	103 Maple Avenu
5	Jones	Renee	05/15/87	30.00	2508 Columbia P
6	Shaw	Michael	07/21/87	35.00	7105 Little Riv
7	Baker	Jeanette	06/22/87	10.00	153 South Lakes
8	Baker	Benjamin	09/08/87	20.00	5602 Lyngate Co
9	Hayes	Cynthia	08/15/88	100.00	9631 Champion C
10	Brown	Nicole	08/15/87	25.00	106 Crestwood D
11	Block	Paul	03/08/87	20.00	1415 South Shor
12	Schultz	Bobby	11/17/87	10.00	1338 Redskin Dr
13	Smith	Larry	01/12/88	100.00	6505 Brandon Av
14	Mills	Ernest	04/30/87	20.00	500 Embarcadero
15	Sand	Lucy	01/01/99	500.00	142 Haven Way
16	Johnson	Lamar	12/01/87	40.00	4005 Williamsbu
17	Roberts	James	05/06/87	25.00	6120 Brandon Av
18	Roberts	Terry	05/06/87	25.00	6120 Brandon Av

TABLE: Unsaved layout | C:MEMBERS.RPD | Selected: 18 of 18

Use ↑ ↓ to locate previous/next record,
END to count, ESC to exit.

Figure 4-8. The record with fields that meet both criteria

Matching on Multiple Criteria

Suppose you want to find records that meet more than one criteria in the same field, such as all members living in California, New York, and Texas. First, change layout modes so it will be easier to see the entire record, including the name of the states. Press F3 (FLIP) to change from "Table" layout to "Form" layout.

Next press CONTROL-R, and then L to select the "Locate" option of the Records menu. Enter M for "Matching records," and the Locate Matching Records screen will appear. Again, the screen will contain the criteria used during the last search. You will need to delete the previous criteria to start a new search.

You could highlight each entry previously made and press DEL. However, there is a faster way to clear all previous entries. In this screen (and in many other entry screens in RapidFile), use the combination CONTROL-DEL to delete all entries.

Enter CONTROL-DEL now. In the Message Area you will see **Clear all Locate settings? Yes No.** Enter Y for "Yes," and the prior entries will be removed. Move the cursor until it is beside the State field; enter

CA

Press RIGHT ARROW once to move the cursor to Match criteria (2); enter

NY

Press RIGHT ARROW once more, and another column, Match criteria (3), will come into view (see Figure 4-9). Enter

TX

RapidFile permits the entry of up to seven different match criteria for any single field name. This provides enough flexibility to find a desired record under almost any circumstances you may encounter.

With the criteria for all three states entered, press F9 to implement the search. The cursor will appear on Askew, the

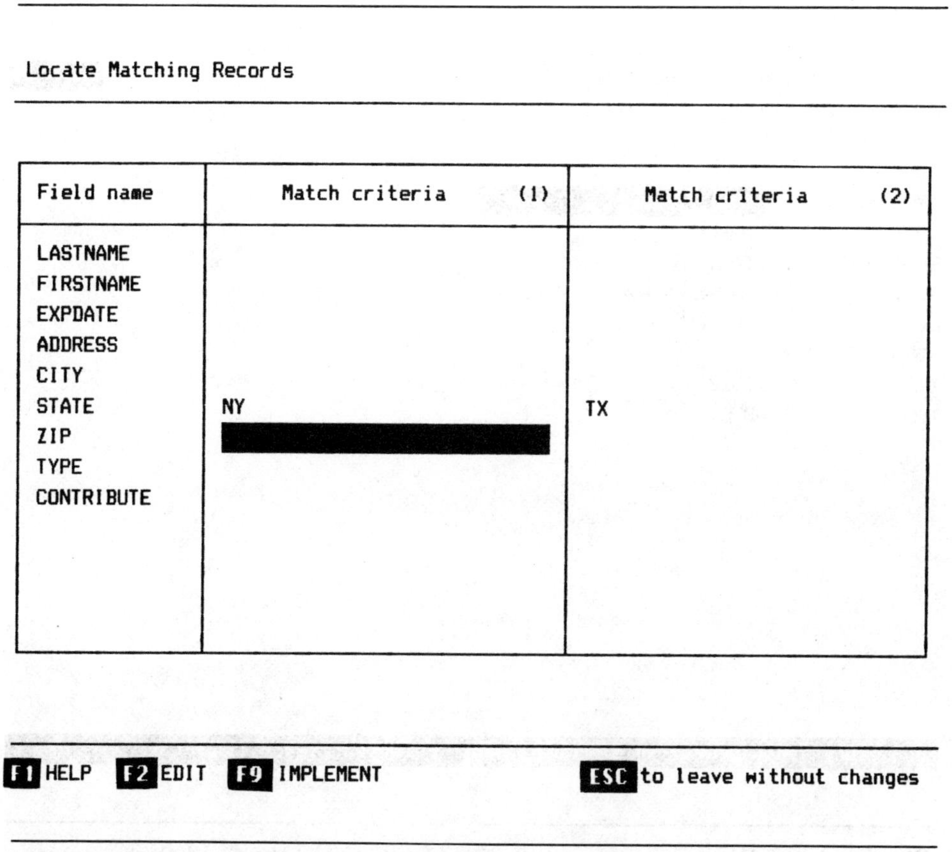

Figure 4-9. Screen with multiple match criteria per field

first member who lives in one of the three states listed (see Figure 4-10). The Message Area contains the message **Use PGUP, PGDN to locate previous/next record, END to count, ESC to exit.** PGUP and PGDN function as UP ARROW and DOWN ARROW function in "Table" layout.

Press PGDN once and the cursor will move to Jones, the second member who meets the specified criteria. Continue

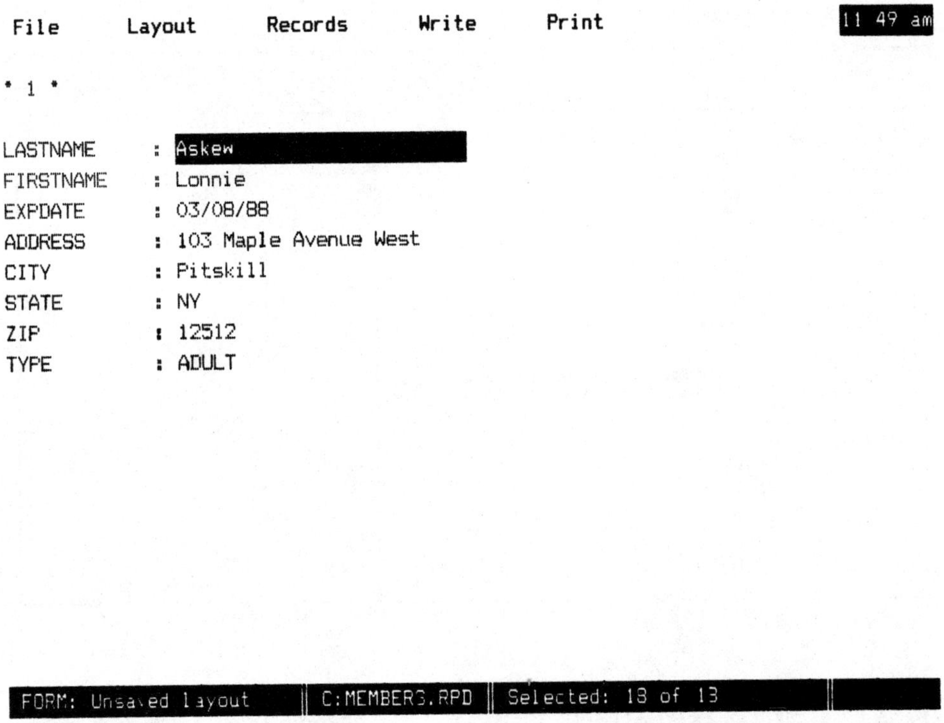

Figure 4-10. First record to meet three criteria in the field State

pressing PGDN repeatedly, and you will see that the cursor highlights only those records of members in the states named. When in "Table" layout you will see the same records highlighted. The only difference is that you must use UP ARROW and DOWN ARROW to move between records when in "Table" layout.

END can be used to count the number of records that meet the specified condition after the "Locate" option has been used. Press END now and you will see **6 records found-press return**

to continue appear in the Message Area. Press RETURN and the search will end.

Complex Matching

You can use RapidFile's ability to match criteria for various fields to set up very complex searches. As an example, suppose that you want to see records of members who live in Texas or California whose membership expires in 1988 and who contributed $25 or more to the association during the last membership drive. Friends of Crabgrass is starting a fund-raising drive in those states, and you would like to send a personalized letter to members who might help your fund-raising prospects by being generous. To perform searches of such a complex nature, you will use math symbols—equal (=), greater than (>) and less than (<)—as a part of the criteria. In this case, what RapidFile needs for search criteria are the State field = TX or CA; an Expdate field > 12/31/87; and a Contribute field >= 25.00. Enter CONTROL-R and then L and M to choose the "Locate" option and to get to the Locate Matching Records screen. Enter CONTROL-DEL and Y (for "Yes") to clear the previous entries. Using the arrow keys to position the cursor and F2 (EDIT) to edit any existing entries, enter the following match criteria:

- In column (1) next to the State field, enter

  TX

- In column (2) next to the State field, enter

  CA

- In columns (1) and (2) next to the Expdate field, enter

  > 12/31/87

- In columns (1) and (2) next to the Contribute field, enter

  >= 25.00

  Your screen should resemble Figure 4-11.

Press F9 to implement the search. By using PGUP and PGDN, you should see only two records, Cynthia Hayes and Larry

Locate Matching Records

Field name	Match criteria (1)	Match criteria (2)
LASTNAME		
FIRSTNAME		
EXPDATE	> 12/31/87	> 12/31/87
ADDRESS		
CITY		
STATE	TX	CA
ZIP		
TYPE		
CONTRIBUTE	>= 25.00	>= 25.00

F1 HELP F2 EDIT F9 IMPLEMENT ESC to leave without changes

Figure 4-11. A screen with complex match criteria

Locate Matching Records

Field name	Match criteria (1)	Match criteria (2)
LASTNAME		
FIRSTNAME		
EXPDATE		
ADDRESS		
CITY		
STATE	VA	NY
ZIP		
TYPE		
CONTRIBUTE		

F1 HELP F2 EDIT F9 IMPLEMENT ESC to leave without changes

Figure 4-12. Match criteria in multiple columns

Smith. No other records in the database meet the specified criteria.

As an alternative to using match criteria in multiple columns, you can also use combinations of criteria within a single column. To do so, you must use the words AND, OR, and NOT to link the desired criteria. Always enter these words surrounded by periods.

An example of how to use this method can be seen by using

Locate Matching Records

Field name	Match criteria (1)	Match criteria (2)
LASTNAME		
FIRSTNAME		
EXPDATE		
ADDRESS		
CITY		
STATE	VA .OR. NY	
ZIP		
TYPE		
CONTRIBUTE		

F1 HELP F2 EDIT F9 IMPLEMENT ESC to leave without changes

Figure 4-13. Different entries with same results

the information in the screens shown in Figures 4-12 and 4-13. Both screens will result in RapidFile locating all members living in Virginia or in New York. The AND, OR, and NOT expressions work the same way they do in basic algebra. AND requires a match with both conditions true, OR requires one condition or the other, and NOT excludes records that match the condition. As an example, you could locate members with contributions greater than $25 and less than $100 by specifying

> 25.00 .AND. < 100.00 in the match criteria column next to the Contribute field. To find members who live in Arizona or Florida, you could specify AZ .OR. FL in the match criteria column next to the State field. To find members living in any state but Illinois, you could enter .NOT. IL in the match criteria column next to the State field. By combining the criteria for matches in the ways described, you can locate precisely defined groups of records.

In most cases RapidFile finds any text that you enter as a search criteria regardless of where that text falls within a field. There are times when this may not be what you want. In searching a City field in a large database, for example, you may want to find persons living in a town named Atlantic. The problem is that if you enter Atlantic next to the City field as a search criteria, you are apt to get records of persons living in Atlantic, Atlantic Beach, Atlantic Bay, Atlantic City, Atlantic Island, and other towns with names that begin with the word *Atlantic*. To locate text containing only the specified word in the field, surround the word with quotation marks when entering it in the criteria column. In this case you would enter

"Atlantic"

in the City field. The examples outlined in Table 4-1 can be used as an aid in building complex matching criteria when dealing with text in a field.

The following summary of hints when entering matching criteria may be helpful in constructing complex searches:

- RapidFile ignores capitalization and spaces before and after text entered as matching criteria. Whether you enter SMITH or Smith or smith, RapidFile will find the record.
- To narrow a text search to specific text, use quotation marks before, after, or on both sides of the text as outlined in Table 4-1.
- The symbols =, <, and > can be used to build comparisons

that cover a range of dates, numeric values, or letters of the alphabet.

- The comparison operators .AND., .OR., and .NOT., can be used to select records that match multiple criteria. Use .AND. to select records that must match both criteria, use .OR. to select records that match one criteria or the other, and use .NOT. to exclude specific criteria. These operators must always be surrounded with periods.

SELECTING RECORDS

In addition to finding records, you will need to know how to select groups of records. Selecting records is akin to filtering a database so that only the selected records appear. By selecting a group of records, you can print only those records or generate totals based on only that group of records.

Table 4-1. Matching Criteria for Text

Example	Selects These Records
Atlantic	Contains Atlantic anywhere in the field
=Atlantic	Contains Atlantic anywhere in the field
"Atlantic"	Contains only the word Atlantic
"Atlantic	Field begins with Atlantic
Atlantic"	Field ends with Atlantic
>At	Alphabetically greater than At
>=At	Alphabetically greater than or equal to At
<At	Alphabetically less than At
<=At	Alphabetically less than or equal to At
""	Contents of cell are blank

Much of the technique behind selecting records will be familiar at this point because the process uses the same matching criteria screens that are used to locate records. Only the menu options used to select records are different. To select records, you will use the "Select" option of the Records menu.

Enter CONTROL-R to open the Records menu, and choose "Select." A submenu opens to reveal five choices (see Figure 4-14).

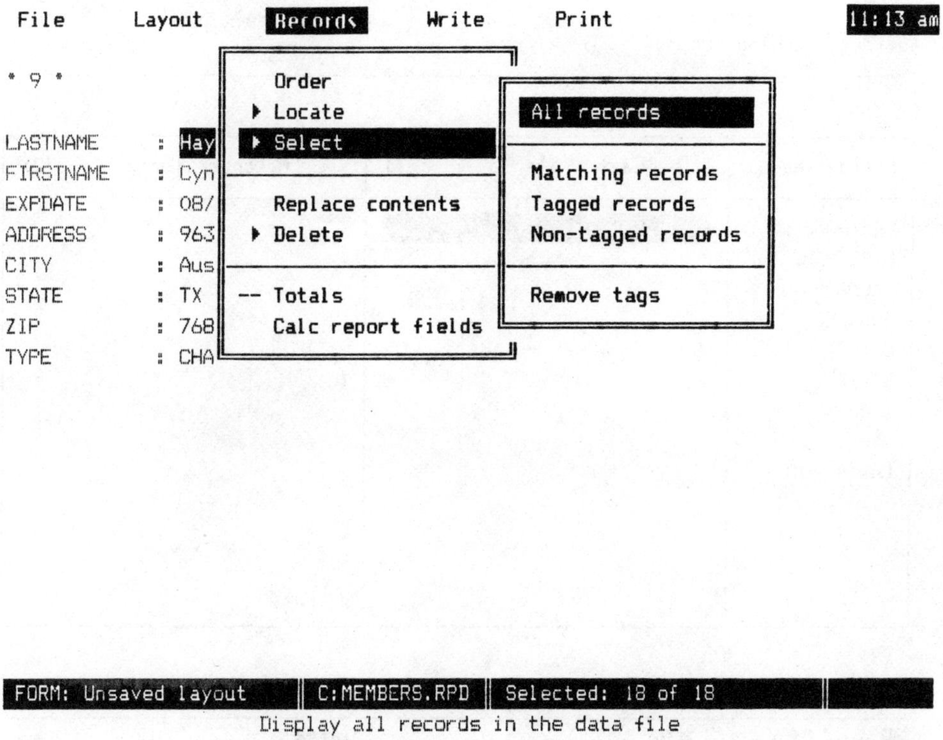

Figure 4-14. The Select submenu

The options "Tagged records," "Non-tagged records," and "Remove tags" are topics for discussion in the next section of this chapter. The option "All records" results in all records being selected. This option is usually used to restore a complete display of the database after the "Select" option has been used to select a group of records.

"Matching records" will allow you to select a group of records by using the same type of criteria that were used to locate records. Enter M for "Matching records." A familiar-looking screen will appear (Figure 4-15). The only difference between

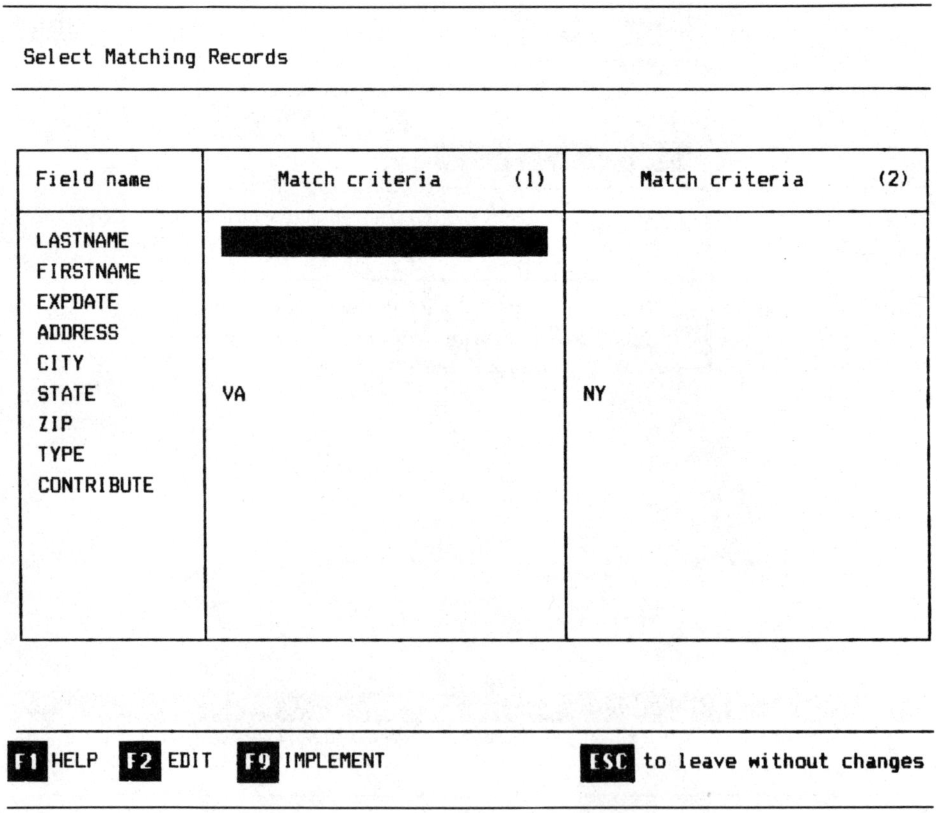

Figure 4-15. The Select Matching Records screen

this screen and the Locate Matching Records screen is the title; Figure 4-15 shows the Select Matching Records screen.

For an example let's use .OR. to select all members living in Chicago or in Los Angeles. First enter CONTROL-DEL, and then enter Y to clear the previous entries. Next move the cursor to Match Criteria (1) next to the City field, and enter the following:

Chicago .OR. Los Angeles

Once you have entered the criteria, press F9 to implement the selection. Using PGUP you will see that three records are available.

This may seem no different than the results yielded by the "Locate" option of the Records menu, but there is an important difference. The chosen records are selected, meaning these are the only records available to other operations within RapidFile —operations such as printing a list or a report. Any records that did not meet the conditions of the selection are hidden from view and will remain hidden until you perform a different selection or until you select all records. As an example of the usefulness of selecting records, suppose that you decide you need a printed copy of the selected records. Turn on your printer and enter CONTROL-P to open the Print menu. Choose "Begin printing" and the Message Area will prompt **All, Current, or Remaining?** Select "All" to print all the selected records. The results will resemble the following:

```
- 1 -

LASTNAME      : Brown
FIRSTNAME     : Nicole
EXPDATE       : 08/15/87
CONTRIBUTE    :  25.00
ADDRESS       : 106 Crestwood Drive
CITY          : Chicago
STATE         : IL
ZIP           : 60610
TYPE          : REGULAR
```

```
- 2 -
LASTNAME      : Block
FIRSTNAME     : Paul
EXPDATE       : 03/08/87
CONTRIBUTE    :  20.00
ADDRESS       : 1415 South Shore Drive
CITY          : Chicago
STATE         : IL
ZIP           : 60617
TYPE          : REGULAR
- 3 -
LASTNAME      : Smith
FIRSTNAME     : Larry
EXPDATE       : 01/12/88
CONTRIBUTE    :  100.00
ADDRESS       : 6505 Brandon Avenue
CITY          : Los Angeles
STATE         : CA
ZIP           : 90055
TYPE          : CHARTER
```

Note that only the selected records are printed. By comparison, if you were to print the file after using the "Locate" option of the Records menu, you would find that all the records in the database would be printed. Try pressing F3 to flip to the "Table" layout. Only the selected records will be visible, as Figure 4-16 shows.

Selecting records is useful when you want to work with a specific portion of a database. One important fact to realize is that the records are still present in the database. They just appear to have vanished because not all records are selected at this time. RapidFile will leave the other records hidden, even if you save the file, exit the program, and reload the file later. To demonstrate this capability, press CONTROL-RETURN to save the file. Then open the File menu with CONTROL-F and enter Q for "Quit," and then Y for "Yes." When you are back in DOS, load the program again by entering

RF

Choose "Retrieve file" from the File menu and highlight MEMBERS to load the file. What you will see, when the file is

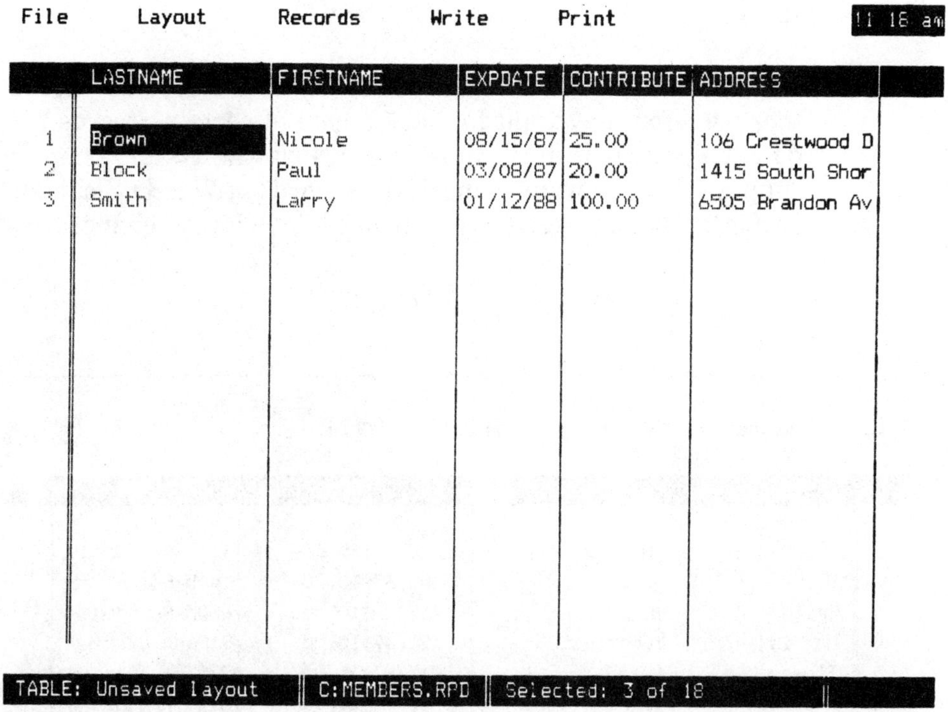

Figure 4-16. "Table" layout with selected records

loaded, are the same three records that were visible when the file was saved.

RapidFile indicates the number of records actually in a database with the words contained at the right side of the Status Bar: **Selected: 3 of 18.** To make all the records available for use, use the option "All records" of the Select submenu.

Enter CONTROL-R and then S to open the Select submenu. Enter A for "All records," and the complete membership database will appear. The Status Bar will display **Selected: 18 of 18,** which indicates that all records are currently selected.

TAGGED AND UNTAGGED RECORDS

RapidFile provides a way to manually mark records for further use. You may want to make a note of certain records that do not necessarily meet any kind of criteria. As an example, suppose that you want to mark the records of Wanda Sloan and Jeanette Baker because they phoned in address changes last

File Layout Records Write Print 11 19 am

	LASTNAME	FIRSTNAME	EXPDATE	CONTRIBUTE	ADDRESS
1	Brown	Nicole	08/15/87	25.00	106 Crestwood D
2	Block	Paul	03/08/87	20.00	1415 South Shor
3	Smith	Larry	01/12/88	100.00	6505 Brandon Av
4	Harris	Charles	02/22/87	10.00	9 Park Circle
5 ♦	Sloan	♦Wanda	♦10/15/87	♦25.00	♦2723 Hunters Wo♦
6	Roberts	Norma	03/08/87	20.00	6120 Brandon Av
7	Askew	Lonnie	03/08/88	25.00	103 Maple Avenu
8	Jones	Renee	05/15/87	30.00	2508 Columbia P
9	Shaw	Michael	07/21/87	35.00	7105 Little Riv
10 ♦	Baker	♦Jeanette	♦06/22/87	♦10.00	♦153 South Lakes♦
11	Baker	Benjamin	09/08/87	20.00	5602 Lyngate Co
12	Hayes	Cynthia	08/15/88	100.00	9631 Champion C
13	Schultz	Bobby	11/17/87	10.00	1338 Redskin Dr
14	Mills	Ernest	04/30/87	20.00	500 Embarcadero
15	Sand	Lucy	01/01/99	500.00	142 Haven Way
16	Johnson	Lamar	12/01/87	40.00	4005 Williamsbu
17	Roberts	James	05/06/87	25.00	6120 Brandon Av

TABLE: Unsaved layout | C:MEMBERS.RPD | Selected: 18 of 18

Figure 4-17. Tagged records

week; you plan to update those records later. You can tag any record by placing the cursor anywhere within the desired record and pressing F5 (TAG). When a record has been tagged, a diamond-shaped symbol will appear at the field boundaries to mark the record. If you are working with forms, the tag appears by the record number.

Place the cursor on the record for Wanda Sloan, and press F5. Perform the same step for the entry for Jeanette Baker, and your screen will resemble Figure 4-17.

Selecting and Locating Tagged Records

Once records have been tagged, they will remain tagged until you remove the tags. (A tag can be removed by placing the cursor on the tagged record and pressing F5 again.) You can use the "Locate" and "Select" options of the Records menu to find or display only records that have been tagged. As an example, open the Records menu with CONTROL-R and choose "Select." Note that, in addition to selecting matching records, you can select tagged or untagged records.

Choose "Tagged records." The database will appear, displaying only the tagged records as shown in Figure 4-18. Using F5, you could move through a database, tagging only those records you want to work with later. Then you could use the "Select" option of the Records menu to narrow the available records to include only the tagged records. If you just wish to see the tagged records but do not want to do any work (like printing reports) with them, use the "Locate" option in place of the "Select" option of the Records menu, and choose "Tagged records" from the submenu that appears.

As an example, open the Records menu with CONTROL-R, and then enter S and A ("All") to restore the entire database. Enter CONTROL-R again to open the Records menu, and then choose

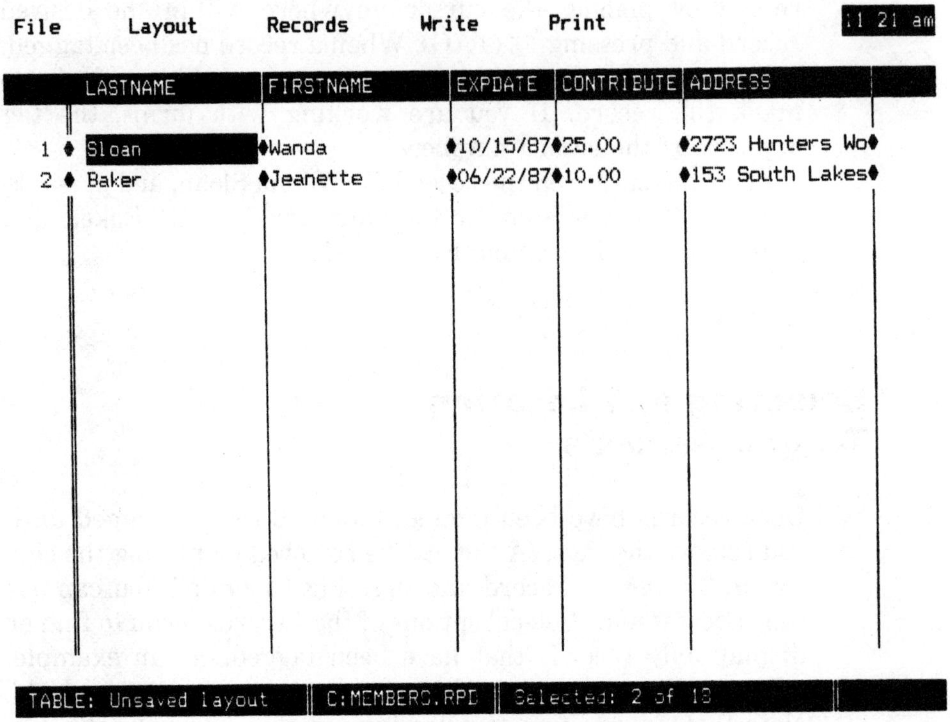

Figure 4-18. A display of tagged records

"Locate" and "Tagged records." The cursor will move to the record for Sloan, and the Message Area will indicate that you can use UP ARROW or DOWN ARROW to locate additional records. Press DOWN ARROW once, and the record for Jeanette Baker will be highlighted.

Removing All Tags

You can remove tags from all tagged records at once by using the "Remove tags" option of the Select submenu. To see how this works, open the Records menu with CONTROL-R and then enter S to open the Select submenu. Choose "Remove tags" and the tags will be removed from the tagged records.

SORTING A FILE

After a database is built, you may need to arrange it in different ways. As an example, consider the needs of the staff at Friends of Crabgrass. Susan, who does the accounting, often wants to refer to a list of members arranged by the size of the contribution. Linda, the association administrator, prefers to keep a list organized in alphabetical order by name, but Frank, who does the mass mailings, wants to keep a list arranged by ZIP code. You can arrange a file by *sorting*—that is, by changing the arrangement of the records to an order that you specify.

If you sorted a file of names arranged in random order, the sorted file would contain all the records that were in the old file, but they would be arranged in alphabetical order (see Figure 4-19).

You must choose a field on which to sort—the chosen field is often referred to as the *key field.* In some cases you will need to sort a database on more than one field. As an example, suppose that you sort a database using the last name as the key field. You may get groups of records with the same last names but with the first names in random order. In such a case you can sort the database, using one field (such as Lastname) as the primary key field and another field (such as Firstname) as the secondary key field.

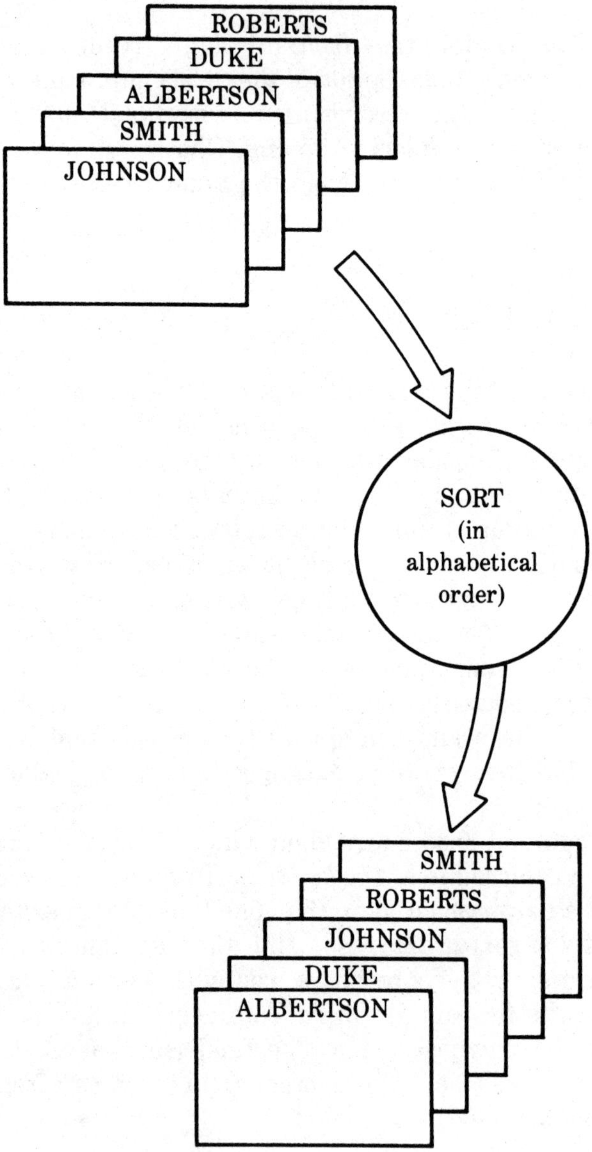

Figure 4-19. Sorting records in a database

To sort a file, open the Records menu with CONTROL-R and then choose the "Order" option. The Order Settings screen will appear (Figure 4-20).

The Order Settings screen provides the ability to sort a file using any field or a combination of fields in either ascending or descending order. The arrow keys are used to move the cursor between the Order and Direction columns. Numbers indicating the sorting order (1, 2, and so on) are placed in the Order column, and the choice "Ascending" or "Descending" is entered in the Direction column.

Order Settings

Field name	Order	Direction
LASTNAME	█	
FIRSTNAME		
EXPDATE		
ADDRESS		
CITY		
STATE		
ZIP		
TYPE		
CONTRIBUTE		

F1 HELP F2 EDIT F9 IMPLEMENT ESC to leave without changes

Figure 4-20. The Order Settings screen

Things are always clearer with an example. To satisfy Susan's request for a list of members arranged in ascending order according to contribution, move the cursor down until it is alongside the Contribute field. Enter 1. The number will appear in the Order column, and **Ascending** will automatically appear in the Direction column. The number indicates the priority of the field that will determine how the database will be sorted. When a database is sorted on a single field, this order has no real meaning. But when you sort a file on more than one field (as you will in later examples), you can use this column to choose which fields will take priority over other fields in the sort.

The Direction column contains **Ascending** as a default entry; RapidFile assumes you wish to sort files in ascending order. *Ascending order* means from A through Z if the sorted field is a text field, from lowest to highest number for numeric fields, and from earliest to latest date for date fields. *Descending order* is the reverse of ascending order; the sequence progresses from Z to A, from highest to lowest, and from latest to earliest. In most cases you will want the database to be sorted in ascending order, and ascending order is fine for our example.

Once the criteria for the sort have been entered in the Order Settings screen, the sort can be performed by pressing F9. Press F9 now, and the file will be sorted. It will reappear, arranged by the size of the contribution, in ascending order as shown in Figure 4-21. Note that records added to a database following a sort are not automatically placed in order. If you want those records to fall into a particular order, you must sort the database again after adding the records.

Sorting on Multiple Fields

So you print the file and pass it along to Susan, who immediately decides that wherever the contributions are for the same amount, the names should appear in alphabetical order.

File Layout Records Write Print 11 26 am

	LASTNAME	FIRSTNAME	EXPDATE	CONTRIBUTE	ADDRESS
1	Baker	Jeanette	06/22/87	10.00	153 South Lakes
2	Harris	Charles	02/22/87	10.00	9 Park Circle
3	Schultz	Bobby	11/17/87	10.00	1338 Redskin Dr
4	Block	Paul	03/08/87	20.00	1415 South Shor
5	Mills	Ernest	04/30/87	20.00	500 Embarcadero
6	Roberts	Norma	03/08/87	20.00	6120 Brandon Av
7	Baker	Benjamin	09/08/87	20.00	5602 Lyngate Co
8	Roberts	James	05/06/87	25.00	6120 Brandon Av
9	Roberts	Terry	05/06/87	25.00	6120 Brandon Av
10	Brown	Nicole	08/15/87	25.00	106 Crestwood D
11	Askew	Lonnie	03/08/88	25.00	103 Maple Avenu
12	Sloan	Wanda	10/15/87	25.00	2723 Hunters Wo
13	Jones	Renee	05/15/87	30.00	2508 Columbia P
14	Shaw	Michael	07/21/87	35.00	7105 Little Riv
15	Johnson	Lamar	12/01/87	40.00	4005 Williamsbu
16	Hayes	Cynthia	08/15/88	100.00	9631 Champion C
17	Smith	Larry	01/12/88	100.00	6505 Brandon Av

TABLE: Unsaved layout ‖ C:MEMBERS.RPD ‖ Selected: 18 of 18

Figure 4-21. File sorted by contribution in ascending order

Look at Figure 4-21. It is clear that for each group of equal amounts, the names are not in alphabetical order. To do this task will require a sort on more than one field.

Enter CONTROL-R and then O to get back to the Order Settings screen. The previous entries will still be present. Move the cursor until it is in the Order column and beside the Lastname field, and enter 2. **Ascending** again appears automatically in the Direction column.

The order that you have entered indicates that the file should be sorted in two ways. First it will be arranged by the amount of the contribution in ascending numeric order. Second, where contribution amounts are equal, the records will be sorted by last name in ascending alphabetical order. To see the results, press F9, and the sorted file will appear (see Figure 4-22).

File　　Layout　　Records　　Write　　Print　　11:27 am

	LASTNAME	FIRSTNAME	EXPDATE	CONTRIBUTE	ADDRESS
1	Baker	Jeanette	06/22/87	10.00	153 South Lakes
2	Harris	Charles	02/22/87	10.00	9 Park Circle
3	Schultz	Bobby	11/17/87	10.00	1338 Redskin Dr
4	Baker	Benjamin	09/08/87	20.00	5602 Lyngate Co
5	Block	Paul	03/08/87	20.00	1415 South Shor
6	Mills	Ernest	04/30/87	20.00	500 Embarcadero
7	Roberts	Norma	03/08/87	20.00	6120 Brandon Av
8	Askew	Lonnie	03/08/88	25.00	103 Maple Avenu
9	Brown	Nicole	08/15/87	25.00	106 Crestwood D
10	Roberts	Terry	05/06/87	25.00	6120 Brandon Av
11	Roberts	James	05/06/87	25.00	6120 Brandon Av
12	Sloan	Wanda	10/15/87	25.00	2723 Hunters Wo
13	Jones	Renee	05/15/87	30.00	2508 Columbia P
14	Shaw	Michael	07/21/87	35.00	7105 Little Riv
15	Johnson	Lamar	12/01/87	40.00	4005 Williamsbu
16	Hayes	Cynthia	08/15/88	100.00	9631 Champion C
17	Smith	Larry	01/12/88	100.00	6505 Brandon Av

TABLE: Unsaved layout　C:MEMBERS.RPD　Selected: 18 of 18

Figure 4-22. File sorted by contribution and last name

Changing Sort Direction

Susan is happy with the printed file you have supplied, but Linda would like to see a list arranged by expiration date with the earliest date at the bottom. To sort in descending order, you will need to change the direction of the sort.

Open the Order Settings screen with CONTROL-R and then enter O. Since you need to sort on the Expdate field this time, all prior entries must be deleted. The same CONTROL-DEL shortcut that was helpful in erasing the Select and Locate screens can be used here. Press CONTROL-DEL, and answer Y for "Yes" to the prompt **Clear all order settings?**

Move the cursor to the Order column beside the Expdate field, and enter 1. Press RIGHT ARROW once to move the cursor to the Direction column. To change the sort direction, press F2 (EDIT). The prompt in the Message Area will ask **Sort this field in which direction? Ascending Descending**. Choose "Descending," and then press F9 to implement the sort. The resulting file will display the records in order of expiration date, with the earliest date at the bottom of the file.

A Shortcut for Single-Field Sorts

If you need to sort a file on only one field, there is a fast way to do so without using the menus. The combination CONTROL-O (letter O, not zero) will sort on the field containing the cursor. To try this, move the cursor to the Lastname field, and press CONTROL-O. The Message Area will display a prompt, asking if you want to sort in ascending or descending order. Choose "Ascending," and the file will be sorted by last name in ascending order as shown in Figure 4-23.

File Layout Records Write Print 11:29 am

	LASTNAME	FIRSTNAME	EXPDATE	CONTRIBUTE	ADDRESS
1	Askew	Lonnie	03/08/88	25.00	103 Maple Avenu
2	Baker	Benjamin	09/08/87	20.00	5602 Lyngate Co
3	Baker	Jeanette	06/22/87	10.00	153 South Lakes
4	Block	Paul	03/08/87	20.00	1415 South Shor
5	Brown	Nicole	08/15/87	25.00	106 Crestwood D
6	Harris	Charles	02/22/87	10.00	9 Park Circle
7	Hayes	Cynthia	08/15/88	100.00	9631 Champion C
8	Johnson	Lamar	12/01/87	40.00	4005 Williamsbu
9	Jones	Renee	05/15/87	30.00	2508 Columbia P
10	Mills	Ernest	04/30/87	20.00	500 Embarcadero
11	Roberts	Terry	05/06/87	25.00	6120 Brandon Av
12	Roberts	James	05/06/87	25.00	6120 Brandon Av
13	Roberts	Norma	03/08/87	20.00	6120 Brandon Av
14	Sand	Lucy	01/01/99	500.00	142 Haven Way
15	Schultz	Bobby	11/17/87	10.00	1338 Redskin Dr
16	Shaw	Michael	07/21/87	35.00	7105 Little Riv
17	Sloan	Wanda	10/15/87	25.00	2723 Hunters Wo

TABLE: Unsaved layout | C:MEMBERS.RFD | Selected: 18 of 18

Figure 4-23. A sort on the field containing the cursor

DELETING RECORDS

RapidFile provides three different ways to delete records: using a shortcut key to delete the current record; deleting all tagged records; and deleting all records that have not been selected. RapidFile also offers a useful capability that allows you to restore, or undo, any deleted records. The option works as long as you have not yet saved the file. Once you save the file, any deletions are permanent.

Deleting a Single Record

To delete one record, simply place the cursor on the desired record and press CONTROL-DEL. As an example, place the cursor on the first record in the file and press CONTROL-DEL. The Message Area will display the prompt **Do you want to delete this record? Yes No.** Choose "Yes." The record will be deleted, and all remaining records will be renumbered and move up one notch throughout the database (see Figure 4-24).

To try the "Undo deletions" feature, open the Delete submenu with CONTROL-R, and then enter D. Select "Undo deletions," and the deleted record will reappear.

Deleting Tagged Records

As an option, you can manually tag a series of records, and then delete those records. To do so, use F5 (TAG) to tag the desired records, and then use the "Tagged records" option of the Delete submenu. Try this now by moving the cursor to records 3, 4, and 5 and pressing F5 at each record to tag all three records.

Open the Delete submenu with CONTROL-R, and then enter D. Choose the "Tagged records" option of the submenu. When the option is chosen, the tagged records will be deleted as shown in Figure 4-25.

Again, recover the deleted records with CONTROL-R, then D, then U for "Undo deletions."

File Layout Records Write Print 07 16 pm

	LASTNAME	FIRSTNAME	EXPDATE	CONTRIBUTE	ADDRESS
1	Baker	Benjamin	09/08/87	20.00	5206 Lyngate Co
2	Baker	Jeanette	06/22/87	10.00	153 South Lakes
3	Block	Paul	03/08/87	20.00	1415 South Shor
4	Brown	Nicole	08/15/87	25.00	106 Crestwood D
5	Harris	Charles	02/22/87	10.00	9 Park Circle
6	Hayes	Cynthia	08/15/88	100.00	9631 Champion C
7	Johnson	Lamar	12/01/87	40.00	4005 Williamsbu
8	Jones	Renee	05/15/87	30.00	2508 Columbia P
9	Mills	Ernest	04/30/87	20.00	500 Embarcadero
10	Roberts	James	05/06/87	25.00	6120 Brandon Av
11	Roberts	Terry	05/06/87	25.00	6120 Brandon Av
12	Roberts	Norma	03/08/87	20.00	6120 Brandon Av
13	Sand	Lucy	01/01/99	500.00	142 Haven Way
14	Schultz	Bobby	11/17/87	10.00	1338 Redskin Dr
15	Shaw	Michael	07/21/87	35.00	7105 Little Riv
16	Sloan	Wanda	10/15/86	25.00	2723 Hunters Wo
17	Smith	Larry	01/12/88	100.00	6505 Brandon Av

TABLE: Standard | C:MEMBERS.RPD | Selected: 17 of 17

Figure 4-24. The file after deletion of Lonnie Askew's record

Deleting All Unselected Records

The final method of deleting records allows you to select a subset of the file based on a matching condition and to delete all records that do not meet that condition. As an example, suppose that you wanted to delete every member whose membership expiration date is 1987.

File Layout Records Write Print 07:18 pm

	LASTNAME	FIRSTNAME	EXPDATE	CONTRIBUTE	ADDRESS
1	Baker	Benjamin	09/08/87	20.00	5206 Lyngate Co
2	Baker	Jeanette	06/22/87	10.00	153 South Lakes
3	Hayes	Cynthia	08/15/88	100.00	9631 Champion C
4	Johnson	Lamar	12/01/87	40.00	4005 Williamsbu
5	Jones	Renee	05/15/87	30.00	2508 Columbia P
6	Mills	Ernest	04/30/87	20.00	500 Embarcadero
7	Roberts	James	05/06/87	25.00	6120 Brandon Av
8	Roberts	Norma	03/08/87	20.00	6120 Brandon Av
9	Roberts	Terry	05/06/87	25.00	6120 Brandon Av
10	Sand	Lucy	01/01/99	500.00	142 Haven Way
11	Schultz	Bobby	11/17/87	10.00	1338 Redskin Dr
12	Shaw	Michael	07/21/87	35.00	7105 Little Riv
13	Sloan	Wanda	10/15/86	25.00	2723 Hunters Wo
14	Smith	Larry	01/12/88	100.00	6505 Brandon Av

TABLE: Standard | C:MEMBERS.RPD | Selected: 14 of 14

Figure 4-25. The file after deletion of Block, Brown, and Harris

First you must select the subset of records that will remain after the deletions. Enter CONTROL-R, S for "Select," and M to get to the Matching Records screen. If there are entries still in the columns from past examples, press CONTROL-DEL, and then enter Y to clear those entries. Place the cursor beside the Expdate field and enter the following:

>= 01/01/88

Next press F9 to implement the selection. Four records will appear.

You can now delete all records that did not meet the selection criteria. Open the Delete submenu with CONTROL-R and then enter D. Choose N for "Non-selected records," and your screen should resemble the one shown in Figure 4-26.

Note the indication within the Status Bar, **Selected: 4 of 4.** There are only four records remaining in the entire database. That would not leave much to work with throughout the rest of this book, so restore the deleted records with CONTROL-R, and then enter D and U for "Undo deletions." Remove the tags that appear with CONTROL-R, and then enter S and R. Finally, with the cursor in the Lastname field, do a quick sort of the file with CONTROL-O followed by RETURN. Save the latest version of the file with CONTROL-RETURN.

GLOBAL REPLACEMENTS TO RECORDS

RapidFile allows you to replace the contents of a field on a record-by-record basis or for all records in a file. As an example, suppose that Friends of Crabgrass decides to change the membership classification in the Type field from REGULAR to ADULT. You could edit the Type field for each record containing REGULAR and enter ADULT in that space instead. But there are easier, less time-consuming ways to replace a field in a selected set of records.

If you are not currently in "Table" layout, change to "Table" layout with F3 (FLIP). (The replacements can be done in "Table" or in "Form" layout, but the changes will be easier to see when in "Table" layout.) Move the cursor to the right until it highlights the first TYPE entry in the database.

Now open the Records menu with CONTROL-R and choose the "Replace contents" option. A message at the bottom of the

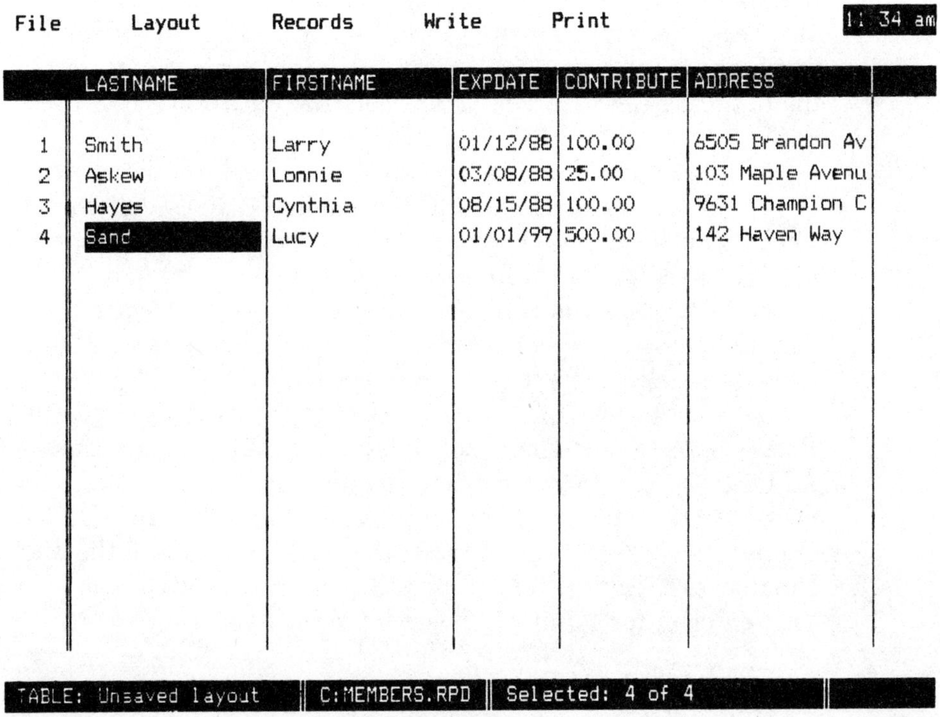

Figure 4-26. The database after deletion of nonselected records

screen will prompt **Type in replacement for the current field, then press Return.** Underneath the message, enter

ADULT

Upon pressing RETURN, a new message will appear at the bottom of the screen: **Replace Contents: Press ↵ to replace,**

↓ to skip current record, END to replace from here on, ESC to cancel. You are presented with one of four choices: to manually accept a replacement (press RETURN), to skip a replacement (press DOWN ARROW), to replace all records remaining in the database (press END), or to abort the entire process (press ESC).

In this case a manual replacement is needed; we do not wish to replace all records—just those having REGULAR in the Type field. The first record falls into this category, so press RETURN once to make the first replacement.

The next record is a student record, so press DOWN ARROW once to bypass this record with no changes. Then press RETURN twice to mark the next two records as ADULT.

Again use DOWN ARROW twice to skip the next two records. Press RETURN six times to change the next six records to ADULT. Press DOWN ARROW twice to skip the next two, and press RETURN twice to change records 16 and 17 to ADULT. Press CONTROL-RETURN to save the latest version of the file. Finally, exit RapidFile for now by entering CONTROL-F, and then enter Q for "Quit" followed by Y for "Yes."

Using Layouts

Chapter 5

RapidFile can display information in various layouts. *Layouts* are arrangements for viewing and printing the data contained in different fields. The first step in working with layouts is to design and implement the layout you want. You can move the fields to different locations on the screen to meet your needs, and you can also hide and show fields as necessary. Once you have rearranged the fields, you can save that arrangement, or layout, to disk. After the records are viewed in the layout, you can select records, sort the file as desired, and print your data.

RapidFile offers six different types of layouts: "Tables," "Forms," "Split table/forms," "Labels," "Quick Reports," and "Custom Reports." This chapter will cover in detail the first four layouts mentioned. "Quick Reports" and "Custom Reports" will be covered in later chapters.

Start RapidFile in the usual manner, and load the database MEMBERS. The file should appear in table layout if you chose the option "Table" the last time you displayed the file. If you did not choose "Table" layout press F3 (FLIP) until the file appears in table form.

At the bottom of the screen on the left side of the Status Bar are the words, **TABLE: Unsaved layout.** Until now you have not been working with any specific layout, so RapidFile has been showing all fields of the database in the manner in which they were entered when the database was designed. Although there is nothing special about this particular layout, it would be helpful to save it now so you can reuse it after working with other layouts throughout this chapter.

SAVING LAYOUTS

To save any layout, use the "Use/Save layout" option of the Layout menu. Press CONTROL-L to open the Layout menu. Press U for "Use/Save layout," and a submenu that offers the choices of using, saving, or erasing a layout appears (see Figure 5-1).

Enter S for "Save layout." A window showing the names of all available layouts appears on the right side of the screen. If no layouts have been created, the window is empty. At the same time at the bottom of the screen, the cursor moves to a highlighted area that requests a name for the layout.

Enter

Standard

and press RETURN. The existing layout is saved under the name Standard. Note that the Status Bar indicates the use of the layout with the words, **TABLE: Standard** at the left side.

DESIGNING A NEW LAYOUT

Now that the original layout has been saved, you can create additional layouts for different needs. Frank, who handles the mail, wants to work regularly with a table layout that shows just the names and addresses of members. He would like the

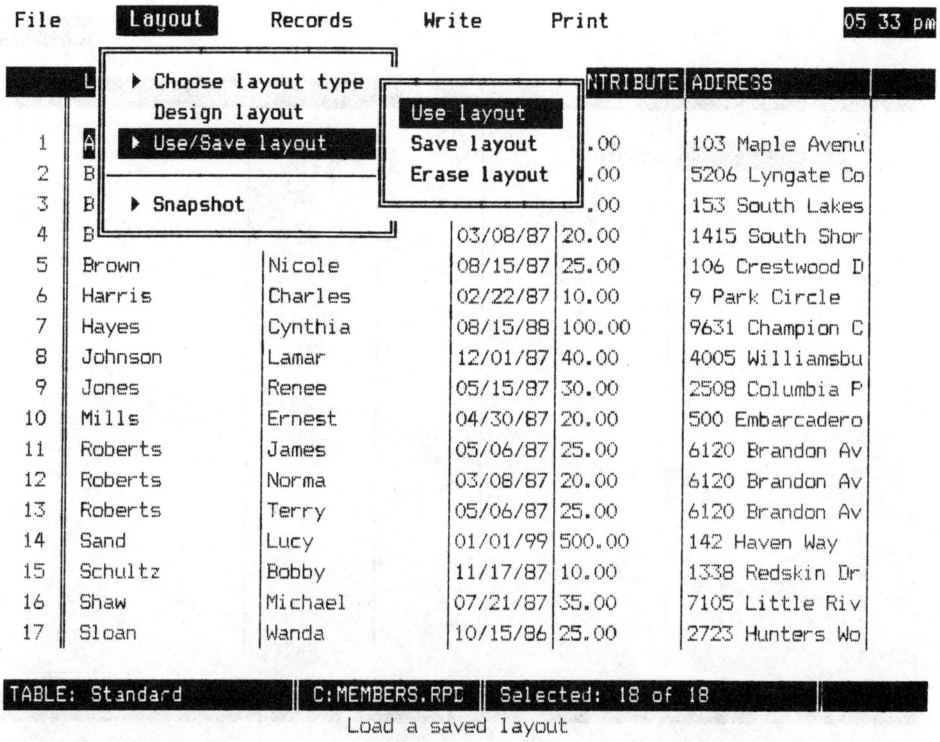

Figure 5-1. The submenu of the Layout menu

fields for the first name and last name to be narrower so more fields fit on a single screen. To satisfy Frank's request, you create a table layout with the expiration date, contribution, and member type fields hidden and the remaining fields narrowed as much as possible.

To design a layout, use the "Design layout" option of the Layout menu. Enter CONTROL-L to open the Layout menu, and

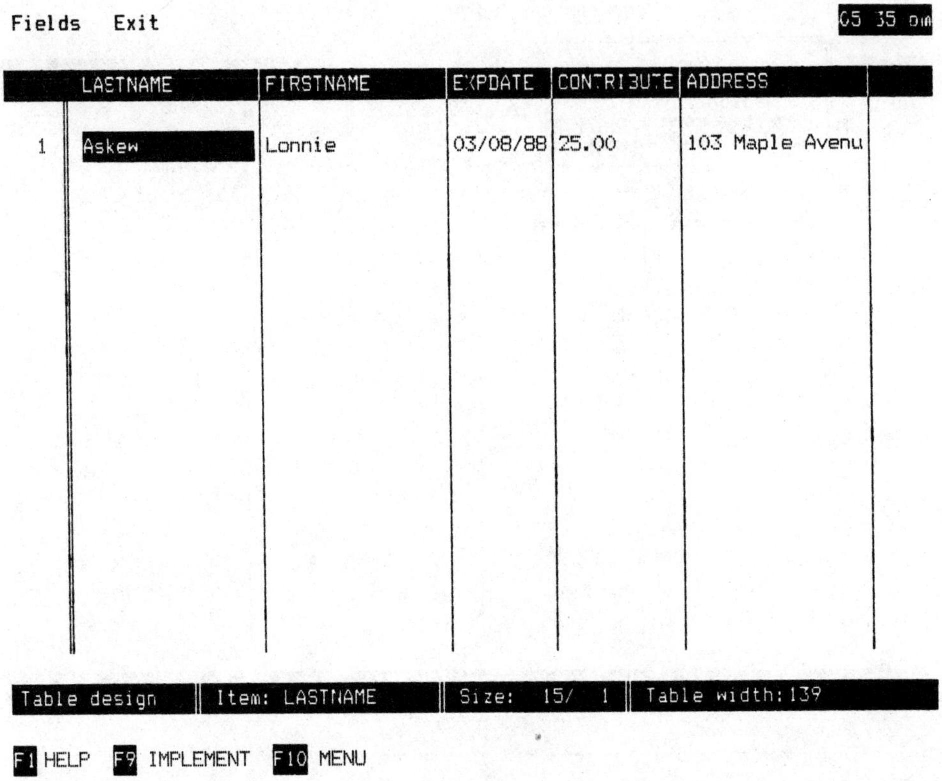

Figure 5-2. The Table Design screen

press D for "Design layout." In this case the Layout design area of RapidFile is called the Table design area, and it appears as shown in Figure 5-2. The screen resembles the table or form you were working with when you chose to design a layout. However, only one record is visible at a time. If necessary, you can see additional records (one at a time) by using the UP ARROW and DOWN ARROW keys when in "Table" layout or by using the PGUP and PGDN keys when in "Form" layout.

At the bottom of the screen, the Status Bar shows the type of operation you are performing (Table design), the name of the field in which the cursor is located, the size of that field, and the width (in characters) of the entire table. (The width reflects the current margin settings.) At the top of the screen are two menu choices: "Fields" and "Exit." Like all menus in Rapid-File, you can open these menus by pressing the CONTROL key with the first letter of the menu name.

Enter CONTROL-F to open the Fields menu. The Fields menu lists seven choices: "Show field," "Remove field," "Width of field," "Height of record," "Field format," "Display all fields," and "Clear layout."

The option "Remove field" allows you to remove a field from the layout; "Show field" allows you to restore a field that has been previously removed. "Width of field" and "Height of record" allow you to control the field widths and record heights, respectively. (These options will be demonstrated shortly.) "Field format" provides control over the ways in which information is displayed in a field. "Display all fields" allows you to restore all fields to a layout, and "Clear layout" allows you to remove all fields in preparation for creating a new layout.

Changing Field Widths

The cursor is in the first field, Lastname (even though it may be temporarily hidden by the menu). Since Frank, the mail handler, wants this field to be narrower than it currently appears, press W for "Width of field." At the bottom of the screen, the Message Area displays a prompt that asks for the new field width. Enter and the field width changes to the new width of 12 characters.

Move the cursor to the Firstname field. Open the Fields menu with CONTROL-F and again choose "Width of field." This time enter

9

to set a field width of nine characters.

Removing Fields

Besides changing the width of a field, you can remove fields during the design of a layout. Removing a field does not destroy any data within a file—it simply hides that data from view for as long as that particular layout is being used. Frank is not interested in the membership expiration date or contribution information, so these fields should be removed from the layout that he will use. Move the cursor to the Expdate field and open the Fields menu with CONTROL-F. Enter R for "Remove field," and the field will vanish from view. The cursor is now highlighting the Contribute field. Remove this field by again entering CONTROL-F, and then R.

Place the cursor in the City field. Open the Fields menu with CONTROL-F and choose "Width of field." This time enter

10

for the width. Move the cursor to the State field, open the Fields menu with CONTROL-F, and choose "Width of field." Since only two letters are needed to display state abbreviations, enter

2

for the width. Your screen should now resemble Figure 5-3.

This layout is looking better to Frank. But addresses are important to him, and the ends of the addresses cannot be seen. Since there is room remaining on the screen to the right of the Zip column, the Address field could be somewhat wider. Move

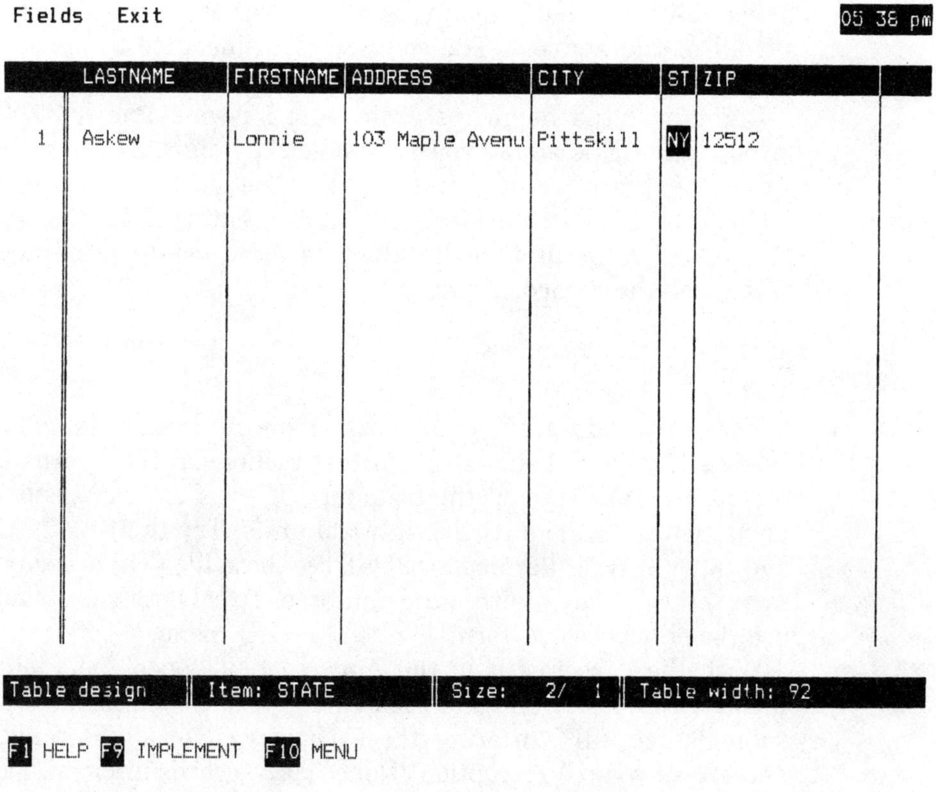

Figure 5-3. The result of hiding and narrowing fields

the cursor to the Address field and open the Fields menu with CONTROL-F. Choose "Width of field" and enter

19

for the width. In this case 19 is the maximum width we can give to the Address field while keeping the Zip field from scrolling off the right side of the screen.

However, it is clear that Frank is still unable to see all of the Address field. Frank admits that he is willing to put up with being able to see half the number of records at a time if he can see all of the address. The solution is to increase the record height.

Right now the height of each record is one line in table layout. RapidFile allows you to change the height by using the option "Height of record" on the Fields menu.

Open the Fields menu with CONTROL-F. Enter H for "Height of record." A prompt in the Message Area asks for the new height for the record. Enter

2

The entire address now appears in the Address field. However, as Figure 5-4 shows, the format is illogical. The words in the address are split at the boundary of the field rather than being moved to the next line in word units. Try the UP ARROW and DOWN ARROW keys and you will see these illogical breaks in many other records within the database. To solve this problem, use the option "Field format" of the Fields menu.

With the cursor still in the Address field, open the Fields menu with CONTROL-F, and then enter F for "Field format." A submenu appears, offering three choices: "None," "Reverse," and "Word wrap." The option "None" leaves words unformatted, the way they appear now. "Reverse" is a special option that reverses two names when they are separated by a comma. This option is useful when you choose to store both the last name and

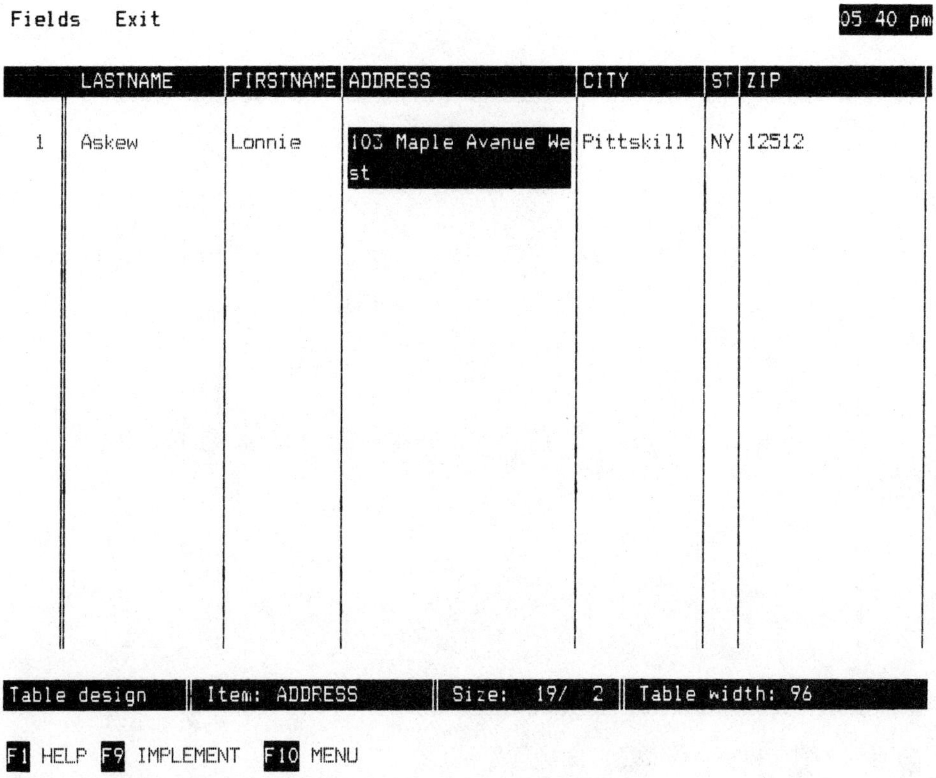

Figure 5-4. Changing record height to display the full address

the first name separated by a comma in the same field. In such cases "Reverse" causes the first name to appear before the last name, even though the names were not stored in the database in that manner.

The option desired in this case is "Word wrap." Choosing this option causes a word to *wrap*, or to move to the following line if it is too long to fit on the existing line.

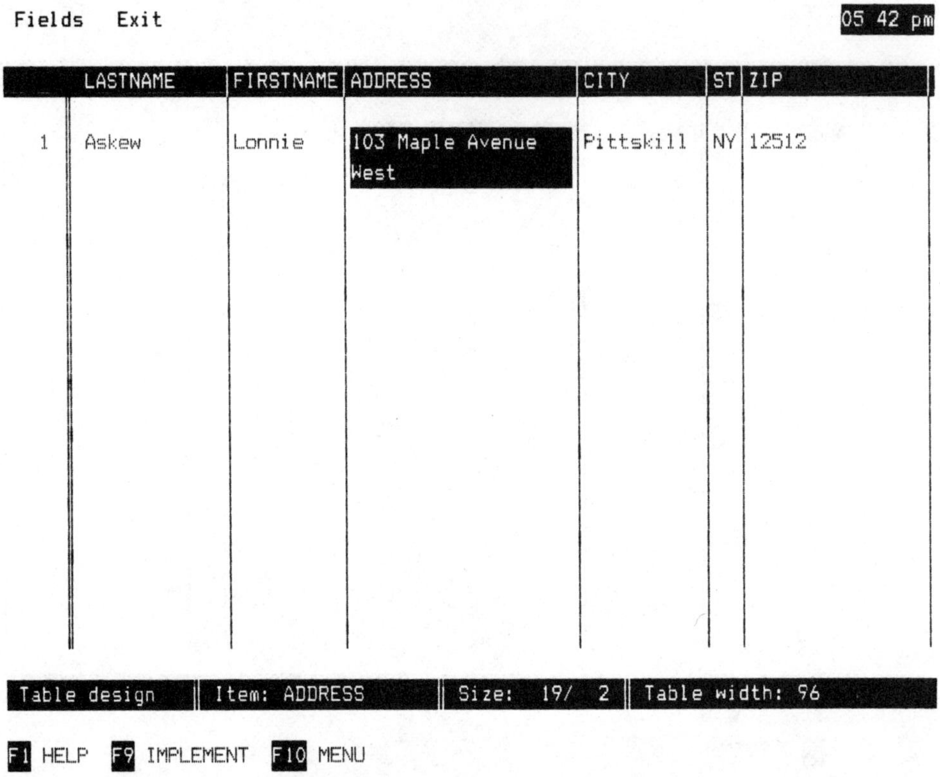

Figure 5-5. Using "Word wrap" to improve the layout of the Address field

Enter W for "Word wrap." The address now appears in a more logical format, as Figure 5-5 shows. If you press UP ARROW and DOWN ARROW you will see that other addresses in the database are also displayed in the improved format.

Frank is happy with this layout. The only remaining step is to save it so that he will be able to call the layout up at any time.

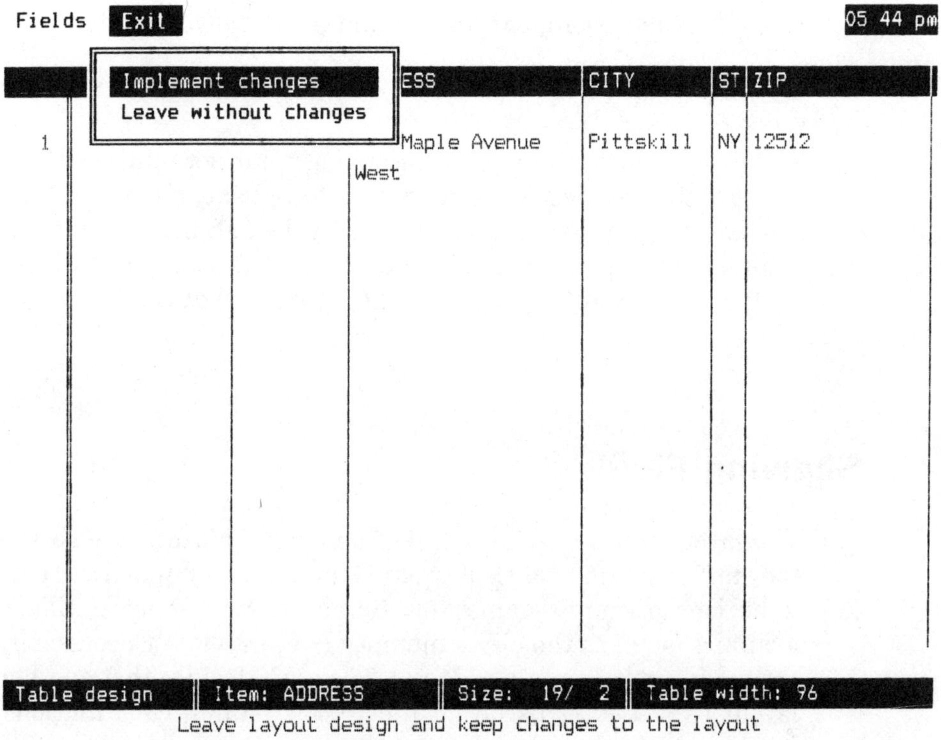

Figure 5-6. The Exit menu

Enter CONTROL-E to open the Exit menu (see Figure 5-6).

The Exit menu offers two choices: "Implement changes" and "Leave without changes." Enter I for "Implement changes." Note that F9 (IMPLEMENT) can be used as a shortcut to implement the changes. The database appears in the new layout, and the RapidFile menu appears at the top of the screen.

Open the Layout menu with CONTROL-L and enter U for "Use/Save layout." From the submenu that appears, choose "Save layout." When prompted for a name for the layout, enter

MAILING

The new layout will be saved in memory but not to disk. When you save the database prior to exiting RapidFile, all layouts that you save are written to disk along with the database. If you exit RapidFile without saving changes to the database, you will lose all the new layouts that you created during that session.

Showing Fields

The layout you designed will do fine for Frank. But the rest of the staff at Friends of Crabgrass is interested primarily in contribution amounts, names of members, and general demographics (such as the city a member lives in but not necessarily the member's complete address). The staff decides that another layout is needed. This layout must show names, contributions, membership expiration dates, cities, and states.

The new layout does not need to provide two lines for each record, and the fields that have been hidden for Frank's layout must now be restored. The option "Display all fields" of the Fields menu is the quickest way to restore a display of all fields. Open the Layout menu with CONTROL-L and choose "Design layout." When the Layout design area appears, open the Fields menu with CONTROL-F.

Note that there are actually two ways the hidden fields can be restored to view. The Fields menu offers the option "Show field," which allows you to name, one at a time, individual fields to be restored to view. As an alternative, "Display all fields" from the same Fields menu restores all the fields at one time.

Since it will be faster to restore all the fields to view, choose "Display all fields."

A warning appears in the Message Area—it indicates that the current layout will be replaced. Since you have saved the layout, there is no danger in replacing it on the screen now; the saved layout can be recalled at any time. Choose "Yes" to confirm the replacement, and the database appears with all fields visible.

For this layout the Address field will not be needed. Move the cursor to the Address field, open the Fields menu with CONTROL-F, and choose the option "Remove field" to remove the field.

Move the cursor back to the Lastname field and change the width to 10 characters by entering CONTROL-F, and then W, and then

10

Perform the same steps for the Firstname field.

Move the cursor to the Contribute field and change the width to 6 characters by entering CONTROL-F, and then W, and then

6

Move the cursor to the State field and change the width to 2 characters in the same manner. Finally, move the cursor to the Zip field and remove the field with CONTROL-F, and then R. Your screen should resemble Figure 5-7.

The revised layout is complete, so press F9 to implement it. The database appears within the confines of the new layout, but remember—the layout is not yet saved. If you were to quit RapidFile without saving this layout and the database file, you would be forced to create the layout again to view the data in this manner.

To save the layout, open the Layout menu with CONTROL-L, and choose "Use/Save layout." From the submenu that appears,

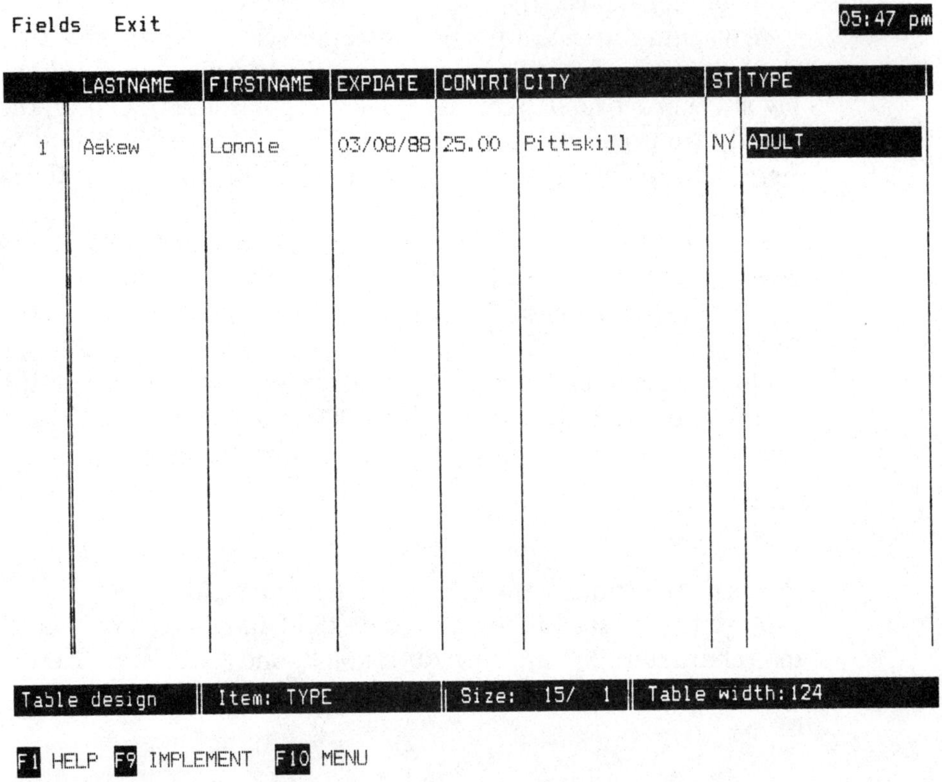

Figure 5-7. The result of hiding Address and Zip and narrowing fields

choose "Save layout." You are again prompted for a name for the layout. This time enter

STAFF

in response to the prompt.

Changing the Display of Dates and Numerals

RapidFile allows you to change the display of dates and numeric values. You will have more room to see how dates and numerals can be displayed if you use a form layout, so press F3 to flip to Form layout. Note that when the form appears on the screen, the Status Bar indicates that you are again working with an unsaved layout because the layouts that you saved previously were table layouts, not form layouts. If you choose to work with both forms and tables, you must save individual layouts for each.

Open the Layout menu with CONTROL-L and choose "Design layout." The Form design area appears as shown in Figure 5-8.

Except for the fact that the table has been replaced with a form, the Form design area resembles the Table design area. UP ARROW and DOWN ARROW move the cursor between fields, and PGUP PGDN can be used to bring other records into view.

Form design is different from table design in an important way: When designing a form layout, RapidFile allows you to move fields around to make a more visually pleasing screen. The F7 (MOVE) key is used to accomplish this task. You may desire, for example, a blank line between the fields Firstname and Expdate and between the fields Zip and Type. To do this, move the cursor to the Type field and press F7. Note the message at the bottom of the screen: **Use ↑ ↓ → ← to drag the field or text into position, then press ↵.** Press the DOWN ARROW key twice to drag the Type field down by two lines, and press RETURN to complete the movement process. Figure 5-9 shows the result.

Move the cursor to the Zip field, press F7, and then press DOWN ARROW once to move the Zip field down by one line. Complete the movement of the field by pressing RETURN. Repeat these steps for the State field, the City field, and the Address field.

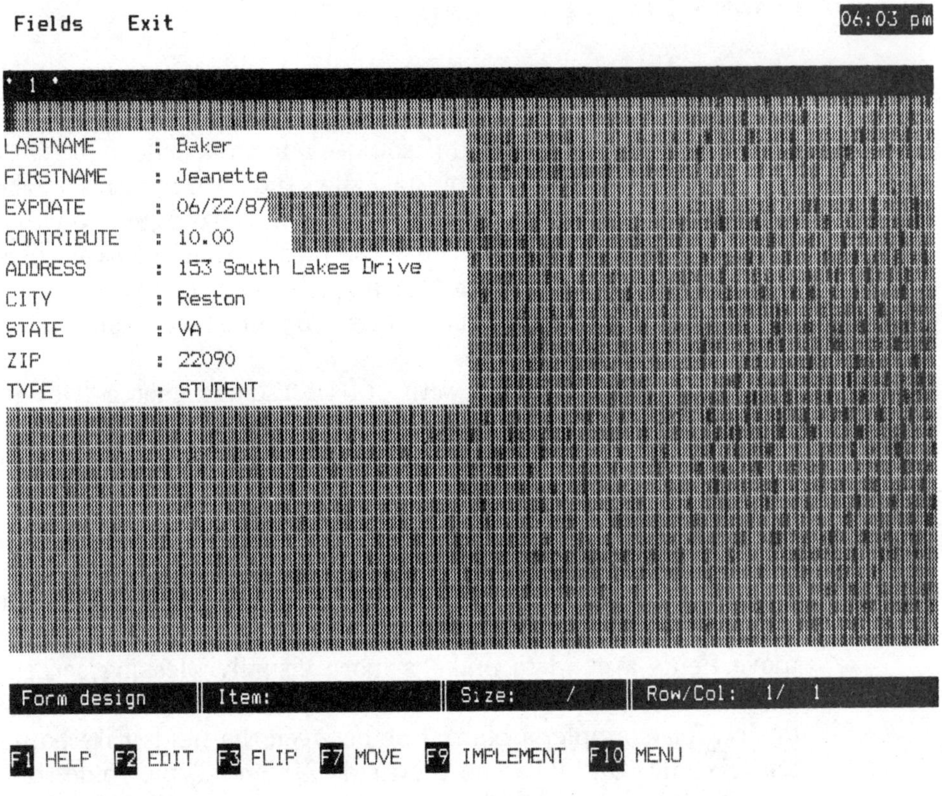

Figure 5-8. The Form Design screen

When you are done, your screen should look like Figure 5-10.

You can also drag fields to the left or right by using the LEFT ARROW or RIGHT ARROW keys. Place the cursor on the E in Expdate and press F7. Use RIGHT ARROW to move the entire

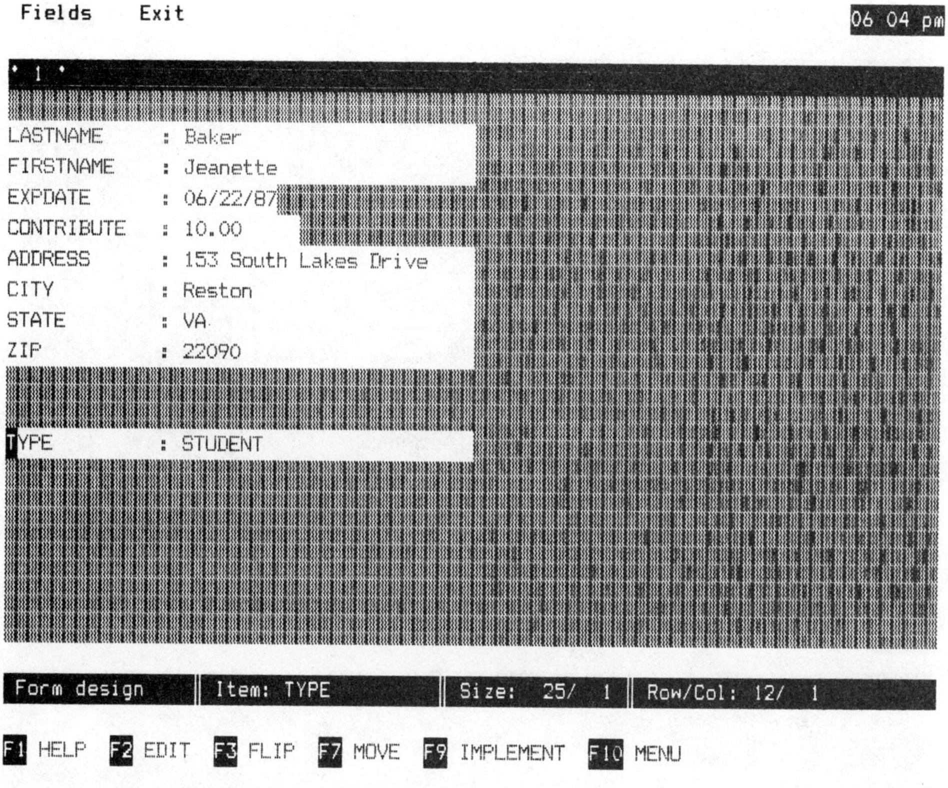

Figure 5-9. Use of F7 to drag Type into a new position

field to the right until it begins two characters to the right of the end of Lastname. Use UP ARROW to move Expdate up two lines. Press RETURN to complete the movement process. Your screen should look like Figure 5-11.

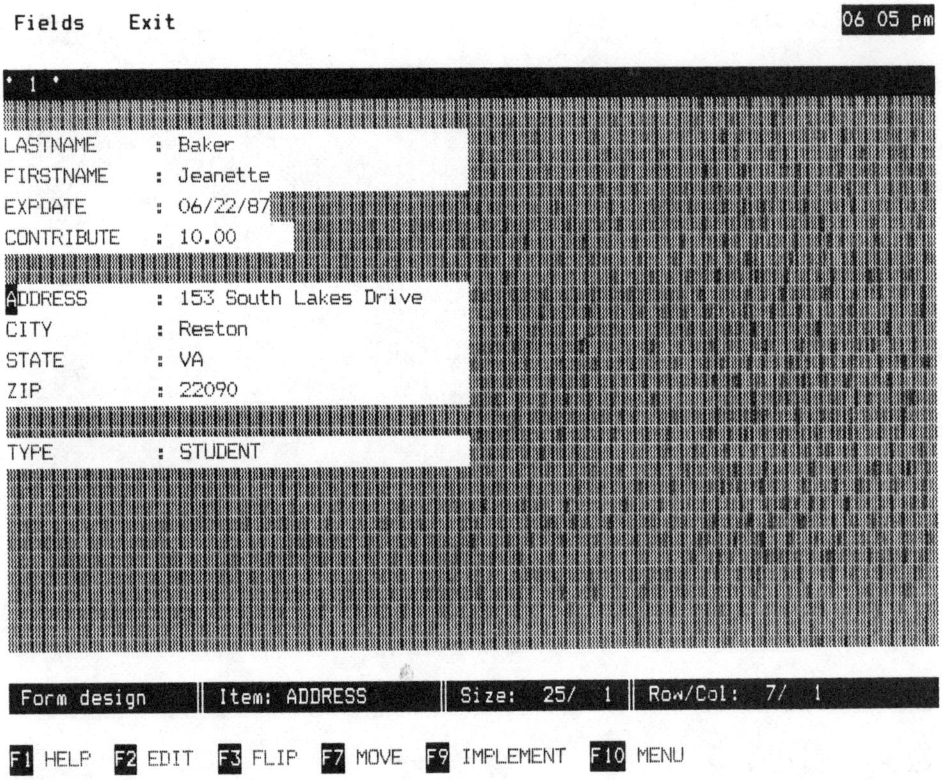

Figure 5-10. The result of dragging Address, City, State, and Zip

Finally, place the cursor on the C in Contribute, press F7, and move the field until it is directly underneath the Expdate field. Again press RETURN to complete the movement process. Your screen should resemble Figure 5-12.

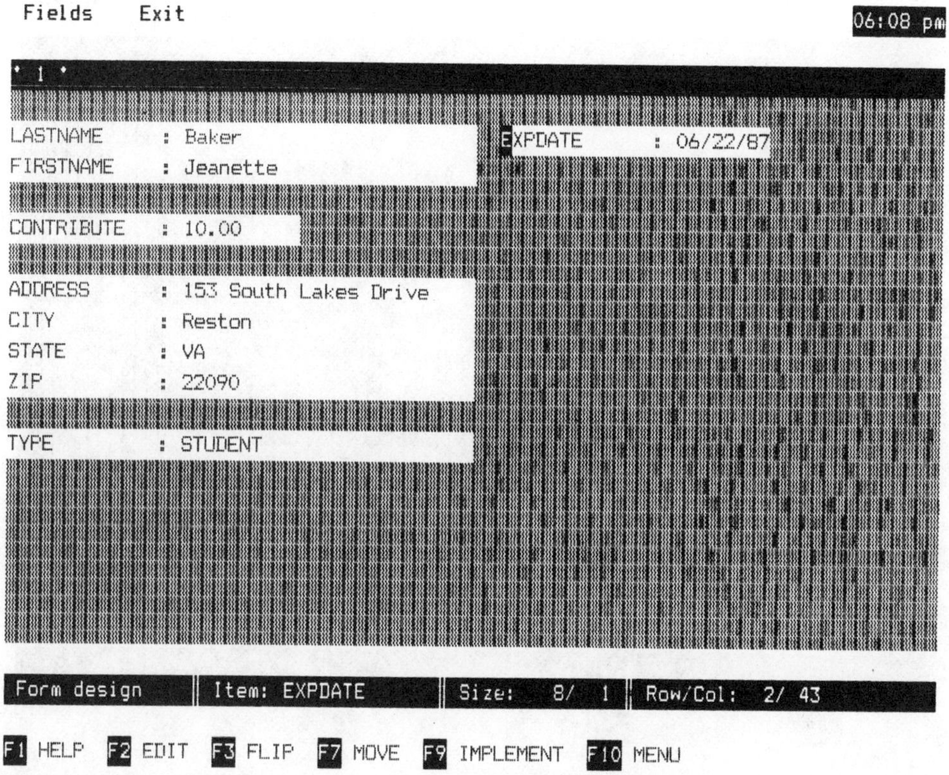

Figure 5-11. Use of F7, RIGHT ARROW, and UP ARROW to reposition Expdate

Now the form looks relatively uncluttered, but there is still the matter of formatting dates and numerals for best appearance. Place the cursor in the Expdate field and open the Fields menu with CONTROL-F. Choose "Field format," and note the

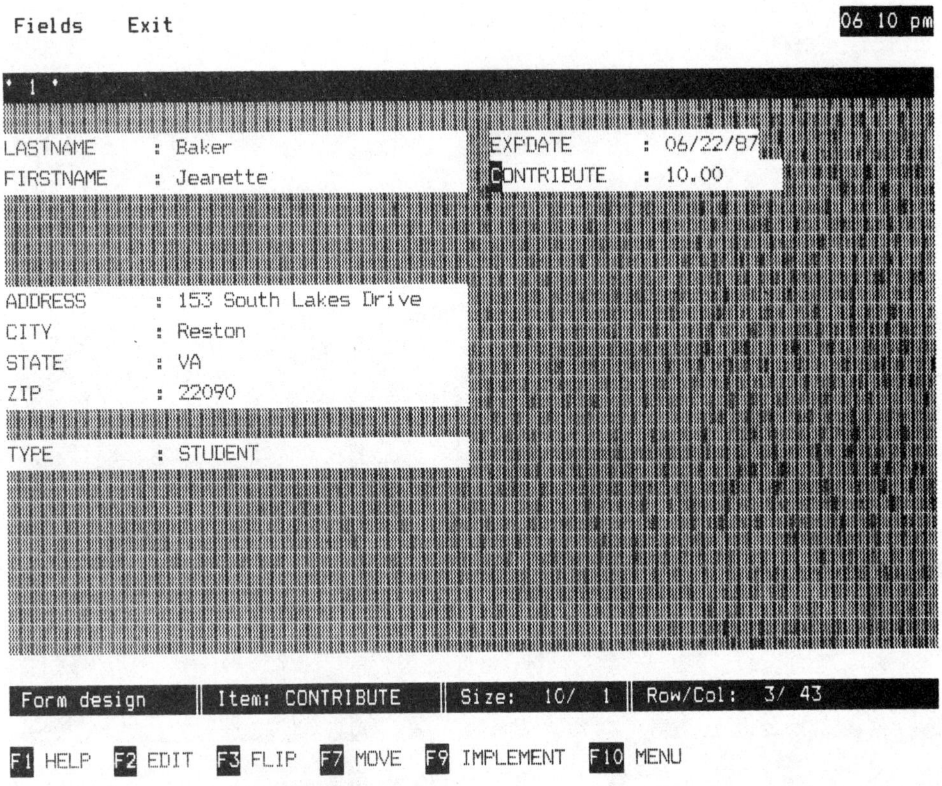

Figure 5-12. Dragging Contribute to a new position

submenu that appears (see Figure 5-13).

This submenu only appears when the field in which the cursor resides is a date field. You have five choices for date formatting:

- "None" (dates are displayed as entered in the database)
- "American" (MM/DD/YY)
- "European" (DD-MM-YY)
- "Written" (dates are spelled out as Month, DD, YYYY)
- "Custom" (a custom-defined date formatting option explained in Chapter 18)

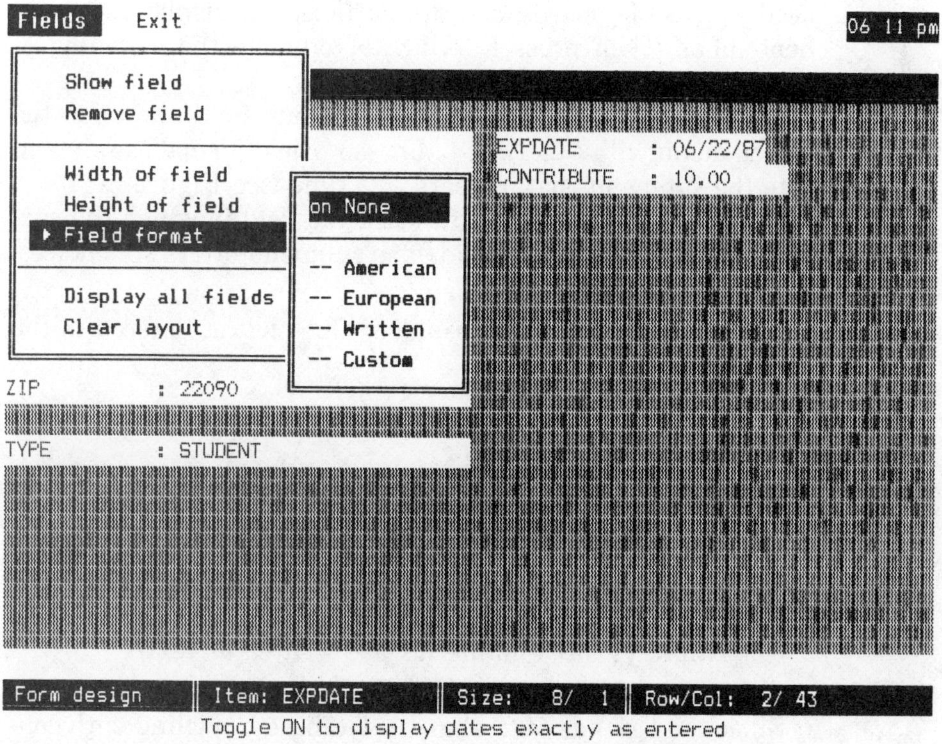

Figure 5-13. The submenu of "Field format" that lists date formats

In this case the staff would like the dates to be spelled out, so choose "Written" from the menu.

The result is not quite so appealing as before—the month, day, and year do not appear completely. The field must be widened to show all of the characters in the new layout. Open the Fields menu with CONTROL-F and choose "Width of field."

The Message Area shows another difference between designing form layouts and designing table layouts: Instead of typing in a number, use LEFT ARROW and RIGHT ARROW to set field width. The form layout allows you to see whether the field is long enough by changing width while displaying actual data.

Press RIGHT ARROW until the entire date appears. You will need at least 18 spaces, a width sufficient to display a date in September. Then press RETURN to complete the widening of the display.

Move the cursor down to the Contribute field and open the Fields menu with CONTROL-F. Choose "Field format" again and note the submenu that appears this time (see Figure 5-14).

This submenu only appears when the field in which the cursor resides is a numeric field. The submenu offers six choices:

- "None" (numerals are displayed flush left as entered in the database)
- "Fixed" (numerals appear with a set number of decimal places)
- "Business" (numerals appear with commas at thousands)
- "Currency" (numerals appear as dollars and cents)
- "Accounting" (negative numerals appear in parentheses)
- "Written" (positive numerals are written as text)

Since the Friends of Crabgrass database is dealing with contributions in U.S. dollars, choose "Currency" from the menu. Once the choice is made, another prompt in the message area asks, **digits after decimal: 0 1 2 3 4 5 6 7 8 9**. Note that the

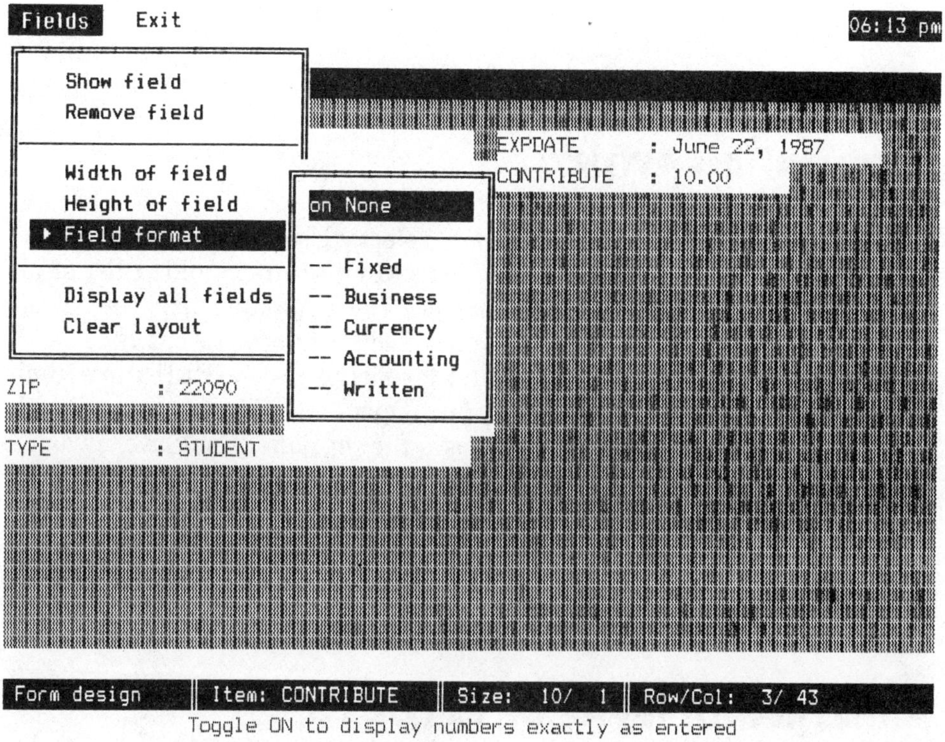

Figure 5-14. The submenu of "Field format" that lists numeric formats

numeral 2 is highlighted. Press RETURN to accept the default value of two decimal places, and a dollar sign appears beside the amount within the field.

Press F9 to implement the layout. A record in the database appears in the chosen form layout. To save the form layout, open the Layout menu with CONTROL-L, and then choose "Use/Save layout." From the next menu that appears, choose "Save layout." When prompted for a name for the layout, enter

MYFORM

REUSING A LAYOUT

To reuse an existing layout, select "Use/Save layout," choose "Use layout," and then press F3 to view an expanded list of all layouts. When you choose from the expanded list, the layout displays and the Status Bar reflects the new layout type.

To try reusing an existing layout, press F3 (FLIP) to switch back to the "Table" layout. Open the Layout menu with CONTROL-L and then choose the option "Use/Save layout." Choose "Use layout" from the submenu, and a list of the saved layouts appears on the right side of the screen. Highlight the layout named "Mailing," press RETURN, and the data appears within the "Mailing" layout created earlier.

PRINTING DIFFERENT LAYOUTS

To print a file, you must select the desired layout in advance. The file will print in the format of the layout that is in use when you select the option "Begin printing" from the Print menu. As an example, open the Print menu with CONTROL-P and choose "Begin printing." The records print in the format defined by the "Mailing" layout, the layout which is currently in effect.

CREATING LABELS

RapidFile allows you to create Label layouts, which are a special kind of form layout designed to print mailing labels, envelopes, and other business labels. Designing a label is similar to designing a form, but Label layout provides options that enhance your control of finished size.

Open the Layout menu with CONTROL-L and select "Choose layout type." The "Label" option shown in the submenu of Figure 5-15 is used to design and select label layouts. After you choose "Label" from the menu, the prompt **Do you want to design a label layout? Yes No** appears at the bottom of the screen. Select "Yes," and a Label design area appears (see Figure 5-16).

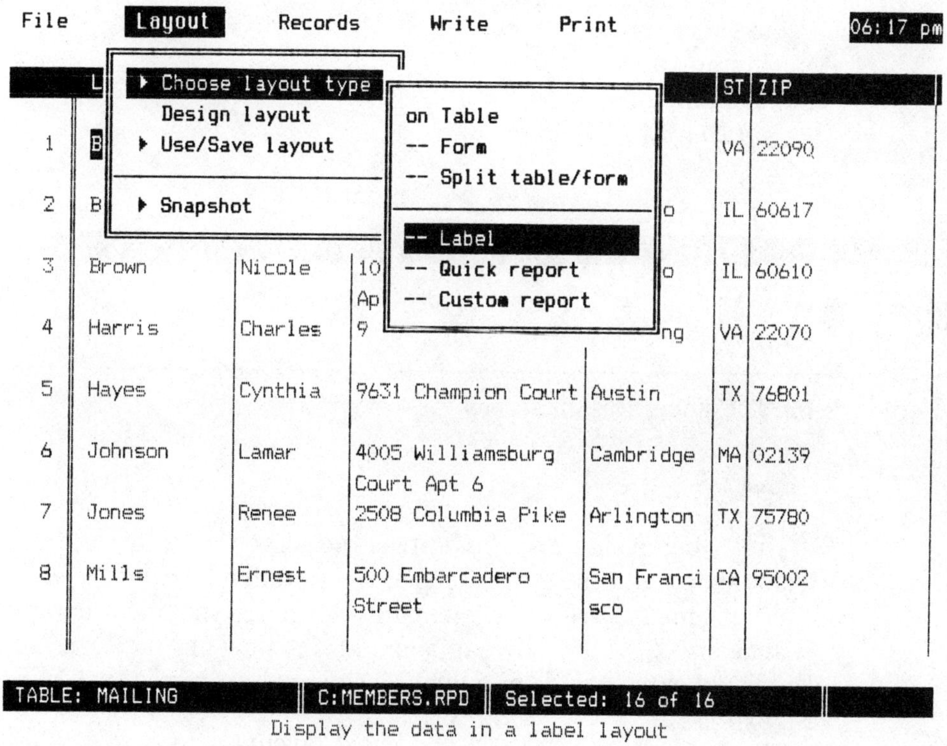

Figure 5-15. Label format created by choosing "Label" from submenu

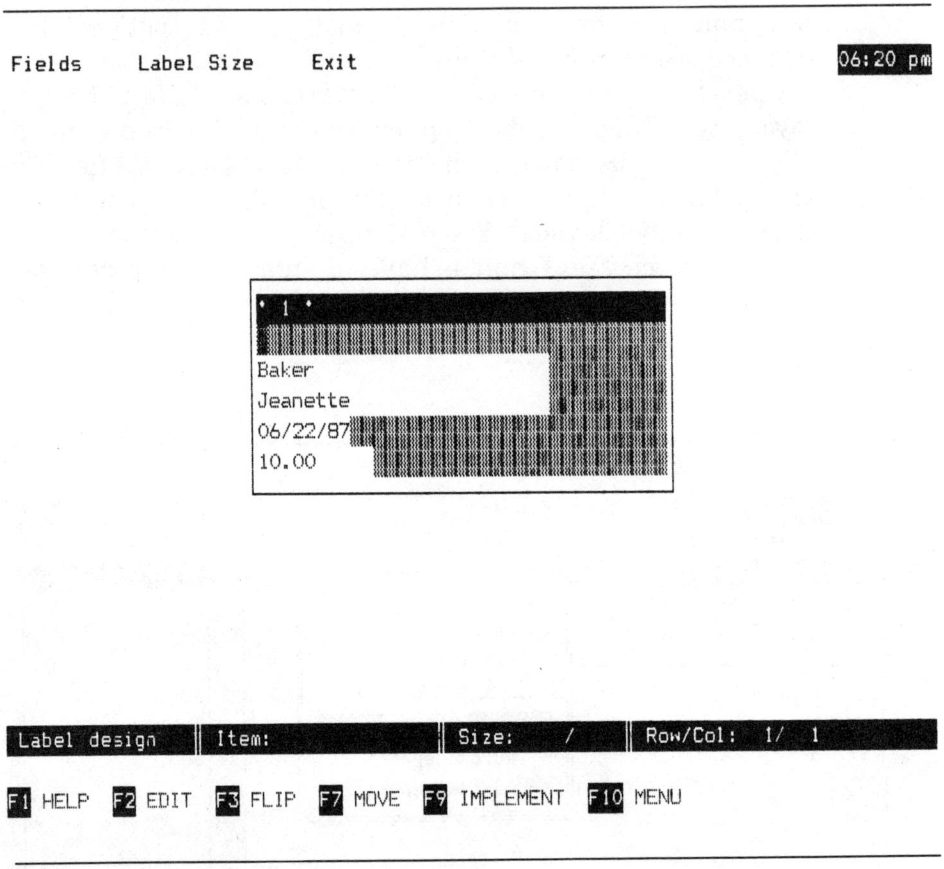

Figure 5-16. The Label Design screen

The Label design area resembles the screen used to design a form layout, and the definitions of the function keys and Fields and Exit menus are the same. One addition is the menu option "Label size," which now appears at the top of your screen. Enter CONTROL-L and the Label Size menu appears as shown in Figure 5-17.

The Label Size menu provides options for changing the size and format of the labels. RapidFile offers nine predefined label

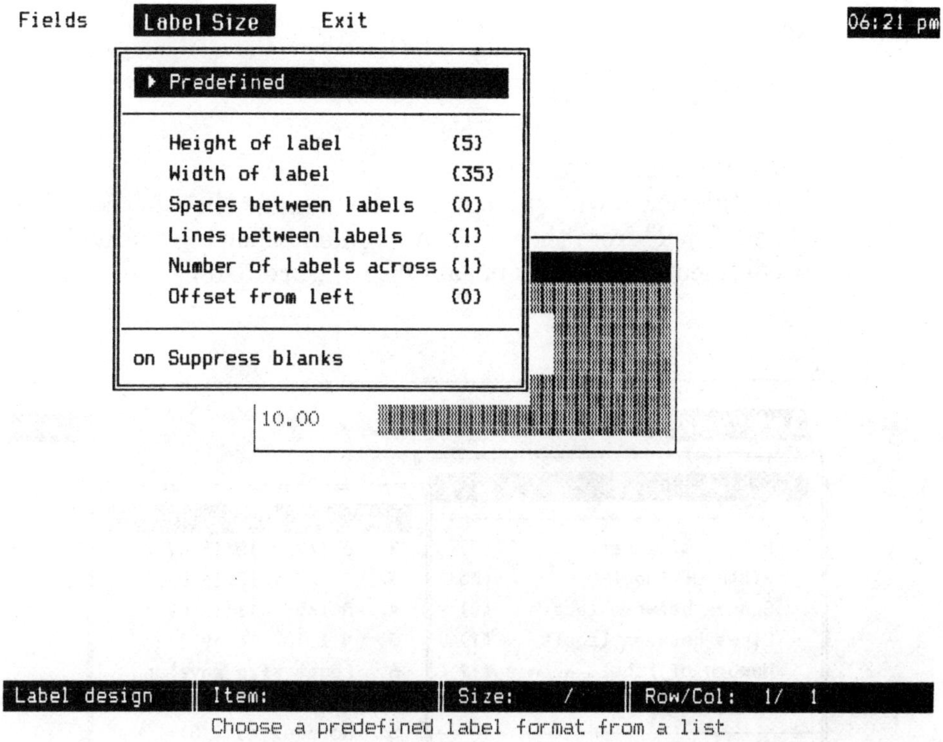

Figure 5-17. The Label Size menu

sizes that match most standard business sizes. You are also given the option of providing your own specifications for labels of unusual size. If you want to design your own nonstandard format, simply highlight the desired options shown and enter the values for your design. Note the option "Suppress blanks" at the bottom of the menu. This option, which is normally on, trims extra blank spaces from the end of a field. By leaving this option turned on, a name that would otherwise appear as

Paul Block

appears as

Paul Block

when the label is printed.

In this case we will opt for a standard size by selecting "Predefined" from the menu. A submenu showing the available predefined label sizes appears (see Figure 5-18).

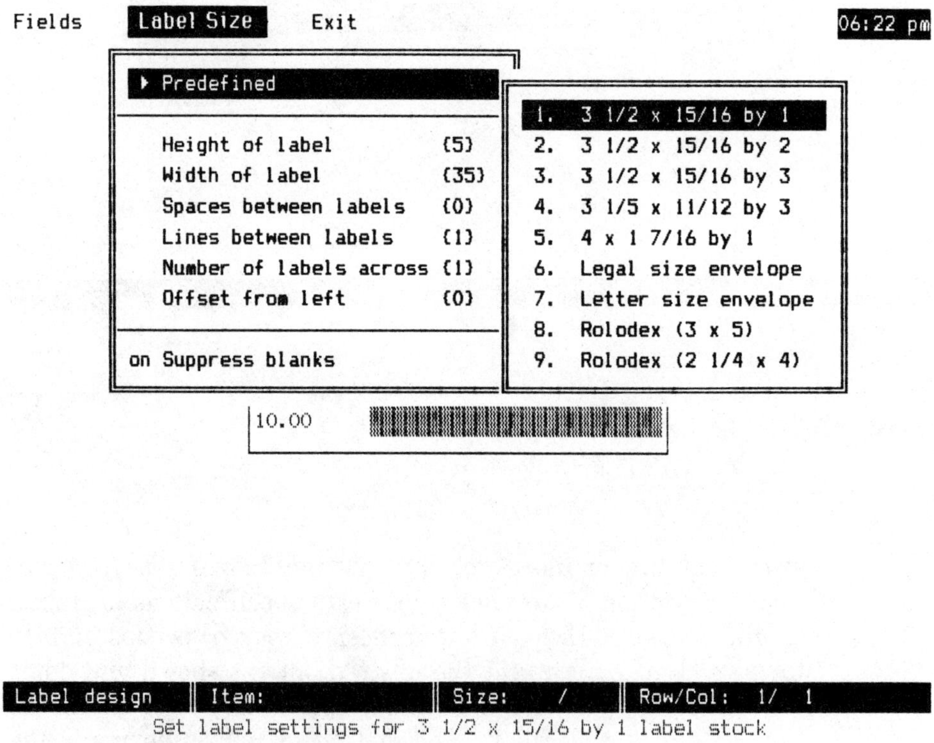

Figure 5-18. The submenu that lists predefined label sizes

Note that the first three options are for the same size. The first option is for one set of labels per page, the second option provides two sets per page (called two-across labels), and the third option provides three-across labels. The remaining options match the sizes indicated in the menu.

For our example, select the fifth option, "4 x 1 7/16 by 1." At the bottom of the screen, RapidFile warns you with the message **Fields that do not fit will be removed. OK to proceed? Yes No.** Select "Yes" and the new label size appears. In this case, because the new label size is larger, more fields appear within the label than appeared on the screen. Compare Figure 5-19 with Figure 5-16 to see the difference.

Since RapidFile has no idea which fields you would like to include in the label, it simply places as many fields as will fit, beginning with the first field in the database. Use the Fields menu to add or remove fields at the cursor location and the F7 (MOVE) key to move fields to different locations on the label.

Try pressing F3 (FLIP). Note that F3 can be used to alternate between the actual names of the fields and the sample record in the database. For our example leave the actual names of the fields on the screen.

Suppose you need a mailing label that shows the name, address, and membership expiration date. Move the cursor to the Firstname field and open the Fields menu with the CONTROL-F keys.

Select the Option "Width of field" and use LEFT ARROW to narrow the Firstname field to ten spaces. (You can tell how wide the field is at any time by looking at the Size designation in the Status Bar at the bottom of the screen.) Press RETURN to complete the change.

Move the cursor to the Lastname field and open the Fields menu with CONTROL-F. Again choose "Width of field," and use LEFT ARROW to narrow the field to 15 spaces. Press RETURN to complete the change. With the cursor still in the Lastname field press F7 (MOVE). Use RIGHT ARROW to move the field to position 15 of the label (check the Row/Column designation on the Status Bar to see in what position you are when moving the

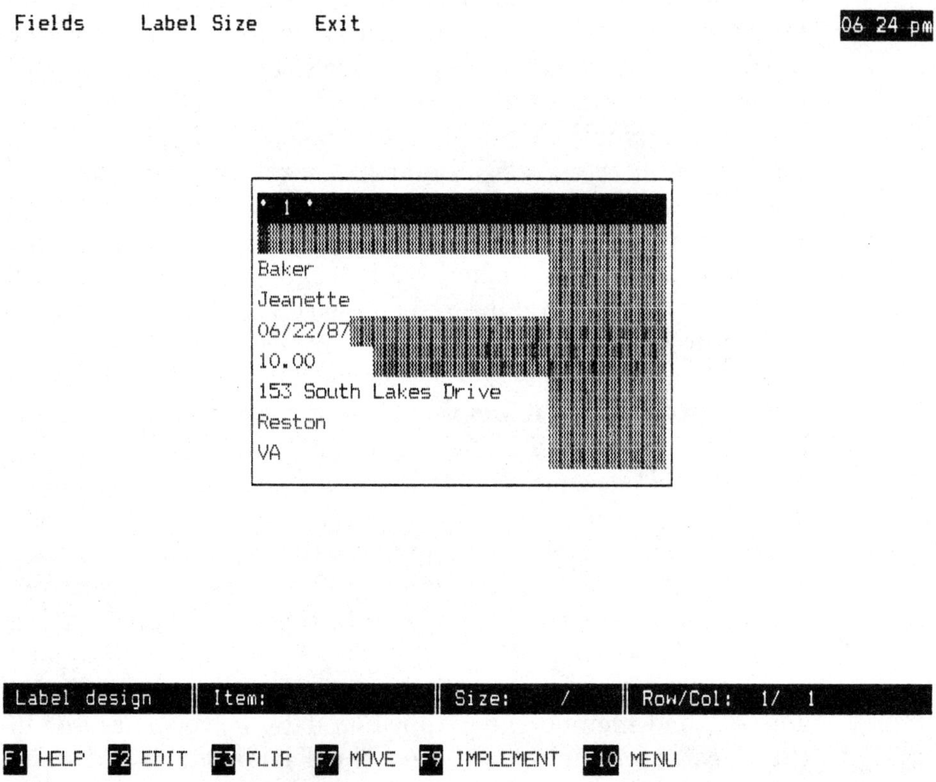

Figure 5-19. Fields added to a label by choosing a label size larger than screen format

field). Press RETURN to complete the movement of the field.

Place the cursor in the Firstname field and press F7 again. Move the field up one line to the same line as the Lastname field; press RETURN. Your label should now look like the one in Figure 5-20.

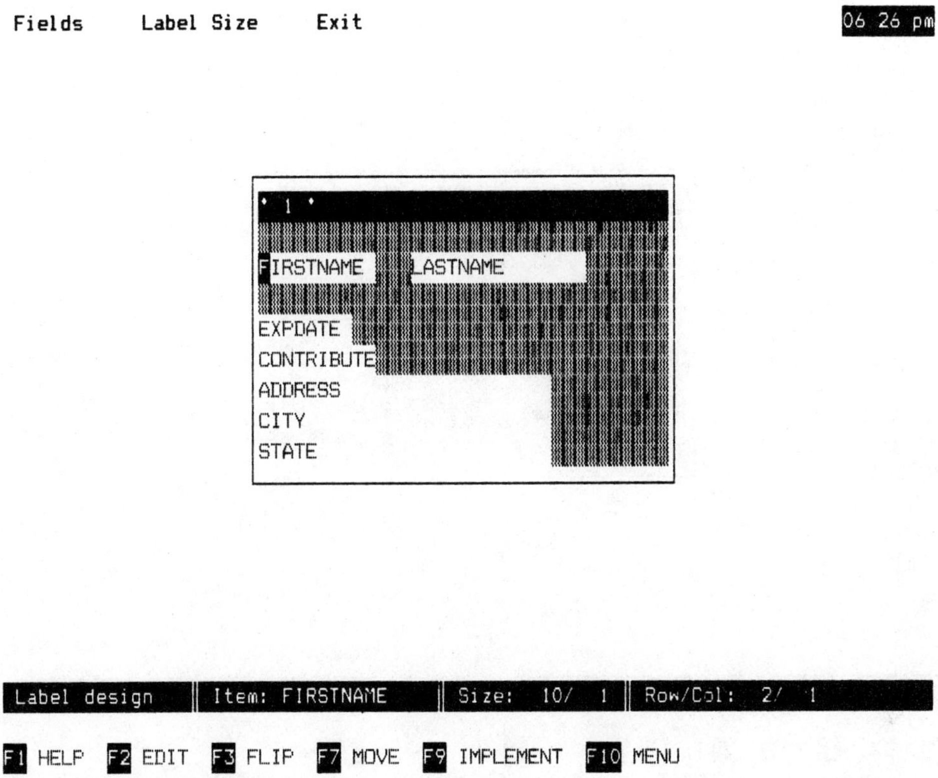

Figure 5-20. Use of F7 to modify field position

Move the cursor to the Contribute field and open the Fields menu with CONTROL-F. Choose "Remove field" to delete the contribution field from the label.

Using the same process as you used to move the Lastname and Firstname fields around on the label, use F7 to move the

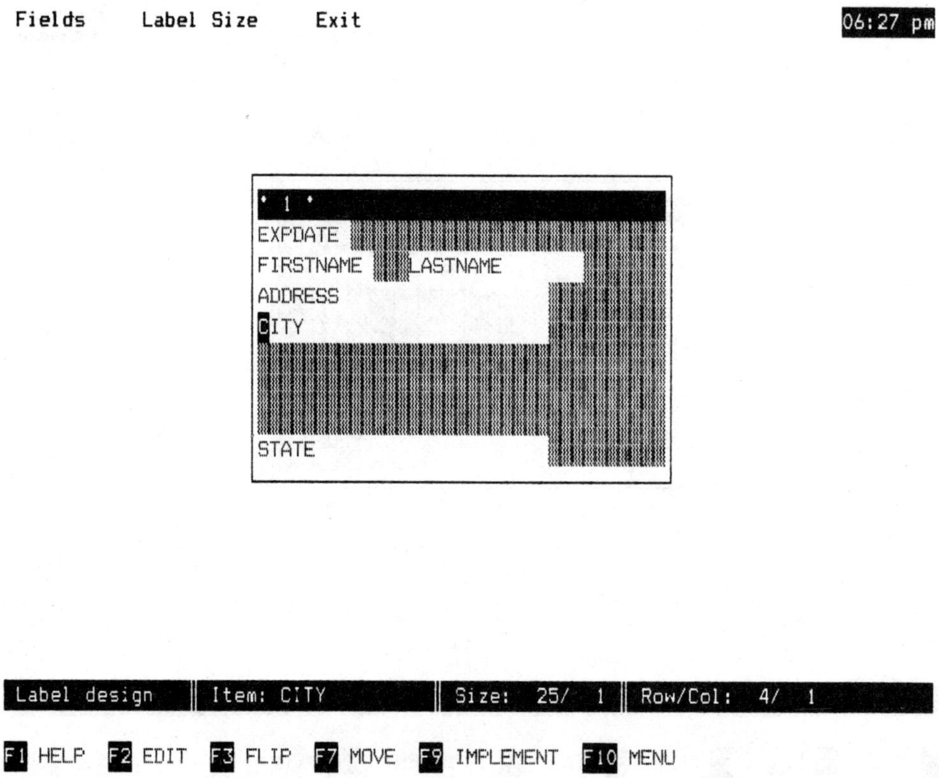

Figure 5-21. The label after the repositioning of Address and City

Expdate field to the top line. This placement is temporary; later you will move Expdate to the bottom of the label.

Next use F7 to move the Address and City fields to the two lines directly underneath the Firstname and Lastname fields. Your label should now resemble the one shown in Figure 5-21.

Place the cursor in the State field and open the Fields menu with CONTROL-F. Select "Width of field" and use LEFT ARROW to change the field width to 2 characters. Press RETURN to complete the change, and then use F7 and the arrow keys to move the State field so it follows the City field by two spaces. Do not forget to press RETURN to complete the process of moving the State field.

With these changes our label is almost complete. Place the cursor at the start of row 5 (check the Row/Column designation of the Status Bar, if necessary). Open the Fields menu with CONTROL-F and choose the "Show field" option. A list of available fields appears on the right half of the screen, as Figure 5-22 shows.

Select Zip from the list. The field appears at the cursor location, and a message at the bottom of the screen indicates that you can now use the arrow keys to change the field width and height. Press LEFT ARROW until the field width narrows to 10 characters, and then press RETURN.

A new message at the bottom of the screen indicates that you can use the arrow keys to drag the field to any desired location on the label. Place the field at row 5, column 18; press RETURN to complete the movement process.

Finally, place the cursor in the Expdate field, and press F7. Move the field to the lower right corner of the label (at row 7, column 25), and then press RETURN to complete the process of moving the field. Your label should resemble Figure 5-23. See how a sample record would appear in the label by pressing F3 (FLIP).

Open the Exit menu with CONTROL-E and select the option "Implement changes." The database appears in the form of the mailing labels, and you can use PGUP and PGDN to view the various records in the format that you have designed.

To see how the labels would print without using paper, open the Print menu with CONTROL-P. Select "Destination" and choose "Monitor/screen" from the submenu. Press ESC to close the submenu and choose "Begin printing." From the prompt that appears at the bottom of the screen, select "All." The records will be "printed" to the screen (you must press RETURN as each screen fills).

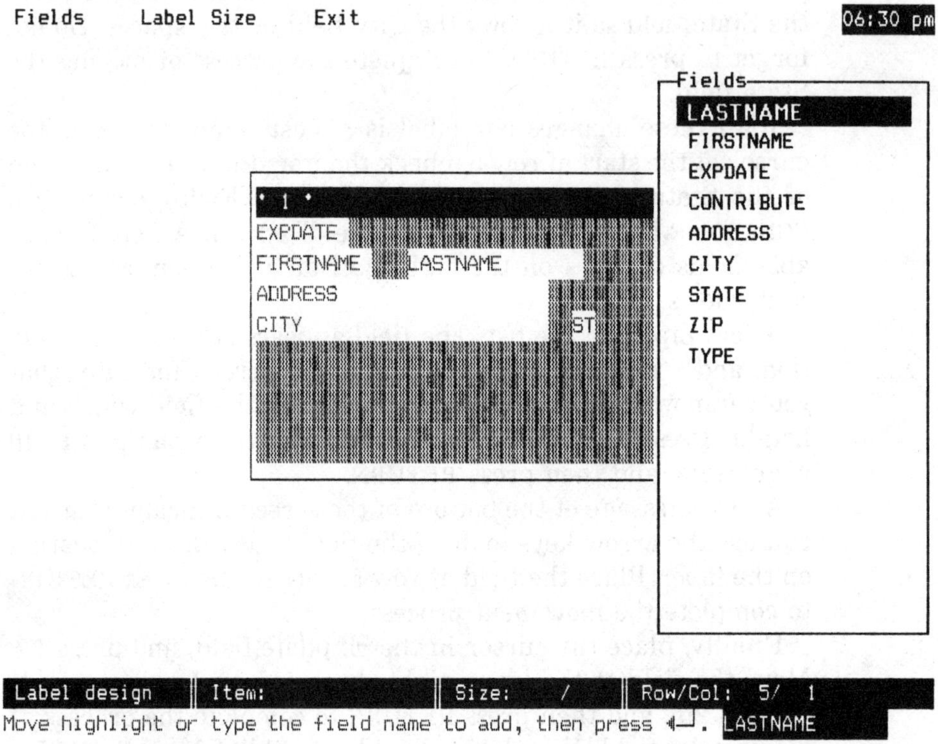

Figure 5-22. A list of available fields produced with "Show field"

SAVE THE FILE TO SAVE THE LAYOUTS

As noted, layouts are saved in memory as you create them, but they are not saved to disk until you save the file. If you were to turn off your computer without saving the file, your layouts

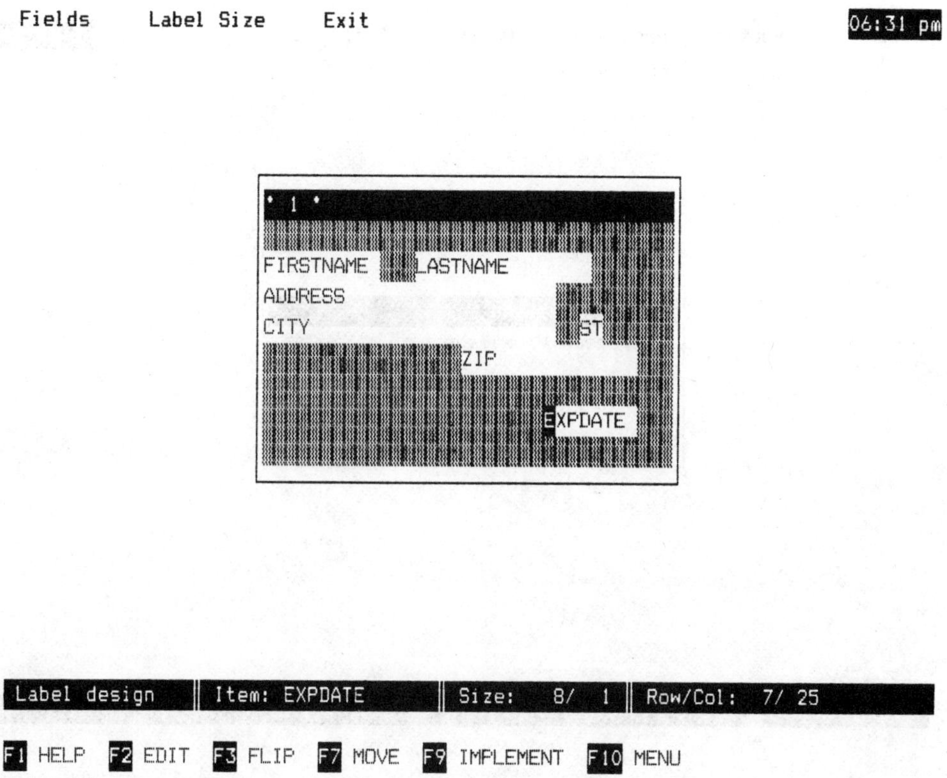

Figure 5-23. The completed label layout

would be lost. To save the layout, open the File menu with CONTROL-F and select the option "Save file." Select MEMBERS for the filename. Once the file has been saved, quit RapidFile with the option "Quit RapidFile" from the File menu.

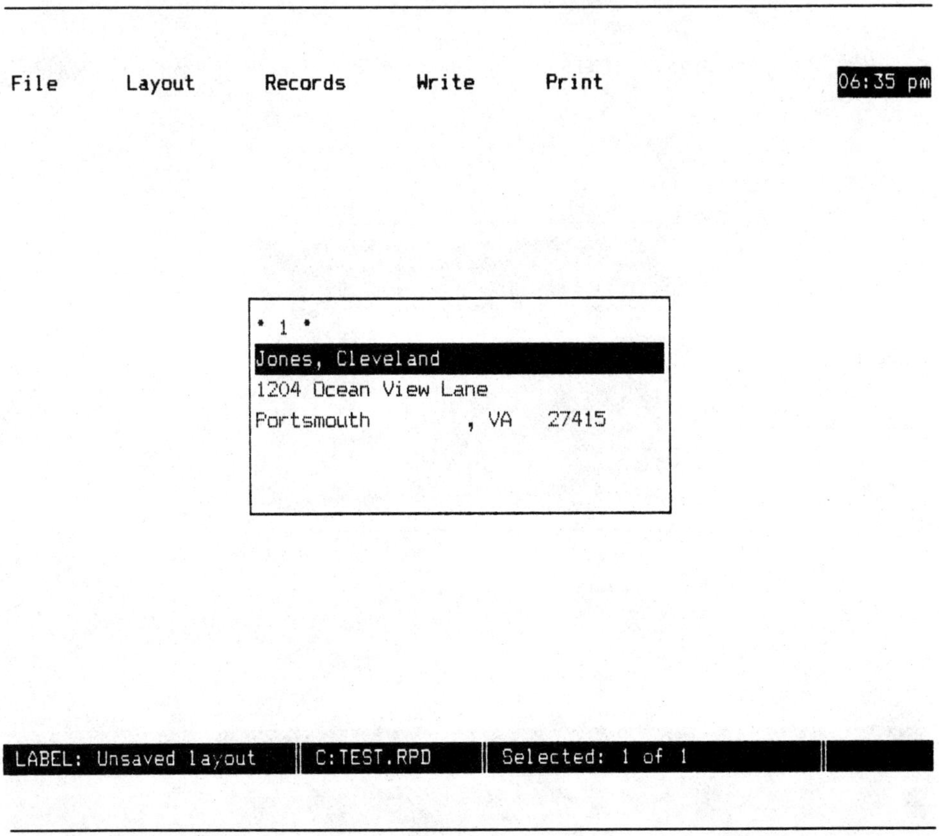

Figure 5-24. A label in the automatic format

AUTOMATIC MAILING LABELS

If you create a database with fields called Name, Address, City, State, and Zip, RapidFile automatically creates a mailing label when you select "Label" from the Layout menu. If the database has a field called Company, it will be included in the automatic label. RapidFile makes certain assumptions about design. The label appears on the screen in the form of the sample shown in Figure 5-24. You can use the label as is or modify the design to your liking.

Simple Reports

Chapter 6

Detailed reports are less trouble with RapidFile than with many other database managers because of RapidFile's ability to use layouts. You can use a layout to show specific data needed for analysis and to print reports based on that specific information.

RapidFile offers two types of reports: Quick Reports and Custom Reports. Quick Reports are columnar printouts with or without numeric information (such as totals or other calculations based on numeric fields). Quick Reports automatically include headings that contain the specified title of the report, the date (set by the system clock), and page numbers for each page.

Custom Reports are reports with varying formats. RapidFile offers more control over where information appears with a Custom Report than with a Quick Report. The data can be printed in columnar or in row formats, with special titles, headings, and areas for calculated totals.

Figure 6-1 shows an example of a Quick Report, and Figure 6-2 shows an example of a Custom Report. Quick Reports will be detailed throughout this chapter, and Custom Reports will be detailed in Chapter 10.

```
                         Report from MEMBERS.RPD on 09/22/86

REC# |LASTNAME           |EXPDATE |CONTRIBUTE|STATE|TYPE
-----+-------------------+--------+----------+-----+----------
   1 |Roberts            |05/06/87|25.00     |AZ   |ADULT
   2 |Baker              |09/08/87|20.00     |CA   |ADULT
   3 |Sloan              |10/15/86|25.00     |VA   |ADULT
   4 |Shaw               |07/21/87|35.00     |FL   |ADULT
   5 |Roberts            |03/08/87|20.00     |AZ   |ADULT
   6 |Jones              |05/15/87|30.00     |TX   |ADULT
   7 |Roberts            |05/06/87|25.00     |AZ   |ADULT
   8 |Block              |03/08/87|20.00     |IL   |ADULT
   9 |Mills              |04/30/87|20.00     |CA   |ADULT
  10 |Johnson, Jr.       |12/01/87|40.00     |MA   |ADULT
  11 |Brown              |08/15/87|25.00     |IL   |ADULT
  12 |Askew              |03/01/88|25.00     |NY   |ADULT
                                   ----------
               Total for ADULT 310.
```

Figure 6-1. Portion of sample Quick Report

```
                      Friends of Crabgrass

                        Membership Report

     Lonnie Askew

     103 Maple Avenue West
     Pittskill NY
                 12512

                          Contribution Amount: $25.00

                          Exp. Date:     March 1, 1988
```

Figure 6-2. Portion of sample Custom Report

To learn more about Quick Reports, load RapidFile (if necessary) and retrieve the MEMBERS database. The file appears in the way that it was last saved, in the form of mailing labels. Recall from the previous chapter that this layout was designed for the ease of mail processing at Friends of Crabgrass. As a result, it does not show the membership contributions, which will be needed in our reports. Open the Layout menu with CONTROL-L and select the option "Choose layout type." Choose "Table" layout from the submenu. Again open the Layout menu with CONTROL-L and choose "Use/Save layout." Select "Use layout" from the submenu, and the list of layouts that you saved during the last session appears (see Figure 6-3).

Standard is the layout you saved before making any changes to the layouts used in the last chapter; select "Standard." The database should appear in a table layout, with the names, expiration dates, contributions, and addresses visible and the remaining fields to the right of the visible fields.

DESIGNING AND PRINTING A QUICK REPORT

To create a Quick Report, you must first design a Quick Report layout. Quick Report layouts are designed by filling in the Quick Report guide, a screen that appears when you tell RapidFile to design a Quick Report. As an example, consider a Quick Report for Friends of Crabgrass. The report must show last names, expiration dates, contribution amounts, and the state of residence for all members. The report needs to be grouped by type of member.

Like all layouts, a Quick Report layout can be chosen from the Layout menu. Open the Layout menu with CONTROL-L and select "Choose layout type." From the submenu select "Quick Report."

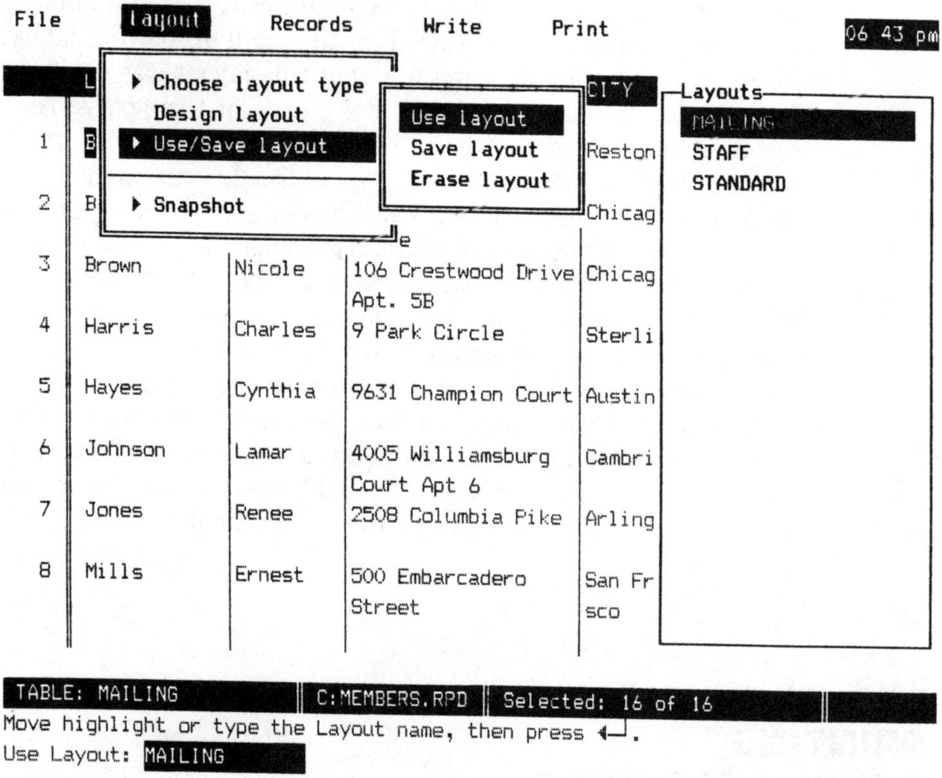

Figure 6-3. The list of available layouts

The first time you select "Quick Report," a prompt appears at the bottom of the screen, asking if you want to design a Quick Report layout (see Figure 6-4). Choose "Yes," and the Quick Report guide appears as shown in Figure 6-5.

The Quick Report guide is divided into halves. The upper half shows one record in the database as an aid so that you can

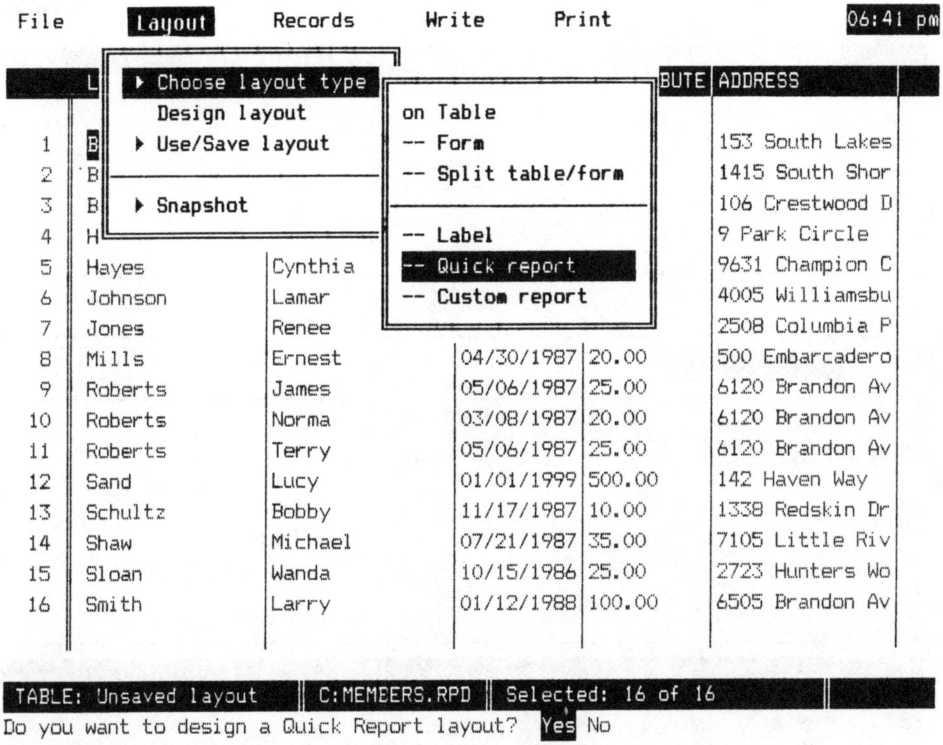

Figure 6-4. The Quick Report layout prompt

see field names while designing the layout for the report. The bottom half of the screen displays various abbreviations that will be used in designing the report. Also note the two menu options, "Fields" and "Exit," shown at the top of the screen. The Fields menu provides options for showing and removing fields from the report, for changing the width of fields and the height

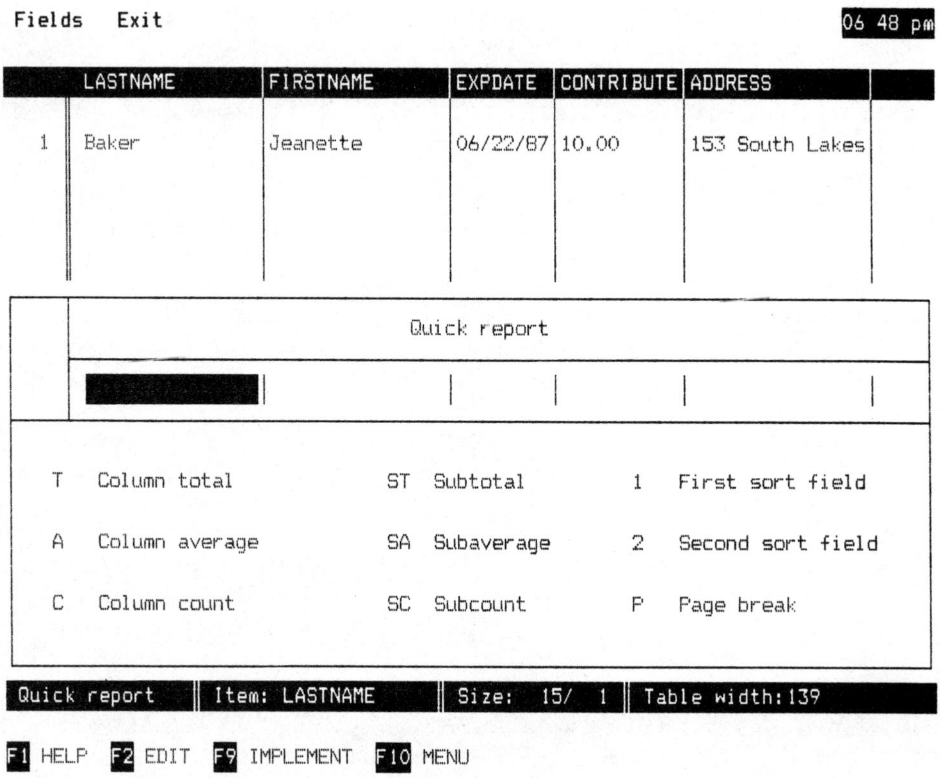

Figure 6-5. The Quick Report guide

of each printed record, and for changing the field format (the ways in which the fields are displayed). The Exit menu is used to exit the Quick Report layout when the report design is complete.

Two steps are involved in designing a Quick Report. First you must hide any unwanted fields and display the remaining fields in the formats desired. Second, you must choose the desired options for sorting, for calculating numeric fields, and for determining page breaks. The abbreviations shown on the lower half of the screen allow you to make these choices.

In this example some fields must be removed. The fields Firstname, Address, City, and Zip are not needed in this report. To remove a field, you must place the cursor in that field and then select "Remove field" from the Fields menu. The cursor should now be in the Lastname field, directly underneath the name of the field. Use the RIGHT ARROW key to move the cursor to the Firstname field.

Open the Fields menu with CONTROL-F and choose the option "Remove fields." The Firstname field will be removed from the fields shown on the upper half of the screen. In a similar fashion remove the fields Address, City, and Zip by placing the cursor in each field, opening the Fields menu with CONTROL-F, and choosing "Remove field" from the menu. The fields Lastname, Expdate, Contribute, State, and Type should remain on the screen.

Only the desired fields are now on screen, but a few changes in field formats would improve the appearance of the report. The State and Type fields are considerably wider than necessary. Use the option "Width of field" of the Fields menu to change field widths.

Place the cursor in the State field and open the Fields menu with CONTROL-F. Choose "Width of field" and enter

5

for the new field width. (In this case a field width of 2 would suffice, but choosing 5 allows the entire heading, State, to appear above the column.)

Move the cursor to the Type field and open the Fields menu with CONTROL-F. Again select "Width of field" and enter a width of 10 for the Type field.

You are now ready to select various options that relate to sort order, numeric calculation, and page breaks. These options are chosen by entering the abbreviations shown in each field at the cursor location. This report will need to be grouped by type of member, with each type of member appearing on a new page. The entire report must show the total contributed and a subtotal of contributed amounts by Type. To produce such a report, the file must be sorted on the Type field, a column total must appear for the Contribute field, and a subtotal must also appear for the Contribute field for each type of membership. By telling RapidFile to provide both totals and subtotals of contributions, the report will provide both a total amount for all records and a subtotal amount for groups of records. By sorting on the Type field, the subtotal amounts will apply to groups of records with the same entry in the Type field.

Place the cursor in the Contribute field. To put the abbreviations in the respective field columns, you must use F2 (EDIT) to edit the entries. In the Contribute field you need the abbreviations T ("Column total") and ST ("Subtotal"). Press F2 (EDIT) and the Edit Panel opens at the bottom of the screen. Enter T, a space, and then the letters ST; press RETURN. The abbreviations appear, automatically separated by a comma, in the proper column underneath the Quick Report heading.

Move the cursor to the Type field. This field will be used to determine both the sort order and the page breaks, so press F2 to open the Edit Panel. Enter the number 1 (to designate "First sort field"), a space, and then the letter P (to designate "Page break"); press RETURN. Again the abbreviations appear in the Type column.

Once you are done designing a Quick Report layout, you must use either the "Implement" option of the Exit menu or, as a shortcut, F9 (IMPLEMENT) to implement the report design. Press F9 now and the file reappears in table layout. Do not be surprised if the file is not sorted in the order you desire. The sort will not occur until you give the command to print the report.

Open the Print menu with CONTROL-P. Select "Begin printing," and the report will be printed as shown in the example in Figure 6-6.

```
                          Report from MEMBERS.RPD on 09/22/86


REC# |LASTNAME        |EXPDATE |CONTRIBUTE|STATE|TYPE
-----+----------------+--------+----------+-----+----------
   1 |Roberts         |05/06/87|25.00     |AZ   |ADULT
   2 |Baker           |09/08/87|20.00     |CA   |ADULT
   3 |Sloan           |10/15/86|25.00     |VA   |ADULT
   4 |Shaw            |07/21/87|35.00     |FL   |ADULT
   5 |Roberts         |03/08/87|20.00     |AZ   |ADULT
   6 |Jones           |05/15/87|30.00     |TX   |ADULT
   7 |Roberts         |05/06/87|25.00     |AZ   |ADULT
   8 |Block           |03/08/87|20.00     |IL   |ADULT
   9 |Mills           |04/30/87|20.00     |CA   |ADULT
  10 |Johnson, Jr.    |12/01/87|40.00     |MA   |ADULT
  11 |Brown           |08/15/87|25.00     |IL   |ADULT
  12 |Askew           |03/01/88|25.00     |NY   |ADULT
                                ----------
                 Total for ADULT 310.

                                         - 1 -


                          Report from MEMBERS.RPD on 09/22/86


REC# |LASTNAME        |EXPDATE |CONTRIBUTE|STATE|TYPE
-----+----------------+--------+----------+-----+----------
  13 |Smith           |01/12/88|100.00    |CA   |CHARTER
  14 |Hayes           |08/15/88|100.00    |TX   |CHARTER
                                ----------
               Total for CHARTER 200.

                                         - 2 -
```

Figure 6-6. Report 1

```
                          Report from MEMBERS.RPD on 09/22/86


REC# |LASTNAME        |EXPDATE |CONTRIBUTE|STATE|TYPE
-----+----------------+--------+----------+-----+----------
  15 |Sand            |01/01/99|500.00    |MD   |LIFETIME
                                ----------
              Total for LIFETIME 500.

                                         - 3 -
```

```
                          Report from MEMBERS.RPD on 09/22/86


REC# |LASTNAME        |EXPDATE |CONTRIBUTE|STATE|TYPE
-----+----------------+--------+----------+-----+----------
  16 |Harris          |02/22/78|10.00     |VA   |STUDENT
  17 |Schultz         |11/17/87|10.00     |VA   |STUDENT
  18 |Baker           |06/22/87|10.00     |VA   |STUDENT
                                ----------
               Total for STUDENT 30.
                                ==========
                  Total for File 1040.
                                         - 4 -
```

Figure 6-6. Report 1 (*continued*)

The report prints on four separate pages, one for each type of member (adult, charter, lifetime, and student). Because subtotals were requested for the Contribute field, a subtotal prints for each page within the report. At the end of the final page of the report, a total for the entire file appears.

SAVING REPORTS

To use a Quick Report repeatedly, you must save the report with an assigned name. To do so, use the option "Use/Save layout" of the Layout menu. Open the Layout menu now with CONTROL-L and select "Use/Save layout." Choose "Save layout" from the submenu. At the bottom of the screen, you are prompted for a name for the report layout. Enter

Report 1

(spaces are allowed in report names), and then press RETURN. The report is saved in memory so you can use it again. Report layouts are saved to disk when you save the database file.

QUICK REPORTS SORTED ON TWO FIELDS

RapidFile also allows you to produce reports sorted on two fields. In this example such an option would be helpful. In cases where the same name appears in a sorted category (such as Type), a second sort field (such as Lastname) would provide additional order to the report.

To choose a second field to sort on, open the Layout menu with CONTROL-L and choose the option "Design layout." The Quick Report guide appears, and the previously entered options are still in effect.

Place the cursor in the Lastname field and press F2 (EDIT). Enter the number 2 to indicate second sort field; press

RETURN. Press F9 (IMPLEMENT) to implement the modified sort order. Check to see that your printer is turned on and ready, and then open the Print menu with CONTROL-P. Choose "Begin printing." The report is printed, and in each group of types the records appear sorted in order of last names.

To save the modified report layout under a different name, open the Layout menu with CONTROL-L and select the option "Use/Save layout." Select "Save layout" from the submenu. Enter

Report 2

as the name of the report.

All Quick Reports are designed in a manner similar to that in the example. "Column total" (abbreviated as T) provides a total of all records printed within the report. "Column average" (A) can be used to provide an average value of a numeric field for all records printed. "Column count" (C) provides a count of the number of records printed within the report. "Subtotal" (ST), "Subaverage" (SA), and "Subcount" (SC) offer totals, numeric averages, and record counts for groups of records determined by the first sort field chosen. By entering the desired abbreviation, you can apply one or more of the selections to any field.

APPLYING SELECTIVE CONDITIONS TO A QUICK REPORT

To produce a report based on selected records within a file, simply select the desired records with the "Select" option of the Records menu, and print the Quick Report layout after the records have been selected. As an example, open the Records menu with CONTROL-R and choose "Select." Choose "Matching records" from the submenu. If any criteria appear in the Match

Criteria columns, delete them with CONTROL-DEL followed by "Yes" to confirm the deletion.

Move the cursor until it is beside the Type field, press F2 (EDIT), and enter

ADULT

Press the RIGHT ARROW key once to move the cursor to the second Match Criteria column, and press F2 again. Enter

STUDENT

and then press F9 to implement the selections. The database appears showing records for only those records having Adult or Student in the Type field.

Check to see that your printer is turned on and ready, and then open the Print menu with CONTROL-P. Choose "Begin printing." The report prints, and records appear for both types.

Before proceeding, restore all records to full view. To do so, open the Records menu with CONTROL-R. Choose "Select," and then choose "All records" from the submenu.

CHANGING THE ORDER OF FIELDS WITHIN A REPORT

Fields often do not appear exactly where you want them in a report. You can move fields to different locations when designing the report by alternately removing and showing fields, which requires the options "Remove field" and "Show field" of the Fields menu.

Suppose that the staff at Friends of Crabgrass wants a report to show the State field following the Lastname field and the Contribute field following the State field. Since this change is

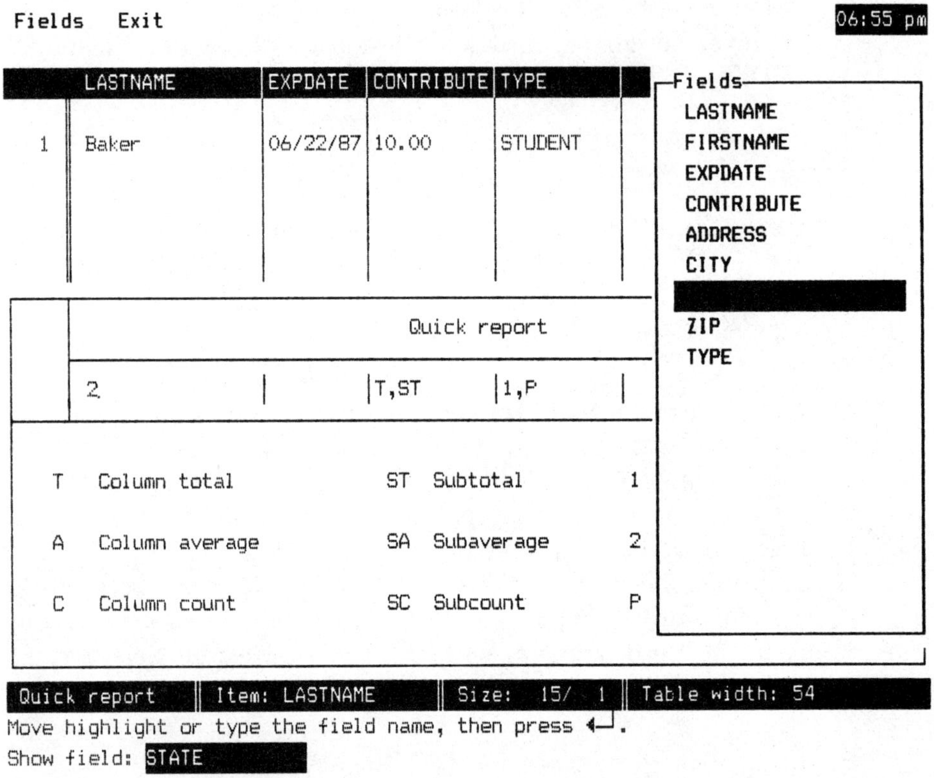

Figure 6-7. Producing a list of fields with "Show Field"

to affect just the Quick Report, the change should be made to the Quick Report layout.

Open the Layout menu with CONTROL-L and select the option "Design layout." First remove the State field from the current location. Move the cursor to the State field, open the Fields menu with CONTROL-F, and select "Remove field."

Next add the State field at the new location, to the right of the Lastname field. Place the cursor at the Lastname field. Use CONTROL-F to open the Fields menu, and choose "Show field" from the submenu. A message at the bottom of the screen asks **Insert field to the left or right of the current field? Left Right.**

This message appears only when you insert a field at the leftmost field location of a table. At all other locations Rapid-File automatically inserts the field to the right of the existing field, without asking first. In this case, since State is to appear to the right of the Lastname field, select "Right." A list of available fields appears on the right side of the screen as Figure 6-7 shows.

Select State from the list. The State field appears in the proper location, to the right of the Lastname field.

Next place the cursor at the Contribute field. Enter CONTROL-F and then R to remove the field. Move the cursor to the State field, and enter CONTROL-F and then S for "Show field." Choose the Contribute field from the list of fields. The field appears in the desired location, and the Quick Report guide resembles Figure 6-8.

Press F9 to implement the changes to the report layout. Then check to see that your printer is turned on and ready, and open the Print menu with CONTROL-P. Choose "Begin printing." The report will print with the columns appearing in the desired order, as shown in Figure 6-9.

PREVIEWING A QUICK REPORT WITHOUT PRINTING

You can view a Quick Report without printing it to see if the appearance of the report is really what you desire. To do this, simply open the Print menu with CONTROL-P, and select "Destination" from the menu and "Monitor/Screen" from the submenu.

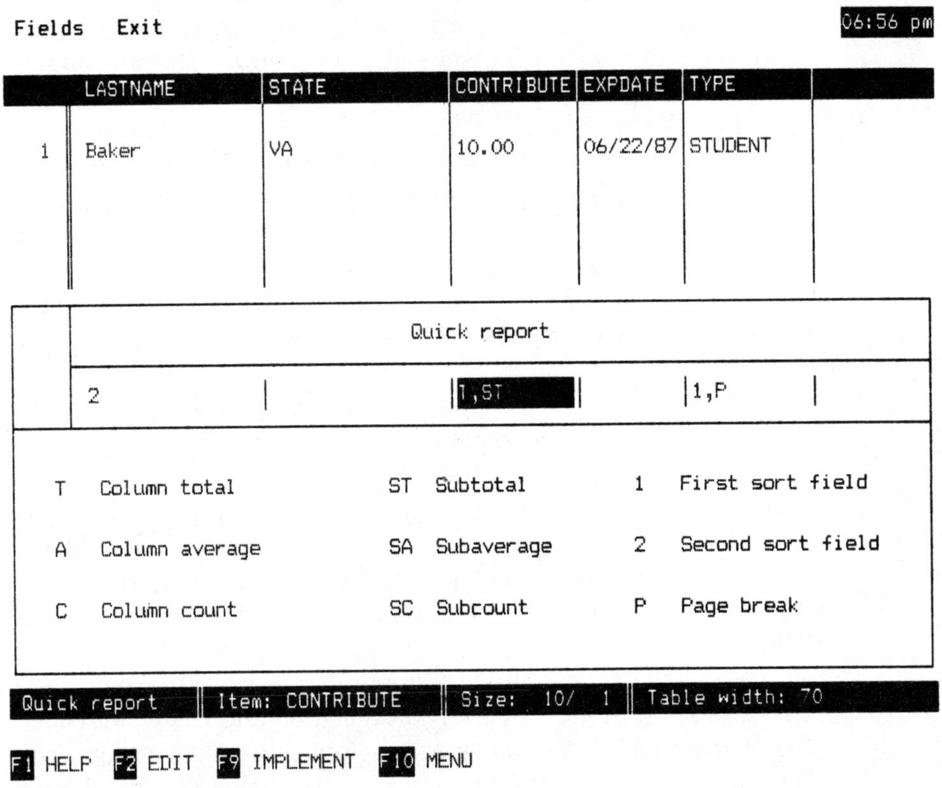

Figure 6-8. The on-screen result of moving State and Contribute

Close the submenu with ESC, and then choose "Begin printing." The report appears on the screen in the same format as it would be printed on paper, although only one screen of information appears at a time. To see each successive screen, press

```
                    Report from MEMBERS.RPD on 09/22/86


REC# |LASTNAME       |STATE          |CONTRIBUTE|EXPDATE |TYPE
-----+---------------+---------------+----------+--------+----------
   1 |Askew          |NY             |25.00     |03/01/88|ADULT
   2 |Baker          |CA             |20.00     |09/08/87|ADULT
   3 |Block          |IL             |20.00     |03/08/87|ADULT
   4 |Brown          |IL             |25.00     |08/15/87|ADULT
   5 |Johnson, Jr.   |MA             |40.00     |12/01/87|ADULT
   6 |Jones          |TX             |30.00     |05/15/87|ADULT
   7 |Mills          |CA             |20.00     |04/30/87|ADULT
   8 |Roberts        |AZ             |25.00     |05/06/87|ADULT
   9 |Roberts        |AZ             |25.00     |05/06/87|ADULT
  10 |Roberts        |AZ             |20.00     |03/08/87|ADULT
  11 |Shaw           |FL             |35.00     |07/21/87|ADULT
  12 |Sloan          |VA             |25.00     |10/15/86|ADULT
                                      ----------
                    Total for ADULT 310.

                               - 1 -



                    Report from MEMBERS.RPD on 09/22/86


REC# |LASTNAME       |STATE          |CONTRIBUTE|EXPDATE |TYPE
-----+---------------+---------------+----------+--------+----------
  13 |Hayes          |TX             |100.00    |08/15/88|CHARTER
  14 |Smith          |CA             |100.00    |01/12/88|CHARTER
                                      ----------
                  Total for CHARTER 200.

                               - 2 -
```

Figure 6-9. New report

```
                                   Report from MEMBERS.RPD on 09/22/86


REC# |LASTNAME          |STATE             |CONTRIBUTE|EXPDATE |TYPE
-----+------------------+------------------+----------+--------+---------
 15  |Sand              |MD                |500.00    |01/01/99|LIFETIME
                                            ----------
                            Total for LIFETIME 500.

                                        - 3 -
```

```
                             Report from MEMBERS.RPD on 09/22/86


REC# |LASTNAME          |STATE             |CONTRIBUTE|EXPDATE |TYPE
-----+------------------+------------------+----------+--------+---------
 16  |Baker             |VA                |10.00     |06/22/87|STUDENT
 17  |Harris            |VA                |10.00     |02/22/78|STUDENT
 18  |Schultz           |VA                |10.00     |11/17/87|STUDENT
                                            ----------
                             Total for STUDENT 30.
                                            ==========
                                Total for File 1040.

                                        - 4 -
```

Figure 6-9. New report (*continued*)

RETURN. Press ESC at any time to cancel the screen operation. After pressing ESC you may elect to cancel or resume the printing by making the appropriate selection from the horizontal prompt in the Message Area.

A SHORTCUT: TOTALING NUMERIC DATA

If you need to obtain totals, averages, or counts for all selected records in a file and you do not actually need a printed report, you do not have to design a Quick Report layout. To quickly obtain numeric totals, averages, and counts, open the Records menu with CONTROL-R, and then choose the "Totals" option. The values you need appear at the bottom of the screen as Figure 6-10 shows.

File   Layout   Records   Write   Print   08:57 am

	LASTNAME	STATE	CONTRIBUTE	EXPDATE	TYPE
8	Jones	TX	30.00	05/15/87	ADULT
9	Askew	NY	25.00	03/08/88	ADULT
10	Johnson, Jr.	MA	40.00	12/01/87	ADULT
11	Brown	IL	25.00	08/15/87	ADULT
12	Block	IL	20.00	03/08/87	ADULT
13	Hayes	TX	100.00	08/15/88	CHARTER
14	Smith	CA	100.00	01/12/88	CHARTER
15	Sand	MD	500.00	01/01/99	LIFETIME
16	Harris	VA	10.00	02/22/87	STUDENT
17	Schultz	VA	10.00	11/17/87	STUDENT
18	Baker	VA	10.00	06/22/87	STUDENT
CNT			18		
TOT			1040.		
AVG			57.7777777		
MIN			10.		
MAX			500.		

QUICK: Report 2 | C:MEMBERS.RPD | Selected: 18 of 18

Figure 6-10. Using "Totals" to see numeric data quickly

Table 6-1 presents a key to the values produced by "Total." As you see, the values include a count of all selected records, the sum of the values, an average of the values, and minimum and maximum values. The values appear at the bottom of every field that has been designated as a numeric field. (Values also appear for calculated totals and for report and field types.) If the file has additional numeric fields hidden to the right, use LEFT ARROW or RIGHT ARROW to bring those fields and the corresponding totals into view.

The "Totals" option acts as a *toggle*—selecting it will turn off the option if it is already on and will turn on the option if it is off. If you want to produce quick totals, averages, and counts for a group of records, use the "Select" option of the Records menu to select those records. Then turn on the "Totals" option.

If you select the "Totals" option and no values appear, you may have defined the fields improperly during the creation of the database. If numbers are entered into a field that is defined as text, RapidFile stores the numbers, but it does not total them. The cure is to use the option "Modify file structure" of the

Table 6-1. A Key to the Values Produced by "Totals"

Description	**Result**
CNT	Provides a count of the number of entries in the numeric field where the count appears
TOT	Provides a total for all values in the numeric field
AVG	Provides an average of the values contained in the numeric field
MIN	Shows the minimum, or smallest, value contained in the numeric field
MAX	Shows the maximum, or largest, value contained in the numeric field

File menu to change the field type from text to numeric. After the field type has been changed, use the "Totals" option again to display the totals.

CUSTOMIZING YOUR PRINT SETTINGS

All the reports printed so far have contained the standard headings and page numbering supplied by RapidFile. RapidFile also offers the flexibility of adding custom titles, headers, and footers. Access these options by choosing "Print settings" from the Print menu.

Open the Print menu with CONTROL-P and select "Print settings." The submenu shown in Figure 6-11 appears. The upper half of the submenu provides toggle (off or on) options for page numbers at the bottom of each page, record numbers at the left side of each page, and line borders between the columns. It also allows you to decide whether the printer should pause before each page and whether repeated data should be omitted. If the option "Omit repeated data" is on, data in a sorted field that is identical to that in the previous record will not print. Selecting any of these options turns the option on if it was off or off if it was on.

The lower half of the submenu allows you to decide if headers print at the top of every page and if footers print at the bottom of every page. "Title" allows you to choose a report title that prints on each page. "Copies" allows you to choose the number of copies to be printed (from 1 to 999). "Printer codes" allows you to enter printer codes applicable to your printer that enable special effects such as compressed or emphasized characters (see your printer manual for details on which codes apply).

For our example, select the "Header" option, delete the existing header, and enter

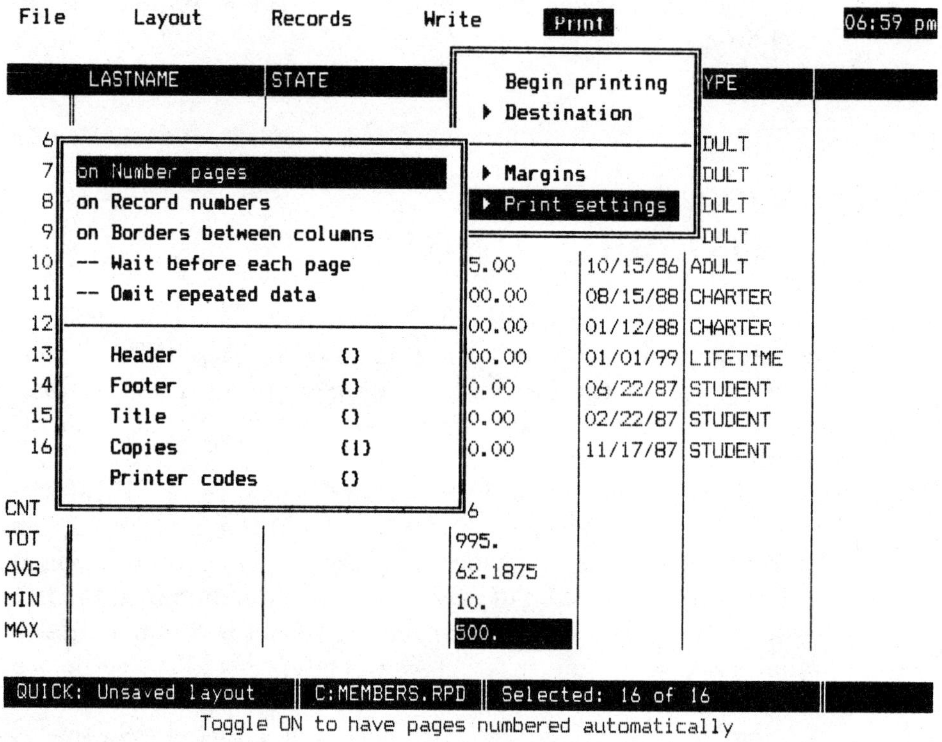

Figure 6-11. The submenu of "Print settings"

Membership Report

as a header. Select "Footer" and enter

Statewide

as the footer. Select "Title" and enter

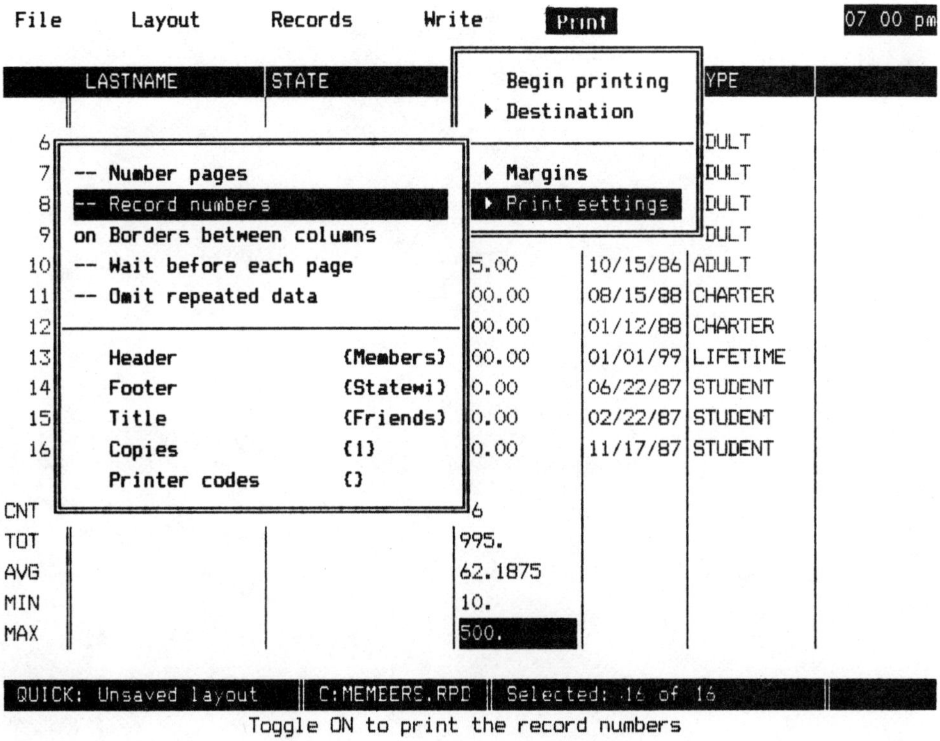

Figure 6-12. The "Print settings" submenu showing elements that will and will not appear on the printed report

Friends of Crabgrass

as a title for the report. Turn off the option "Record numbers." The submenu should resemble Figure 6-12.

Press ESC to close the submenu, and choose "Begin printing." Each page of the report contains the header, footer, and title that you defined.

Managing Your Files

Chapter 7

Once you have created a database, you will probably need to make changes to the design of it. Despite the best planning, the need for additional fields or for changes to existing fields will arise. With RapidFile no database design is cast in stone. You can easily add new fields or change the design of an existing field.

In addition to helping you manage the characteristics of a database, RapidFile also allows you to manage other files by doing many tasks usually achieved through DOS—tasks such as erasing and renaming files. To change a database or manage other files, the RapidFile user accesses options provided by the File menu (see Figure 7-1).

In addition to being used to create new databases, the "Create" option of the File menu is also used to create a new field within an existing database. The option "Modify structure" is used to change existing field types and to delete fields, and "Disk/directory" provides a menu of additional choices relating to displaying directories, erasing and renaming files, and accessing DOS to perform other tasks.

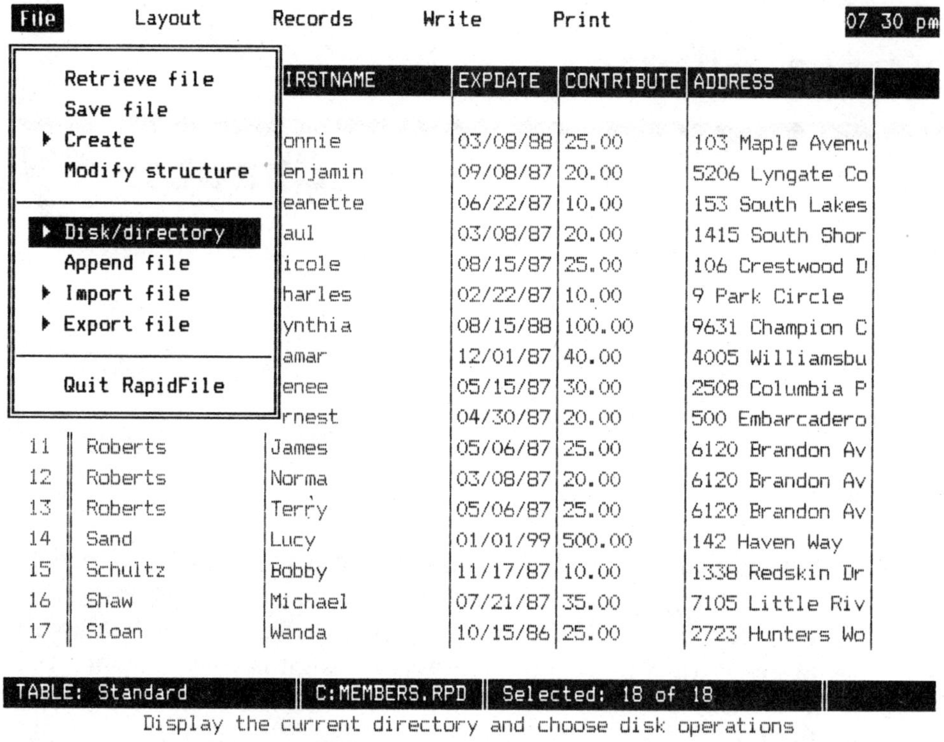

Figure 7-1. The File menu allows the user to change a database and manage files

CHANGING A DATABASE DESIGN

If you have not done so, start RapidFile and load the database MEMBERS. If necessary, open the Layout menu, and choose "Table layout" to view the file in columnar form.

Adding a Field

As an example of how "Create" allows you to restructure a database, add another field to MEMBERS that contains the amount of a member's contribution in the previous year. The option adds a field to the right of the present cursor location, so position the cursor before choosing "Create." (You have the option of removing the new field if you do not like the placement after you have added it.)

Place the cursor in the Contribute field. Open the File menu with CONTROL-F and select "Create." A submenu asks if you desire an additional field for the current database or a new file. Select "Additional field" from the submenu.

A prompt at the bottom of the screen asks for a new name for the field. Enter

LASTYEAR

as the new field name. The next prompt to appear at the bottom of the screen asks **Choose the field type: Text Numeric Date Calculated Report**. Select "Text" from the available options. If the use of "Text" seems incorrect for contributions, you are observant, but choose "Text" nevertheless. The new column for the Lastyear field appears to the right of the existing Contribute column.

As indicated in the following, add amounts in the new Lastyear field next to the appropriate member names.

LASTNAME	LASTYEAR
Askew	25.00
Baker	10.00
Baker	0.00
Block	20.00
Brown	30.00
Harris	10.00
Hayes	20.00
Johnson, Jr.	20.00

Jones	25.00
Mills	20.00
Roberts	25.00
Roberts	20.00
Roberts	20.00
Sand	100.00
Schultz	0.00
Shaw	20.00
Sloan	20.00
Smith	40.00

You will use these values in this and successive chapters to demonstrate various calculation capabilities of RapidFile.

Once you have entered the numbers, save your changes to the file with CONTROL-RETURN. Then open the Records menu with CONTROL-R and select "Totals." Your screen should look like Figure 7-2. Values similar to those that appear in the Contribute field should appear in Lastyear. No values appear, however, because you followed the instructions given for the purpose of the example and entered "Text" as the field type. How can you correct the field type?

Changing the Database Structure

Although the Lastyear field contains numbers, RapidFile was unable to calculate them because the field was not designated as a numeric field. As a text field, Lastyear is useless for calculation. Fortunately, RapidFile provides an option for changing the structure, or design, of the database, and field type is one of the elements that you can redefine.

Open the File menu with CONTROL-F. Select the option "Modify structure." The on-screen database will be replaced with the File Structure Table (Figure 7-3).

File Layout Records Write Print 09 51 am

	LASTNAME	FIRSTNAME	EXPDATE	CONTRIBUTE	LASTYEAR
8	Johnson, Jr.	Lamar	12/01/87	40.00	20.00
9	Jones	Renee	05/15/87	30.00	25.00
10	Mills	Ernest	04/30/87	20.00	20.00
11	Roberts	James	05/06/87	25.00	25.00
12	Roberts	Norma	03/08/87	20.00	20.00
13	Roberts	Terry	05/06/87	25.00	20.00
14	Sand	Lucy	01/01/99	500.00	100.00
15	Schultz	Bobby	11/17/87	10.00	0.00
16	Shaw	Michael	07/21/87	35.00	20.00
17	Sloan	Wanda	10/15/86	25.00	20.00
18	Smith	Larry	01/12/88	100.00	40.00
CNT				18	
TOT				1040.	
AVG				57.7777777	
MIN				10.	
MAX				500.	

TABLE: Unsaved layout | C:MEMBERS.RPD | Selected: 18 of 18

Figure 7-2. "Totals" yields no values in Lastyear because Lastyear was defined as a text field

The File Structure Table shows the settings for the fields of the database and for the layout currently in use. The *field settings,* which occupy the left half of the screen, specify the field names and field types for the fields of the database. Field settings also specify expressions you have provided in calculated fields and report fields. (Report fields are covered in Chapter 9.)

File Structure Table

Field Settings			Preset Layout Settings		
Field name	Type	Expression	Field Format	Table size	Form size
LASTNAME	Text		None	15	25/1
FIRSTNAME	Text		None	15	25/1
EXPDATE	Date		None	8	8/1
CONTRIBUTE	Numeric		None	10	10/1
ADDRESS	Text		None	15	25/1
CITY	Text		None	15	25/1
STATE	Text		None	15	25/1
ZIP	Text		None	15	25/1
TYPE	Text		None	15	25/1
LASTYEAR	Text		None	15	25/1

F1 HELP F2 EDIT F9 IMPLEMENT ESC to leave without changes

Figure 7-3. The File Structure Table

The *preset layout settings,* which occupy the right half of the screen, reflect the preset field sizes and formats. RapidFile uses the presets when you show a field during layout design and when you choose the option "Display all fields" from the Fields menu. By changing the preset layout settings, you can change the appearance of new layouts you create for the database to a format that is more to your liking. However, changing the presets does not change the current layout.

To change any of the settings within the File Structure Table, use the arrow keys to move the cursor to any position on the screen. Once you have moved the cursor to the desired location, press F2 (EDIT). In the case of field names, expressions, and table and form sizes, type in the desired names, expressions, or numbers after pressing F2. To alter values in the columns Type and Field Format, pressing F2 reveals a list of appropriate options at the bottom of the screen.

On the screen under the column Field Settings, the column called Field Name contains the names of the fields. The Type column contains one of the five acceptable data types (text, numeric, date, calculated, or report). The column called Expression can contain data that RapidFile will automatically enter in each field for every new record created. The Expression column can also contain a math formula, such as Contribute % Lastyear or Sales + Tax, to provide calculated results based on other fields.

Under Preset Layout Settings, you can select various options for the Field Format column. The options that are available depend on the type of field. Text fields accommodate the format options "None," "Reverse," and "Word wrap"; date fields accommodate the options "None," "American," "European," "Written," and "Custom"; and numeric fields accommodate the options "None," "Fixed," "Business," "Currency," "Accounting," and "Written." The columns Table Size and Form Size allow the entry of numbers that change the preset table size or the preset form size. The form size is entered as two numbers separated by a slash, such as 25/1. The first number refers to the width (in characters) of the field format. The second number refers to the height (in lines) of the field. Fields in a table layout can range from 1 to 72 characters in width. Fields in a form layout can range from 1 to 254 characters in width.

In the present case the field Lastyear needs to be changed from a text field to a numeric field so RapidFile can calculate the desired values. Place the cursor in the Type column next to the field name Lastyear. Press F2. The following options appear at the bottom of the screen: **Choose the field type: Text Numeric Date Calculated Report**. Select "Numeric" from the list of options, and then press F9 to implement the changes. The database reappears.

Open the Records menu and choose the "Totals" option. Because this option is a toggle, doing so will turn it off. Open the Records menu and again choose "Totals." This time, the values for the Lastyear field appear, as Figure 7-4 shows.

File Layout Records Write Print 09 53 am

	LASTNAME	FIRSTNAME	EXPDATE	CONTRIBUTE	LASTYEAR
8	Johnson, Jr.	Lamar	12/01/87	40.00	20.00
9	Jones	Renee	05/15/87	30.00	25.00
10	Mills	Ernest	04/30/87	20.00	20.00
11	Roberts	James	05/06/87	25.00	25.00
12	Roberts	Norma	03/08/87	20.00	20.00
13	Roberts	Terry	05/06/87	25.00	20.00
14	Sand	Lucy	01/01/99	500.00	100.00
15	Schultz	Bobby	11/17/87	10.00	0.00
16	Shaw	Michael	07/21/87	35.00	20.00
17	Sloan	Wanda	10/15/86	25.00	20.00
18	Smith	Larry	01/12/88	100.00	40.00
CNT				18	18
TOT				1040.	425.
AVG				57.7777777	23.6111111
MIN				10.	0
MAX				500.	100.

TABLE: Unsaved layout | C:MEMBERS.RPD | Selected: 18 of 18

Figure 7-4. "Totals" yields values when Lastyear is defined as a numeric field

Adding Calculated Fields

RapidFile offers calculated fields, which are fields that contain information based on calculations of numeric data. The contents of a calculated field can be based on a calculation between two fields or based on a calculation between one field and some fixed value. As an example, consider a sales database that contains a calculated field that multiplies the amount of a sale by a state sales tax. A database of rental properties could contain a calculated field based on one field containing the rental amount and another field containing the number of months of the lease. In the following example you will create a calculated field that shows the percentage of increase or decrease for contributions. Such an amount can be calculated by dividing the Contribute field by the Lastyear field and multiplying the result by 100.

The first step in the example is to add the new field. With the cursor in the Lastyear field, open the File menu with CONTROL-F and select the "Create" option. From the submenu that appears, choose "Additional field." For the name of the field, enter

CHANGED

For the field type choose "Calculated" from the list of options at the bottom of the screen.

Another menu, which appears at the bottom of the screen, now asks **Choose calculation type: Add Subtract Multiply Divide Percent.** The options are self-explanatory. You can base the contents of the calculated field on addition, subtraction, multiplication, division, or the formula to figure percentages. Select "Percent" from the options list. The field list shown in Figure 7-5 appears, and the prompt at the bottom of the screen asks you to select the field that you want to use first in the percentage calculation.

Select the Contribute field from the fields list. At the bottom of the screen the next prompt asks **Will the calculation be a**

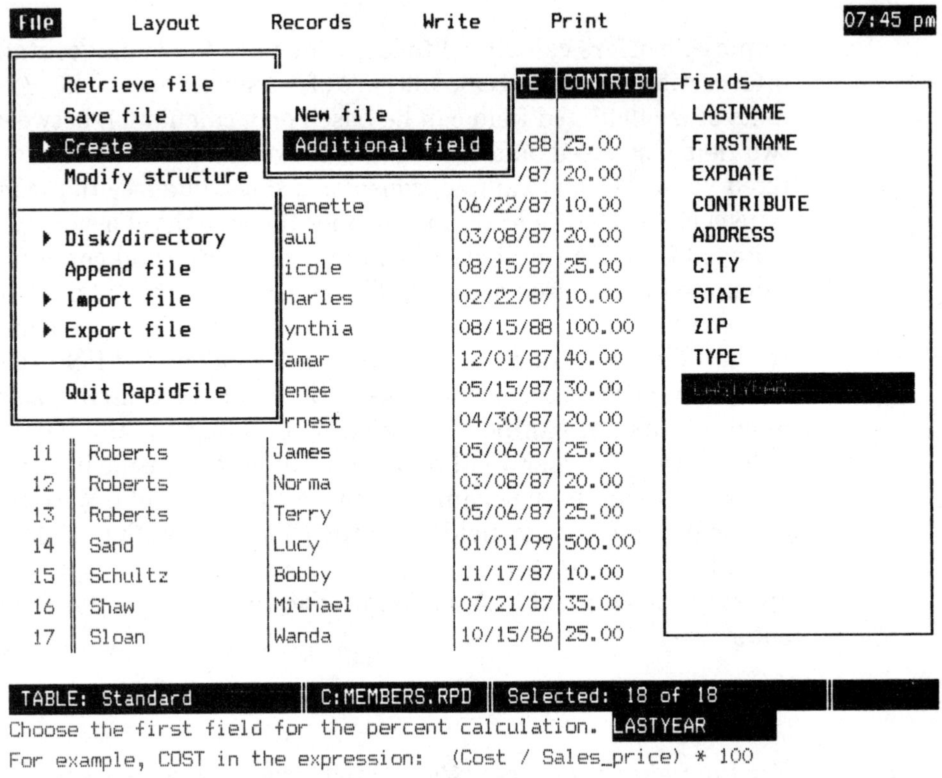

Figure 7-5. The prompt asks for the field to use first in the calculation of percentage

percentage of a field or a number? Choose "Field." The list of fields again appears, and the prompt at the bottom of the screen now asks for the second field to use in the percentage calculation. Select Lastyear from the list of fields. The database reappears with the new field, Changed, that contains the percentage values (see Figure 7-6).

File Layout Records Write Print 07 51 pm

	FIRSTNAME	EXPDATE	CONTRIBUTE	LASTYEAR	CHANGED
1	Lonnie	03/08/88	25.00	25.00	100.00
2	Benjamin	09/08/87	20.00	10.00	200.00
3	Jeanette	06/22/87	10.00	0.00	1000.00
4	Paul	03/08/87	20.00	20.00	100.00
5	Nicole	08/15/87	25.00	30.00	83.33
6	Charles	02/22/87	10.00	10.00	100.00
7	Cynthia	08/15/88	100.00	20.00	500.00
8	Lamar	12/01/87	40.00	20.00	200.00
9	Renee	05/15/87	30.00	25.00	120.00
10	Ernest	04/30/87	20.00	20.00	100.00
11	James	05/06/87	25.00	25.00	100.00
12	Norma	03/08/87	20.00	20.00	100.00
13	Terry	05/06/87	25.00	20.00	125.00
14	Lucy	01/01/99	500.00	100.00	500.00
15	Bobby	11/17/87	10.00	0.00	1000.00
16	Michael	07/21/87	35.00	20.00	175.00
17	Wanda	10/15/86	25.00	20.00	125.00

TABLE: Standard | C:MEMBERS.RPD | Selected: 18 of 18

Figure 7-6. The new field, Changed, shows the results of a percentage calculation

PERFORMING AUTOMATED DATA ENTRY

If you often or always enter the same information into a particular field, use the Expression column of the File Structure Table to automate the data entry process. In the case of the database for Friends of Crabgrass, most members fall into the category "regular" when it comes to type of member, so it would be a time-saving aid if Regular appeared in the Type field for every new record. The person entering the data could then change the entry if the new member happened to fall into one of the other categories.

To make this change, open the File menu with CONTROL-F and select the option "Modify structure." Confirm that you have read the prompt, which reminds you to save changes to your existing file. When the File Structure Table appears, move the cursor to the Expression column beside the Type field, and then press F2. At the bottom of the screen, you see the following prompt: **Type the expression for the current field, then press ↵**. Enter

"REGULAR"

(including the quotation marks), and press RETURN. Note that any text that is to be repeatedly entered as a result of this technique must be surrounded by quotation marks. It is not necessary to surround numbers entered into numeric or calculated fields with quotation marks.

Once the entry has been made, press F9 to implement the change. Use the RIGHT ARROW key to bring the type field into view. No change is immediately apparent, but if you move the cursor past the last record in the database as if you wanted to add a new record, you see that the notation Regular has automatically been entered in the field of the blank record (see Figure 7-7). You can cancel the addition of the new record by moving the cursor back up into the existing database.

You can continue to edit the entries in the File Structure Table to perform automated data entry for specific groups of records. This technique can be handy for entering groups of records with the same city, state, and ZIP code or records with similar repetitive data.

File Layout Records Write Print 09:56 am

	CITY	STATE	ZIP	TYPE
3	Reston	VA	22090	STUDENT
4	Chicago	IL	60617	ADULT
5	Chicago	IL	60610	ADULT
6	Sterling	VA	22070	STUDENT
7	Austin	TX	76801	CHARTER
8	Cambridge	MA	02139	ADULT
9	Arlington	TX	75780	ADULT
10	San Francisco	CA	95002	ADULT
11	Phoenix	AZ	80555	ADULT
12	Phoenix	AZ	80555	ADULT
13	Phoenix	AZ	80555	ADULT
14	Annapolis	MD	18955	LIFETIME
15	Herndon	VA	22070	STUDENT
16	Annandale	FL	30508	ADULT
17	Reston	VA	22091	ADULT
18	Los Angeles	CA	90055	CHARTER
19				REGULAR

TABLE: Unsaved layout | C:MEMBERS.RPD | Selected: 19 of 19

Figure 7-7. The results of automated data entry

DELETING FIELDS

Fields can be deleted from the File Structure Table by highlighting the field name with the cursor and pressing CONTROL-DEL. (All the current fields in our file are needed, so do not try this with the database MEMBERS.) If you perform such a step, RapidFile prompts for confirmation by displaying a message at the bottom of the screen that reads **Do you really want to delete this field from the file? Yes No.** You must select the "Yes" option to delete the field. Once you delete a field, all the data that was in that field is lost, and the field is simultaneously removed from any layouts that contained it. Remember that any expressions that used the field will be invalid.

APPENDING DATA FROM ANOTHER FILE

RapidFile provides a way to add (or append) records from a different database into the one you are currently using. If you wish to see how this works, you will need another file from which to append the records. To save time, use the sample database called SALES, which is on the Sample Data/Utility disk provided with RapidFile. Open the File menu with CONTROL-F and select "Disk/directory." Choose the option "Access DOS" from the submenu, and the DOS prompt appears. If you are using a hard disk, use the DOS command COPY to copy the file SALES.RPD from the Sample Data/Utility disk onto your hard disk. If you are using floppy disks, temporarily place the Sample Data/Utility disk in drive A. Use the DOS command COPY to copy the file SALES.RPD from the Sample Data/Utility disk onto your data disk in drive B, and replace the Sample Data/Utility disk with the RapidFile program disk when done.

At the DOS prompt type

EXIT

and press RETURN to get back to RapidFile. To append records from another file, enter CONTROL-F and then use the option "Append file" of the File menu. From the list of available files

Append File

Source Fields on Disk		Target Fields in Current File
Buyer	-▸	LASTNAME
Address	-▸	FIRSTNAME
City	-▸	EXPDATE
State	-▸	CONTRIBUTE
ZIP	-▸	ADDRESS
Item	-▸	CITY
Cost	-▸	STATE
Retail_Price	-▸	ZIP
Date_Sold	-▸	TYPE
Payment_#1	-▸	LASTYEAR
Date_#1	-▸	CHANGED

F1 HELP F2 EDIT F9 IMPLEMENT ESC to leave without changes

Figure 7-8. The Append File screen

that appears, select SALES. Once you have selected the file to append, the Append File screen appears, as shown in Figure 7-8.

The left side of the screen contains the field names within the file you are appending, or the *source file.* The right side of the screen contains the names of the fields in the file that you are appending to, also known as the *target file.*

This short exercise will demonstrate, however, how you can append data from another file and discard the results later. You can change the fields from the source file by moving the cursor to the desired field, pressing F2, and then selecting a new field from a list that appears.

Consider how the Address field in the source file is currently headed for the Firstname field in the target file. In the exercise that follows, you will rearrange the fields so that fields that contain similar data are together. Fields relating to money will be together, for example, and so will fields about names. Move the cursor down to the Address field and press F2. A list of available fields appears on the right side of the screen (see Figure 7-9). Now proceed as follows:

1. Highlight Buyer and press RETURN. This tells RapidFile to prepare to move all entries from the SALES file under Buyer to both the Lastname and the Firstname fields of the MEMBERS database.
2. Move the cursor to City and press F2. From the list of fields that appears, select Date_#1. This tells RapidFile to replace the source field you highlighted with the field you chose from the list of available fields on the far right.
3. Move the cursor to State and press F2. From the list of fields, select Payment_#1.
4. Move the cursor to ZIP and press F2. From the list of fields, select Address.
5. Move the cursor to Item and press F2. From the list of fields, select City.
6. Move the cursor to Cost and press F2. From the list of fields, select State.
7. Move the cursor to Retail_Price and press F2. From the list of fields, select Zip.

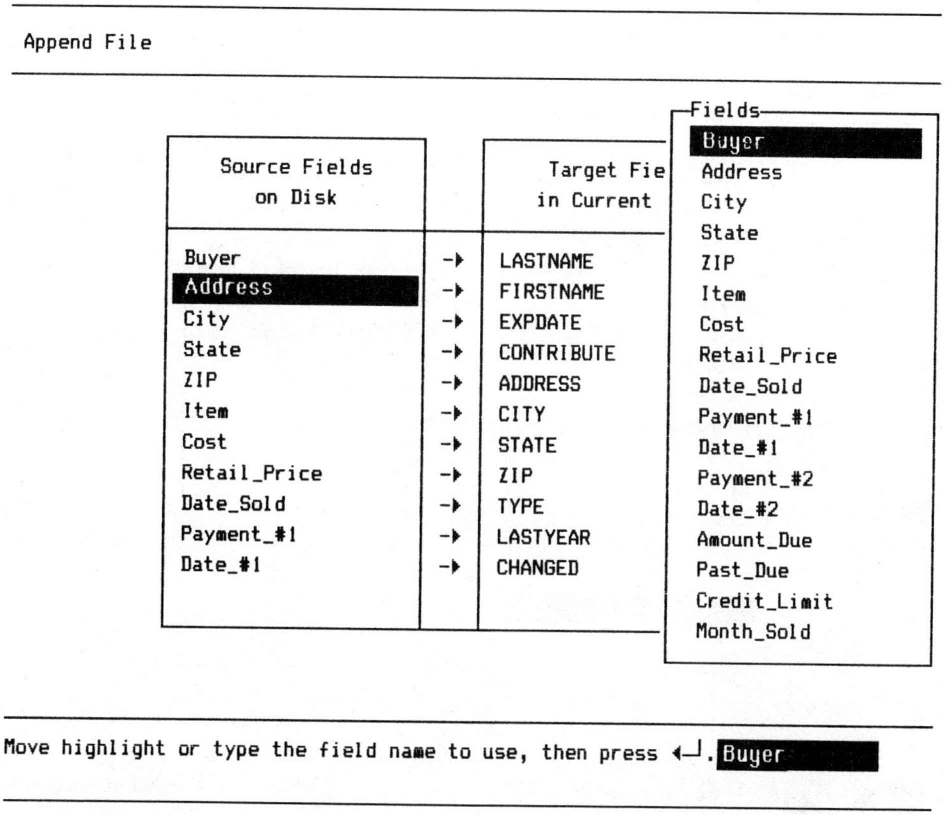

Figure 7-9. Pressing F2 in the Append File screen allows you to assign a different source field to the target field

If you do not want to add the data in a particular field, you can delete that field from the list of source fields with the DEL key. Move the cursor to the final source-field names ("Date_Sold," "Payment_#1," and "Date_#1"), and delete each entry by pressing DEL. Your screen should now resemble the one shown in Figure 7-10.

Append File

Source Fields on Disk		Target Fields in Current File
Buyer	-▸	LASTNAME
Buyer	-▸	FIRSTNAME
Date_#1	-▸	EXPDATE
Payment_#1	-▸	CONTRIBUTE
Address	-▸	ADDRESS
City	-▸	CITY
State	-▸	STATE
ZIP	-▸	ZIP
	-▸	TYPE
	-▸	LASTYEAR
	-▸	CHANGED

F1 HELP F2 EDIT F9 IMPLEMENT ESC to leave without changes

Figure 7-10. The result of rearranging source fields

The number of target fields determines how many fields from the source file are displayed, but all fields in the source file are available for inserting.

Press F9 to implement the addition. The records from the SALES file are appended to the MEMBERS file. During the append process, a count appears at the bottom of the screen, indicating the number of records that have been added. When the process is complete, you see the following prompt at the bottom of the screen: **Do you want to append another file? Yes No.**

Select "No," and the database MEMBERS appears. Try the PGDN key, and you see that the new records have been added. You do not really want these records, however, so open the File menu with CONTROL-F, and choose "Retrieve file." Answer "No" to the prompt **Save before continuing?**, and highlight MEMBERS from the list of files. The modified file is discarded when the older version of the database is again loaded from disk.

PERFORMING DISK AND DIRECTORY FUNCTIONS

RapidFile allows you to perform a number of operations that are performed from DOS. RapidFile also allows you to temporarily access DOS and to quickly return to the RapidFile program. These types of operations are available through the "Disk/directory" option of the File menu.

Open the File menu now with CONTROL-F and select "Disk/directory." A submenu appears along with a directory of files (see Figure 7-11). If the directory contains more files than you can view at once, use the PGUP and PGDN keys to view them all.

The submenu offers the options "Data drive" (to change the disk drive in use for the data files), "Change" (to change the directory path), "Sort" (to change the display order of the directory), "Print" (to print a listing of the directory), "Erase file," "Rename file," and "Access DOS."

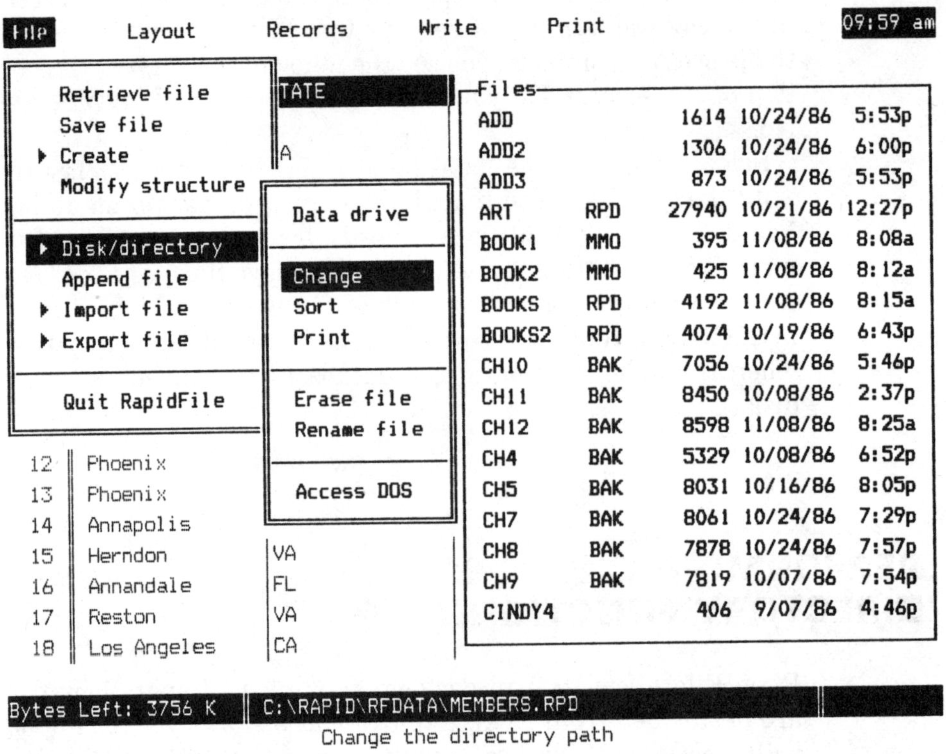

Figure 7-11. The submenu of "Disk/directory"

Changing Data Drives and Data Directories

Selecting the option "Data drive" results in a prompt at the bottom of the screen. The prompt shows your available disk drives. (The number of drives shown by this prompt depends on your hardware configuration.) Highlight the desired drive and press

RETURN. On a dual-drive system, RapidFile normally uses drive B for your data unless you tell the program otherwise by using this option of the Disk/directory menu. If you installed RapidFile on your hard disk, the program is using the hard-disk drive that you specified as part of the installation process.

If you use a hard disk or if you use subdirectories on your floppy disks, selecting the "Change" option of the menu allows you to change directory paths. If you used the installation program provided with RapidFile to install the program on your hard disk, you have a directory named RAPID and a subdirectory of that directory, which is named RFDATA. By selecting "Change" and highlighting the desired directory, you can alternate between the *parent directory* (RAPID) and the *child subdirectory* (RAPID/RFDATA). To keep the display of files to a minimal clutter, hard-disk users should keep the database files in the child subdirectory. The concepts of directories and subdirectories are explained in your DOS manual.

Sorting a Directory

The "Sort" option of the File menu changes the manner in which the directory is displayed. Select "Sort" now and note the following prompt at the bottom of the screen: **Display directory sorted by: Name Extension Size Date Time**.

Highlight any of the choices and press RETURN to display the directory in the indicated fashion. As an example, select "Size" and your directory reappears sorted by the size of the file. Figure 7-12 shows an example of this arrangement.

Printing a Directory

To print a directory, first check to see that your printer is ready, and then select "Print" from the submenu. The directory prints in a format that allows two columns per sheet of paper.

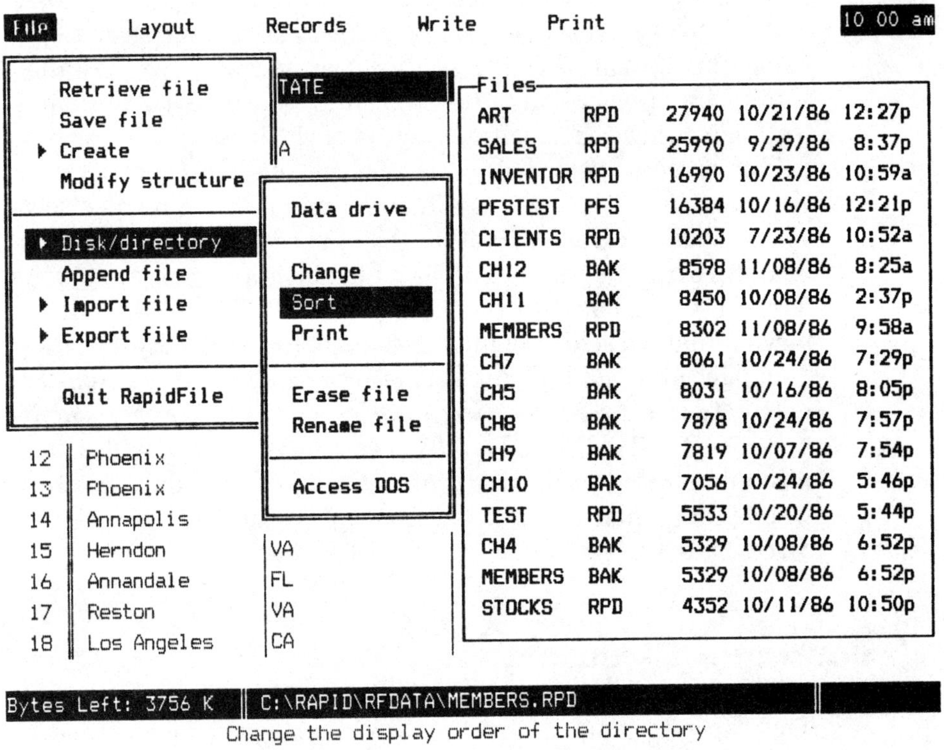

Figure 7-12. A directory sorted by size

The filenames on the printout are sorted in the same manner as the files are sorted on the screen.

Erasing and Renaming Files

Use the options "Erase file" and "Rename file" of the File menu to erase or rename files. When you select either of these options, you may highlight in the directory list the file to be erased or renamed, or you may type the name of the file instead of highlighting it. If you wish to perform some housekeeping on your hard disk, use the "Change" option of the menu to switch to other directories, and then use "Erase file" to get rid of unwanted files in the other directories.

Accessing DOS

Use the option "Access DOS" of the File menu to exit to DOS without quitting RapidFile. This can be a handy option for performing DOS functions such as copying a file or formatting a disk or for running another program and then returning to RapidFile. Selecting "Access DOS" results in the appearance of the DOS prompt. Perform the desired DOS functions or run another program in the usual manner. At the DOS prompt type

EXIT

to return to RapidFile.

To see how this works, select the option "Access DOS." The RapidFile screen vanishes, and something like the following takes its place:

Type EXIT to return to RapidFile.
The IBM Personal Computer DOS
Version 2.10 (C)Copyright IBM Corp 1981, 1982, 1983

C>

You are now back in DOS, but RapidFile remains in a portion of your computer's memory. Try entering the following command:

COPY MEMBERS.RPD TEST.TMP

and the message **(1) files copied** shows that the file has been copied with the DOS command COPY. If you prefer, try running another program. (Do not try loading a memory-resident program, however—see the warning at the end of the chapter.) If you are using a hard disk, you will have to use the DOS command CD \ to change to the directory containing the program you wish to run. Be sure to switch back to the RapidFile data directory afterward by entering

CD \RAPID \RFDATA

at the DOS prompt.

The fact that RapidFile remains in memory when you use "Access DOS" limits what programs you can run. RapidFile requires 256K of memory. Subtract this figure from the amount of your computer's available memory, and then subtract the amount of memory consumed by any memory-resident software that you may be using. The figure that remains is the amount of memory currently available for use by other programs. If your computer has only 256K of memory, you probably cannot run additional programs, but you probably can use most DOS functions like COPY and FORMAT because these functions use little memory.

At the DOS prompt type

EXIT

and press RETURN. The RapidFile screen reappears, and you are again ready to work within RapidFile. If you would like to try the option "Erase file," select it now to get rid of the file you just copied. Open the File menu with CONTROL-F, choose the option "Disk/directory," and then choose "Erase file." From the list of files that appears in the directory, highlight TEST.TMP and press RETURN. Answer the **OK to continue?** prompt by selecting "Yes," and the file is erased. Press ESC to close the submenu.

A Warning About Accessing DOS

Do not use the option "Access DOS" to load programs that are memory resident. (These programs are also known as *TSRs*, which stands for *terminate and stay resident.*) Memory-resident programs are those that "pop up" at the touch of a key combination that contains SHIFT, CONTROL, or ALT. If you load a memory-resident program from "Access DOS," the TSR may overwrite portions of RapidFile that are temporarily stored in the memory of your computer. When you try to return to RapidFile, you may be in for unpleasant results. Your computer may freeze, requiring a complete reboot of the system. If you do not know whether a program is a TSR, save your database before you use the option "Access DOS" of RapidFile to run another program.

The Basics of the Memo Writer

Chapter 8

Until now, all tasks performed with RapidFile have revolved around the use of the program as a database (or file) manager. Although RapidFile performs this task well, it is not limited to database management alone. A major component of the program is the memo writer, a powerful word processing program that can be used alone or in conjunction with the file manager of RapidFile. The memo writer rates on a par with many low-end word processors for the IBM PC and IBM compatibles. It will format text using a variety of margins and tab settings. You can select variable line spacing, justified or nonjustified text, and differing type styles. The memo writer also offers headers and footers, full search-and-replace capabilities, and options for inserting text from other documents.

What is probably the most powerful feature of the memo writer is the fact that it is integrated with the file manager of RapidFile so that you can arrange fields from a database file within a memo writer document. The data contained in various records within the database can then be merged automatically with the memo writer document. Using this technique, you can create form letters based on the records within a RapidFile database. You can also use the memo writer to add large fields to a database file. As an example, a medical database might contain a field that summarizes a patient's illness in a one- or two-paragraph description. Normally, fields within RapidFile are limited to a maximum of 254 characters in length. But, using the memo writer, you can go beyond this limit in field size.

STARTING THE MEMO WRITER

There are two ways to start the memo writer. Use the first method if you are using the file manager of RapidFile and the other method if you are using the memo writer without the file manager. To load the memo writer from DOS, enter

RF MEMO

Access the memo writer from the file manager with the option "Write memo" of the Write menu. There is an important difference between the two methods: If you load the memo writer from within the RapidFile file manager, you are limited to a document size of about 8K (roughly four single-spaced pages of text); if you load the memo writer directly from DOS without loading the file manager, you will have about 64K of memory available for the document (about 32 single-spaced pages of text). The limit of 8K should not pose a significant problem when using both the file manager and the memo writer simultaneously because most simultaneous uses do not demand long documents. Form letters, for example, do not usually run four pages in length.

Load RapidFile and press CONTROL-W to open the Write menu. (Your screen should look like Figure 8-1.)

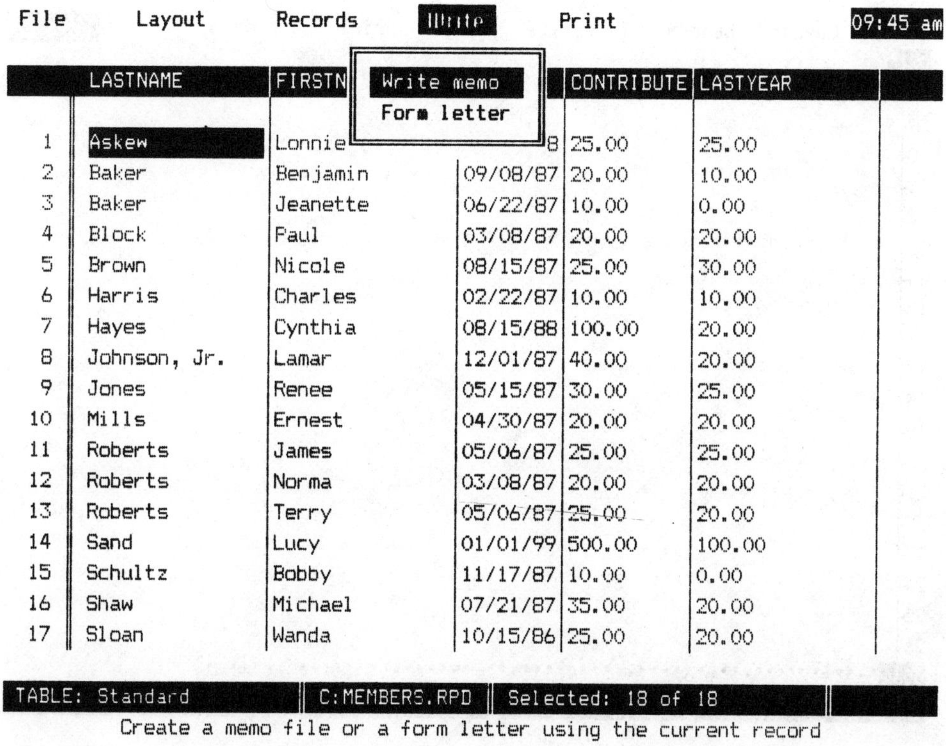

Figure 8-1. The Write menu

The Write menu provides two options: "Write memo" and "Form letter." "Write memo" places you in the memo writer, ready to write a document or form letter; "Form letter" permits the current database to be used with a document to generate form letters.

Select the option "Write memo" and the memo writer's Menu Bar appears as shown in Figure 8-2.

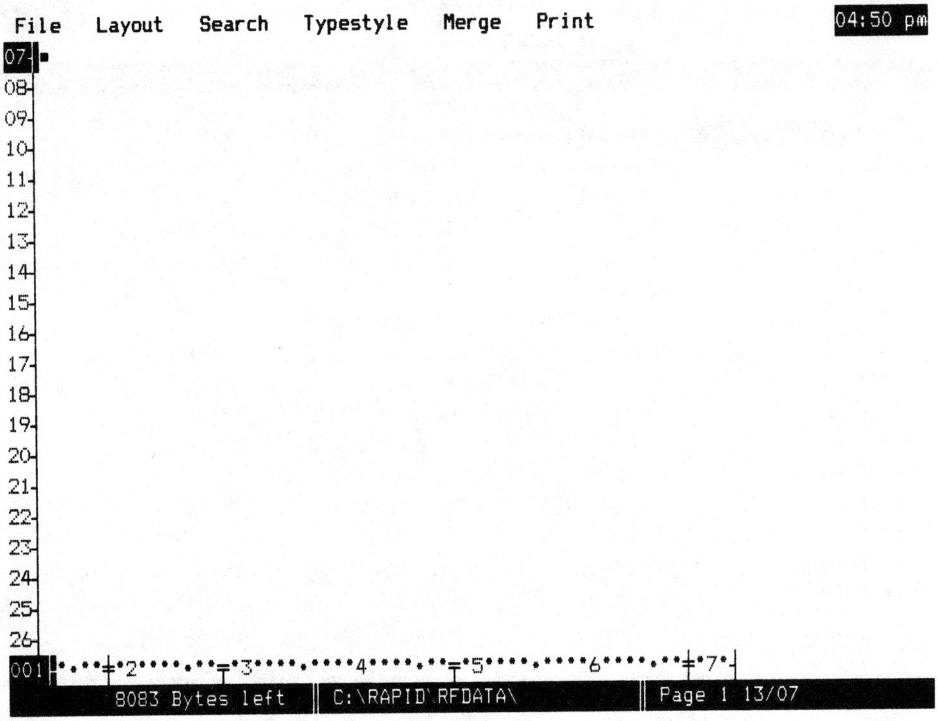

Figure 8-2. The memo writer's Menu Bar

The screen you see when using the memo writer contains five specific areas: the Menu Bar, the Horizontal Ruler, the Vertical Ruler, the Status Bar, and the Message Area. The Status Bar and Message Area occupy the same areas at the bottom of the screen as they do in the file manager of RapidFile. However, the Status Bar provides somewhat different information when in the memo writer. It displays amount of memory (bytes) remaining, name of the file being edited (if any), and page number, line number, and cursor position within a document. As in the file manager, the Message Area displays various messages, which appear when using the memo writer.

The Horizontal Ruler marks the horizontal position of the cursor on the screen, and the Vertical Ruler shows the vertical position of the cursor. Both rulers also serve as a reference guide for formatting documents while you are editing. Note that the Horizontal Ruler begins at cursor position 12 and ends at position 72, and the Vertical Ruler begins at line 7. These preset values, or *default values*, can be changed by customizing your copy of RapidFile (more about customizing appears in Chapter 18).

The Menu Bar provides six different menus: File, Layout, Search, Typestyle, Merge, and Print.

The File menu of the memo writer offers options for retrieving and saving memo files, clearing a file from the screen or inserting another file into the existing one, performing directory operations, and exiting the memo writer. The Layout menu provides choices for formatting documents by offering settings relating to tabs, margins, page breaks, and indentation. The Search menu performs search and search-and-replace operations, and the Typestyle menu offers options for choosing different type styles. The Merge menu is used to combine written documents with records in the database and to generate form letters. The Print menu, similar to the Print menu offered by the file manager, is used to print documents and to control print settings.

TEXT ENTRY

To enter text within the memo writer, you type—just as you would on most typewriters—but with one significant difference. It is not necessary to press RETURN at the end of each line as it is with most typewriters. Simply keep typing as you approach the end of a line, and any words too long to fit on one line will be placed on the next line automatically. This process is known as *word wrap.*

To provide enough text to work with the features of the memo writer, type the letter shown in Figure 8-3.

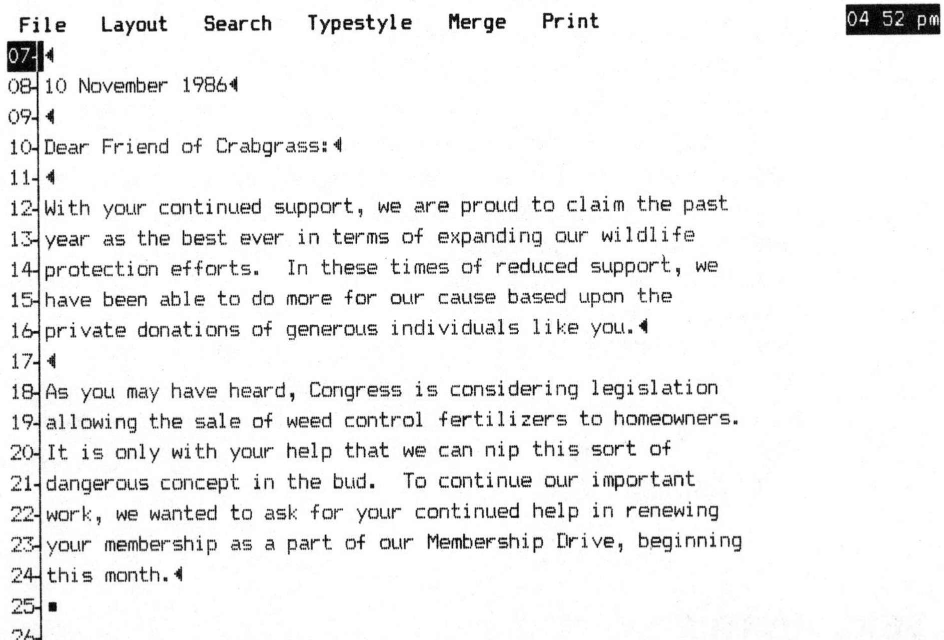
File Layout Search Typestyle Merge Print 04 52 pm

10 November 1986

Dear Friend of Crabgrass:

With your continued support, we are proud to claim the past year as the best ever in terms of expanding our wildlife protection efforts. In these times of reduced support, we have been able to do more for our cause based upon the private donations of generous individuals like you.

As you may have heard, Congress is considering legislation allowing the sale of weed control fertilizers to homeowners. It is only with your help that we can nip this sort of dangerous concept in the bud. To continue our important work, we wanted to ask for your continued help in renewing your membership as a part of our Membership Drive, beginning this month.

001 7388 Bytes left C:\RAPID\RFDATA\ Page 1 13/07

Figure 8-3. The text of a letter

DELETING TEXT

Text that is no longer desired (such as typographical errors) can be removed by moving the cursor to the appropriate position with the arrow keys and using BACKSPACE or DEL to remove the offending characters. The memo writer is normally in an *insert mode* of operation, meaning that any characters to the right of the cursor are pushed to the right by new characters that are entered at the cursor location. You can switch back and forth between insert and *overwrite mode* by pressing the INS key. In overwrite mode each character typed replaces one existing character at the cursor. The mode is indicated by the shape of the cursor when in the memo writer. When in insert mode, the cursor is a large block; when in overwrite mode, it is a narrow underline.

MOVING AROUND THE SCREEN

It may be obvious that the arrow keys can be used for movement around the screen. However, these keys are often not the fastest way to move around a document—particularly if the document is long. The HOME and END keys move the cursor to the beginning and the end of a line, respectively. PGUP and PGDN scroll up and down by a screenful of text at a time. The combination of the CONTROL key and the LEFT ARROW key moves the cursor left a word at a time, and the combination CONTROL-RIGHT ARROW moves the cursor right by a word at a time. CONTROL-HOME moves to the start of a document, and CONTROL-END moves to the end of a document. These are just some of the more popular ways of quickly getting around in a memo writer document. A complete list of cursor-movement key combinations is provided in Table 8-1.

Table 8-1. Cursor Movement Keys

Key Pressed	Result
LEFT ARROW	Cursor left one character
RIGHT ARROW	Cursor right one character
UP ARROW	Cursor up one line
DOWN ARROW	Cursor down one line
CONTROL-LEFT ARROW	Prior word
CONTROL-RIGHT ARROW	Next word
CONTROL-UP ARROW	Prior sentence
CONTROL-DOWN ARROW	Next sentence
HOME	Start of line
END	End of line
CONTROL-HOME	Start of document
CONTROL-END	End of document
PGUP	Scroll up by one screen
PGDN	Scroll down by one screen
CONTROL-PGUP	Prior page
CONTROL-PGDN	Next page
CONTROL-grey−	Prior paragraph
CONTROL-grey+	Next paragraph
TAB	Cursor to next tab stop
SHIFT-TAB	Cursor to prior tab stop

INSERTING NEW TEXT

To insert additional text in an existing document, simply place the cursor at the location where the text is to be inserted, make sure you are in the insert mode, and begin typing. As an example, press the INS key until you are in insert mode (in insert mode the cursor is shaped like a rectangular block). Then move the cursor to the start of the word "support" in the second sentence of the first full paragraph. Type governmental

and add a space after the word. Note that as you add the word, the memo writer automatically reformats (rearranges) the paragraph when a line grows too long.

SAVING A FILE

Save a memo writer document with the option "Save" of the File menu. As with many operations, the memo writer keeps your document in memory until you give a command to save the file to disk. To avoid accidental loss of typed text because of a power failure or similar problem, it is wise to save documents regularly when working with the memo writer.

Open the File menu with CONTROL-F and select "Save file" from the menu. A list of available memo files appears on the right side of the screen, and you are asked to enter a filename at the bottom of the screen.

Enter

CRAB1

as the name of the file. The file is saved and the menus disappear, leaving the memo writer document. As an option, use the same shortcut that you use in the file manager to save the document—enter the key combination CONTROL-RETURN.

PRINTING A DOCUMENT

Printing a document created with the memo writer is almost identical to the process of printing a database file. Open the Print menu with CONTROL-P. Using the Print menu, select the desired printer settings and the destination (a DOS text file or the printer). Make sure the printer is ready, and then choose "Begin printing" from the Print menu to print the document.

DELETING BLOCKS OF TEXT

For deleting one or two characters or even an entire word, holding down the BACKSPACE key or DEL may work well enough. But you will want a faster method of removing large amounts of text. RapidFile allows you to mark large blocks of text, which can then be deleted with DEL. To mark text, place the cursor at the beginning of the text to be deleted, press F6 (HIGHLIGHT), move the cursor to the end of the text to be deleted, and press RETURN.

To illustrate, suppose you decide to delete the first five words in the second paragraph, "As you may have heard." To highlight the text, place the cursor at the start of the word "As" in the sentence and press F6. The following prompt appears at the bottom of the screen: **Use (cursor keys) to extend the highlighted area, then press ↵**. Move the cursor to the space preceding the word "Congress." As you move the cursor, the words are highlighted on your screen. When highlighting text, you can move the cursor by using any of the cursor-movement methods outlined in Table 8-1. These keys and key combinations allow you to quickly highlight large areas of text, if necessary. Once the words are highlighted, press the DEL key to remove the highlighted text. The remaining text automatically reformats.

A Helpful Hint About Deleted Text

When you delete a block of text by highlighting the block and then pressing DEL, it is not permanently discarded; it is temporarily stored in an area of memory. You can recall the last block of text that was deleted by pressing F2 (EDIT). The deleted text reappears at the cursor location, and you can then press ESC to clear the highlighting. This technique works only with text that is deleted by highlighting a block of text. It will not work with text that has been deleted by pressing BACKSPACE or DEL.

MOVING AND COPYING BLOCKS OF TEXT

Use the same highlighting procedure along with F7 (MOVE) and F8 (COPY) to move and copy blocks of text to other locations within the document. To move or copy a block of text, place the cursor on the first character of the text to be moved or copied, press F6, move the cursor to the last character in the block of text, and press RETURN. Then move the cursor to the new location for the text. Press F7 if the text is to be moved; press F8 if the text is to be copied.

As an example, suppose you decide that the last sentence of the second paragraph works better if it precedes the first sentence. To move the text, place the cursor at the start of the last sentence in the second paragraph, press F6, and move the cursor to the end of the sentence. Press RETURN to complete the marking of the text.

Next, place the cursor at the start of the first sentence in the second paragraph and press F7 (MOVE). The highlighted text moves to the new location. The highlighting remains until you either press F6 again to begin highlighting or until you press another key.

If you pressed RETURN upon the completion of the last sentence when you originally typed the second paragraph, your text may not be properly formatted now because there is a return (indicated by the small triangle) at the end of what is now the first sentence of the second paragraph. If this is the case, move the cursor to the return symbol and use the DEL key to delete the return. Then add two spaces between the period

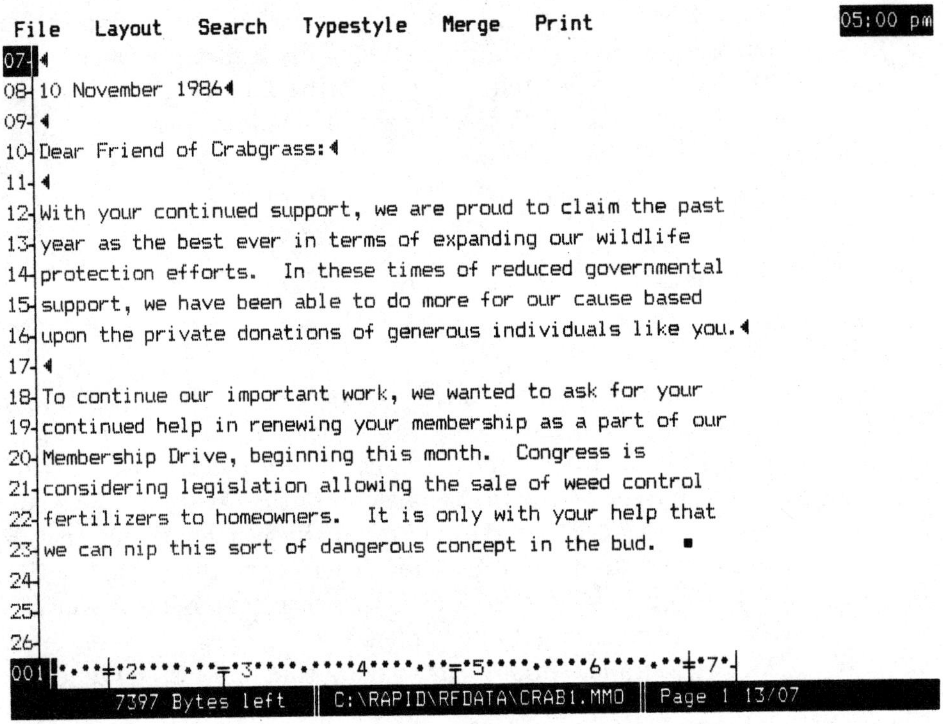

Figure 8-4. Rearranged text

and the start of the word "Congress." The paragraph is now properly formatted. Your text should now resemble Figure 8-4.

USING THE LAYOUT MENU OPTIONS

You can easily change margins, tabs, and other basic page formatting settings by using the options of the Layout menu, which is shown in Figure 8-5.

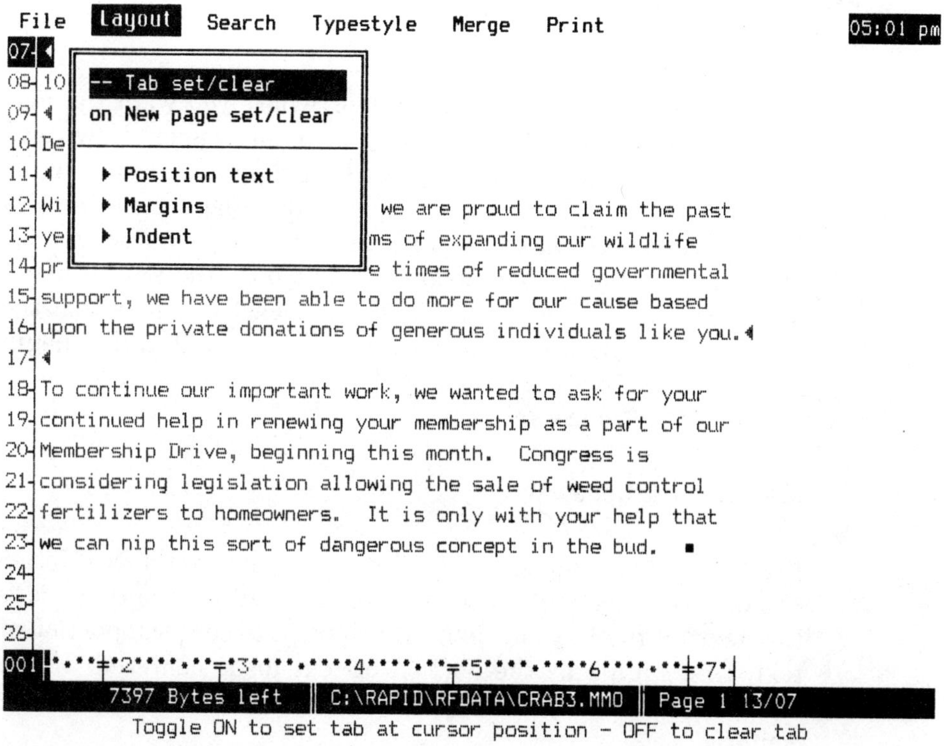

Figure 8-5. The Layout menu

The Layout menu provides options for setting and clearing tabs; for setting page breaks (places where the printer will index to a new sheet of paper); for setting margins and indentation; and for positioning text to be flush left, flush right, justified, or centered. The top two options ("Tab set/clear" and "New page set/clear") are toggles, meaning that selecting the options sets or clears the tab or page break at the cursor location. The lower three menu options reveal submenus with additional choices.

Setting Page Breaks and Centering Text

To set a page break, place the cursor where you want the new page to begin. Then, from the Layout menu, select "New page set/clear." As an example, suppose that the membership letter for Friends of Crabgrass needs a second page containing a form for the renewal of memberships. Place the cursor on the line following the second paragraph, and open the Layout menu with CONTROL-L. Select "New page set/clear" and note that the line numbers beside the cursor on the Vertical Ruler begin again at line 7, which indicates the start of a new page. Press RETURN once and type

Membership Renewal

Press RETURN at the end of the line. This text would look better centered on the page. You can center text with the option "Position text" of the Layout menu. If you want to center a portion of text, first highlight the portion of text to be centered. If you do not highlight a portion of text, the entire document will be centered.

In this case only the line containing the words "Membership Renewal" is to be centered. Highlight the text by placing the cursor at the start of the word "Membership" and pressing F6. Then move the cursor to the end of the line and press RETURN.

Open the Layout menu with CONTROL-L and select "Position text." The submenu shown in Figure 8-6 appears.

The available options for positioning text are "Center" (text centered between margins), "Left flush" (even left margin, right side of the text jagged), "Right flush" (even right margins, left side of the text jagged), and "Justify" (both sides of the text even). Note that "Center," "Left flush," and "Right flush" have a visible effect on your text while it is on the screen, but "justify" does not—it looks identical to flush-left text until it is printed.

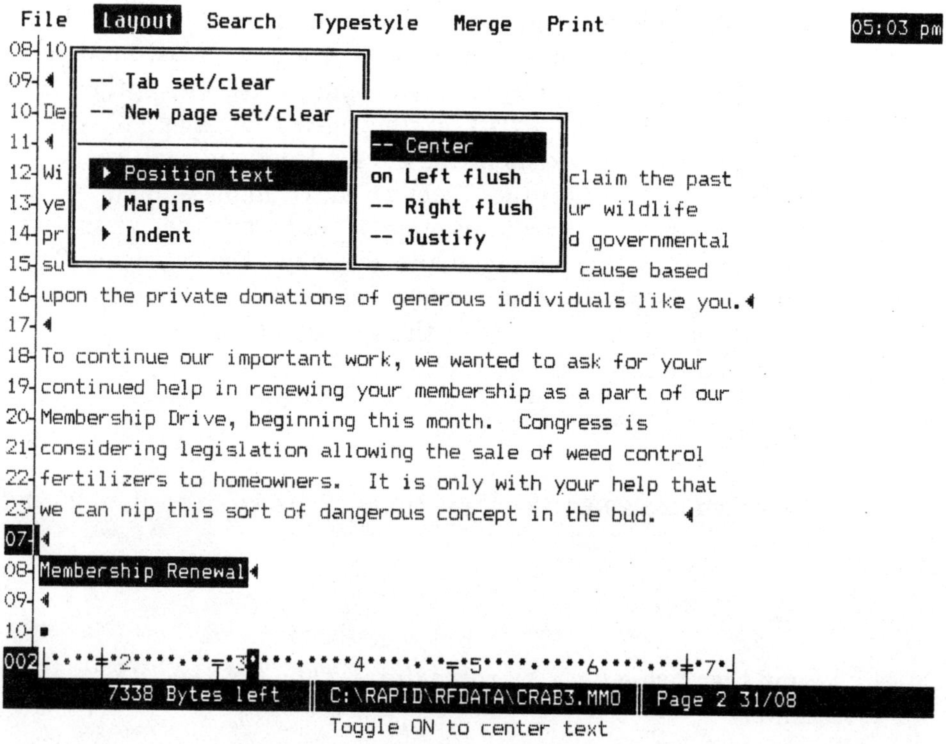

Figure 8-6. The submenu for "Position text"

Select "Center" from the submenu. The highlighted text is centered, but the other text within the memo remains flush left.

Setting Tabs

Tabs are provided by the memo writer at cursor locations 17, 27, 47, and 67. Tabs are indicated on the Horizontal Ruler by a small vertical line underneath a double horizontal line. You may not like the standard tabs provided by the memo writer, so you will want to know how to clear and set new tabs. To do so, just move the cursor to the location of the existing or new tab. Then open the Layout menu and choose the option "Tab set/clear." If a tab exists at the cursor location, it will be cleared. If no tab exists at the cursor location, a tab is set.

To continue with the Friends of Crabgrass membership form, move the cursor to position 17 and clear the existing tab by opening the Layout menu and choosing "Tab set/clear." Then move the cursor to position 20, and set a tab by again choosing the option "Tab set/clear" of the Layout menu.

At the tabbed position (20), enter

NAME:

and then press RETURN three times. Tab over to position 20 and enter

ADDRESS:

and then press RETURN three times. Tab over to position 20 and enter

AMOUNT:

Your screen should resemble the one shown in Figure 8-7.

Setting Margins

RapidFile's memo writer uses standard margins of 12 and 72, top and bottom margins of 6 lines from each edge of the page, a page length of 66 lines, and single spacing. Each of these values can be changed by using the "Margins" option of the Layout menu.

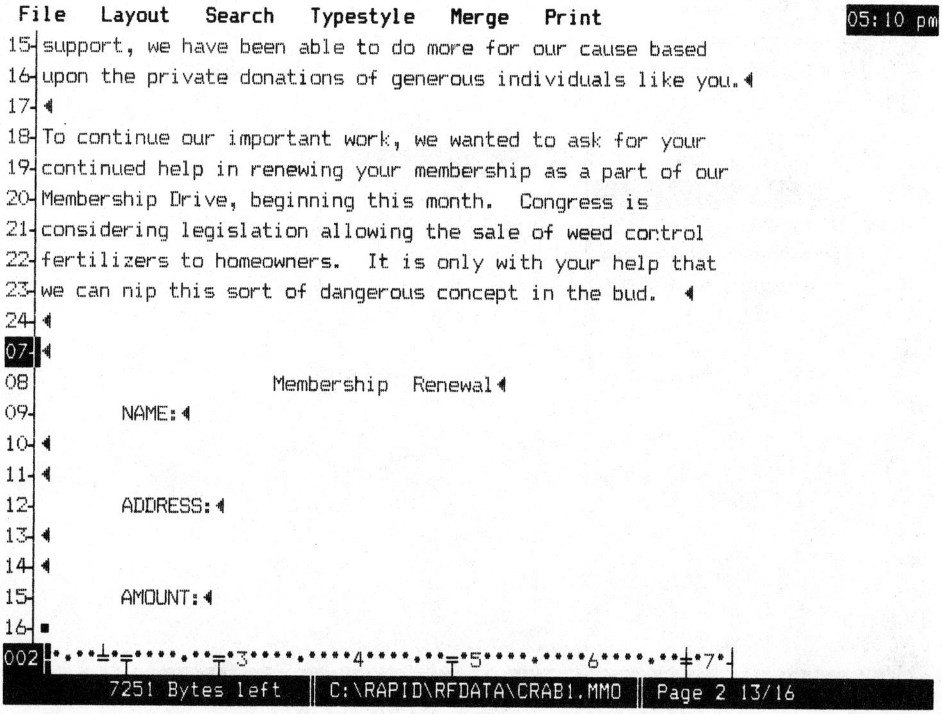

Figure 8-7. The membership form

Open the Layout menu with CONTROL-L and select the "Margins" option. The submenu shown in Figure 8-8 appears.

To change any of the desired values, select the option and enter the new value desired. As an example, select the option "Right margin" from the submenu. A prompt at the bottom of the screen displays the following: **Type the setting for the right margin, then press ↵. 72.** Enter

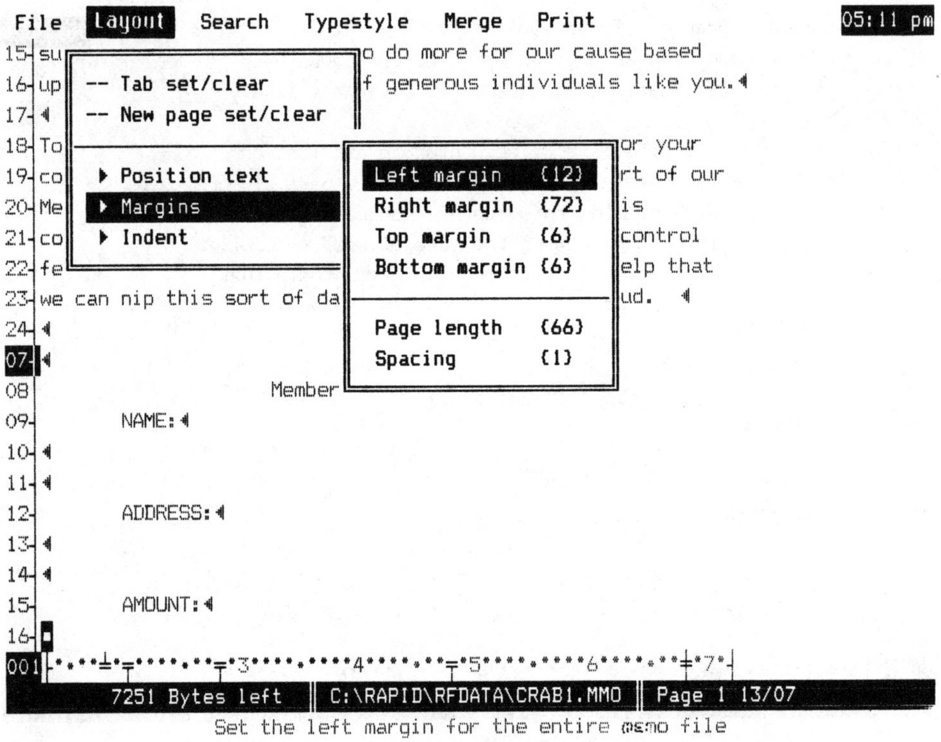

Figure 8-8. The submenu of "Margins"

When you press RETURN to enter the value, there will be no immediate visible change in the right margin. But keep viewing the text, and press ESC twice to close the menus. Once the menus are closed, the text reformats to accommodate the new, narrower right margin.

Open the File menu with CONTROL-F and select the option "Save file." Highlight CRAB1 and press RETURN. Answer "Yes" to the prompt to replace the old file.

LEAVING THE MEMO WRITER

To exit the memo writer, open the File menu and choose the option "Leave memo writer." If you started the memo writer from DOS, you return to DOS. If you started the memo writer from the file manager, you return to the file manager.

BUILDING A FORM LETTER

By using a form letter, you can combine the body of a standard letter with names, addresses, and other pertinent data contained within a database.

Preparing the Database

Before preparing the form letter, prepare the database file as necessary. If the fields within the file contain the information in the manner in which you want it to print within the form letter and if you want to print all the records in the file, then no preparation is needed. In some cases, however, you may want to select a group of records and print form letters for only those names. If this is the case, you must first select those records by using the appropriate "Select" option of the Records menu. If you prefer that certain fields display their contents in a special format (such as written dates or as currency), you must design and use an appropriate layout before generating the form letter. Also, if the form letters should be printed in any particular order, sort the database as required.

Designing the Form Letter

Once you have the desired layout, have selected the records, and have chosen the sort order (if any), you are ready to design the form letter. The design process consists of simply placing the desired fields in the locations of the letter. As an example, suppose that the letter you typed for Friends of Crabgrass can be used as a form letter if the appropriate names and addresses are placed at the top. If you have not already done so, load the database MEMBERS by using the option "Retrieve file" of the File menu. Open the Write menu with CONTROL-W. This time, instead of choosing the option "Write memo," select "Form letter." After RapidFile copies your records to a text file, the memo writer's screen replaces the database.

Open the File menu with CONTROL-F and choose the option "Retrieve file." From the list of filenames, select CRAB1.

Any form letter that you build must contain spaces for the fields that are to be inserted. For a name, address, city, state, and ZIP code, four lines are needed (the city and state can occupy the same line). Place the cursor at the start of the document with CONTROL-HOME and press RETURN four times to add four new lines.

Now move the cursor to the top of the file again. Press CONTROL-M and the Merge menu appears (see Figure 8-9).

The Merge menu offers three options: "Insert field," "Display form letters," and "Print form letters." You must use "Insert field" to place the desired fields at the desired locations in the form letter.

With the cursor on the first line of the form letter, select "Insert field" and a list of the fields within the database appears on the right side of the screen (see Figure 8-10).

Since the member's first name should appear as the first entry on the line, select the Firstname field. The first name for one of the members in the database appears on the screen.

Place the cursor at the end of the member's name and press the spacebar once to add a space between the first name and

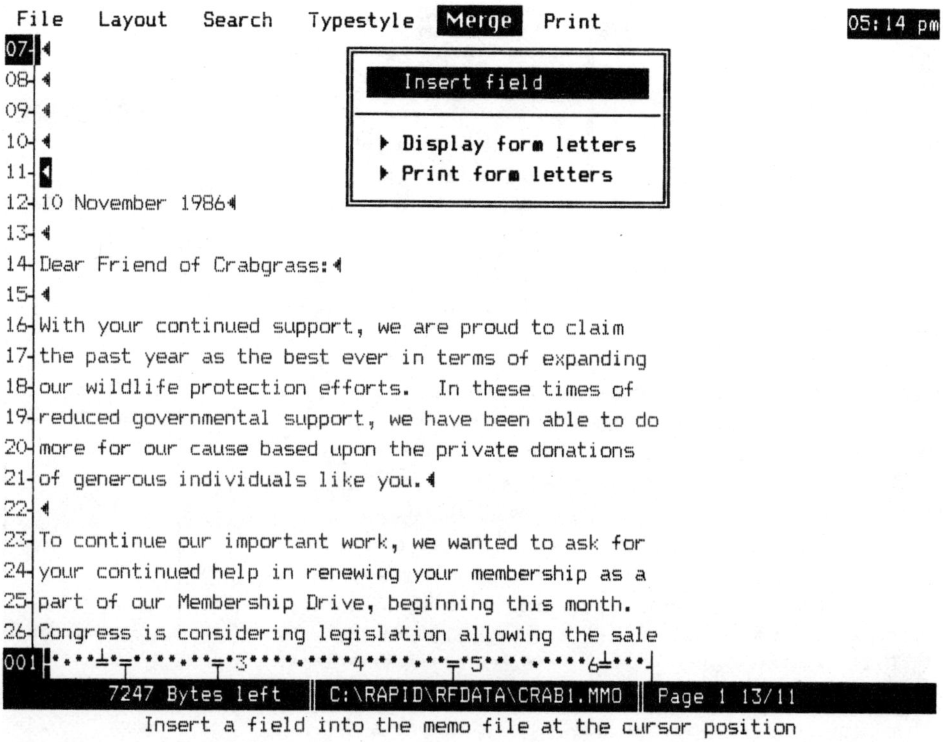

Figure 8-9. The Merge menu

the last name, which will be added. Then open the Merge menu with CONTROL-M, choose "Insert field," and select the Lastname field. A last name appears.

Move the cursor to the start of the second line. Open the Merge menu with CONTROL-M, choose "Insert field," and select the Address field. The address for the sample record appears below the name.

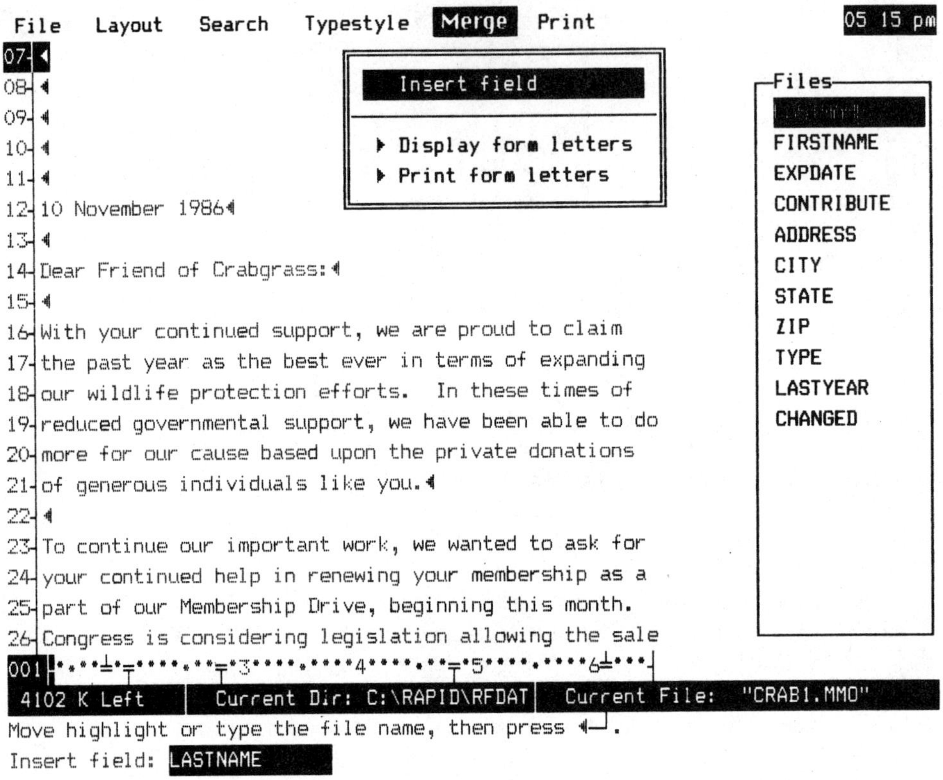

Figure 8-10. After selecting "Insert field," a list of the database fields appears

Place the cursor at the start of the third line and open the Merge menu with CONTROL-M. Select "Insert field" and choose City from the list of fields. Move the cursor past the end of the name of the city that appears, and press the spacebar once to add a space between the city and the state. Then open the Merge menu with CONTROL-M, choose "Insert field," and select the State field.

After the abbreviation for a state appears, move the cursor to the start of the fourth line. Open the Merge menu with CONTROL-M, choose "Insert field," and select the ZIP field. Your screen should now resemble the one shown in Figure 8-11.

The form letter is now ready for printing. To ensure that you are satisfied with the appearance, however, you can display the form letters before printing. To do this, use the option "Display form letters" of the Merge menu.

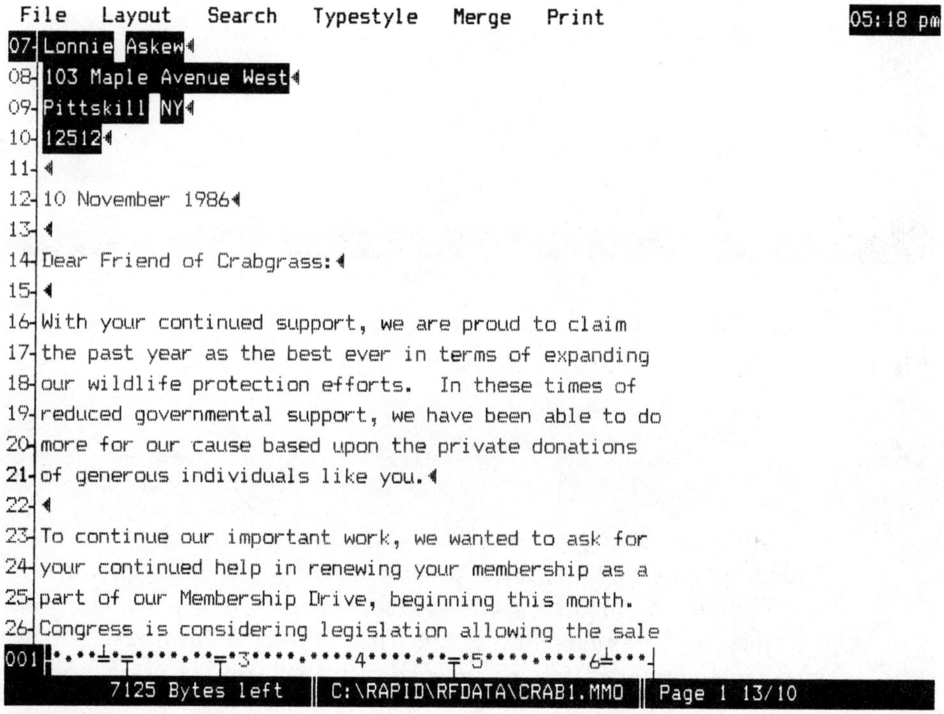

Figure 8-11. The form letter after insertion of database fields

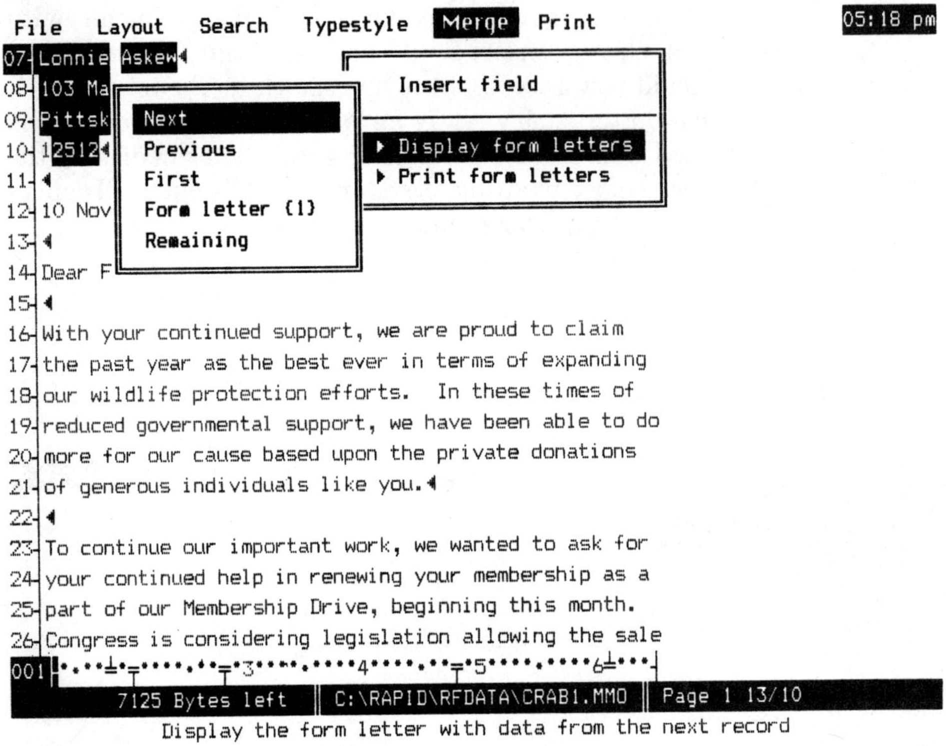

Figure 8-12. The submenu of the option "Display form letters"

Open the Merge menu with CONTROL-M and select "Display form letters." The submenu shown in Figure 8-12 appears.

The submenu offers choices that allow you to see the next letter; the previous letter; the first letter; a numbered letter (where you specify the record number to be used); or all remaining letters, one by one. Try selecting "Next," and then "Previous" to see the names and addresses for different records. Also note that the record number is displayed in the Message Area at the bottom of the screen. For your reference, note that pressing F3 (FLIP) alternates between the display of a sample record and the names of the actual fields within the form letter.

Open the Merge menu and select "Display form letters." From the submenu choose "Remaining." At the bottom of the screen, you see the prompt **Press any key to see the next form letter.**

Strike any key and the next form letter appears. You can continue to view successive form letters by pressing any key repeatedly. Pressing ESC at any time cancels the display of form letters.

Printing Form Letters

To print form letters, you will use the option "Print form letters" of the Merge menu. Open the Merge menu with CONTROL-M and select "Print form letters." Note the submenu that appears (see Figure 8-13).

The submenu offers three choices: "Current," "Remaining," and "All." Use "Current" to print the specific record appearing on the screen. "Remaining" prints all records from the current one onward, and the option "All" prints all selected records.

Turn on your printer and select "Current." The form letter prints with the name and address that currently appear on your screen at the top of the page. The appearance of the letter should be similar to the sample shown in Figure 8-14. If you care to print the rest of the records, choose "Remaining" from the menu.

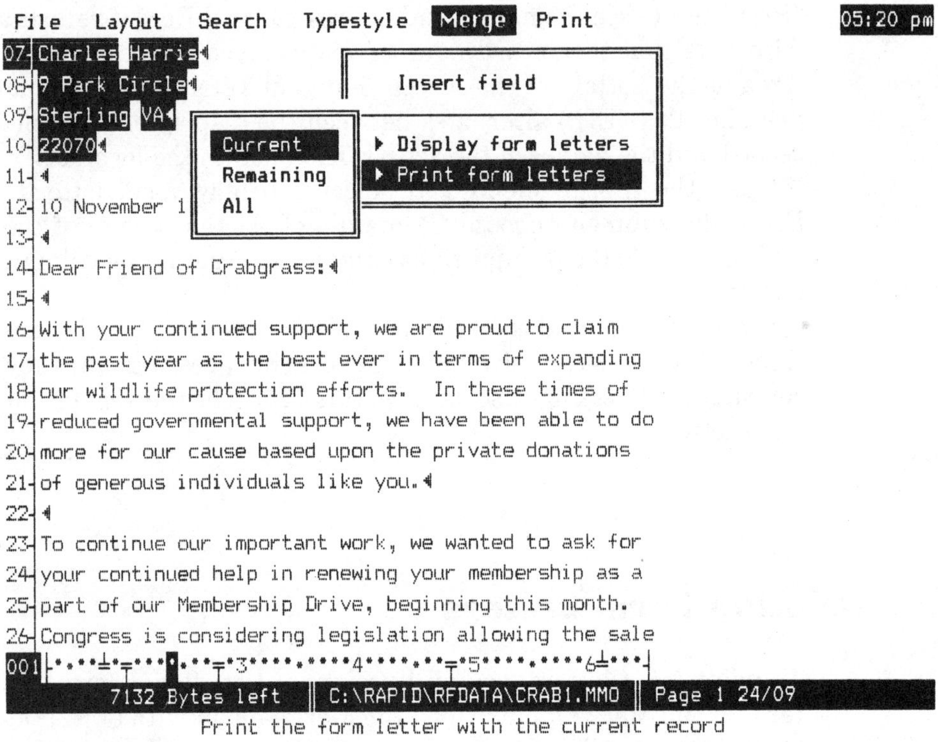

Figure 8-13. The submenu of the option "Print form letters"

USING THE MEMO WRITER WITH FIELDS WITHIN A DATABASE

The memo writer can interact with a RapidFile database in another important manner. It can be used to create memos that are, in effect, extensions of fields of the database. By using the

```
Ernest Mills
500 Embarcadero Street
San Francisco CA
95002

10 November 1986

Dear Friend of Crabgrass:

With your continued support, we are proud to claim the past
year as the best ever in terms of expanding our wildlife
protection efforts.  In these times of reduced governmental
support, we have been able to do more for our cause based
upon the private donations of generous individuals like you.

To continue our important work, we wanted to ask for your
continued help in renewing your membership as a part of our
Membership Drive, beginning this month.  Congress is
considering legislation allowing the sale of weed control
fertilizers to homeowners.  It is only with your help that
we can nip this sort of dangerous concept in the bud.
```

Figure 8-14. A sample form letter

memo writer to create memos that are "linked" to the fields of a database, you can store large amounts of textual material within a field and search for information contained within the text. This makes RapidFile quite useful for applications that require fields with large amounts of textual material, such as medical histories, bibliographic descriptions of library books, or legal depositions.

As an example, consider a small database of book titles. Each record must contain the book title, the author's name, and a short description of the contents. The descriptions may run several sentences, which is more than the 254-character limit of a field (and more than the field-length limitation of many other database managers). With the memo writer you can store all of the descriptive text in a memo and link that memo to the field within the database. This is easily done by placing the cursor in the desired field and pressing F4 (ZOOM). Once F4 is pressed, the memo writer screen appears, and the text can be typed. After the text has been entered, pressing F4 again exits the memo writer. If the text exceeds the 254-character limit, RapidFile prompts you for a name under which to store the memo on disk. The memo is then linked to the appropriate field in the database file.

To see an example, you will create a new database. First exit from the memo writer by opening the File menu and selecting the option "Leave memo writer." Open the file manager's File menu with CONTROL-F and select the "Create" option. Choose "New file" from the submenu. All fields in this database will be text fields, so select "Text" for type of field when prompted. Call the first field Title, the second field Author, and the third field Description. Once you have defined the fields, select "Add data" from the options shown at the bottom of the screen.

To create the first record, enter

Using dBASE III Plus

in the Title column. In the Author column enter

Jones, E.

Your database should resemble the one shown in Figure 8-15, and your cursor should be in the Description column.

Instead of simply entering text, press F4 (ZOOM). The view of the database is replaced by the memo writer. You can now type a complete description, which can be considerably longer than 254 characters—the Status Bar indicates the amount of text you can type. The indication **LINKED 8093 Bytes left** shows that you have approximately 8K of available space (or about four single-spaced pages). Enter the following description:

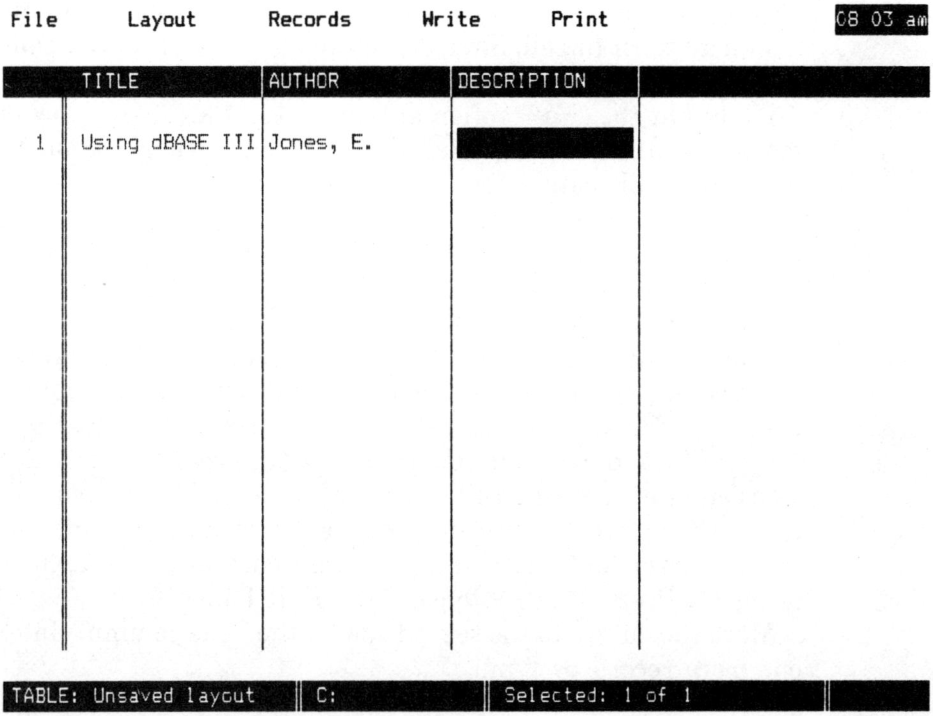

Figure 8-15. Creating a new database

1. Programming. 2. Computer language. Covers use of dBASE III PLUS, database management software for the IBM PC and compatible computers. Chapters on designing, displaying database; using the Screen Painter; generating reports; using Query Files; installation on a hard disk; and using networking commands.

Once you have finished typing the text, press F4 again. This message comes to the bottom of your screen: **Current memo too large to fit in cell. Save this memo and link it to the cell? Yes No.**

Highlight the "Yes" option and press RETURN. A window of memo filenames appears, and you are asked to enter a name for the file. In this case enter

BOOK1

as the memo filename.

Once you have entered a name for the memo file, the database reappears. Note that the Description field contains the name of the memo file and a portion of the text stored in the file. Press F2 (EDIT) and the Edit Panel opens to reveal the first 254 characters of the memo file (see Figure 8-16). You cannot edit the entire contents without pressing F4 to go back into the memo writer, but you can see a large portion of the text by using F2. Press RETURN to close the Edit Panel.

Move the cursor to the second row in the Title column. Enter one more record by typing

dBASE III Tips and Traps

in the Title column. In the Author column enter

Andersen, Cooper, & Dempsey

With the cursor in the Description column, press F4 to use the memo writer, and then enter the following text:

1. Computer language. 2. Usage techniques. Covers use of dBASE III, database management software for IBM PCs and compatibles. Written in concise tips-and-traps format. Techniques on planning applications; data entry and updating; relating databases; customizing screen displays; generating reports; and interfacing with other software.

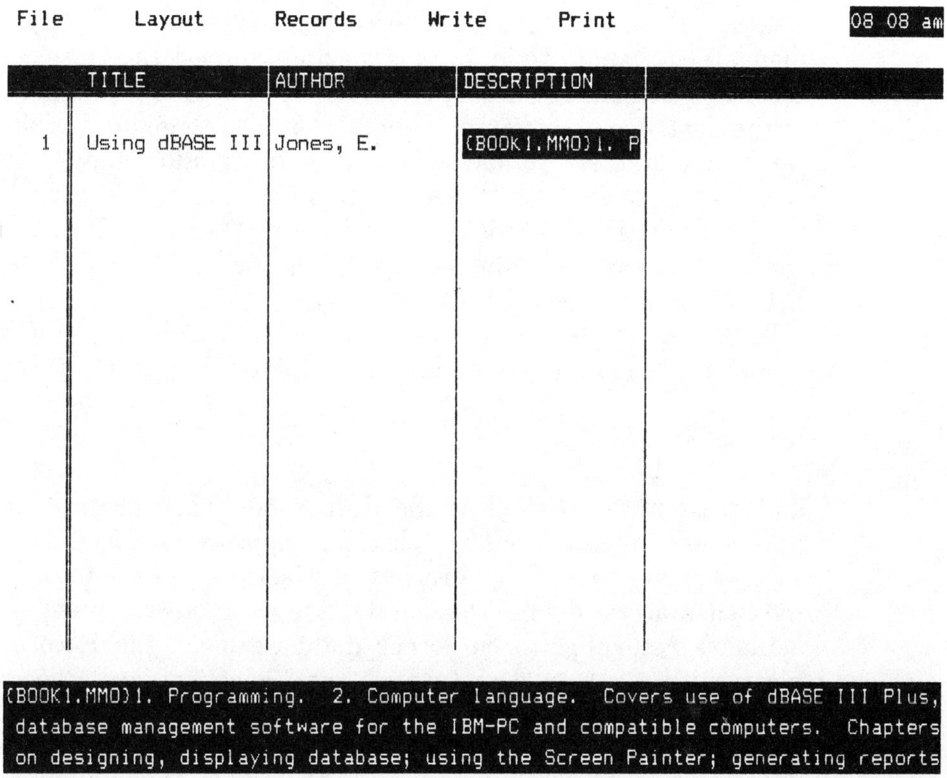

Figure 8-16. The Edit Panel displays a portion of the memo file

Press F4 to store the memo. Answer "Yes" to the prompt to link the memo to the database, and enter the name

BOOK2

as the name of the memo file. The database reappears in table layout and contains both records.

A major advantage of using RapidFile in this manner is that although the data in the description fields is stored in separate memo files, RapidFile maintains the ability to locate and select records based on that information. If you wanted to find a book in the database, for example, and all you had to go on was the word "techniques" somewhere in the description field, you could set criteria for a "Select" option based on that term. To try it, open the Records menu with CONTROL-R and choose "Select." Choose "Matching records" from the submenu, and the Select Matching Records screen appears.

With the cursor next to the Description field in the Match Criteria (1) column, press F2 (EDIT). Enter the word

techniques

and press RETURN to close the Edit Panel. Then press F9 to implement the selection. The database appears (see Figure 8-17) and shows that one record has been selected on the basis of the fact that the memo file contains the word "techniques."

Before returning to our other database, open the Records menu with CONTROL-R and choose the "Select" option. Choose "All records" from the submenu to restore the full view of the database. Finally, save the file by opening the File menu with CONTROL-F and selecting the option "Save file." Enter

BOOKS

as the name of the database.

Hints and a Warning

You can use fields containing linked memo files just as you would use other fields in a database. They can be included in reports or used as locate or select criteria to isolate a single

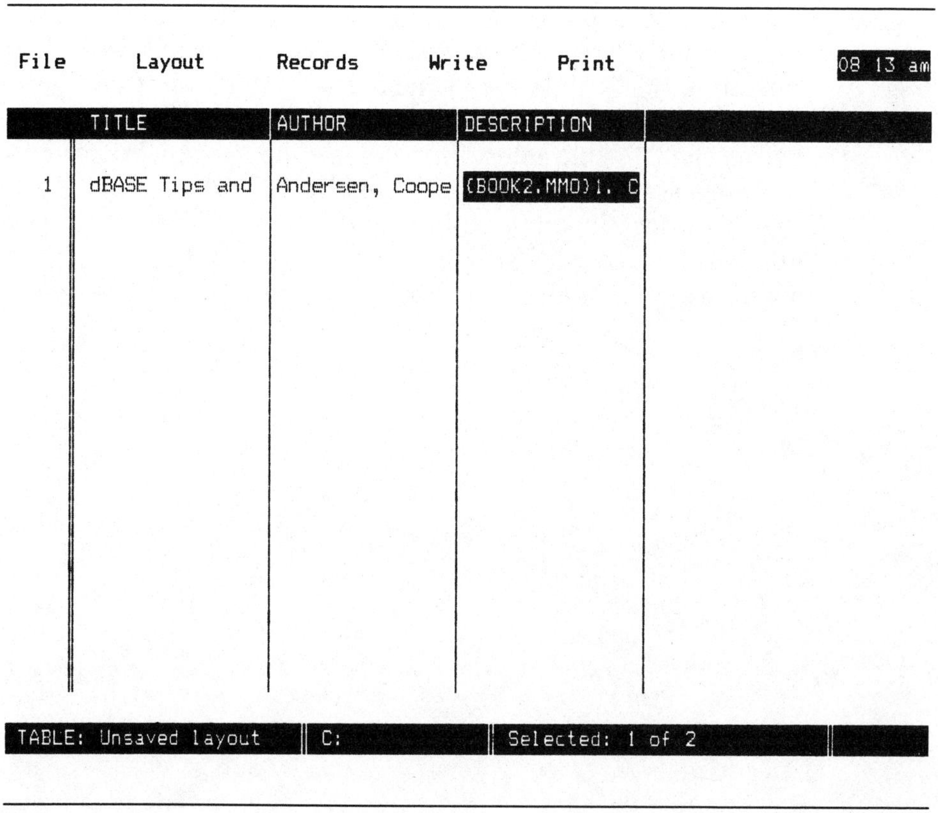

Figure 8-17. RapidFile highlights the record selected as a result of searching the memo file

record or a group of records. However, there is one significant drawback to the use of linked memo files for storing fields containing large amounts of text: Each memo file creates a file with the extension .MMO on the disk. Besides being limited in terms of disk space, floppy disks are limited to 112 directory entries, or filenames, per disk. If your database approaches 100 records in size and each record uses a memo file, you will soon reach the limit of files that can be stored on the disk. If you are using a hard disk, storage space is less of a problem, but you can still quickly clutter up a hard disk with hundreds of memo files. One alternative is to try to keep the large textual entries within the 254-character limit and use the F4 (ZOOM) key only when necessary for the largest textual descriptions. Also note that when locating or selecting records based on search criteria applied to a record that is linked to a memo writer document, only the first 254 characters of the memo are searched.

Complex Reports

Chapter 9

Chapter 6 covered the topic of Quick Reports, which are reports that provide information from a database in columnar form. Although Quick Reports offer a number of formatting options, there are times when you need more flexible formatting than you can obtain in a Quick Report. Custom Reports offer greater control over formatting than is provided by Quick Reports. Using Custom Reports, you can print the data in columnar form or in a line-oriented form, much like data is viewed when using the "Form" layout option of RapidFile. You can add customized titles, headers, footers, and titled areas containing the results of calculations. Figure 9-1 shows the first page of a Custom Report created with RapidFile.

```
                         Friends of Crabgrass
                          Membership Report

             10/24/86                                 05:04 pm

Total Contributed                           Total Last Year

Last Name      Askew
First Name     Lonnie
Contributed Amount 25.00                    Last Years Amount 25.00
State NY

Last Name      Baker
First Name     Benjamin
Contributed Amount 20.00                    Last Years Amount 10.00
State CA

Last Name      Baker
First Name     Jeanette
Contributed Amount 10.00                    Last Years Amount 0.00
State VA

Last Name      Block
First Name     Paul
Contributed Amount 20.00                    Last Years Amount 20.00
State IL

Last Name      Brown
First Name     Nicole
Contributed Amount 25.00                    Last Years Amount 30.00
State IL

Last Name      Harris
First Name     Charles
Contributed Amount 10.00                    Last Years Amount 10.00
State VA

Last Name      Hayes
First Name     Cynthia
Contributed Amount 100.00                   Last Years Amount 20.00
State TX
```

Figure 9-1. Sample Custom Report

CUSTOM REPORT SECTIONS

Custom Reports are created in a significantly different manner than Quick Reports. RapidFile views each part of a Custom Report as a horizontal area known as a *section.* There are separate sections for titles, headers, footers, subtotals and totals, and for the data that composes the actual report. These report sections determine what the report contains and how it appears when printed. The various report sections are illustrated in Figure 9-2. Each report section serves a particular purpose and appears in a particular area, as indicated in Table 9-1.

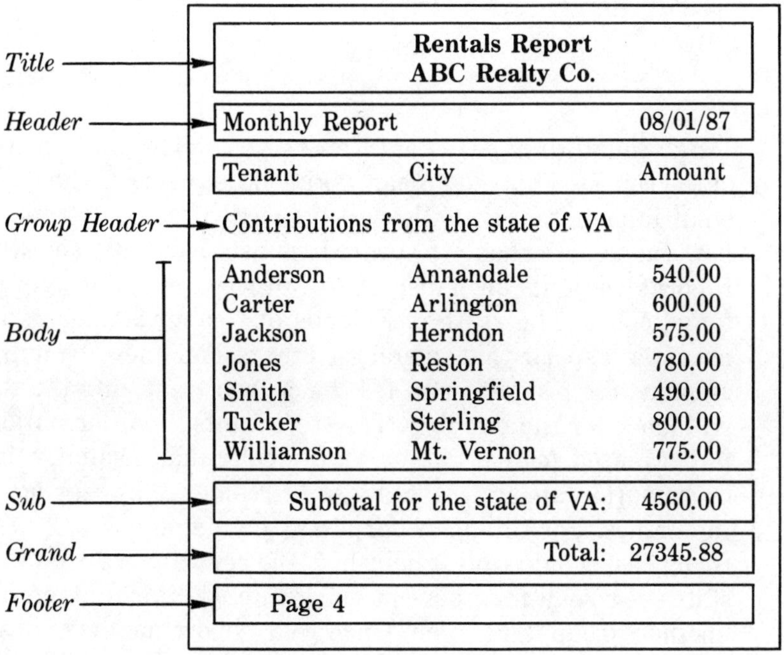

Figure 9-2. Report sections

Table 9-1. Report Sections and Descriptions

Section Name	Description
Title	Appears at start of report.
Header	Appears at start of each page.
Group Header	Appears following the header and following the subtotals and subcounts of each section.
Body	Contains the actual records from the database. RapidFile enters as many records as will fit on a page according to the format that you lay out for one record.
Sub	Contains subtotals and subcounts that appear for each group of records within a specified category.
Grand	Contains statistics that summarize all records in the report and appears at the end of the report.
Footer	Appears at the bottom of every page. Often used for page numbers.

Before building a Custom Report, you should plan the design of the report. This may mean asking other users of the database what information actually will be needed from the report and how the report should appear. It is usually best to outline the report's contents on paper before proceeding to design a Custom Report. The staff at Friends of Crabgrass, for example, needs a report that displays the last names, contribution amounts for last year and for the current year, and the state of residence for the member. The staff wants the information in a line-oriented format rather than a columnar format, with the contribution amounts and states of residence appearing below the names. For financial purposes, the managers at Friends of Crabgrass would find it helpful if the report were organized by state—Arizona members in one group, California members in another group, and so on. Once your report has been designed on paper, your outline should resemble the Custom Report you will design using RapidFile. An outline for the report described for use at Friends of Crabgrass is shown in Figure 9-3.

There is one major similarity between Custom Reports and Quick Reports. Both types of reports will print information based on how you tell RapidFile to reveal that information. If you want certain records to appear in a report, then you should take whatever steps are necessary to select records so that the

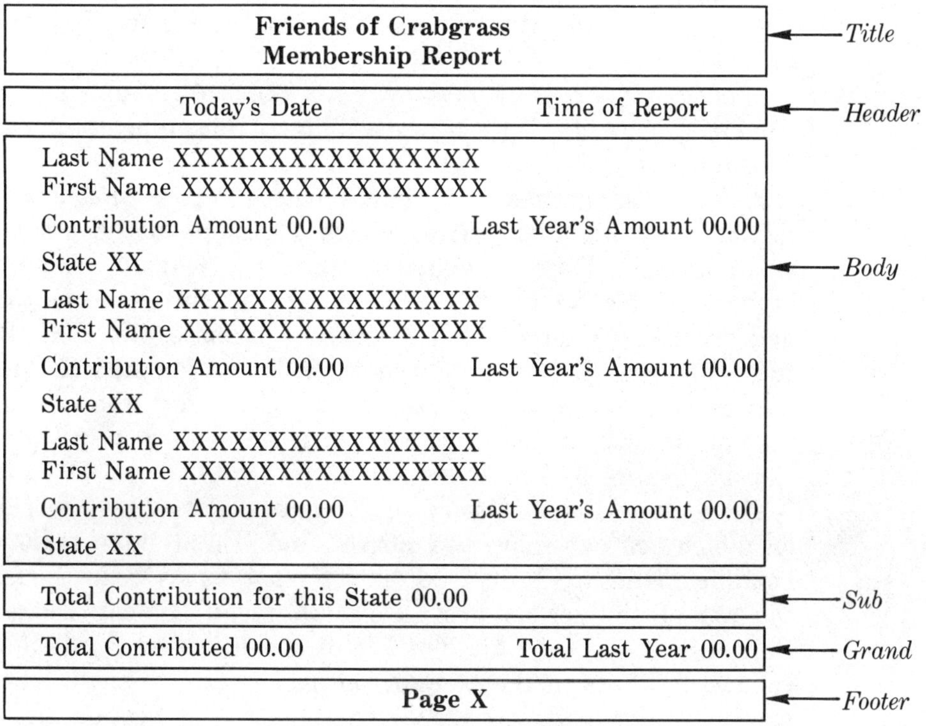

Figure 9-3. Sample outline for Custom Report

records you desire appear. Once records have been selected, you can proceed to use the Report layouts, whether they are Quick Reports or Custom Reports, to produce the report you need.

DESIGNING A CUSTOM REPORT

To design the Custom Report for Friends of Crabgrass, start RapidFile (if it is not already started) and load the database MEMBERS. Custom Reports are a type of layout, so you will create them by using the option "Choose layout type" of the Layout menu.

Open the Layout menu now with CONTROL-L, and select "Choose layout type." From the submenu that appears, select "Custom Report."

Because you have never created a Custom Report for this particular database, RapidFile displays a prompt at the bottom of the screen: **Do you want to design a Custom Report layout? Yes No.** Select "Yes." (If this were not the first time you had created a Custom Report for the database MEMBERS, RapidFile would immediately show the layout for the last Custom Report created.) Once you have selected "Yes," the view of the database is replaced with the design screen for the Custom Report (Figure 9-4).

The Custom Report Design screen appears as a blank screen on which you can move the cursor around and enter various headings, titles, and other report information. A Menu Bar at the top of the screen provides three menu choices: Fields, Report Section, and Exit. The Fields menu is used to add and remove fields from the body of the report and to change the way in which fields are displayed. The Report Section menu allows you to define areas of the screen as the report sections described in Table 9-1. The Exit menu allows you to save changes to the Custom Report layout or to leave the design

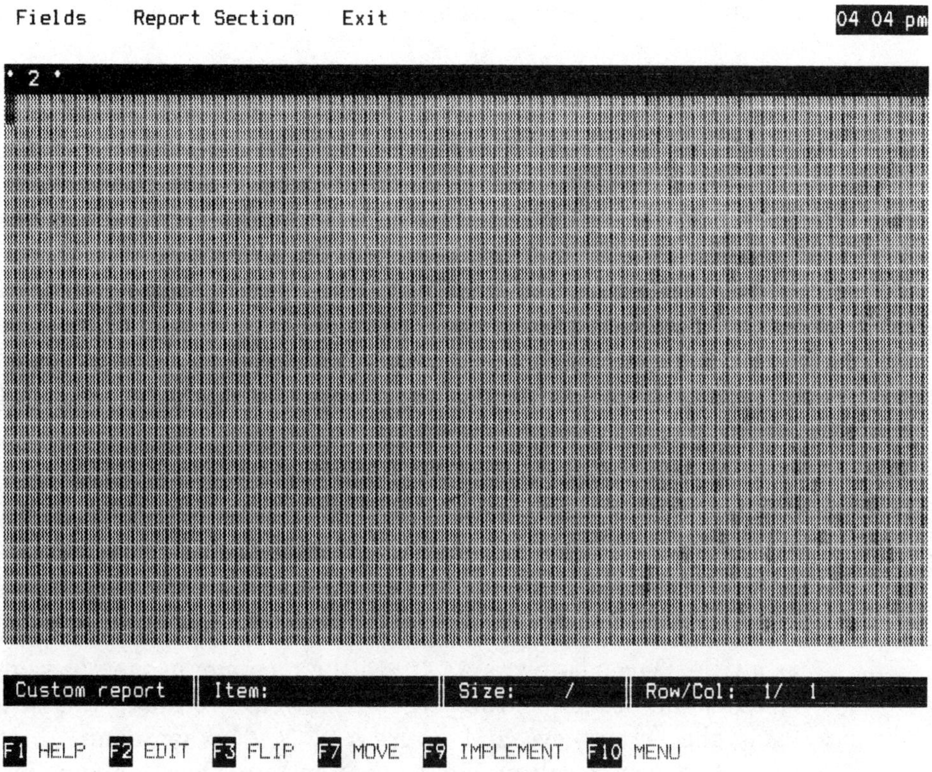

Figure 9-4. The Custom Report Design screen

screen without saving any changes. Laying out the Custom Report can be broken down into a three-step process: First, place the desired titles, headers, footers, and body of the report, and identify these areas by using the Report Section menu. Second, place the fields in the proper places within the body of the report by using the Fields menu. Finally, implement the changes to the report design with the Exit menu's "Implement" option or with the F9 (IMPLEMENT) key.

Laying Out the Report

In our example, both a title and a header are needed. As indicated in Table 9-1, a title prints only at the start of a report, but a header prints at the start of every page within a report. RapidFile allows you to move titles and headings around on the screen, so you need not be too concerned with precise locations as you are entering the desired titles and headings for the first time.

To enter the report title, press F2 (EDIT). A prompt appears at the bottom of the screen: **Type the text to add, or edit existing text, then press ↵**. Enter

Friends of Crabgrass

as a title. Once you press RETURN, the message in the Message Area at the bottom of the screen asks you to position the title using the arrow keys and to press RETURN when done. Move the title to row 2, column 25 (you can tell your location by viewing the Row/Col designation on the right side of the Status Bar). Press the RETURN key after moving the title to complete the positioning.

Move the cursor two lines down to line 4 and press F2. For the first line of the header, enter

Membership Report

After pressing RETURN, move the heading to row 4, column 26, and press RETURN to complete the positioning.

Move the cursor down two lines and press F2. For the second line of the header, enter

@DATE

and press RETURN. The symbol @DATE is used by RapidFile to indicate that the current date, which is stored in the computer's clock, should be printed at this location on the report. Two other helpful symbols are @TIME, which tells RapidFile to print the current time, and @PN, which specifies a page number that begins with page 1 and increases with each page printed.

Move @DATE to row 5, column 15, and press RETURN to complete the placement. Next move the cursor to row 5, column 50, and press F2. Enter the symbol

@TIME

and press RETURN, and then press RETURN again to indicate that the position is fine as it is. Your screen should resemble the one shown in Figure 9-5.

Move the cursor down two lines and press F2. As a field title, enter the words

Last Name

and press RETURN. Move the title to row 7, column 2, and press RETURN.

Move the cursor down one line and press F2. As a field title, enter the words

First Name

and press RETURN. Press RETURN again to indicate that the position is fine as it is.

Move the cursor down one line and press F2. As a field title, enter the words

Contribution Amount

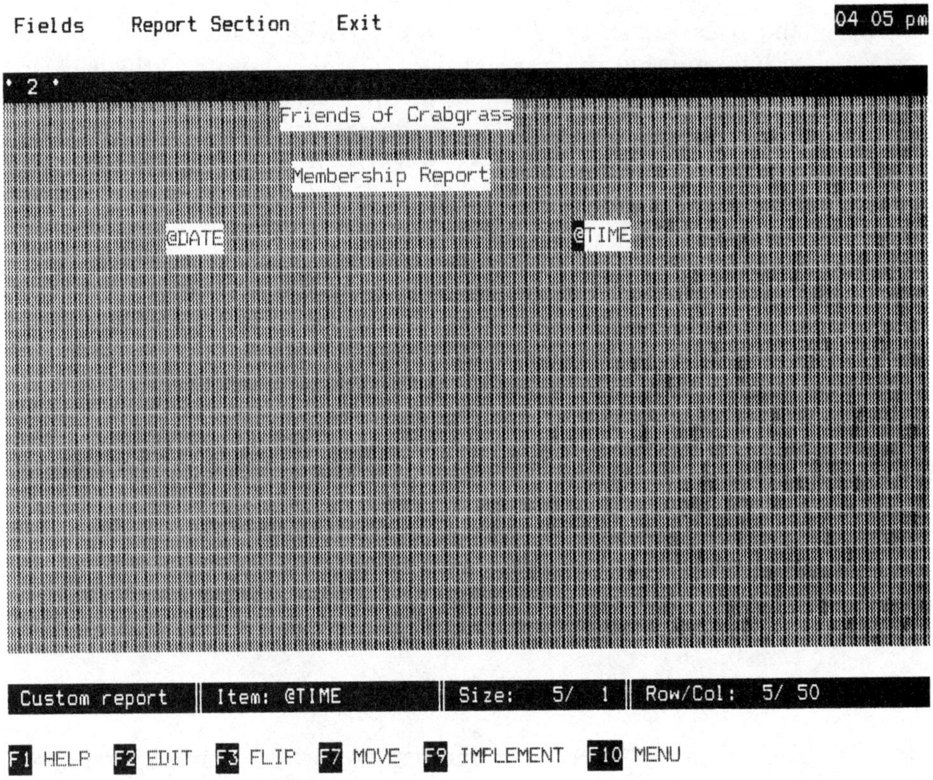

Figure 9-5. Partially completed Custom Report

and press RETURN. Move the title to row 10, column 2, and press RETURN.

Press F2. As a field title, enter the words

Last Year's Amount

and press RETURN. Move the title to row 10, column 40, and press RETURN.

Move the cursor down one line and press F2. As a field title, enter the word

State

and press RETURN. Move the title to row 12, column 2, and press RETURN.

Move the cursor down one line and press F2. As the title for the grand total, type the words

Total Contributed

and press RETURN. Move the title to row 16, column 2, and press RETURN.

Press F2. As a second grand total, enter the words

Total Last Year

and press RETURN. Move the title to row 16, column 40, and press RETURN.

For a page footer containing the page number, move the cursor down one line and press F2. Enter the symbol

@PN

and press RETURN. Move the page number code to row 18, column 30, and press RETURN. Your screen should resemble the one shown in Figure 9-6.

You are now ready to indicate the sections of the report by using the various options of the Report Section menu. Place the cursor on row 1, and open the Report Section menu with CONTROL-R. Figure 9-7 shows the Report Section menu.

The Report Section menu provides options for specifying each of the report sections identified in Table 9-1. At the bot-

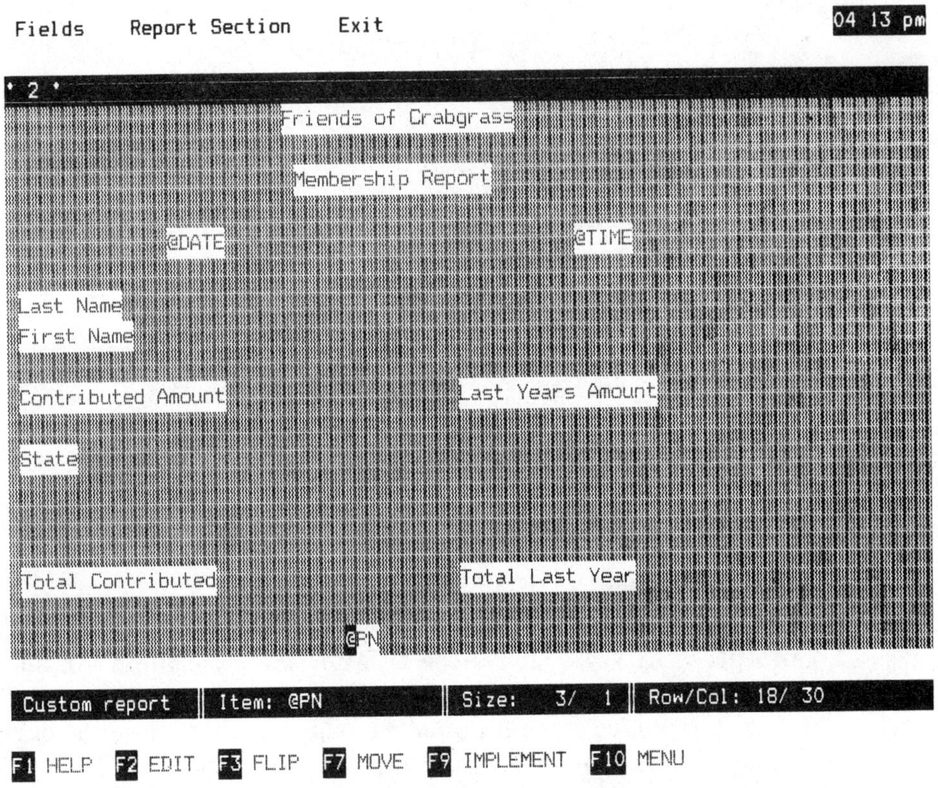

Figure 9-6. Custom Report with all titles, headers, and footers

tom of the menu are options for erasing a previously defined section and for allowing the display of sections on the screen.

Select the "Title" option. Row 1 is highlighted, and a message at the bottom of the screen provides the instruction: **Move cursor to last line of the report section, then press ↵.**

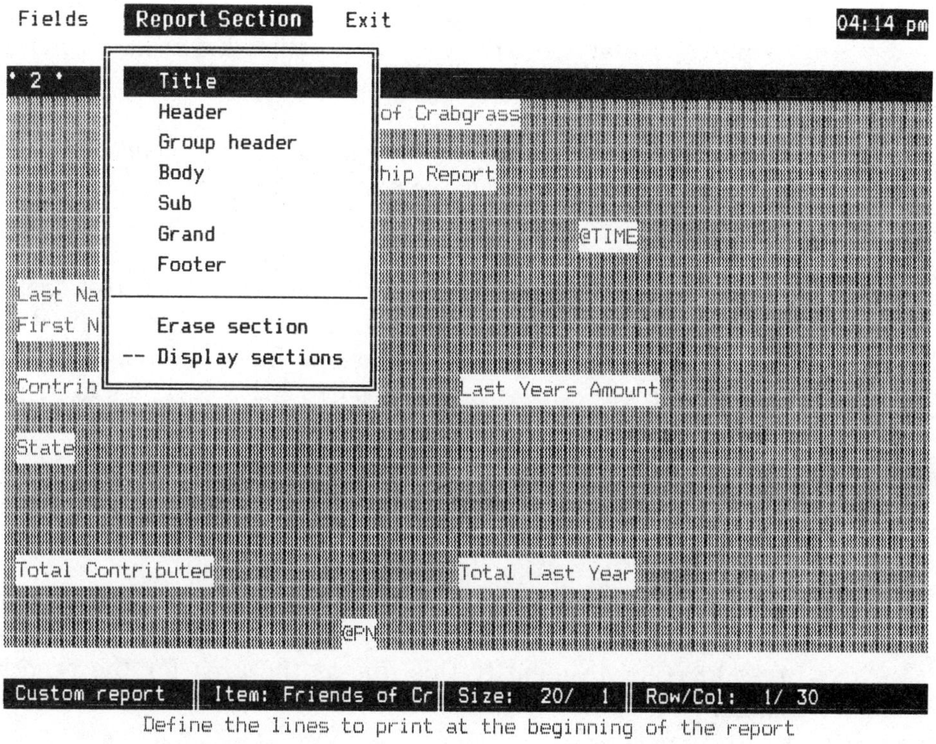

Figure 9-7. The Report Section menu

Highlight three lines for the title section and press RETURN. This gives the report blank lines above and below the title.

Move the cursor down to row 4, open the Report Section menu with CONTROL-R, and select the "Header" option. Again the message in the Message Area asks you to move the cursor to the last line of this section. In this case, you must include row 5 in the section as the date and time abbreviations are also a part of the report header and the extra (last) line will provide a line of white space at the bottom of the header. From line 4 move the cursor down three lines, and press RETURN to identify the report header.

Move the cursor down to row 7, open the Report Section menu, and select the "Body" option. This option identifies the beginning of the area that will contain all the actual data appearing in the report.

Move the cursor down to row 13, so that the entire area from the field Last Name down to one line beyond the State field is highlighted. (The extra line provides a line space between the records that will appear on the report.) Press RETURN to identify this as the area of the body of the report.

Move the cursor to row 16, open the Report Section menu, and select the option "Grand." In this case two lines are sufficient, so move the cursor down one line and press RETURN to identify this line as the area for the grand totals.

Move the cursor to row 17, open the Report Section menu, and select the "Footer" option. In this case one line is sufficient, so press RETURN to identify this line as the area for the report footers.

Adding the Fields

Once the design of the report sections has been provided, you must tell RapidFile where the fields will appear within the report. To do so, use the options of the Fields menu, which is shown in Figure 9-8. Place the cursor at row 7, column 15, and open the Fields menu with CONTROL-F.

The options shown perform the same tasks as were previously described for Fields menus used in other parts of RapidFile. To place a field within a report, simply place the cursor at the

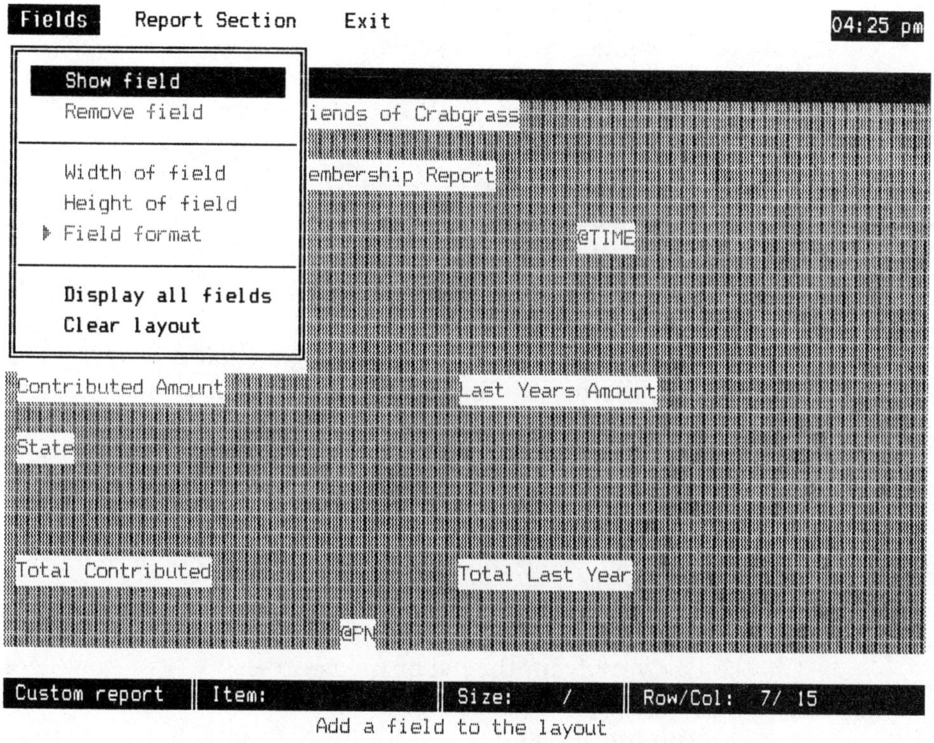

Figure 9-8. The Fields menu

desired location for the field contents, choose the option "Show field," and select the desired field from the list of fields that appears.

The cursor is currently at the location for the contents of the Last Name field. Select the option "Show field," and choose Last Name from the fields list. The contents of a sample record within the database appears at the cursor location, and the message in the Message Area asks you to use the arrow keys to set the field width and height.

As the message indicates, you have the ability to change both the width and height of the field when placing a field in a Custom Report by using the arrow keys. In this example the field size is fine without any changes, so press RETURN.

Another message at the bottom of the screen asks you to use the arrow keys to drag the field to the proper position. Again, the current location is fine, so just press RETURN.

Move the cursor down one line to row 8, column 15. This location will contain the first name, so open the Fields menu with CONTROL-F, and choose the option "Show field." Select First Name from the list of fields. Press RETURN twice to confirm that the size and the location of the field are correct.

Move the cursor down one line, open the Fields menu, and select the option "Show fields." Choose Contribute from the list of fields. Press RETURN to accept the size of the field. Then use the arrow keys to drag the field to row 10, column 21, and press RETURN to implement the new location.

Open the Fields menu and select the option "Show fields." Choose Lastyear from the list of fields. Press RETURN to accept the size of the field. Then use the arrow keys to drag the field to row 10, column 58, and press RETURN to implement the new location.

Move the cursor down one line, open the Fields menu, and select "Show fields." Choose State from the list of fields. The width shown is a bit large for a two-character abbreviation, so use the LEFT ARROW key to narrow the field size to two characters, and then press RETURN to implement the new size of the field. Then use the arrow keys to drag the field to row 12, column 8, and press RETURN to implement the new location.

Exiting the Report

Once the fields have been selected with the options of the Fields menu, you can proceed to implement the layout of the report.

Open the Exit menu with CONTROL-E and select the option "Implement changes." A sample record appears within the report format to show how the fields will be laid out within the actual report (see Figure 9-9).

To see how the report actually prints, open the Print menu with CONTROL-P and select "Begin printing." The report prints according to the design of the Custom Report. The report should resemble the example shown in Figure 9-1, which is the first page of the report.

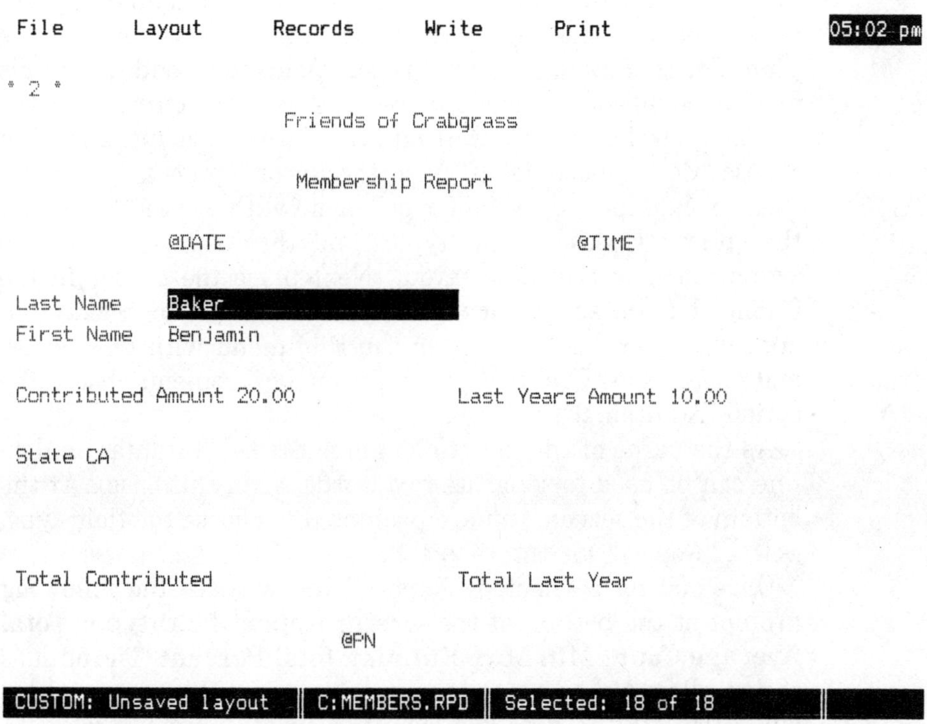

Figure 9-9. A sample record within the report format

USING REPORT FIELDS

RapidFile offers *report fields,* a special type of field designed to provide a summary for groups of records within a report. Report fields can be used with Quick Reports or with Custom Reports. Because they constitute a more advanced use of RapidFile, they are covered in this chapter. Report fields do not contain information for each record within a database. Instead, a report field contains a total for all selected records or a subtotal for a group of records. The total or subtotal is based on numeric values in another field. As an example, you will create a report field in the Custom Report used by Friends of Crabgrass. The report field will present subtotals by state. When the State field is sorted, a subtotal for the contributed amounts will be provided in the report field each time the contents of the State field changes. If you use report fields to provide subtotals and subcounts for a group of records, you must first sort the database so that records fall into the desired groups, and then choose "Calc report fields" from the Records menu.

As an example, open the Layout menu with CONTROL-L, select the option "Choose layout type," and then choose "Table" to switch back to the table layout. Next place the cursor in the Changed field, so the new field you are about to create will appear beside this field. Open the File menu with CONTROL-F and choose the "Create" option. From the submenu choose the option "Additional field."

As the name of the new field, enter State_Total (an underline can be used to separate two words, as in this case). At the bottom of the screen, you are prompted to choose the field type. Select "Report" for the field type.

Once you have selected "Report," you will see the following prompt at the bottom of the screen: **Report field type: Total Average Count Min Max Running-total Percent.** The options shown allow you to choose the ways in which the report fields will calculate the data for the appropriate group of records. Descriptions of the available options are in Table 9-2.

Table 9-2. Types of Report Fields

Field Type	Purpose
Total	Sums the field contents for the group or for all selected records.
Average	Averages the field contents for the group or for all selected records.
Count	Counts the number of records (nonblank entries) in the field or the group or for all selected records.
Minimum	Provides the minimum value within the group or the minimum for all selected records.
Maximum	Provides the maximum value within the group or the maximum for all selected records.
Running Total	Provides the current total (the running total) for a given field.
Percent	Provides the percentage of the value for a group of records.

Since you want the report field to provide totals for each state, select the "Total" option. A list of fields appears, and the prompt at the bottom of the screen now asks **Calculate the total for which field?** This prompt is asking you to define the numeric field from which to derive the totals. Select Contribute from the list of fields.

The next prompt in the Message Area asks **Calculate the total of all records or by groups of records? All Group.** In this case the results you desire are totals for each state, so select "Group." You are then asked to choose the field to use to group the records. Highlight State from the list of fields.

Once the field for the groups has been chosen, a warning appears at the bottom of the screen that says **You must select Calc Report Fields to update report statistics. Press ↵ to continue.**

Two more report fields are needed for the database, to indicate the desired grand totals for contributions and for last year's contributions. Open the File menu with CONTROL-F, and choose the "Create" option. From the submenu that appears, choose the "Additional field" option. For the name of the field, enter **Total_Contrib**. For the type of field, select "Report." Since this report field is to provide totals of the contributions, select the "Total" option. Then choose Contribute from the list of fields that appears.

The next prompt in the Message Area asks whether you wish the totals to be calculated by groups of records or by all records. Since this is a grand total, choose the "All" option. Finally, press RETURN to confirm the warning message about selecting the "Calc report fields" option to update the report statistics.

To add the final report field, again open the File menu with CONTROL-F, and choose the "Create" option. From the submenu that appears, choose the "Additional field" option. For the name of the field, enter **Total_Lastyr**. For the type of field, select "Report." Since this report field is to provide totals of the last year's contributions, select the "Total" option. Then choose Lastyear from the list of fields that appears.

The next prompt in the Message Area asks whether you wish the totals to be calculated by groups of records or by all records. Select the "All" option. Finally, press RETURN to confirm the warning message about selecting the "Calc report fields" option to update the report statistics.

Press RETURN, and the database reappears, containing the new field. Note that the fields are empty. To provide the desired totals, you must use the option "Calc report fields" of the Records menu. Also, if you are providing subtotals (which are totals for individual groups of records), you must sort the database on the desired group before calculating.

Open the Records menu with CONTROL-R and choose the "Order" option. Delete any existing entries in the Order Settings screen by pressing CONTROL-DEL and then choosing "Yes."

Enter 1 for the order next to the State column. Then press F9 to implement the sort.

Open the Records menu again and choose the option "Calc report fields." The values for each group of states in the database appear as shown in Figure 9-10. At the bottom of the database, the grand totals will appear in the report fields.

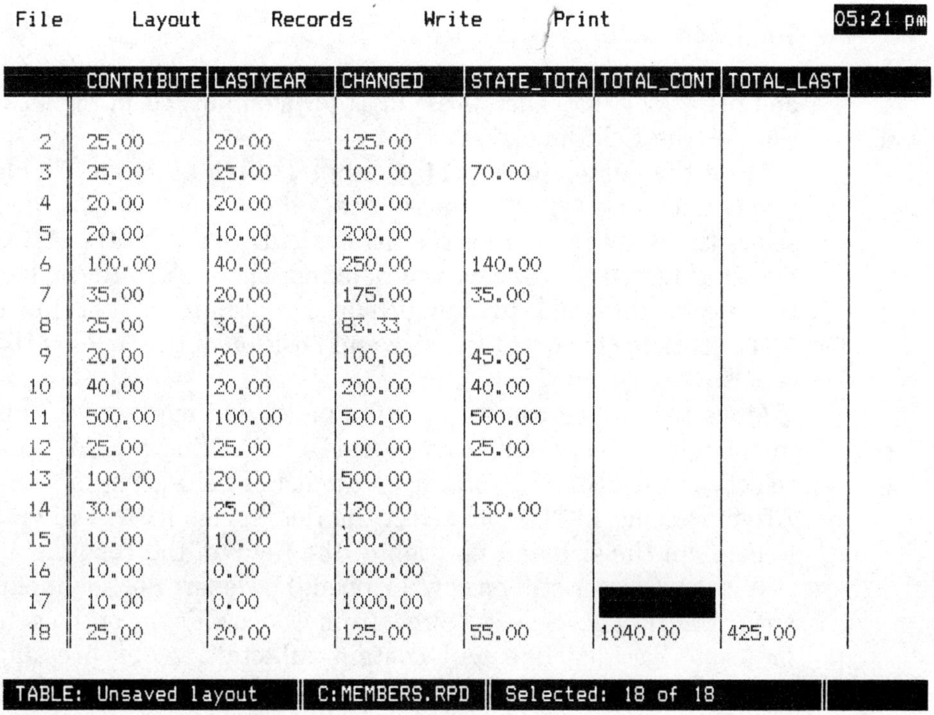
File Layout Records Write Print 05:21 pm

	CONTRIBUTE	LASTYEAR	CHANGED	STATE_TOTA	TOTAL_CONT	TOTAL_LAST
2	25.00	20.00	125.00			
3	25.00	25.00	100.00	70.00		
4	20.00	20.00	100.00			
5	20.00	10.00	200.00			
6	100.00	40.00	250.00	140.00		
7	35.00	20.00	175.00	35.00		
8	25.00	30.00	83.33			
9	20.00	20.00	100.00	45.00		
10	40.00	20.00	200.00	40.00		
11	500.00	100.00	500.00	500.00		
12	25.00	25.00	100.00	25.00		
13	100.00	20.00	500.00			
14	30.00	25.00	120.00	130.00		
15	10.00	10.00	100.00			
16	10.00	0.00	1000.00			
17	10.00	0.00	1000.00			
18	25.00	20.00	125.00	55.00	1040.00	425.00

TABLE: Unsaved layout | C:MEMBERS.RPD | Selected: 18 of 18

Figure 9-10. The database report fields

Use this type of field as a part of a report to provide totals, counts, or other numeric values within the report. To see how this works, open the Layout menu with CONTROL-L and select the option "Choose layout type." From the submenu choose "Custom Report." The previously designed Custom Report appears.

Open the Layout menu again with CONTROL-L and choose the option "Design layout" to redesign the existing Custom Report layout. The design screen for the Quick Report appears.

Move the cursor to row 14, column 2, and press F2 (EDIT). Enter the words

Total For State

and press RETURN. Then press RETURN again to accept the location for the field label.

Move the cursor to row 14, column 13, and open the Fields menu with CONTROL-F. Choose the "Show field" option, and select the State field from the list of fields that appears. After pressing RETURN to accept the field, use the RIGHT ARROW key to narrow the field to a width of two columns, and press RETURN twice to accept the size and position of the field on the report.

Move the cursor to row 14, column 19, and open the Fields menu with CONTROL-F. Choose the option "Show field" and select the field State_Total from the list of fields that appears. After pressing RETURN to select the field, press RETURN twice to confirm the size and position of the field on the report.

With the cursor still on row 14, open the Report Section menu with CONTROL-R. Select "Sub" from the available options to indicate that this line will contain subtotals. After pressing RETURN to select the option, press RETURN again to confirm the size of this report section.

Subsections are printed after groups of records, so RapidFile next requests the name of the field you will sort to group records: **This section is printed only when there is a change**

in:. The prompt is accompanied by a list of fields. You want the report to print a subtotal whenever the State field changes, so select the State field from the list of fields. Notice that, in this case, the report field in the subsection also totals records by state.

Move the cursor to row 16, column 20, open the Fields menu, and select the "Show fields" option. Choose Total_Contrib from the list of fields. Press RETURN to accept the size of the field. Then position the field at row 16, column 20, and press RETURN to accept the new location.

Move the cursor down one line, open the Fields menu, and select the "Show fields" option. Choose Total_Lastyr from the list of fields. Press RETURN to accept the size of the field. Then use the arrow keys to drag the field to row 16, column 56, and press RETURN to accept the new location.

The report fields that you just added to the report must be identified as grand sections of this Custom Report, so open the Report Section menu with CONTROL-R. Choose "Grand" from the menu. One line is fine for this section, so press RETURN.

Press F9 (IMPLEMENT) to implement the changes made to the Custom Report. Open the Records menu with CONTROL-R and choose "Calc report fields" to update the report fields. Then open the Print menu with CONTROL-P and then choose "Begin printing." The printed report, which contains subtotals for each state, resembles the example shown in Figure 9-11.

USING SNAPSHOTS

By now it should be obvious that creating the right type of report for your needs can be a complicated process. You must select the desired records, choose the proper layout, and—if necessary—sort the database. To make such tasks easier when performed on a repetitive basis, RapidFile offers a snapshot capability. *Snapshots* are used to make a "permanent record on

```
                         Membership Report

           10/24/86                                     05:43 pm

Last Name      Baker
First Name     Jeanette

Contributed Amount 10.00                 Last Years Amount 0.00

State VA

Last Name      Schultz
First Name     Bobby

Contributed Amount 10.00                 Last Years Amount 0.00

State VA

Last Name      Sloan
First Name     Wanda

Contributed Amount 25.00                 Last Years Amount 20.00

State VA

Total For: VA     55.00
Total Contributed 1040.00                Total Last Year 425.00


Paul

 Contrib
```

Figure 9-11. Sample report with subtotals

disk" of the various factors used to produce a report. These factors include the layout settings (with the print settings in use), the sort order (if any), and the criteria used to select records. By using a snapshot, you can easily save all the settings necessary to produce a particular report. The settings can then be reloaded at another time to produce the same type of report with a minimal amount of effort. Snapshots are loaded, saved, and erased by selecting the "Snapshot" option of the Layout menu.

Open the Layout menu with CONTROL-L and choose the "Snapshot" option. The submenu shown in Figure 9-12 appears.

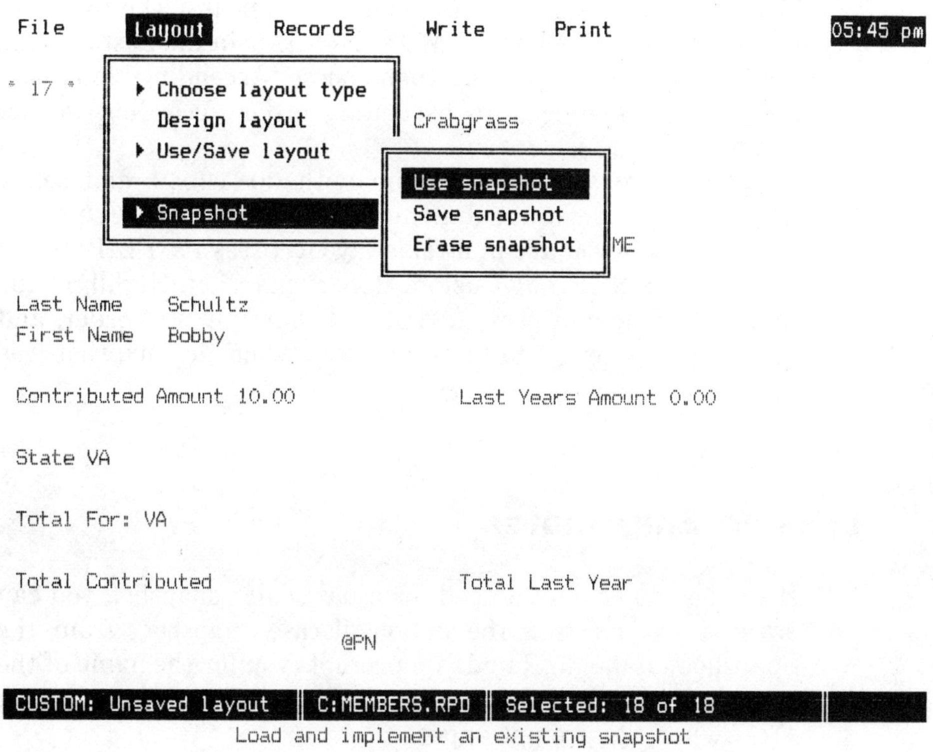

Figure 9-12. Snapshot submenu

The submenu options allow you to use an existing snapshot, to save a snapshot under a new name, or to erase an existing snapshot. For an example, select the option "Save snapshot." You will be prompted for the name of the snapshot. Enter

STATES-REPORT

as the name. The database reappears and the snapshot is saved as a part of the database file when the file is saved.

To see the effects of the snapshot, open the Layout menu with CONTROL-L and select the option "Choose layout type." Choose the "Table" option from the submenu that appears. The database reappears in "Table layout." With the cursor in the Last_Name field, press CONTROL-O, and then choose "Ascending" to re-sort the file alphabetically in ascending order according to last name.

Again, open the Layout menu with CONTROL-L and select "Snapshot." From the submenu choose the option "Use snapshot." Because you are in a table layout, press F3 (FLIP) to see the STATES-REPORT Custom Report snapshot. Highlight the snapshot name and press RETURN. The layout, sort order, and print settings revert to those in effect when the snapshot was saved.

Erasing Snapshots

If you no longer have a need for a particular snapshot, you can erase it by selecting the option "Erase snapshot" from the Snapshot submenu. RapidFile prompts you for the name of the snapshot to erase, and you must confirm the action by selecting "Yes" when the prompt appears.

Dealing with Expressions

Chapter 10

RapidFile permits the use of expressions (which are math formulas or equations) to control the display of data in calculated fields. Prior portions of this book have introduced the use of expressions to provide calculated amounts (such as percentages) based on the contents of various fields within a database. But prior chapters have just touched the surface in revealing the range of customized information that can be produced through the use of expressions with RapidFile. Expressions are based on math equations, but they are not limited to handling numbers alone. You can use expressions to add or multiply two numbers, to subtract one date from another (leaving the number of days between the two), or to add one string of text to another string of text to produce a phrase that will be used as a part of a form letter.

USING CUSTOM CALCULATED EXPRESSIONS

Custom calculated expressions are used with calculated fields, which are defined within the File Structure Table. To create these expressions, you must modify the structure of the database file.

Chapter 7 provided an introduction to the use of calculated fields, with the addition of the Changed field to the database MEMBERS. (Recall that you used Changed to show the percentage of increase of membership contributions.) The expression used to perform the calculation, (Contribute/Lastyear) * 100, is a numeric expression. A numeric expression is just one of three types of expressions that can be used by RapidFile. The following are the three types:

- *String Expressions.* These are expressions that work with text, numbers, or dates and produce strings of text as a result. Examples of string expressions used within RapidFile might include "Ms. " + Lastname, where "Ms. " is a string of characters and Lastname represents a text field.
- *Numeric Expressions.* These are expressions dealing with numbers linked by one or more math operators (+, −, *, /). Examples of numeric expressions include Rental_Amount * 12, Contribute + Lastyear, Contribute − 15.00, and Hourly_Salary * 7.70.
- *Date Expressions.* These expressions work with dates or with dates added to or subtracted from numbers. An example of a date expression is Expdate + 30, which could provide the indication of the end of a grace period that lapses 30 days beyond an expiration date.

This chapter will offer examples of the use of expressions within the two types of calculated fields not yet demonstrated in this text: date expressions and string expressions. After getting a feel for the use of the expressions with the examples, you can begin to plan how to use expressions to add flexibility to your own database applications.

Using a Date Expression

As an example, suppose that it would help the staff at Friends of Crabgrass if there were a simple way to tell at a glance how many days remained in a membership. A date expression could be used within a calculated field to display this information. To gain the greatest flexibility with date expressions, you will need to know RapidFile's date functions. These functions operate with dates and provide an output of dates or numbers (depending on the type of function). The date functions are listed in Table 10-1.

From the table you might surmise that you could subtract the value of the date function, DATE( ), from the value of the contents of the Expdate field to determine the number of days between the two. To try this, start RapidFile, load the database MEMBERS, open the Layout menu with CONTROL-L, and select "Table" layout. A new calculated field must be created to store the results of the data calculations, so open the File menu with CONTROL-F and select the option "Modify structure." The database is replaced with the File Structure Table (see Figure 10-1).

To add a new field, move the cursor down to the last field and press the DOWN ARROW key once more. The following prompt appears at the bottom of the screen: **Type the field name, then press ↵.**

Enter Time_Left for the name of the new field, and the field is added to the File Structure Table. All that remains to be done to use the field for calculations is to change the type of the field and to enter a valid expression in the Expression column.

Move the cursor to the Type column and press F2 (EDIT). At

Table 10-1. Date Functions

Function	Meaning
TODAY( )	In a calculated field, this provides the system clock date when the record is added or edited. In a calculated date field, the record is updated when the record is added or edited.
DATE( )	Provides the system clock date when any information is added or changed in a record. The date does not change when the file is loaded.
DATE#("MM/DD/YY")	Use this format to enter a date constant in an expression.
DAY(Date Field)	Provides the numeric value for the day, which is a part of the date contained within the date field.
DAY$(Date Field)	When used in a calculated text field, this outputs the name of the day of the week.
MONTH(Date Field)	Provides the numeric value for the month, which is a part of the date contained within the date field.
YEAR(Date Field)	Provides the numeric value for the year, which is a part of the date contained within the date field.

the bottom of the screen, you are prompted to select one of the five valid field types (Text, Numeric, Date, Calculated, or Report).

Since this will be a calculated field, select the "Calculated" option. The next prompt to appear asks **What type of output will this calculation have? Numeric Data Text.**

Select "Numeric" from the available options. The next prompt to appear asks how many decimal places should appear. Since you are referring to whole numbers (of days), select zero for the number of decimal places. Once you have made the selection, the designation Calc,N0 appears in the Type column.

File Structure Table

Field Settings			Preset Layout Settings		
Field name	Type	Expression	Field Format	Table size	Form size
LASTNAME	Text		None	15	25/1
FIRSTNAME	Text		None	15	25/1
EXPDATE	Date		None	8	8/1
CONTRIBUTE	Numeric		None	10	10/1
ADDRESS	Text		None	15	25/1
CITY	Text		None	15	25/1
STATE	Text		None	15	25/1
ZIP	Text		None	15	25/1
TYPE	Text		None	15	25/1
LASTYEAR	Numeric		None	10	10/1
CHANGED	Calc,N2	(CONTRIBUTE	None	10	10/1

F1 HELP F2 EDIT F9 IMPLEMENT ESC to leave without changes

Figure 10-1. The File Structure Table

Move the cursor to the Expression column and press F2. The following prompt appears at the bottom of the screen: **Type the expression for the current field, then press ↵.**

Enter

Expdate-Date

File Structure Table

Field Settings			Preset Layout Settings		
Field name	Type	Expression	Field Format	Table size	Form size
EXPDATE	Date		None	8	8/1
CONTRIBUTE	Numeric		None	10	10/1
ADDRESS	Text		None	15	25/1
CITY	Text		None	15	25/1
STATE	Text		None	15	25/1
ZIP	Text		None	15	25/1
TYPE	Text		None	15	25/1
LASTYEAR	Numeric		None	10	10/1
CHANGED	Calc,N2	(CONTRIBUTE	None	10	10/1
STATE_TOTAL	Rprt.2	TOTAL:CONTR	None	10	10/1
TIME_LEFT	Calc,N0	EXPDATE-DAT	None	10	10/1

F1 HELP F2 EDIT F9 IMPLEMENT ESC to leave without changes

Figure 10-2. The File Structure Table with changes

and press RETURN. This expression tells RapidFile to subtract the current date (as determined by the computer's clock) from the expiration dates of the memberships. Your File Structure Table should now resemble the one shown in Figure 10-2.

Finally, press F9 (IMPLEMENT) to implement the changes

File Layout Records Write Print 07:31 pm

	TYPE	LASTYEAR	CHANGED	STATE_TOTA	TIME_LEFT
1	ADULT	25.00	100.00	25.00	510
2	ADULT	10.00	200.00		328
3	STUDENT	0.00	1000.00		250
4	ADULT	20.00	100.00	45.00	144
5	ADULT	30.00	83.33		304
6	STUDENT	10.00	100.00		130
7	CHARTER	20.00	500.00		670
8	ADULT	20.00	200.00	40.00	412
9	ADULT	25.00	120.00	130.00	212
10	ADULT	20.00	100.00		197
11	ADULT	25.00	100.00	70.00	203
12	ADULT	20.00	100.00		144
13	ADULT	20.00	125.00		203
14	LIFETIME	100.00	500.00	500.00	4461
15	STUDENT	0.00	1000.00		398
16	ADULT	20.00	175.00	35.00	279
17	ADULT	20.00	125.00	55.00	0

TABLE: Unsaved layout | C:MEMBERS.RPD | Selected: 18 of 18

Figure 10-3. Result of using a date expression in a calculated field

to the database structure. Within a moment the database (in table layout) appears. Use the RIGHT ARROW key to bring the new field into view, and you see a display that shows the number of days between the current date and the expiration date (see Figure 10-3). Negative numbers would indicate that the members have let their memberships expire.

Using a String Expression

Use the plus sign as a part of a string expression to combine words into phrases. The strings can come from the contents of a field, or they can be literal characters that you include as a part of the expression, such as "Dear Mr./Ms." To add the field Greeting, which combines a salutation and the first and last names, try the following:

Open the File menu with CONTROL-F and select the option "Modify structure." The File Structure Table replaces the database.

Instead of adding a new field, you can delete the field previously used to calculate the dates. Move the cursor down to the field Time_Left and press the DEL key. A prompt appears at the bottom of the screen: **Type the field name, then press ↵.**

Enter Greeting as the name of the new field. Move the cursor to the Type column and press F2. From the list of available field types, select Calculated. Then, from the list of types of outputs, select Text.

Move the cursor to the Expression column and press F2. Delete the prior expression and enter the following expression:

"Dear Mr./Ms. " + Firstname + " " + Lastname

Note that you *must* use quotation marks or apostrophes when you are typing actual text that is to be a part of the expression or when you want to insert blank spaces. Do not enter quotation marks around the field names.

Once the expression has been entered, press F9 to implement the changes to the structure. Move the cursor to any desired record and press F2. As Figure 10-4 shows, you see the results

File Layout Records Write Print 07 34 pm

	TYPE	LASTYEAR	CHANGED	STATE_TOTA	GREETING
1	ADULT	25.00	100.00	25.00	Dear Mr./M
2	ADULT	10.00	200.00		Dear Mr./M
3	STUDENT	0.00	1000.00		Dear Mr./M
4	ADULT	20.00	100.00	45.00	Dear Mr./M
5	ADULT	30.00	83.33		Dear Mr./M
6	STUDENT	10.00	100.00		Dear Mr./M
7	CHARTER	20.00	500.00		Dear Mr./M
8	ADULT	20.00	200.00	40.00	Dear Mr./M
9	ADULT	25.00	120.00	130.00	Dear Mr./M
10	ADULT	20.00	100.00		Dear Mr./M
11	ADULT	25.00	100.00	70.00	Dear Mr./M
12	ADULT	20.00	100.00		Dear Mr./M
13	ADULT	20.00	125.00		Dear Mr./M
14	LIFETIME	100.00	500.00	500.00	Dear Mr./M
15	STUDENT	0.00	1000.00		Dear Mr./M
16	ADULT	20.00	175.00	35.00	Dear Mr./M
17	ADULT	20.00	125.00	55.00	Dear Mr./M

Dear Mr./Ms. Norma Roberts

Figure 10-4. Result of a calculated expression using text

of the entire expression in the Edit Panel. If you wanted to use this greeting, you could widen the new field or include it as a part of a form layout or a form letter produced with the memo writer.

RULES CONCERNING EXPRESSIONS

Keep in mind these general rules as you work with expressions:

1. Expressions containing multiple operators are calculated following a specific order of precedence. Negation (placing a minus sign in front of a number) has first priority, and then exponentiation (raising a number to a power), and then multiplication and division, and then addition and subtraction. You can modify the order of precedence by placing parts of the expression within parentheses. Operations enclosed within parentheses are always performed first.
2. Expressions used in calculated fields can refer only to data in that same record, not to data in other records at the same time. A calculated field, for example, could show the result of one record's cost field plus that same record's tax field. The calculated field could not show one record's cost field plus a different record's cost field.
3. The type (text, numeric, or date) of the calculated field depends on the output of the calculation and not on the kinds of data used to perform the calculation. In the example shown in this chapter you calculated a number based on dates. The input provided was two date values, but the output of the calculated field was a number.
4. Expressions are limited to a maximum of 254 characters.
5. Field names used as a part of an expression should not contain symbols that could be mistaken for a math or string operator. As an example, you might have a database with three fields named Sales, Tax, and Sales-Tax, respectively. This would not be a good idea, because the name Sales-Tax in an expression could be taken by RapidFile as an instruction to subtract the value in the Tax field from

the value in the Sales field. Other symbols to stay away from when naming fields include +, −, *, /, <, >, =, and %.

Expressions can be used for numerous tasks, and additional advanced functions can be combined with expressions within calculated fields to produce a variety of data on your screen or in the form of a report. Many of these functions are beyond the scope of a beginner's book, so they are not covered in this text. More information on the advanced functions and expressions can be found in your RapidFile documentation. If you need powerful math and logical operations with your data, looking into the use of such features may prove worth your time.

Advanced Use of the Memo Writer

Chapter 11

The memo writer portion of RapidFile, introduced in Chapter 8, can handle a variety of word processing tasks. It offers advanced features, including full search-and-replace capabilities, headers and footers, special print options, and macros. This chapter will delve into those advanced features. Before continuing, start RapidFile. Open the Write menu with CONTROL-W and select the option "Write memo." When the memo writer menu appears, open the File menu with CONTROL-F and select the option "Retrieve file." Choose CRAB1 from the list of available files to recall the document you created in Chapter 8.

You will not be using the form letter in this chapter, so place the cursor at the start of the document, press F6 (HIGHLIGHT), move the cursor down three lines, and press the DEL key to delete the name fields.

CHANGING TYPE STYLES

The Typestyle menu offers various type styles that can be used within a document. You can apply different type styles to characters in one of two ways: as you type by turning on an option and proceeding to type, or by highlighting text that has been typed already and then selecting an option. The available type styles are shown in the Typestyle menu (see Figure 11-1).

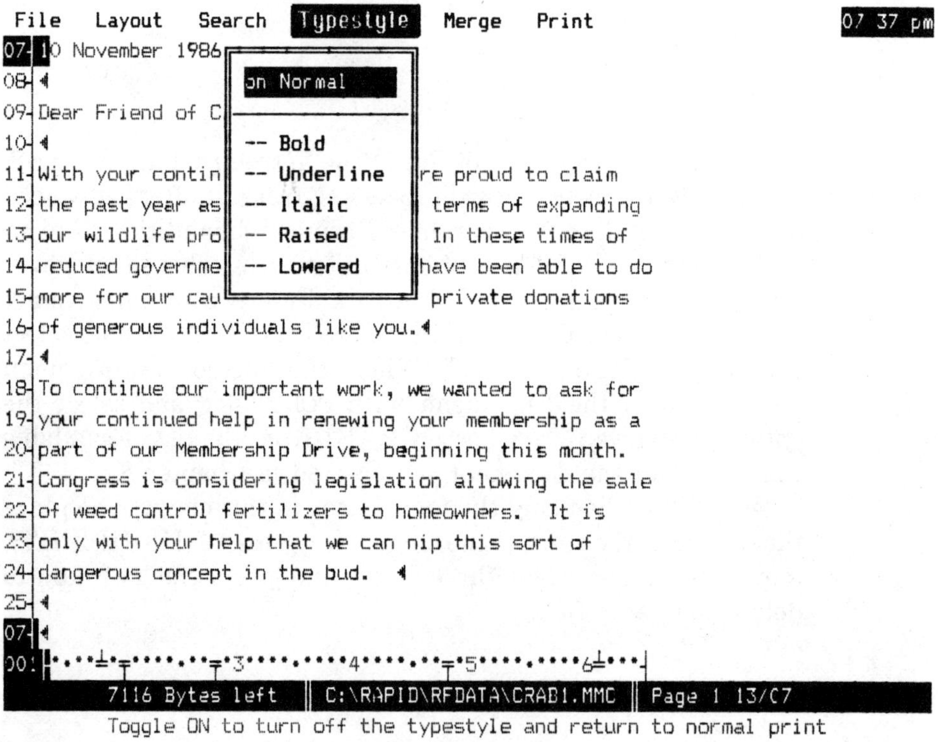

Figure 11-1. The Typestyle menu

The available menu options are "Normal," "Bold," "Underline," "Italic," "Raised," and "Lowered." It is possible to select more than one option at a time. For example, text could be underlined and bold at the same time. All of the options within the Typestyle menu are toggles, meaning that if the option is on when you first select it, it will be turned off the next time you select it. Likewise, if the option is off when you first select it, it will be turned on the next time. Raised and lowered text are also referred to as *subscript* and *superscript* in the word processing world. Raised text is commonly used to enter the trademark symbol, to indicate numbers raised to a power, and to indicate footnotes. Lowered text is commonly used within scientific formulas.

To illustrate, place the cursor on the line following the second paragraph of the letter. Open the Typestyle menu with CONTROL-T and select the "Underline" option. Then type the words

This is underlined

Open the Typestyle menu again with CONTROL-T and choose the "Bold" option. Then type the words

And this is bold

Open the Typestyle menu and select "Normal" to change back to normal text. If you have a color or graphics monitor, you will notice that the underlined and bold words are displayed in different colors. Table 11-1 shows how common type styles will be displayed on the IBM monochrome monitor and on color monitors that follow the normal IBM color graphics specifications. These are the default values for the display. You can change these values to colors more to your liking by changing the customization settings of RapidFile. (Chapter 19 describes this process in detail.)

To use the Typestyle menu options with existing text, highlight the text to be changed by the option, and then select the option. As an example, place the cursor at the start of the

Table 11-1. Display of Type Styles

Type Style	Color-Display Attribute	Monochrome-Display Attribute
Underlined	Yellow	Underlined
Normal text	White	Normal
Bold	Bright white	Bold
Italic	Red	Underlined
Raised	Sky blue	Bold
Lowered	Blue	Bold
Combinations	Violet	Bold

second paragraph of text and press F6 (HIGHLIGHT). Move the cursor to the end of the word "work" and press RETURN. Open the Typestyle menu with CONTROL-T and select the "Italic" option. The highlighted text changes to italic format. You can see how the document will print by using the option "Begin printing" of the Print menu to print the document. If the results do not look italic, see the next section.

A Note About Your Printer

Type style options produce different results on different printers. What is more, all printers do not support such options. Dot matrix printers, for example, usually will not produce raised or lowered text. Some printers print bold and underlined text, but do not print italics. Even if your printer does support all these features, you must still tell RapidFile during the installation process which printer you are using. If you have not told RapidFile which printer you are using, then RapidFile is most likely using a generic printer configuration file that supports only the basic printer features. To run the Printer Installation program, you must exit RapidFile, and return to the DOS prompt. If you are using a floppy-based system, insert the Sample Data/Utility disk; if you are using a hard disk, switch to the subdirectory called RAPID by entering the command

CD \RAPID

Enter

PRINTER

to run the Printer Installation program, and follow the instructions that appear on the screen.

FINDING AND REPLACING TEXT

RapidFile offers search-and-replace functions that allow you to find a word or phrase, find a word or phrase and replace it with other words, or erase every occurrence of a word or phrase. These options are found within the Search menu, which is shown in Figure 11-2.

The first three options—"Find," "Replace," and "Erase"—are used to search for, replace, or delete words that match a specified word or phrase. The next two options, "Whole word only" and "Ignore case," are toggles that can be set to on or off by selecting the option. "Whole word only" causes the search or replacement to be limited to complete words, so a search for "At" will not also turn up "Atkinson," "Atlantic," and "Attack." "Ignore case" tells RapidFile to find the word regardless of whether letters appear in uppercase or lowercase. When "Ignore case" is set to off, the memo writer searches for text exactly as it is entered.

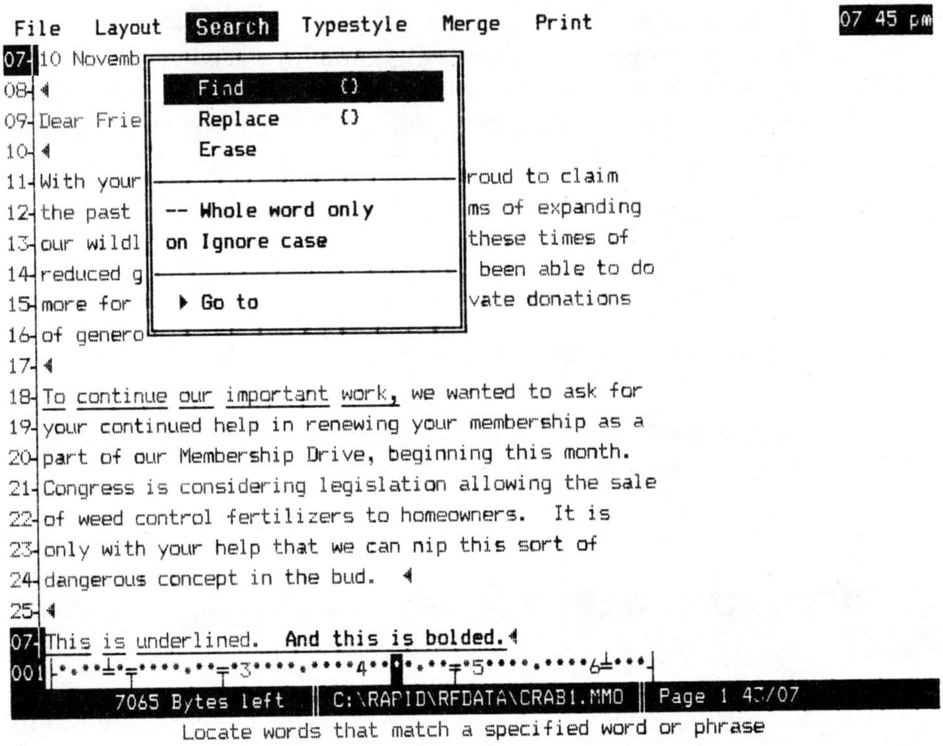

Figure 11-2. The Search menu

The option "Go to," when selected, displays a submenu with three choices: "Page," "Tag," and "Highlight." These options enable you to quickly move the cursor to a specific page number, to a highlighted block of text, or to a tagged character within a document. (Any one character in a document can be tagged by moving the cursor to the character and pressing the

F5 (TAG) key.) Use any of the options by highlighting the option and then pressing RETURN.

As an example, open the Search menu with CONTROL-S and choose the "Find" option. The following prompt appears at the bottom of the screen: **Type the find criteria, then press ↵.**

Enter the word

we

and then press RETURN. The cursor moves to the first occurrence of the word. Press the DOWN ARROW key repeatedly, and the cursor moves to each subsequent occurrence, including cases in which the two letters occur as a part of the word "weed." Press the ESC key to halt the search and press CONTROL-HOME to move the cursor back to the start of the document. Open the Search menu again and select the option "Whole word only" to turn on this toggle. Then select the "Find" option again and, to continue the same search, press RETURN when the prompt for the search text appears. This time, repeated pressing of DOWN ARROW shows only those occurrences of "we" where the letters constitute an entire word. Press ESC to end the search and use CONTROL-HOME to return to the start of the document.

Note that the search feature of RapidFile's memo writer searches in a forward direction only, beginning from the cursor location. If you want to search through the entire document, you must move the cursor to the start of the document before beginning the search.

The "Replace" option operates in a manner similar to "Find"— it prompts you for both the search text and the replacement text. As an example, open the Search menu and select "Replace." You are prompted at the bottom of the screen to enter the "Find" criteria. Enter the word

help

Another prompt appears below the first one, asking for the replacement text. Enter the word

support

Once you have entered the term, notice that the cursor moves to the first occurrence of the word and additional options appear at the bottom of the screen. You have the option of performing the replacement and finding the next occurrence (by pressing RETURN), of skipping this replacement and finding the next occurrence (by pressing DOWN ARROW), of replacing all occurrences (by pressing END), of making this replacement and halting the search (by pressing HOME), or of halting the search without making the replacement (by pressing ESC).

Press the END key and you see the prompt **Replace all "help" with "support" Yes No.** Select the "Yes" option and the replacements are made.

The "Erase" option of the Search menu can be used in a manner identical to the "Find" option. After you have entered your search text, you are prompted to confirm each erasure.

Using Wildcards with the Search Options

As a part of a search, you can use *wildcards*, which are characters used as symbols for one or more characters. RapidFile permits two wildcards as a part of a search: the question mark (which stands for any character) and the quotation mark (which represents a delimiter—a space, a comma, a carriage return, or a parenthesis). For example, the search text "H?ll" locates the names "Hall" and "Hill." The search text "der" locates all words ending in the letters "der" when followed by a space, comma, carriage return, or parenthesis (but not by another character).

USING PRINT SETTINGS

The memo writer offers additional formatting options within the Print Settings submenu of the Print menu. Open the Print menu with CONTROL-P and choose the option "Print settings." The Print Settings submenu appears (see Figure 11-3).

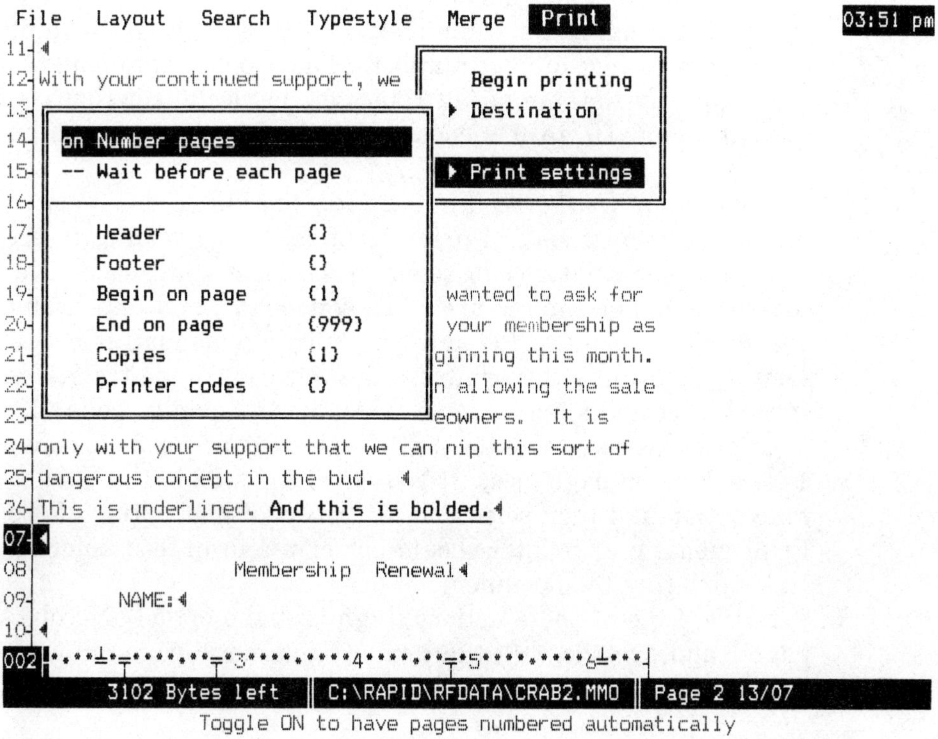

Figure 11-3. The Print Settings submenu

The first two options, "Number pages" and "Wait before each page," are toggle options—selecting either option turns the option off or on. "Number pages" selects whether page numbers appear at the bottom of each page of the document. "Wait before each page," when on, causes the printer to pause before beginning to print each page of the document. If you are using a cut-sheet printer, this option should be turned on to permit time for the loading of each sheet.

The "Header" option is used to create a line of text that appears at the top of each printed page. The "Footer" option creates a line of text that prints at the bottom of every page. "Begin on page" and "End on page" allow you to specify a starting and an ending page number. Use these options to limit printing to a range of page numbers. The "Copies" option allows you to specify the number of copies of the document that you want to print. Up to 999 copies of a single document can be specified.

The option "Printer codes" permits the entry of a printer code to perform a special print function. If you wish to insert more than one printer code, separate the codes with spaces. The codes that can be entered are entirely dependent on your brand and model of printer. Refer to your printer manual, if necessary, to determine the printer codes used by your printer for special effects. As an example, consider the printer code 012. Most printers recognize the ASCII value 012 as a code to cause a form feed or page eject. If you enter 012 within the printer code option and then select the "Begin printing" option of the Print menu, your printer should perform a form feed before it starts printing the document.

To try some of these options, highlight the option "Number pages" and press RETURN to turn off automatic page numbering. Select the "Header" option and enter

Friends of Crabgrass, 1987

as the header.

Select the "Footer" option of the menu and enter

Mid-Atlantic Chapter

as the footer. Select the "Copies" option and enter 2 for the number of copies. Finally, if you have an Epson or Epson-compatible printer, select "Printer codes" and enter

15

Press ESC to close the submenu and select "Begin printing" from the Print menu.

The document produced by your printer should include the chosen header and footer at the top and bottom of the page. Two copies should be printed and, if you entered the printer code for an Epson-compatible printer, you should have a document that was printed using compressed characters.

WRITING A MEMO USING A SINGLE RECORD

At times you may want form-letter capabilities without generating a pile of form letters. You may need to write a single letter to a name and address that happen to be in a database file. In such cases it is not neccessary to build a form letter for just one name and address. You can write a memo and insert fields from a single record by placing the cursor at that record before switching to the memo writer.

To try this, open the File menu with CONTROL-F and choose "Leave memo writer" to get back to the file manager portion of RapidFile. As an example, perhaps you need to write a personal note to Ms. Lucy Sand, inviting her to a local speech at an upcoming membership function.

The first step is to place the cursor on the desired record within the database, so place the cursor anywhere on the record for Lucy Sand.

Once the record is highlighted, use the Write menu to get into the memo writer. Open the Write menu with CONTROL-W and select the option "Write memo." The memo writer screen appears.

You can now type the desired letter, inserting fields with the option "Insert field" of the Merge menu. As an example, type the current date at the left margin and then press RETURN twice. Open the Merge menu with CONTROL-M, select "Insert field," and choose the Greeting field. Once you select the field, the contents of the field appear at the cursor location.

Press the END key to move the cursor to the end of the line. Then press RETURN twice more and type the following words:

Our organization is having an upcoming conference in

Open the Merge menu with CONTROL-M, choose "Insert field," and select the field City from the list of fields that appears. The city name is inserted into the document at the cursor location. If this were an actual letter, you could continue typing the desired text, save the letter with the option "Save file" of the File menu, and print the letter with the option "Begin printing" of the Print menu.

READING IN ANOTHER FILE

You can also combine documents by reading the contents of one document into another. The option "Insert file" of the File menu can be used to perform this task. To do so, place the cursor at the location where you wish to insert the text of the other file, select "Insert file" of the File menu, and specify the name of the incoming file.

To demonstrate this process, read a previously written file, CRAB1, into the letter you are writing at this time. Place the cursor at the end of the document and press RETURN to move to a new line. Open the File menu with CONTROL-F and select "Insert file."

A list of files appears and the prompt at the bottom of the screen asks you to select a file from the list, or type in a name. Highlight CRAB1 and press RETURN.

Another prompt appears at the bottom of the screen: **Insert file: "CRAB1.MMO" OK to continue? Yes No.** Select the "Yes" option, and the other document appears below the existing document.

Note that when you insert a document into an existing document, the formats (typefaces and layout settings) of the inserted document are carried into the existing document. You may or may not want the formatting, so change the formatting as necessary once the desired document has been read into the existing file.

READING FOREIGN FILES

You can read text files into RapidFile that have been created with other word processors, although the results may vary and this capability is not supported by the RapidFile documentation. For best results the file from the other program should be a normal ASCII file that contains no special formatting characters. Many word processors (including MultiMate, WordPerfect, and Microsoft Word) have options allowing you to write a standard ASCII text file without any special formatting codes. You can then read these files into a RapidFile memo writer document.

To read a foreign file into a memo writer document, perform the same steps outlined previously, but type the entire name of the file. If the filename does not have an extension, then you must end the filename with a period. By entering a filename with a period and no extension, you tell RapidFile to read the file by that name that does not have the normal extension .MMO.

SAVING HIGHLIGHTED TEXT

On some occasions you will want to save a block of text to a separate memo file. You can easily do this by highlighting the block of text in the normal manner with F6 (HIGHLIGHT) and then choosing the option "Save file" of the File menu. Once the option has been chosen, RapidFile asks (in the Message Area) whether you want to save the entire file or just the highlighted block. Choose the option "Highlighted block." Then you are asked to supply a name for the new file. You can enter a new name or you can enter the name of an existing file. If you name an existing file, RapidFile appends the highlighted text at the end of the file you name.

To exit the memo writer, open the File menu with CONTROL-F and select the option "Leave memo writer." Answer "No" to the prompt **Save before continuing** to discard the changes made in this chapter. Then open the File menu and select the "Quit" option to exit RapidFile.

RapidFile to Lotus

Chapter 12

RapidFile has options of particular interest to users of Lotus 1-2-3 or Symphony. You can readily exchange information between worksheets of the two Lotus packages and RapidFile databases by using the "Import" and "Export" options of the File menu. This chapter will cover how to export RapidFile data to a Lotus 1-2-3 or Symphony worksheet. Chapter 13 will cover how Lotus 1-2-3 (or Symphony) worksheet data can be imported into a RapidFile database. If you are familiar with Lotus 1-2-3, you may want to take advantage of RapidFile's ability to use menus like those in 1-2-3 instead of the pull-down menus that are standard when RapidFile is first started. You can change the RapidFile menus to a horizontal format that is similar to that used by the Lotus packages. Details about how to do this are provided in Chapter 19.

WHY TRANSFER?

Because Lotus 1-2-3 offers database management capabilities, some users of 1-2-3 may wonder why RapidFile should be considered as a complementary package. Using RapidFile in such a fashion can be well worth the effort because RapidFile overcomes many of the limitations of 1-2-3 as a database manager. Lotus 1-2-3, for example, has limited sorting capabilities. A 1-2-3 database can be sorted according to a maximum of only two sort ranges, or fields. RapidFile allows you to sort on up to 15 different fields.

The 1-2-3 program is also limited in terms of reporting capabilities. You must purchase an optional product, the 1-2-3 Report Writer, to approach the levels of reports possible with RapidFile. In addition, data entry can be difficult for novice users when using 1-2-3. By using RapidFile instead, novices can create a form layout that provides a simple means of data entry. Once the data has been entered, the data can be transferred to the 1-2-3 worksheet for analysis.

Lotus 1-2-3 also lacks any capability for powerful word processing and for the generation of form letters and mailing labels. If you have names and addresses stored within a 1-2-3 worksheet, you can better manage that data if it is exported to a RapidFile database. And by the nature of the database design, a Lotus 1-2-3 database will always be limited in size by the amount of memory present in your computer. Because RapidFile uses virtual memory for storage on disk, it allows up to 64,000 records in a single database. To manage large amounts of information and to perform advanced math on parts of it, you can store the data in RapidFile and transfer portions of the file to Lotus 1-2-3 for your spreadsheet analysis.

TRANSFERRING DATA FROM RAPIDFILE TO LOTUS 1-2-3

Transferring data from RapidFile to Lotus 1-2-3 consists of the following four steps:

1. Prepare the database for export by selecting the desired

records, implementing any desired sort order, and changing the layout so that only the desired fields are visible.

2. Export the file by using the option "Export file" of the File menu.
3. Copy the resultant .WKS worksheet file onto your Lotus 1-2-3 or Symphony data disk or into the appropriate subdirectory.
4. When in Lotus 1-2-3 or Symphony, load the worksheet file in the usual manner.

PREPARING THE RAPIDFILE DATABASE FOR THE TRANSFER

When you tell RapidFile to export records in a database to a Lotus 1-2-3 worksheet, RapidFile translates all selected records into a worksheet compatible with 1-2-3. The new worksheet is in the same order as the records in the RapidFile database. All fields that are shown in the layout in use are included in the exported worksheet.

You can often save much time and effort by customizing the layout and sort order so that the resultant 1-2-3 worksheet contains only those fields you need within the worksheet. If only a portion of the RapidFile database is to be exported to Lotus 1-2-3, use the "Select" option of the Records menu to identify match criteria for the records to be exported. If you work with large RapidFile databases, keep in mind the memory limitations of a 1-2-3 worksheet. You may find that an entire RapidFile database, when exported to 1-2-3 format, will not fit into a single worksheet. A 1-2-3 worksheet is limited to a maximum of 2048 records. (RapidFile will check the number of selected records before performing a Lotus 1-2-3 export and will warn you if the number of records exceeds 2048.) If the RapidFile database exceeds these limits, you must break the database into smaller pieces by selecting groups of records and exporting each group to 1-2-3 as a separate worksheet file.

Consider the database MEMBERS as an example. For purposes of analysis suppose that you want the names, states, and numeric data in the file in the form of a 1-2-3 spreadsheet so that you can use 1-2-3 to graph membership data. The spreadsheet data needs to be sorted in alphabetical order by last name and by first name when the last names are identical. Two steps prepare the file: You must sort it in the desired order and you must establish a layout containing only the names, states, and numeric data.

Start RapidFile if necessary and load the database MEMBERS. If the file does not appear in a table layout, use the option "Choose layout type" of the Layout menu to select "Table" layout.

Open the Layout menu with CONTROL-L and select the option "Design layout." When the Layout design area appears, highlight the State_Total field with the cursor and open the Fields menu with CONTROL-F. Select the option "Remove field" to delete the field from the layout.

Using "Remove field" again, remove the Address, City, Zip, Type, and Greeting fields from the layout.

In the 1-2-3 worksheet you want the State field next to the Firstname field. To move the field while still in RapidFile, you must remove the State field from the current location and use the option "Show field" of the Fields menu to insert the field at the new location. Move the cursor to the State field, open the Fields menu, and select the "Remove field" option to remove the State field.

Move the cursor back to the Firstname field, open the Fields menu, and select the option "Show field." Select "State" from the list of fields to insert the State field in the new location in the layout.

Press F9 to implement the new layout. Open the Layout menu again with CONTROL-L and select the option "Use/Save layout."

Choose "Save layout" from the submenu and enter

LOTUS

as the name of the new layout.

The final step in preparing the database for the 1-2-3 worksheet is to sort the database in the desired order. Open the Records menu with CONTROL-R and choose the "Order" option. Delete any prior entries that remain in the Order Settings screen. Enter 1 in the Order column next to the Lastname field, and enter 2 in the Order field next to the Firstname field. Then press F9 to implement the sort order. Your file should appear, and it should resemble Figure 12-1.

EXPORTING DATA

Exporting the data is likely to be the simplest step in the entire process. You will use the option "Export file" of the File menu to export a database to 1-2-3 format.

Open the File menu with CONTROL-F and select "Export file." A submenu appears (see Figure 12-2).

The submenu offers options for exporting files to dBASE II, dBASE III (or dBASE III PLUS), pfs:FILE, Lotus 1-2-3, and to a format that is comma-delimited. The option "Lotus 1-2-3" is used to export files to both Release 1A and Release 2 of Lotus 1-2-3 and to Symphony. The remaining options, which refer to other software packages, are covered in future chapters.

Select the option "Lotus 1-2-3" of the menu. A window of files appears on the right side of the screen, and you are prompted at the bottom of the screen to enter a name for the exported file (see Figure 12-3).

Note that RapidFile assumes you would like to give the file the same name it currently has (MEMBERS). If the assumption is correct, RapidFile automatically adds the extension

File Layout Records Write Print 08 22 am

	LASTNAME	FIRSTNAME	STATE	EXPDATE	CONTRIBUTE
1	Askew	Lonnie	NY	03/01/88	25.00
2	Baker	Benjamin	CA	09/08/87	20.00
3	Baker	Jeanette	VA	06/22/87	10.00
4	Block	Paul	IL	03/08/87	20.00
5	Brown	Nicole	IL	08/15/87	25.00
6	Harris	Charles	VA	02/22/87	10.00
7	Hayes	Cynthia	TX	08/15/88	100.00
8	Johnson, Jr.	Lamar	MA	12/01/87	40.00
9	Jones	Renee	TX	05/15/87	30.00
10	Mills	Ernest	CA	04/30/87	20.00
11	Roberts	James	AZ	05/06/87	25.00
12	Roberts	Norma	AZ	03/08/87	20.00
13	Roberts	Terry	AZ	05/06/87	25.00
14	Sand	Lucy	MD	01/01/99	500.00
15	Schultz	Bobby	VA	11/17/87	10.00
16	Shaw	Michael	FL	07/21/87	35.00
17	Sloan	Wanda	VA	10/15/86	25.00

TABLE: Lotus | C:MEMBERS.RPD | Selected: 18 of 18

Figure 12-1. RapidFile database prepared for export

.WKS when you press RETURN to accept the name. You can also provide a different name if you desire. In this case press RETURN to accept the name provided. The translation process begins, and this prompt appears at the bottom of the screen: **EXPORTING file MEMBERS.WKS. 18 out of 18 records translated.**

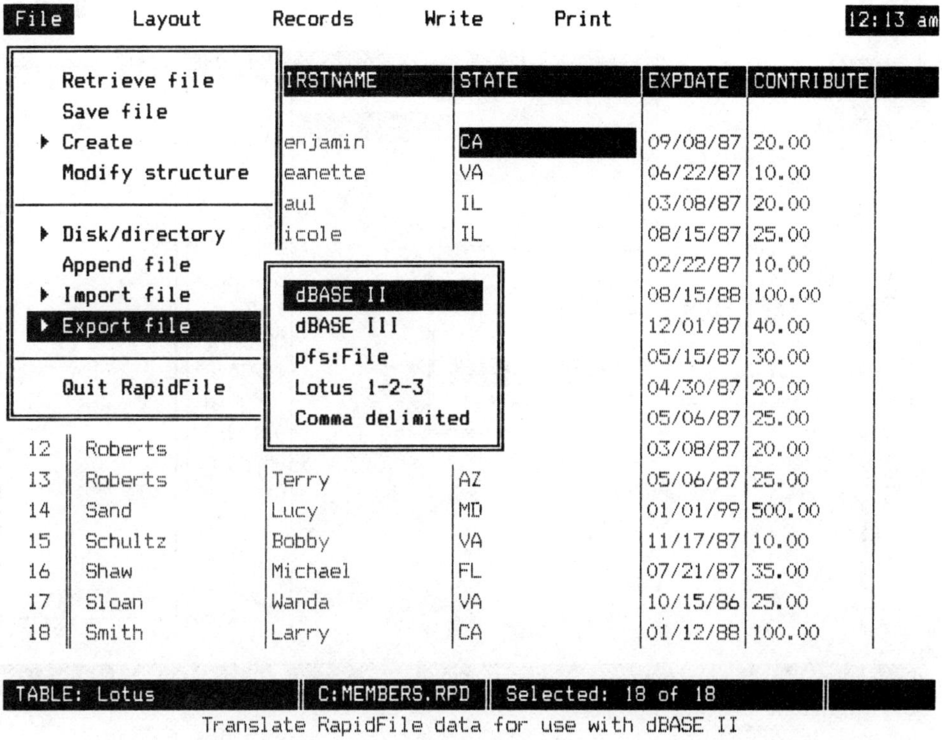

Figure 12-2. The submenu for exporting files

To return to the matter of filename extension, RapidFile assigns the extension .WKS to a file compatible with 1-2-3. (You can override this choice by specifying your own name and extension.) Release 1A of Lotus 1-2-3 expects files to have the .WKS extension. Release 2 of Lotus 1-2-3 reads files with either the extension .WKS or the extension .WK1. Files that have been

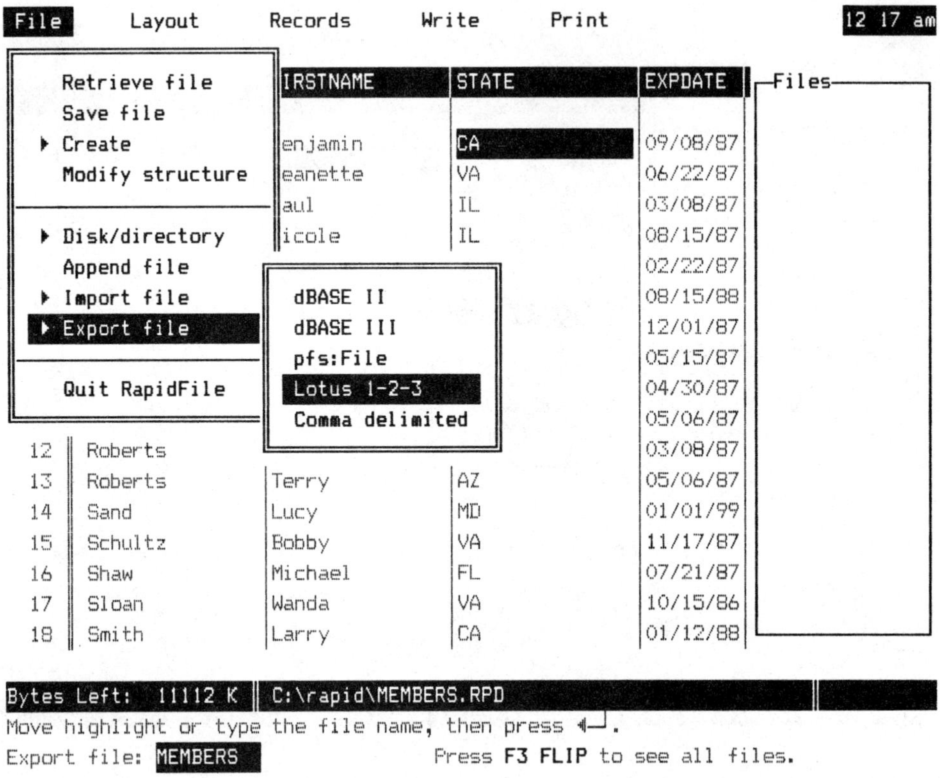

Figure 12-3. The prompt asks for the name of the exported file

exported from RapidFile and are compatible with 1-2-3 can also be used in Symphony without any additional steps. Simply use the usual commands to retrieve the file when in Symphony, but specify the extension .WKS as a part of the filename. (Unless told otherwise, Symphony expects files to have the extension .WR1.) Once you save the file in Symphony, it will be saved in Symphony format with the extension .WR1.

The exported files are usually stored in the default directory.

If you are using a floppy-based system, the default directory is on drive B. If you are using a hard-disk system, the default directory is C:\RAPID\RFDATA, unless you have used the option "Disk/directory" of the File menu to select another directory. Use the appropriate DOS commands to copy the exported 1-2-3 files onto your 1-2-3 data disk or into the appropriate subdirectory of the hard disk that you use with 1-2-3.

USING THE FILE IN LOTUS 1-2-3

Once you have copied the file onto the appropriate data disk or appropriate subdirectory, you can load Lotus 1-2-3 in the usual manner and get into the 1-2-3 worksheet. Use "/ File Retrieve" to display the directory of 1-2-3 files. From the directory, highlight the desired file (in this case, MEMBERS.WKS) and press RETURN. The spreadsheet is loaded and appears as shown in Figure 12-4.

The example highlights a common but easily solved problem with exporting files to 1-2-3. Unless told otherwise, Lotus 1-2-3 assumes a width of nine characters per column. If an existing column in 1-2-3 is not wide enough to display all the RapidFile data, one of two things happens. If the data is text, it is truncated. If the data is in the form of numbers or dates, the data is displayed as a series of asterisks. Column D of the spreadsheet displays asterisks because dates in Lotus 1-2-3 default to a display that spells out the month using a three-letter abbreviation, and a nine-character column is not wide enough to show the date.

Solve this problem in one of two ways: widen the column in question or widen every column in the 1-2-3 worksheet. In this case widen just the date column. Place the cursor on the date column, and then use "/ Worksheet Column Set-Width." Enter

A1: 'Askew READY

	A	B	C	D	E	F	G	H
1	Askew	Lonnie	NY	*********	25	25	100	
2	Baker	Benjamin	CA	*********	20	10	200	
3	Baker	Jeanette	VA	*********	10	0	1000	
4	Block	Paul	IL	*********	20	20	100	
5	Brown	Nicole	IL	*********	25	30	83.33	
6	Harris	Charles	VA	*********	10	10	100	
7	Hayes	Cynthia	TX	*********	100	20	500	
8	Johnson,	Lamar	MA	*********	40	20	200	
9	Jones	Renee	TX	*********	30	25	120	
10	Mills	Ernest	CA	*********	20	20	100	
11	Roberts	James	AZ	*********	25	25	100	
12	Roberts	Norma	AZ	*********	20	20	100	
13	Roberts	Terry	AZ	*********	25	20	125	
14	Sand	Lucy	MD	*********	500	100	500	
15	Schultz	Bobby	VA	*********	10	0	1000	
16	Shaw	Michael	FL	*********	35	20	175	
17	Sloan	Wanda	VA	*********	25	20	125	
18	Smith	Larry	CA	*********	100	40	250	
19								
20								

Figure 12-4. The database MEMBERS in the Lotus 1-2-3 worksheet

for a new column width, and the dates appear in Lotus 1-2-3 format. Perform the same steps to widen the lastname column, but choose a column width of 14 characters, to show the longest last name.

One other change would improve the appearance of the spreadsheet. Columns E and F, which contain the contribution amounts for this year and last year, could easily be displayed in currency format. Move the cursor to location E1 of the work-

E1: (C2) 25 READY

	A	B	C	D	E	F	G
1	Askew	Lonnie	NY	01-Mar-88	$25.00	$25.00	100
2	Baker	Benjamin	CA	08-Sep-87	$20.00	$10.00	200
3	Baker	Jeanette	VA	22-Jun-87	$10.00	$0.00	1000
4	Block	Paul	IL	08-Mar-87	$20.00	$20.00	100
5	Brown	Nicole	IL	15-Aug-87	$25.00	$30.00	83.33
6	Harris	Charles	VA	22-Feb-87	$10.00	$10.00	100
7	Hayes	Cynthia	TX	15-Aug-88	$100.00	$20.00	500
8	Johnson, Jr.	Lamar	MA	01-Dec-87	$40.00	$20.00	200
9	Jones	Renee	TX	15-May-87	$30.00	$25.00	120
10	Mills	Ernest	CA	30-Apr-87	$20.00	$20.00	100
11	Roberts	James	AZ	06-May-87	$25.00	$25.00	100
12	Roberts	Norma	AZ	08-Mar-87	$20.00	$20.00	100
13	Roberts	Terry	AZ	06-May-87	$25.00	$20.00	125
14	Sand	Lucy	MD	01-Jan-99	$500.00	$100.00	500
15	Schultz	Bobby	VA	17-Nov-87	$10.00	$0.00	1000
16	Shaw	Michael	FL	21-Jul-87	$35.00	$20.00	175
17	Sloan	Wanda	VA	15-Oct-86	$25.00	$20.00	125
18	Smith	Larry	CA	12-Jan-88	$100.00	$40.00	250
19							
20							

Figure 12-5. Completed Lotus worksheet

sheet. Use "/ Range Format Currency," and press RETURN to accept the default value of two decimal places. Enter a period to anchor the range at location E1, move the cursor to location F18, and then press RETURN. The amounts reformat to appear as shown in Figure 12-5.

At this point you could use the appropriate 1-2-3 commands to add columnar totals and headings and to graph the data.

HOW RAPIDFILE DATA APPEARS IN LOTUS 1-2-3

RapidFile data appears in a Lotus 1-2-3 worksheet in one of two possible formats: as labels or as numbers. RapidFile exports all fields that are defined as text in the database as labels to the 1-2-3 worksheet. All RapidFile fields defined as numeric, calculated, or date fields are defined as numbers in the 1-2-3 worksheet.

Even dates are stored in the 1-2-3 worksheet as numbers— this is the way dates are normally handled in Lotus 1-2-3. (The actual number stored is a representation of the number of days from January 1, 1900. For example, the first date displayed in the 1-2-3 worksheet in Figure 12-5 is actually the numeric value 32,203. It is the formatting used by Lotus 1-2-3 that causes this number to appear as a date.)

The Lotus 1-2-3 method of date formatting can cause problems because 1-2-3 is incapable of displaying dates prior to the year 1900. If you build a genealogical database of ancestors in RapidFile, for example, and you export the file to 1-2-3, any birthdates prior to the year 1900 are translated to negative numbers. Lotus 1-2-3 does not display these as dates, regardless of the width of the column.

Note that formats for numbers in a 1-2-3 or Symphony worksheet are not translated. You may have numbers formatted as currency with a specific number of decimal places when in 1-2-3, for example. When those numbers are imported into RapidFile, however, the currency and decimal-place formatting will not necessarily match the 1-2-3 formats. You must use the formatting options within RapidFile to choose the desired methods of displaying your data.

One final tip: If you use the memo writer to create large fields that contain text as a part of your RapidFile database, only the first 254 characters of the memo files that are linked to the database will be exported to the 1-2-3 worksheet. What is more, the text will appear in the worksheet column as one long label. To keep the label from being overwritten on the screen by successive columns when in the 1-2-3 worksheet, rearrange the fields while still in RapidFile so that the field containing the large amounts of text appears as the last field in the layout.

Lotus to RapidFile

Chapter 13

This chapter will discuss importing data from any one of three products of the Lotus Development Corporation: Lotus 1-2-3, Release 1A; Lotus 1-2-3, Release 2; and Symphony. Importing files from Release 1A of 1-2-3 is a simple process. Release 2 of 1-2-3 and Symphony require an extra step that complicates the process only slightly: These files should be converted back to the format of Release 1A before being transferred to RapidFile. This can be easily done with the Translate Utility of Symphony and Lotus 1-2-3, Release 2.

What RapidFile clearly does best is database management, and what 1-2-3 clearly does best are spreadsheet-related tasks. So if you require complex math analysis, do it while the data is in 1-2-3. (Unlike 1-2-3, RapidFile is not limited to 2048 records, so you should not find it necessary to limit the size of the 1-2-3 or Symphony worksheet before exporting the worksheet to RapidFile.) As an example of a worksheet that can be exported to RapidFile, consider the worksheet shown in Figure 13-1.

The sample worksheet is typical of a 1-2-3 worksheet in that certain fields (or columns, as they are referred to when in spreadsheet form) contain headings in the form of labels, numeric data, and formulas that result in the display of

B6: 290 READY

	A	B	C	D	E	F
1			ABC Trading Company			
2			Stock Transactions			
3						
4	Stock	Shrs	Per Share	Amount	Commission	Buyer
5						
6	IBM	290	125.625	$36,431.25	$3,643.13	Johnson, William
7	JJR	100	30.250	$3,025.00	$302.50	Atkins, Charles
8	DCD	400	56.700	$22,680.00	$2,268.00	Bennington, Sue
9	CVB	350	43.000	$15,050.00	$1,505.00	Robertson, Nancy
10	ZQX	150	38.780	$5,817.00	$581.70	Boyer, James
11	CGG	400	39.000	$15,600.00	$1,560.00	Thompson, Linda
12	THM	100	80.500	$8,050.00	$805.00	Rowe, Mike
13	QRT	300	37.725	$11,317.50	$1,131.75	Williams, Yvonne
14	KDK	700	55.000	$38,500.00	$3,850.00	Robertson, Nancy
15	ZDD	200	42.100	$8,420.00	$842.00	Johnson, William
16						
17	Totals	2990	N/A	$164,890.75	$16,489.08	
18						
19	Averages	299	54.868	$16,489.08	$1,648.91	
20						

Figure 13-1. Sample Lotus worksheet

numeric data. In the example the figures in columns B and C are actual values, but the figures in columns D and E are calculated from formulas entered in those columns. Columns A and F contain labels, or text entries. The totals and averages at the bottom of the worksheet are also based on formulas stored in cells at the bottom of the worksheet. When RapidFile converts the worksheet, the necessary calculations stored in the worksheet formulas are performed for the existing data within the worksheet. The RapidFile database that results from the conversion does not contain 1-2-3 formulas. Instead, the RapidFile database contains the numbers that appear as a result of those formulas.

TRANSFERRING A LOTUS WORKSHEET TO RAPIDFILE

To transfer data from Lotus 1-2-3 to RapidFile, perform the following four steps:

1. Copy the 1-2-3 worksheet (.WKS) file to the data disk or subdirectory containing your RapidFile data. (Be sure to specify the filename extension .WKS or .WK1.)
2. Import the file by using the option "Import file" of the File menu.
3. Edit the File Structure Table of the new database, if necessary, to change field names and types of fields.
4. Make any desired changes to the layout, sort order, and settings of the new database.

PREPARING LOTUS 1-2-3 FILES FOR USE WITH RAPIDFILE

If you are using Release 1A of Lotus 1-2-3, simply save the worksheet in the usual manner and copy the worksheet file to the data disk or subdirectory that contains your RapidFile data.

If you are using Lotus 1-2-3, Release 2, translate the file from the format of Release 2 to the format of Release 1A. To do so, load the Lotus program by inserting your Lotus System Disk in drive A or by switching to the hard-disk subdirectory that contains the Lotus 1-2-3 program. Enter

LOTUS

at the DOS prompt.

```
            Lotus Translate Utility  Version 2.01
   Copyright 1985 Lotus Development Corporation  All Rights Reserved

What do you want to translate FROM?

        1-2-3, release 1A
        1-2-3, release 2
        dBase II
        dBase III
        DIF
        Jazz
        SYMPHONY, release 1.0
        SYMPHONY, release 1.1
        VISICALC

      Move the menu pointer to your selection and press [RETURN].
             Press [ESCAPE] to leave the Translate Utility.
                  Press [HELP] for more information.
```

Figure 13-2. The Lotus Translate Utility screen

When the Lotus Access menu appears, enter T to select the "Translate" option. The Lotus Translate Utility screen appears as shown in Figure 13-2.

The Translate Utility first asks from which file you wish to translate. Use the DOWN ARROW key to highlight "1-2-3, release 2" and press RETURN to choose the option. You are then asked to which format you wish to translate. The choice "1-2-3, release 1A" is highlighted. Press RETURN to accept the option.

After pressing RETURN, a warning screen appears. The screen lists various differences between the two versions of 1-2-3. Press the ESC key to bypass this screen, and another screen listing the available files to be translated appears (see Figure 13-3).

Use the arrow keys to highlight the desired file, and press RETURN. The Lotus Translate Utility displays the same filename with a different extension: .WKS. The screen asks if this filename is acceptable for the translated file. Press RETURN to accept the filename, and answer "Yes" to the prompt **Proceed With Translation**, which appears next.

The file is translated to the format of 1-2-3, Release 1A. Press the ESC key twice to leave the Translate Utility. The worksheet file, with the extension .WKS, resides in the Lotus subdirectory of your hard disk or on the data disk containing your 1-2-3 worksheets. Copy the file to the data disk or subdirectory that contains your RapidFile databases.

PREPARING SYMPHONY FILES FOR USE WITH RAPIDFILE

If you are using Symphony, you must use a translation utility similar to the one provided with Lotus 1-2-3, Release 2, to translate Symphony files to the format of 1-2-3, Release 1A. If Symphony files are read directly into RapidFile by using RapidFile's "Import" option without being translated to 1-2-3 format, the results may or may not be acceptable.

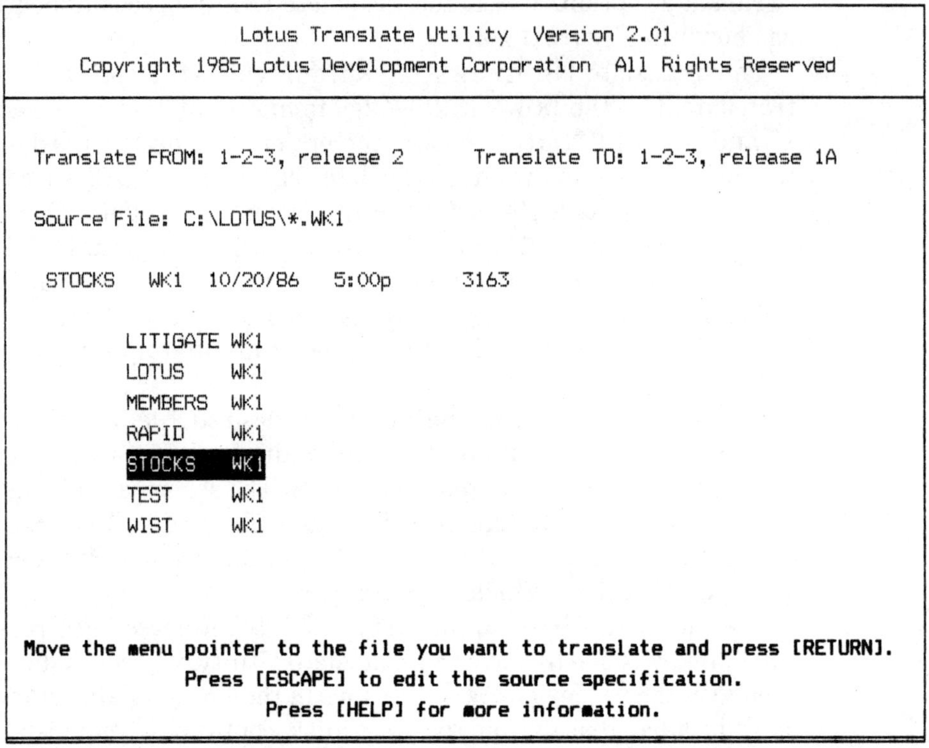

Figure 13-3. Available Lotus 1-2-3 files shown in the Translate Utility

To use the Symphony Translate Utility, load the Symphony program. Insert your Symphony Program Disk in drive A or switch to the hard-disk subdirectory that contains the Symphony program. Enter

ACCESS

at the DOS prompt.

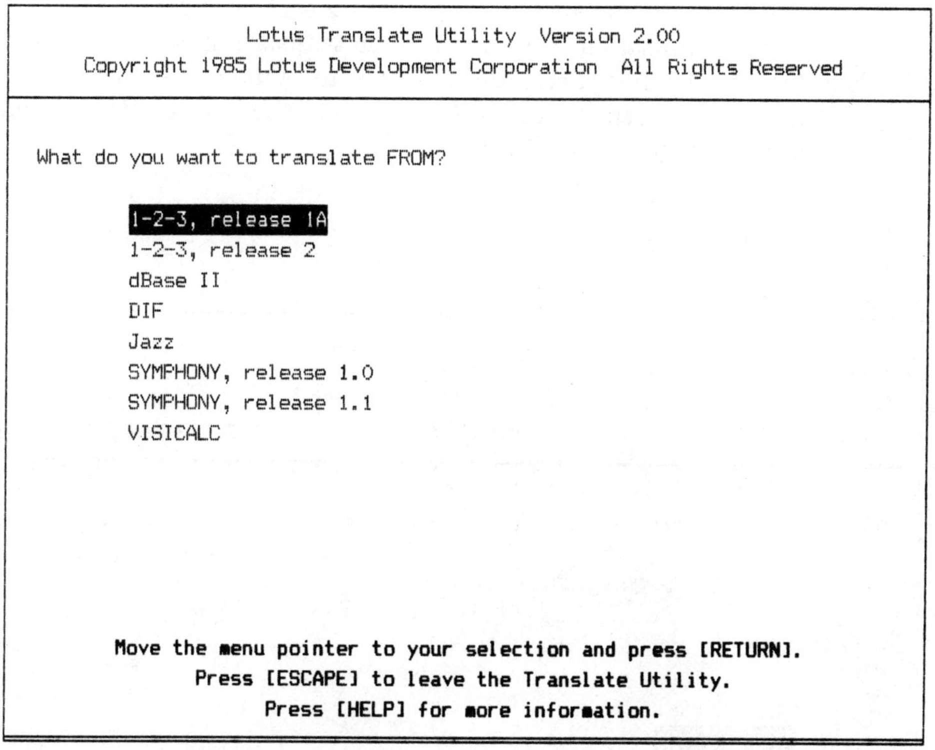

Figure 13-4. The Lotus Translate Utility screen

When the Symphony Access menu appears, enter F to select the option "File-Translate." The Lotus Translate Utility screen appears as shown in Figure 13-4.

The Translate Utility first asks from which file you wish to translate. Use the DOWN ARROW key to highlight the release of Symphony that you are using, and press RETURN to choose the option. You are then asked to which format you wish to translate. The choice "1-2-3, release 1A" is highlighted. Press

RETURN to accept this option.

After pressing RETURN, a warning screen appears that lists various limitations that apply when translating Symphony files to 1-2-3 format. Press the ESC key to bypass this screen, and another screen listing the available files to be translated appears (see Figure 13-5).

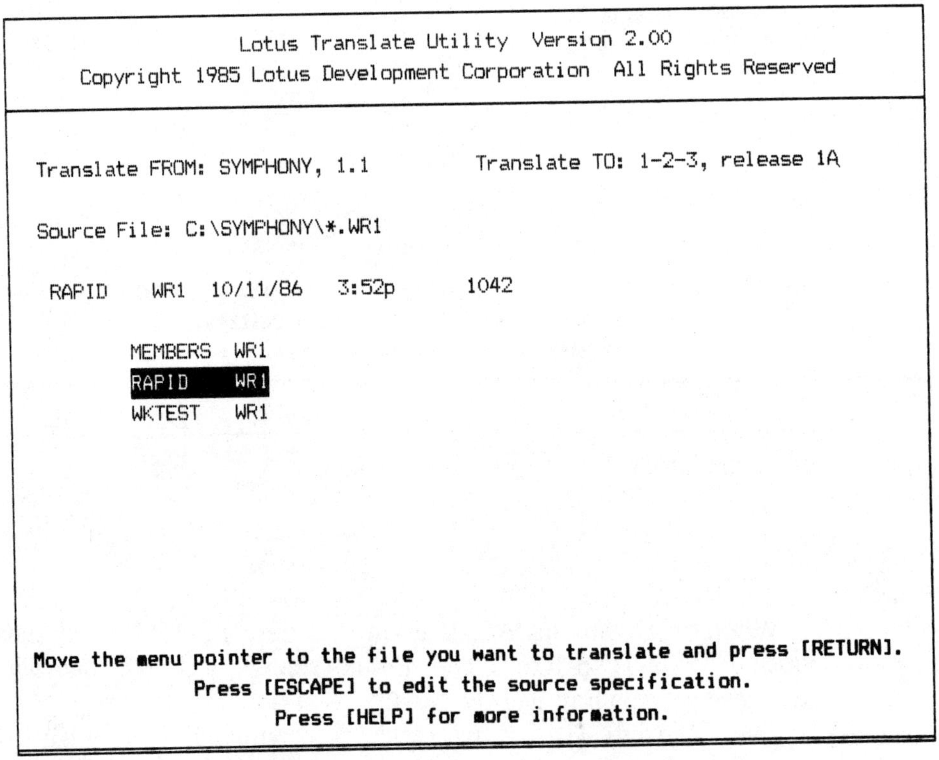

Figure 13-5. Available Symphony files shown in the Translate Utility

Use the arrow keys to highlight the desired file, and press RETURN. The Translate Utility displays the same filename, with a different extension: .WKS. The screen asks if this filename is acceptable for the translated file. Press RETURN to accept the filename, and answer "Yes" to the prompt **Proceed With Translation**, which appears next.

The file is translated to the format of 1-2-3, Release 1A. Press the ESC key twice to leave the Translate Utility. The worksheet file, with the extension .WKS, resides in the Symphony subdirectory of your hard disk or on the data disk containing your Symphony worksheets. Copy the file to the data disk or subdirectory that contains your RapidFile databases.

IMPORTING THE WORKSHEET INTO RAPIDFILE

Start RapidFile and choose "Import file" from the File menu. A submenu appears (see Figure 13-6).

The submenu that appears provides options for importing files from dBASE II, dBASE III, and dBASE III PLUS; Friday!; pfs:FILE or PFS:Professional; Lotus 1-2-3; or files with a format that is comma-delimited. The option "Lotus 1-2-3" is used to import files from Lotus 1-2-3 or from Symphony. The remaining options are covered in future chapters.

Select "Lotus 1-2-3" from the menu. A window of files that contains the extensions .WKS or .WK1 appears on the right side of the screen. (Lotus 1-2-3, Release 1A, usually stores files with the extension .WKS.) At the bottom of the screen, you are prompted to enter the name of the file. Select a file by highlighting a name or enter a filename by typing the entire name and extension.

In this example the file STOCKS.WKS is selected. Once a file name has been selected, the translation process starts and RapidFile displays the number of records translated at the bot-

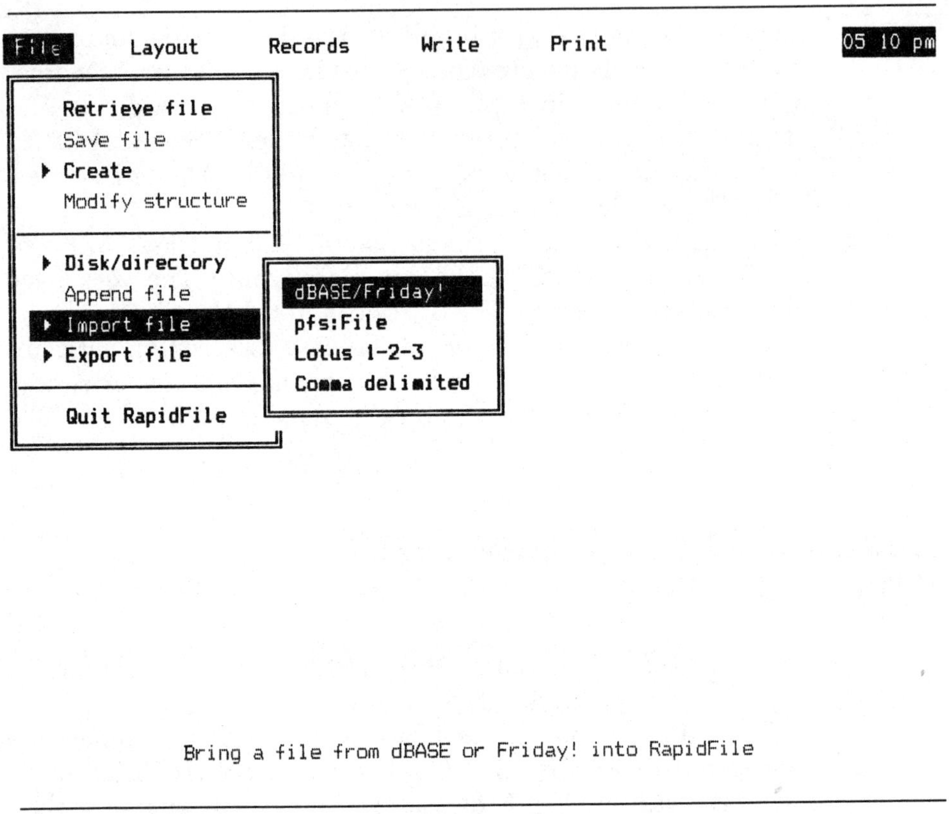

Figure 13-6. Submenu of "Import file"

tom of the screen. When the process is complete, a new database matching the structure of the 1-2-3 worksheet appears on the screen. The database that resulted from the STOCKS worksheet described previously is shown in Figure 13-7.

Once the file is in RapidFile, you may want to edit it to take full advantage of RapidFile's capabilities. The field names within the new database are Field1, Field2, Field3, and so on because Lotus 1-2-3 does not provide a method for explicitly

File Layout Records Write Print 05 29 pm

	Field1	Field2	Field3	Field4
1			ABC Trading Com	
2			Stock Transacti	
3				
4	Stock	Shrs	Per Share	Amount
5				
6	IBM	290	125.625	36431.25
7	JJR	100	30.25	3025
8	DCD	400	56.7	22680
9	CVB	350	43	15050
10	ZQX	150	38.78	5817
11	CGG	400	39	15600
12	THM	100	80.5	8050
13	QRT	300	37.725	11317.5
14	KDK	700	55	38500
15	ZDD	200	42.1	8420
16				
17	Totals	2990	N/A	164890.75

TABLE: Unsaved layout C:STOCKS.RPD Selected: 19 of 19

Figure 13-7. A Rapidfile database imported from Lotus 1-2-3

naming fields (columns). A more serious problem occurs if you attempt to use the "Totals" option of the Records menu to obtain totals and averages for the numbers. If your imported Lotus 1-2-3 file has a design like the one in the example, you will not obtain any totals because all the fields are text fields.

Consider the File Structure Table that appears for the database STOCKS when the option "Modify structure" of the File menu is used (Figure 13-8 shows the table). Although the 1-2-3 fields containing the number of shares, stock prices, and commission amounts are clearly numeric, RapidFile designated the fields as text fields. It did so because the labels at the top of the 1-2-3 columns were entered as text, so the translation process caused the new fields to be text to maintain those labels. Since you want to use the numbers as values, make the necessary changes to the File Structure Table to display numeric fields.

File Structure Table

Field Settings			Preset Layout Settings		
Field name	Type	Expression	Field Format	Table size	Form size
Field1	Text		None	15	25/1
Field2	Text		None	15	25/1
Field3	Text		None	15	25/1
Field4	Text		None	15	25/1
Field5	Text		None	15	25/1
Field6	Text		None	15	25/1

F1 HELP F2 EDIT F9 IMPLEMENT ESC to leave without changes

Figure 13-8. The File Structure Table for an imported Lotus 1-2-3 file

Also change the field names so they indicate the purpose of each field. If this is done, the 1-2-3 labels are no longer necessary and can be deleted from the RapidFile database. In our example the field names assigned during the translation process are replaced with more descriptive field names, and the field types for the fields No_Shares, Per_Share, Amount, and Commission have been changed to numeric fields, as shown in Figure 13-9.

File Structure Table

Field Settings			Preset Layout Settings		
Field name	Type	Expression	Field Format	Table size	Form size
STOCK	Text		None	15	25/1
NO_SHARES	Numeric		None	10	10/1
PER_SHARE	Numeric		None	10	10/1
AMOUNT	Numeric		None	10	10/1
COMMISSION	Numeric		None	10	10/1
BUYER	Text		None	15	25/1

F1 HELP F2 EDIT F9 IMPLEMENT ESC to leave without changes

Figure 13-9. The modified File Structure Table

You may also want to delete certain records from the RapidFile database. Any rows in the 1-2-3 worksheet that contain blank lines or headers for the columns appear as unwanted records in the RapidFile database. You can easily delete these records by tagging them with the F5 (TAG) key, and then using the "Delete" option of the Records menu to delete all tagged records. When these changes are made to the database in the example, the result is as shown in Figure 13-10.

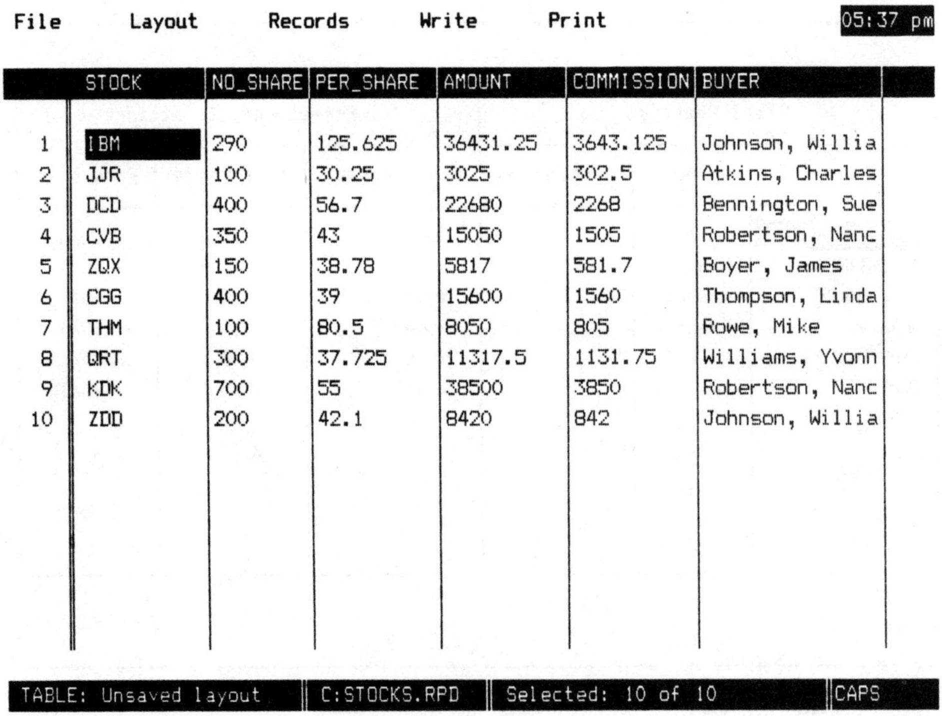

File   Layout   Records   Write   Print   05:37 pm

	STOCK	NO_SHARE	PER_SHARE	AMOUNT	COMMISSION	BUYER
1	IBM	290	125.625	36431.25	3643.125	Johnson, Willia
2	JJR	100	30.25	3025	302.5	Atkins, Charles
3	DCD	400	56.7	22680	2268	Bennington, Sue
4	CVB	350	43	15050	1505	Robertson, Nanc
5	ZQX	150	38.78	5817	581.7	Boyer, James
6	CGG	400	39	15600	1560	Thompson, Linda
7	THM	100	80.5	8050	805	Rowe, Mike
8	QRT	300	37.725	11317.5	1131.75	Williams, Yvonn
9	KDK	700	55	38500	3850	Robertson, Nanc
10	ZDD	200	42.1	8420	842	Johnson, Willia

TABLE: Unsaved layout | C:STOCKS.RPD | Selected: 10 of 10 | CAPS

Figure 13-10. RapidFile database after changes are completed

HELPFUL HINTS

You can save some clean-up work to the RapidFile database by doing some preparation within the worksheet before importing 1-2-3. For example, Lotus 1-2-3 macros will clutter your database by appearing as fields of text. As discussed, headers entered as labels present the same problem. While in the 1-2-3 worksheet, you may want to specify a range of data that contains only the information you need and export that range of data to a separate worksheet file. Then translate that file to RapidFile format with the "Import" option of the File menu and add the necessary field names to the database.

To export a range of a 1-2-3 worksheet as a separate worksheet file, simply get into your worksheet in the usual manner and use "/ File Xtract." Select "Formulas" as the next option, and then enter a name for the new worksheet. Finally, place the cursor at the start of the range of cells to be stored in the new worksheet, enter a period to anchor the range, move the cursor to the end of the range of cells, and then press RETURN. The new worksheet is created, and you can now use it within RapidFile.

One major advantage of performing this type of preparation before you leave 1-2-3 is that if you transfer columns of numbers that do not contain any headings to RapidFile, they will be imported into the new database as numeric fields. It will then be unnecessary to use the option "Modify structure" to change fields from text to numeric to obtain proper totals.

Matching Worksheet and Database Fields

One of the most common problems that occurs when transferring data between 1-2-3 and RapidFile is that the fields of the worksheet and the database do not match exactly. For example, a 1-2-3 worksheet may contain fields (columns) for last name, first name, address, city, state, ZIP code, and salary. A RapidFile database may contain fields for last name, first name, date hired, salary, address, city, state, and ZIP code. In such cases, import the worksheet into RapidFile and then append records from the newly created RapidFile database into another existing RapidFile database. Use the option "Append file" of the File menu to perform this task. The alternative is to rearrange the columns while in 1-2-3 to match the design of the database. Unless you are proficient at moving columns in 1-2-3, you will probably find it less troublesome to match the fields while in RapidFile.

Users of Symphony should also keep in mind that you cannot translate Symphony files that are password-protected to 1-2-3 format. If you are using a password-protected Symphony worksheet, extract the range of data to another worksheet that is not password-protected. Then use the Translate Utility provided with Symphony to translate the file to 1-2-3 format.

The dBASE Connection

Chapter 14

RapidFile shares files with versions of dBASE with a minimal amount of difficulty. RapidFile can import files from dBASE II, dBASE III, dBASE III PLUS, and Friday!—all products of Ashton-Tate. RapidFile has the ability to export files to dBASE II, dBASE III, and dBASE III PLUS. You cannot transfer data from RapidFile back to Friday!, but this limitation should not present a problem. If you are upgrading to RapidFile from Friday!, you will probably want to convert all your Friday! files to RapidFile format and discontinue the use of Friday! in favor of RapidFile. Files are transferred between RapidFile and other Ashton-Tate products using the options "Import file" and "Export file" of the File menu.

THE STEPS OF A RAPIDFILE-TO-dBASE TRANSFER

Transferring data from RapidFile to dBASE consists of the following four steps:

1. Prepare the database for export by selecting the desired records, implementing any desired sort order, and changing the layout so only the desired fields are visible.
2. Export the file, using the option "Export file" of the File menu.
3. Copy the resultant .DBF database file onto your dBASE data disk or into the appropriate subdirectory.
4. When in dBASE, load the database in the usual manner.

PREPARING THE RAPIDFILE DATABASE FOR THE TRANSFER

When you tell RapidFile to export records to dBASE, RapidFile translates all selected records into a dBASE-compatible database that is in the same order as the records in the RapidFile database. All fields shown in the layout in use are included in the exported database. If necessary, customize the layout so that the resultant dBASE database contains only those fields you need. If only a portion of the RapidFile database is to be exported to dBASE, use the "Select" option of the Records menu to identify match criteria for the records to be exported to dBASE.

EXPORTING THE FILE TO dBASE

As an example, export the database MEMBERS to a dBASE III PLUS database. (The dBASE III option of the "Import file" and "Export file" submenus can be used for dBASE III or for dBASE III PLUS.) Start RapidFile, if necessary, and load the database MEMBERS. Open the Layout menu with CONTROL-L and select the option "Use/Save layout."

Choose "Use layout" from the next submenu and select "Mailing" from the list of available layouts. The database appears in the "Mailing" layout that you designed previously (see Figure 14-1).

File Layout Records Write Print 07:01 pm

	LASTNAME	FIRSTNAME	ADDRESS	CITY	ST	ZIP
1	Askew	Lonnie	103 Maple Avenue West	Pittskill	NY	12512
2	Baker	Benjamin	5206 Lyngate Court	Berkeley	CA	95264
3	Baker	Jeanette	153 South Lakes Drive	Reston	VA	22090
4	Block	Paul	1415 South Shore Drive	Chicago	IL	60617
5	Brown	Nicole	106 Crestwood Drive Apt. 5B	Chicago	IL	60610
6	Harris	Charles	9 Park Circle	Sterling	VA	22070
7	Hayes	Cynthia	9631 Champion Court	Austin	TX	76801
8	Johnson, Jr.	Lamar	4005 Williamsburg Court Apt 6	Cambridge	MA	02139

TABLE: Unsaved layout | C:MEMBERS.RPD | Selected: 18 of 18

File: "MEMBERS.RPD" saved. Remaining space = 3362 K bytes.

Figure 14-1. Database MEMBERS in "Mailing" layout

To export the file to a database compatible with dBASE III or dBASE III PLUS, open the File menu with CONTROL-F and select the option "Export file." From the submenu select "dBASE III." (Another option on this menu can be used to produce files for use with dBASE II, if desired.)

A list of files with the extension .DBF appears on the right side of your screen, if any are present on your disk. At the same time you are prompted in the Message Area to enter the name of the file. In this case enter

DBASE

and press RETURN.

A database compatible with dBASE III and dBASE III PLUS is created and stored on the default drive. The filename includes the extension .DBF. Copy this file onto your dBASE data disk or into the hard-disk subdirectory that contains your dBASE files.

USING THE FILE WITHIN dBASE

Load dBASE III or dBASE III PLUS in the normal manner and open the database with the command USE DBASE from the dot prompt. Enter

BROWSE

and you see the dBASE database as shown in Figure 14-2.

One major advantage quickly becomes apparent: you need not worry about translating the RapidFile layout to column (field) locations in dBASE. When the option "Export file" of the RapidFile menu is used to create a dBASE-compatible file, the file automatically receives a structure that is a precise match of

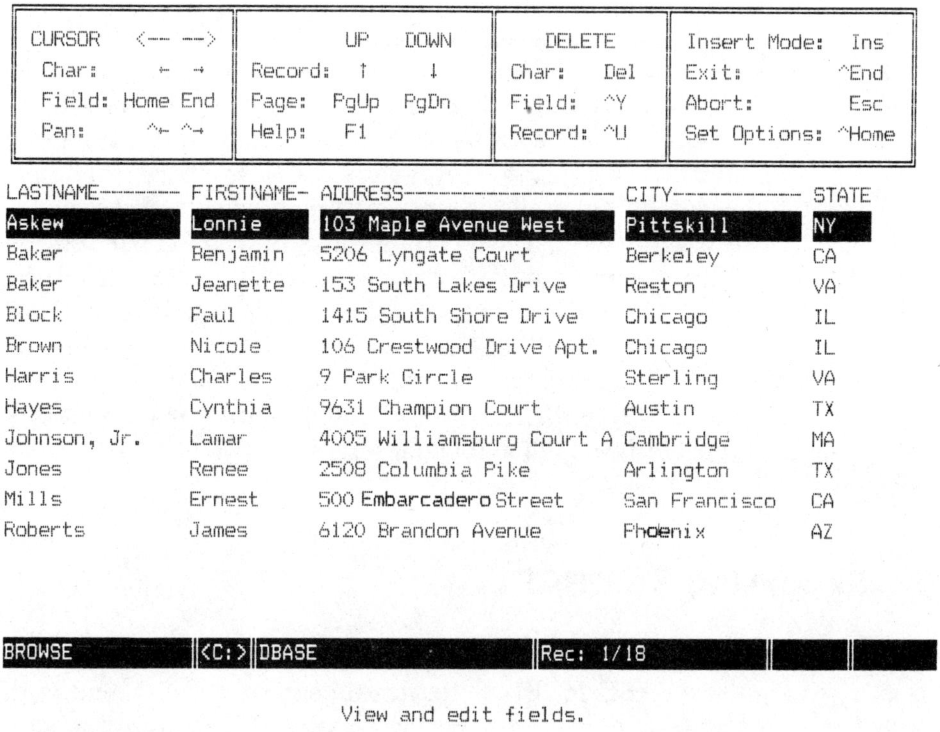

Figure 14-2. dBASE III or dBASE III PLUS database imported from RapidFile

the RapidFile layout. If you wish to add the records to an existing dBASE database that has the same field names but a different structure than that of the RapidFile database, use the APPEND FROM command within dBASE to transfer the records from one database to another. (Details about this process are in your dBASE documentation.)

A Warning

RapidFile permits up to 250 fields per database, but dBASE III and dBASE III PLUS are limited to 128 fields per database. Since dBASE III and dBASE III PLUS are relational databases that can work with more than one database at a time, you can split a large RapidFile database into more than one dBASE database by designing different layouts that contain the desired fields and using those layouts when exporting the files. Choose one or more common fields to include in all the layouts, and then use the relational commands in dBASE III or dBASE III PLUS to link the various databases on the common fields. Also, dBASE has a record limit of 4000 characters (compared to RapidFile's limit of 7500), so limit each record in the exported layout to 4000 characters.

Exporting To dBASE II

The process of exporting is nearly identical if you are exporting a file to dBASE II. From RapidFile open the File menu with CONTROL-F and select the option "Export file." From the submenu select "dBASE II." Enter a name for the dBASE II-compatible file and the file is created. You can copy that file to your dBASE II data disk or to the dBASE subdirectory, load dBASE II, and open the file by using the dBASE command USE <filename>. Enter

BROWSE

and the dBASE II display of the database is similar to the one shown with dBASE III or dBASE III PLUS (see Figure 14-3).

Note that there are limitations in transferring a RapidFile database to dBASE II because of the limitations of dBASE II. dBASE II does not support a specific type of field for dates as do RapidFile, dBASE III, and dBASE III PLUS. If your RapidFile database contains dates, they will be stored as

RECORD # :00001				
LASTNAME--------	FIRSTNAME-	ADDRESS----------------------	CITY----------	ST
Askew	Lonnie	103 Maple Avenue West	Pittskill	NY
Baker	Benjamin	5206 Lyngate Court	Berkeley	CA
Baker	Jeanette	153 South Lakes Drive	Reston	VA
Block	Paul	1415 South Shore Drive	Chicago	IL
Brown	Nicole	106 Crestwood Drive Apt. 5B	Chicago	IL
Harris	Charles	9 Park Circle	Sterling	VA
Hayes	Cynthia	9631 Champion Court	Austin	TX
Johnson, Jr.	Lamar	4005 Williamsburg Court Apt	Cambridge	MA
Jones	Renee	2508 Columbia Pike	Arlington	TX
Mills	Ernest	500 Embarcadero Street	San Francisc	CA
Roberts	James	6120 Brandon Avenue	Phoenix	AZ
Roberts	Norma	6120 Brandon Avenue	Phoenix	AZ
Roberts	Terry	6120 Brandon Avenue	Phoenix	AZ
Sand	Lucy	142 Haven Way	Annapolis	MD
Schultz	Bobby	1338 Redskin Drive	Herndon	VA
Shaw	Michael	7105 Little River Lane	Annandale	FL
Sloan	Wanda	2723 Hunters Woods Plaza	Reston	VA
Smith	Larry	6505 Brandon Avenue	Los Angeles	CA

Figure 14-3. dBASE II database imported from RapidFile

numeric fields in dBASE II in the format YYYYMMDD. For example, November 14, 1988, would be stored as the number 19881114. This format makes it easy to sort the data, but it is obviously not the most visually pleasing format.

dBASE II is also fairly limited in the number of fields that can be present in a database. The maximum in dBASE II is 32 fields per record; RapidFile allows 250 fields per record. If you export a RapidFile database containing more than 32 fields to dBASE II, only the first 32 fields appear in the dBASE database. To get around this problem, split the RapidFile database into more than one dBASE II database by designing different layouts that contain the desired fields. Use those layouts to export to more than one dBASE II database file. Choose one or more common fields to include in all the layouts, and use the relational commands of dBASE II to link the various databases on the common fields.

Large Text Fields and dBASE

Suppose you are working with a layout that contains large text fields (such as a form with a comment field) and you link memo writer files to those fields to store more than 254 characters in a field. When you export the database to any dBASE program, only the first 254 characters of the memo appear in the dBASE database. The resultant text is stored in a character field with a length of 254 characters. Figure 14-4 shows BOOKS, the RapidFile database created in Chapter 8, after export to dBASE III PLUS. Note that the comment field is contained within a dBASE character field with a maximum length of 254 characters.

The export process does not automatically make use of the memo fields that can be used within dBASE III and dBASE III PLUS. If you are exporting a RapidFile database to dBASE III or dBASE III PLUS and you desperately wish to use the contents of linked memo writer files in the dBASE memo fields, perform the following additional steps:

1. Get into the RapidFile memo writer, open the File menu, and retrieve the memo file that you wish to store within a memo field in the dBASE database.

2. Open the Print menu, select "Destination," and choose "Disk" to write a DOS text file. Close the submenu with ESC and select the option "Begin printing." The resulting file has the same filename as the memo file, but it has the extension .TXT.

```
TITLE:       dBASE Tips and Traps

AUTHOR:      Andersen, Cooper, & Dempsey

DESCRIPTIO   (BOOK2.MMO)1. Computer language.  2. Usage techniques.  Covers use o
             f dBASE III, database management software for IBM PCs and compatible
             s.  Written in concise tips and traps format.  Techniques on plannin
             g applications; data entry and updating; relating

EDIT         ||<C:>||BOOKS             ||Rec: 1/2         ||Ins ||
```

Figure 14-4. Database BOOKS exported to dBASE III PLUS

3. Exit RapidFile and copy the file you just created (the file with the extension .TXT) to the dBASE data disk or subdirectory. Load dBASE in the normal manner and open the database. Move to the record to which you wish to add the memo, place the cursor in the memo field, and press CONTROL-PGDN to enter the dBASE Word Processor.
4. Press CONTROL-K R. At the top of the screen, a prompt appears that asks for the filename. Enter the name of the file with the .TXT extension that you created when in RapidFile.

5. The memo text is read into the dBASE database, and you can press CONTROL-END to store the modified record. (If the margins are not what you would like them to be, you will find it to be less trouble to change the left margin to zero in RapidFile and then print the memo to disk before transferring the file to dBASE III or dBASE III PLUS.)

You have to go through this process for every linked memo file in RapidFile that you want to store in a dBASE memo field. Obviously, it is time-consuming, and you must decide whether having the added text in the dBASE III database is worth the added effort.

TRANSFERRING dBASE OR FRIDAY! TO RAPIDFILE

Suppose you are going in the other direction, from an existing dBASE or Friday! database to RapidFile. The steps in this process are

1. While in dBASE, perform any preparation necessary to bring the file within the size limitations of RapidFile. This should be necessary only with very large dBASE III or dBASE III PLUS databases that contain more than 64,000 records.
2. Copy the database file onto your RapidFile data disk or into the subdirectory named \RAPID \RFDATA.
3. Start RapidFile and choose "Import file" from the File menu. Select the option "dBASE/Friday!" from the submenu and enter the appropriate filename. The file is translated to RapidFile format and displayed in a table layout.

```
Structure for database: C:lawyers.dbf
Number of data records:        98
Date of last update   : 07/17/86

Field  Field Name  Type       Width    Dec
    1  NAME        Character     50
    2  ADDRESS1    Character     30
    3  ADDRESS2    Character     15
    4  CITY        Character     15
    5  STATE       Character      2
    6  ZIP         Character     10
    7  CONTACT     Character     32
    8  TITLE       Character     15
    9  CTLNAME     Character     15
   10  PHONE       Character     12
   11  LARGE       Logical        1
   12  COMMENTS    Memo          10
   13  SENTFLYER   Logical        1
   14  MEDIUM      Logical        1
** Total **                     210
```

Figure 14-5. Sample dBASE III PLUS database structure

Suppose, for example, that the design (or structure) of a dBASE III PLUS database used to maintain a mailing list is as shown in Figure 14-5.

When the steps outlined previously are used to import this dBASE III PLUS database into RapidFile, the resulting file structure is as shown in Figure 14-6. A record from the actual file appears in Figure 14-7, where it is shown in form layout.

Note that any dBASE files present on your data disk or in the default directory (the files with the extension .DBF) now appear in RapidFile's directory display. You can load files with .DBF extensions directly by using the option "Retrieve file" from the File menu. The first time you save the file it will be saved in RapidFile format with the extension .RPD.

File Structure Table

Field Settings			Preset Layout Settings		
Field name	Type	Expression	Field Format	Table size	Form size
NAME	Text		None	15	25/1
ADDRESS1	Text		None	15	25/1
ADDRESS2	Text		None	15	25/1
CITY	Text		None	15	25/1
STATE	Text		None	15	25/1
ZIP	Text		None	15	25/1
CONTACT	Text		None	15	25/1
TITLE	Text		None	15	25/1
CTLNAME	Text		None	15	25/1
PHONE	Text		None	15	25/1
LARGE	Text		None	15	25/1

F1 HELP F2 EDIT F9 IMPLEMENT ESC to leave without changes

Figure 14-6. File structure of imported file in RapidFile

About the Data

After transferring data from an existing dBASE database to a RapidFile database, you may want to edit the entries in the File Structure Table to change the field formats. Note that logical fields in a dBASE III or dBASE III PLUS database are translated to text fields in RapidFile and that they contain the letter T (for true) or F (for false).

```
File      Layout      Records      Write      Print                    06:56 pm

* 1 *

NAME          : Amram and Hahn, P.C.
ADDRESS1      : 1155 15th Street, NW
ADDRESS2      : Suite 1100
CITY          : Washington
STATE         : DC
ZIP           : 20005
CONTACT       : Managing Partner
TITLE         :
CTLNAME       : Counselor
PHONE         : 555 1212
LARGE         : F
SENTFLYER     : T
MEDIUM        :


FORM: Unsaved layout   || C:LAWYERS.RPD || Selected: 98 of 98 ||
```

Figure 14-7. Record within imported dBASE file

Dealing with Memo Fields

If you are using memo fields within a dBASE III or dBASE III PLUS database, the memo fields are not translated during the import process. The fields are simply dropped from the RapidFile database created during the translation. If you must use the memo field data in a RapidFile database, do so by adding a text field to the RapidFile database to hold linked memo writer files, and then perform the following steps:

1. Load dBASE III or dBASE III PLUS in the normal manner and open the database. Edit the record containing the memo field you wish to transfer to the RapidFile database. Place the cursor in the memo field and enter CONTROL-PGDN to access the dBASE Word Processor.
2. Press CONTROL-K W to access a prompt at the top of the screen that asks for the filename of the text file you want to write. Enter the name you choose and it receives the extension .TXT unless you specify a different extension. In this case use the default extension .TXT.
3. Exit dBASE and copy the text file you just created onto your RapidFile data disk or into the subdirectory \RAPID \RFDATA. Load RapidFile and retrieve the database that has been imported from dBASE.
4. Place the cursor on the desired record at the new field you added to store the memo text and press F4 (ZOOM). The memo writer screen appears.
5. Open the File menu with CONTROL-F and choose the option "Retrieve file." When prompted for a filename, enter the name of the text file you created in dBASE, and be sure to include the extension .TXT. The contents of the dBASE memo field appear in the memo writer. A graphic character may be at the end of the file. Delete it by placing the cursor on the character and pressing the DEL key. Press F4 again to exit the memo writer and return to the layout. When you confirm the save process, the file is stored with the same name you assigned the file when in dBASE, but it has the extension .MMO.

Clearly, this is a complicated process, and it must be repeated for every record in the dBASE database if you wish to have the contents of the memo fields in your RapidFile database. Unfortunately, the only other option is to enter the data manually into RapidFile text fields. If the memos in dBASE are not lengthy, entering them manually may be less time consuming.

The pfs Connection

Chapter 15

RapidFile has the ability to transfer files to pfs:FILE, a database manager produced by Software Publishing Corporation. A form-oriented file manager, pfs:FILE has a loyal following because it is easy to use. However, it lacks many of the capabilities that RapidFile has, including the ability to display data using a number of different layouts, the ability to sort on numeric or date fields, and the ability to generate complex reports without the use of an optional, extra-cost software package. If you have been a regular user of pfs:FILE, you will probably find it to your advantage to translate all your pfs:FILE databases to RapidFile format and to work with them in RapidFile. If you maintain file compatibility with others who are using pfs:FILE, you will find that moving back and forth between the two packages is a simple matter.

IBM Filing Assistant, a database manager sold by IBM Corporation, is similar to pfs:FILE. All procedures outlined within this chapter can also be used with IBM Filing Assistant. Note that files can be translated between RapidFile and PFS:Professional in the same manner.

```
Employee #: 002                               Hired: 85/01/06
Name:Andy Robinson
Address:1515 Great White Way
City:New York                                 State: NY                Zip: 11413
Job Title:Assistant Manager
Salary:1700

File: EMPLOYEE                        FORM 2                                Page 1

F2-Print Form    F3-Remove Form    F5-Date    F6-Time                  F10-Continue
```

Figure 15-1. Employee database in pfs:FILE

TRANSFERRING A pfs:FILE DATABASE TO RAPIDFILE

A transfer of a pfs:FILE database to RapidFile encompasses the following two steps:

1. Copy the pfs:FILE database file to your RapidFile data disk or into the hard-disk subdirectory containing your RapidFile data files (\RAPID \RFDATA).

2. Start RapidFile and choose "Import file" from the File menu. Select the option "pfs:FILE" from the submenu and enter the appropriate filename. The file is translated to RapidFile format and appears in a table layout.

As an example, consider the pfs:FILE database shown in Figure 15-1, which is used to maintain a list of employees. When the steps outlined previously are used to import the database into RapidFile, the resulting file contains a file structure as shown in Figure 15-2. The same record is shown as it appears in a form layout in the RapidFile database in Figure 15-3.

File Structure Table

Field Settings			Preset Layout Settings		
Field name	Type	Expression	Field Format	Table size	Form size
Employee:	Text		None	15	25/1
Hired:	Text		None	15	25/1
Name:	Text		None	15	25/1
Address:	Text		None	15	25/1
City:	Text		None	15	25/1
State:	Text		None	15	25/1
Zip:	Text		None	15	25/1
Job_Title:	Text		None	15	25/1
Salary:	Text		None	15	25/1

F1 HELP F2 EDIT F9 IMPLEMENT ESC to leave without changes

Figure 15-2. File Structure Table for imported pfs:FILE database

Figure 15-3. Sample record in form layout in RapidFile

About the Data

Because pfs:FILE is limited to storing and displaying data as character fields, you will probably want to make some changes to the design of the database once it has been imported into RapidFile. Although fields in a pfs:FILE database may have been used to store numeric values, they will still be imported as text fields, which means you are not able to perform any calculations on those fields. Choose the option "Modify structure" of the File menu to get to the File Structure Table and change any fields containing numbers to numeric fields. In terms of capacity, pfs:FILE is more limited than RapidFile, so you will not run into any problems with pfs:FILE databases being too large for RapidFile.

TRANSFERRING A RAPIDFILE DATABASE TO pfs:FILE

Transfer a RapidFile database to pfs:FILE by following these four steps:

1. Prepare the database for export by selecting the desired records, by implementing any desired sort order, and by changing the layout so that only the desired fields are shown.
2. Export the file, using the option "Export file" of the File menu.
3. Copy the resultant file onto your pfs:FILE data disk or into the appropriate subdirectory.
4. Load pfs:FILE and select the database file in the usual manner.

PREPARING THE RAPIDFILE DATABASE FOR THE TRANSFER

When you tell RapidFile to export records in a database to a pfs:FILE database, RapidFile translates all selected records into a pfs:FILE-compatible database in which the records appear in the same order as they do in RapidFile. All fields shown in the layout in use are included in the exported database. If necessary, customize the layout so that the resultant pfs:FILE database contains only those fields you need. You are limited to a maximum of 32,000 records in a pfs:FILE database, whereas RapidFile can handle more than 64,000 records. pfs:FILE also stores all data as character fields, so you will not be able to perform sorts or totals on numeric data once you are using the data in pfs:FILE. If only a portion of the RapidFile database is to be exported, use the "Select" option of the Records menu to identify match criteria for the records to be exported to the pfs:FILE database.

EXPORTING THE FILE TO pfs:FILE

As an example, export the database MEMBERS to a pfs:FILE database by using the option "pfs:FILE" of the "Import file" and "Export file" submenus. Start RapidFile, if necessary, and open the database MEMBERS. Open the Layout menu with CONTROL-L and select the option "Use/Save layout."

Choose "Use layout" from the next submenu and select "Mailing" from the list of available layouts. The file appears in the "Mailing" layout you designed previously (see Figure 15-4).

To export the file to a pfs:FILE-compatible database, open the File menu with CONTROL-F and select the option "Export file." From the submenu select "pfs:FILE."

A list of files with the extension .PFS (if any are present) along with any files having no extensions appears on the right side of your screen. At the same time you are prompted in the Message Area to enter the name of the file. For the purposes of the example, enter

PFSTEST

File Layout Records Write Print 07:01 pm

	LASTNAME	FIRSTNAME	ADDRESS	CITY	ST	ZIP
1	Askew	Lonnie	103 Maple Avenue West	Pittskill	NY	12512
2	Baker	Benjamin	5206 Lyngate Court	Berkeley	CA	95264
3	Baker	Jeanette	153 South Lakes Drive	Reston	VA	22090
4	Block	Paul	1415 South Shore Drive	Chicago	IL	60617
5	Brown	Nicole	106 Crestwood Drive Apt. 5B	Chicago	IL	60610
6	Harris	Charles	9 Park Circle	Sterling	VA	22070
7	Hayes	Cynthia	9631 Champion Court	Austin	TX	76801
8	Johnson, Jr.	Lamar	4005 Williamsburg Court Apt 6	Cambridge	MA	02139

TABLE: Unsaved layout | C:MEMBERS.RPD | Selected: 18 of 18

File: "MEMBERS.RPD" saved. Remaining space = 3362 K bytes.

Figure 15-4. "Mailing" layout

and press RETURN. The file is created, and it is assigned the name PFSTEST.PFS. Copy this file onto your pfs:FILE data disk or into the appropriate hard-disk subdirectory.

```
LASTNAME Askew
FIRSTNAME Lonnie
ADDRESS 103 Maple Avenue West
CITY Pittskill
STATE NY
ZIP 12512
TYPE ADULT

--------------------------------------------------------------------------------
File: C:MEMBERS.PFS                 FORM 1                              Page 1

F2-Print Form     F3-Remove Form     F5-Date     F6-Time               F10-Continue
```

Figure 15-5. Imported database in pfs:FILE

USING THE FILE WITHIN pfs:FILE

If you have pfs:FILE, load the program in the normal manner and select option 4, "Search/Update," from the pfs:FILE Function menu. As a filename, enter

PFSTEST.PFS

(include a drive letter if you are using a hard disk), and press F10 to proceed.

The pfs:FILE form appears. Press PGDN and then F10 to display the first record in the database. In the case of the database MAILING, which you exported to pfs:FILE format, the pfs:FILE form resembles Figure 15-5.

About the Data

Since pfs:FILE defines all information as text, the fields contain character data in the format in which it was exported from RapidFile. Dates maintain the format of the RapidFile layout, but you cannot sort on them when in pfs:FILE. Fields of text can contain up to the maximum allowable pfs:FILE field size, which is 254 characters. Memo fields linked to a field in RapidFile will not be exported to a pfs:FILE database.

Interfacing with Other Software

Chapter 16

The ability to exchange information with other programs enhances the power of RapidFile. In addition to the specific packages discussed in previous chapters, RapidFile can exchange data with many other personal computer programs. One limitation to RapidFile's ability to transfer programs, however, is that the other programs must be able to transfer information in a format acceptable to RapidFile.

You can transfer information between RapidFile and other programs using the *comma-delimited format,* a common method of file transfer among IBM-compatible PCs. Comma-delimited format files are files composed of ASCII text in a special format. The acronym ASCII stands for American Standard Code for Information Interchange, an international method of representing information in computers. Text files created by word processors and by RapidFile when you select "Disk" as the print destination during a printing operation are stored as ASCII files. You will use ASCII files if you merge the contents of a RapidFile database with a document created by a word processor.

ABOUT COMMA-DELIMITED FORMAT

ASCII files in comma-delimited format are composed of records in which the fields are surrounded by quotation marks and are separated from other fields by commas. Each record occupies a separate line, so each record is followed by a carriage return. Comma-delimited files have the form shown in Figure 16-1. The options "Export file" and "Import file" of the File menu can be used to transfer files in comma-delimited format. To export a RapidFile database in comma-delimited format, perform the following steps:

1. Prepare the database for export by selecting the desired records, choosing a sort order (if necessary), and changing the layout so that the desired fields are visible.
2. Export the file, using the "Export file" option of the File menu.
3. Copy the resultant file (which receives the extension .TXT, unless you specify otherwise) to the data disk or subdirectory that will be used with the other software package.
4. Load the other software package and perform the steps necessary with that package to import a comma-delimited file.

As an example, use a predefined layout with the database MEMBERS to export a file in comma-delimited format. The "Mailing" layout of the database MEMBERS contains seven specific fields and will serve as the layout in the example. Load RapidFile, if necessary, and retrieve the database MEMBERS. Open the Layout menu with CONTROL-L and select the option "Use/Save layout." Choose "Use layout" from the submenu and highlight MAILING from the list of predefined layouts. The table form changes to the "Mailing" layout that you defined previously.

```
"Askew","Lonnie","103 Maple Avenue West","Pittskill","NY","12512","ADULT"
"Baker","Benjamin"$"5206 Lyngate Court","Berkeley","CA","95264","ADULT"
"Baker","Jeanette","153 South Lakes Drive","Reston","VA","22090","STUDENT"
"Block","Paul","1415 South Shore Drive","Chicago","IL","60617","ADULT"
"Brown","Nicole","106 Crestwood Drive Apt. 5B","Chicago","IL","60610","ADULT"
"Harris","Charles","9 Park Circle","Sterling","VA","22070","STUDENT"
"Hayes","Cynthia","9631 Champion Court","Austin","TX","76801","CHARTER"
"Johnson","Lamar","4005 Williamsburg Court Apt 6","Cambridge","MA","02139","ADULT"
"Jones","Renee","2508 Columbia Pike","Arlington","TX","75780","ADULT"
"Mills","Ernest","500 Embarcadero Street","San Francisco","CA","95002","ADULT"
"Roberts","James","6120 Brandon Avenue","Phoenix","AZ","80555","ADULT"
"Roberts","Norma","6120 Brandon Avenue","Phoenix","AZ","80555","ADULT"
"Roberts","Terry","6120 Brandon Avenue","Phoenix","AZ","80555","ADULT"
"Sand","Lucy","142 Haven Way","Annapolis","MD","18955","LIFETIME"
"Schultz","Bobby","1338 Redskin Drive","Herndon","VA","22070","STUDENT"
"Shaw","Michael","7105 Little River Lane","Annandale","FL","30508","ADULT"
"Sloan","Wanda","2723 Hunters Woods Plaza","Reston","VA","22091","ADULT"
"Smith","Larry","6505 Brandon Avenue","Los Angeles","CA","90055","CHARTER"
```

Figure 16-1. A comma-delimited file

To export this file in comma-delimited format, open the File menu with CONTROL-F and choose "Export file." From the submenu choose "Comma delimited." A window of files with the extension .TXT appears and you are prompted to enter a filename. Enter

COMMAS.TXT

and press RETURN. The file is translated into the comma-delimited format.

Use the DOS command TYPE from the DOS level to examine the contents of the file. To get to DOS, open the File menu with CONTROL-F and choose "Disk/directory." Then choose "Access DOS" from the submenu. From the DOS prompt enter

TYPE MEMBERS.TXT

and the file is displayed on your screen. It should resemble Figure 16-1. From the DOS prompt enter

EXIT

to get back to RapidFile.

Many other database management programs and some programs for mainframes and minicomputer systems are capable of dealing with data that is stored in comma-delimited format. Some of the more popular packages that can accept data in comma-delimited format include R:base 4000, R:base 5000, and PC-FILE III. You will need to refer to the operator's manuals provided with the particular software package to determine precisely how comma-delimited files can be read by the software package you are using.

Some programs use fixed field lengths and allocate disk space based on the field lengths specified in the program for each record. If the program to which you are exporting data uses fixed field lengths, trim the field widths in the layout of the RapidFile database to the minimum possible to save disk space.

IMPORTING FILES

You can import foreign files that are stored in the comma-delimited format by following a process that is similar to the one used to export files. To import files, perform the following steps:

1. Perform the steps necessary with the other package to create a comma-delimited file. Copy that file to your RapidFile data disk or hard-disk subdirectory.
2. Start RapidFile and choose "Import file" from the File menu. Select "Comma delimited" from the submenu and enter the appropriate filename. The file is translated to RapidFile format and displayed in a table layout.

Once you have transferred the data into RapidFile, you will probably want to edit the File Structure Table. To do so, choose the option "Modify structure" of the File menu. Comma-delimited files do not contain any formatting and field identification information, so you will have to identify numeric and date fields in the new database. The fields receive the names Field_1, Field_2, Field_3, and so on. You will probably want to change the field names so they are more descriptive of the contents.

TRANSFERRING ASCII TEXT FILES TO OTHER WORD PROCESSORS

In addition to exporting data in a comma-delimited format, you can also export data as ordinary ASCII text by specifying the "Disk" option when choosing a destination for printing. This option will prove useful if you must insert data from a RapidFile database as a part of a report written with another word processor. Most PC-based word processors offer an option for reading in a file of ASCII text. (If you prefer to use the memo writer of RapidFile for all your correspondence, you can read text files from a database into a memo writer document as well.)

As an example, suppose that in a document for the Friends of Crabgrass you want to show the records for members in the database who live in California. Because you are familiar with it, use the RapidFile memo writer in this instance. But be aware that you could follow the same steps with most PC-based word processors.

Start RapidFile and retrieve the database MEMBERS. Press F3 (FLIP) until the database is visible in form layout. (Use form layout in this example only so all field contents are visible when the records are printed to disk.) Open the Records menu with CONTROL-R and choose "Select." Choose "Matching records" from the submenu and the view of the database is replaced with the Select Matching Records screen.

Delete any previous entries with CONTROL-DEL, and then enter

CA

in the first column next to the State field. Press F9 to implement the selection, and the file shows only those records with members living in California.

Open the Print menu with CONTROL-P and choose the "Destination" option. Select "Disk" from the submenu, press ESC to close the submenu, and choose "Begin printing." When prompted, select "All" for the records to be printed. Since you have already selected only those records with CA in the State field, RapidFile prints those specific records. The records are also written to a disk file named MEMBERS.TXT.

Open the Write menu with CONTROL-W and choose the option "Write memo." When the memo writer screen appears, type the following sentence:

All staff should be prepared to receive written inquiries or telephone calls from the following members:

Add two carriage returns after the end of the last line and open the File menu with CONTROL-F. Use the option "Insert file" of the File menu to read in the file of names you just created while in the file manager of RapidFile.

When you choose "Insert file," you see a prompt at the bottom of the screen that asks for the name of the file to be inserted. Enter

MEMBERS.TXT

and press RETURN. Answer "Yes" to the prompt **OK to continue**, and the records are read into the file (see Figure 16-2).

A large number of extra carriage returns precede and follow the data. Delete these by highlighting them with F6 and

```
File   Layout   Search   Typestyle   Merge   Print                     07:18 pm
All staff should be prepared to receive written inquiries or telephone
calls from the following members:◄
◄
◄
◄
◄
 - 1 -     ◄
 ◄
 LASTNAME      : Baker◄
 FIRSTNAME     : Benjamin◄
 ADDRESS       : 5206 Lyngate Court◄
 CITY          : Berkeley◄
 STATE         : CA◄
 ZIP           : 95264◄
 - 2 -     ◄
 ◄
 LASTNAME      : Mills◄
 FIRSTNAME     : Ernest◄
 ADDRESS       : 500 Embarcadero Street◄
 CITY          : San Francisco◄
001 ...1.....2.....3.....4.....5.....6.....
      7338 Bytes left   | C:\RAPID\              | Page 1 01/01
```

Figure 16-2. Memo writer document with file data

pressing the DEL key. The result is a complete document, consisting of both written text and data from a RapidFile database. If this were an actual application, you could proceed to complete the letter as desired. For now, choose "Leave memo writer" from the File menu (answer "No" to the prompt **Save the file?**). Then open the Records menu with CONTROL-R, choose "Select," and then choose the option "All records" to restore a view of all records to the database.

As a general rule, most word processors have an option for reading in an ASCII file that has been printed to disk in the same manner that was used in the example. Using this technique, you can merge data from a RapidFile database with your word processor's documents. If it is not obvious how to read in ASCII text, check the operator's manual of your word processor.

TRANSFERRING DATA BETWEEN RAPIDFILE AND FRAMEWORK II

Users of Ashton-Tate's integrated software Framework II will find it a simple matter to transfer RapidFile data to a Framework II database. The transfer is simple because Framework II can read data in dBASE III format, and it can write data in comma-delimited format. To transfer a RapidFile database to Framework II, simply export the file by choosing "Export file." Then choose the option "dBASE III" of the submenu that appears. The resultant .DBF file can then be copied to the Framework II data disk or to the appropriate hard-disk subdirectory. Framework II users should load the dBASE database onto the Framework II desktop in the usual manner, highlight the frame, and press F5 (RECALC). Framework II converts the file into a Framework II database.

To export a Framework II database to RapidFile, employ the usual Framework II commands to highlight the frame containing the database. Then open the Disk menu of Framework II with CONTROL-D and choose the "Export file" option. From the next menu that appears, choose "dBASE delimited." Framework II creates a comma-delimited file, which can be read into RapidFile by using the option "Import file" of the File menu as described previously in this chapter.

One caution for users of Framework II: The maximum size of a Framework II database is limited by the amount of memory in your PC. RapidFile, by comparison, is limited to 64,000 records. It is possible to have a RapidFile database that is too large to be imported into Framework II. In such cases Framework II imports as much of the file as it can handle and then displays a warning message indicating the number of records that are present in the Framework II database. If database size becomes a problem, divide the RapidFile database into smaller pieces by selecting groups of records and exporting them as individual files. For example, use the "Select" option of the Records menu to select all records with last names from A through L and export those names to one dBASE database, and then select records with last names from M through Z and export those records to another dBASE database. The databases could then be read individually into Framework II.

Automating Your Work with Macros

Chapter 17

RapidFile provides *macros*, which are combinations of keystrokes that can automate many of the tasks you normally perform with a program. Macros allow you to record a sequence of characters as a single key combination. You can save the macro and use it later to "play back" the character sequence by pressing the same single key combination. When the macro is played back, RapidFile performs as if you had manually typed the characters contained within the macro.

Using macros, a single key combination can hold a complex series of commands for the file manager, the memo writer, or both. You can store frequently used phrases, names, or complete paragraphs of text in a macro. And you are not limited to one key combination. You can use various combinations of ALT, SHIFT, and CONTROL for macros. If you must print daily reports or perform similar repetitive tasks, you can save many keystrokes by using macros.

If you use commercially available keyboard enhancers like Superkey and ProKey, you are familiar with the advantages of automating your work with macros. Users of other keyboard enhancers may wonder whether they should simply continue to use such products instead of using RapidFile's macro capability. The advantage of using the macro capability within RapidFile is twofold. First, the memory that the enhancer would consume is available to RapidFile. Second, you avoid any possible conflicts between the operation of RapidFile and the memory-resident keyboard enhancer. Memory-resident programs have, in the past, been known to conflict with various Ashton-Tate software packages, and as of this writing Ashton-Tate recommends against the use of them with Ashton-Tate products. During the writing of this book, Borland's SideKick and Superkey were both used with RapidFile with no ill effects. However, that experience is no guarantee that you will not encounter problems using memory-resident packages with RapidFile.

THE THREE TYPES OF RAPIDFILE MACROS

RapidFile offers three types of macros: Program Macros, Data File Macros, and Memo Macros. Program Macros are assigned to key combinations of CONTROL, ALT, or SHIFT and one function key. As an example, a Program Macro could be assigned to the key combination ALT-F1 or SHIFT-F10. Program Macros work anywhere in the RapidFile program. When you save Program Macros, they are saved in a file named RF.MAC.

Data File Macros work within the file manager of RapidFile. Such macros are saved along with the database file when it is saved. Data File Macros can be assigned any combination of ALT and an alphabetic key.

Memo Macros work within the memo writer portion of RapidFile. Such macros are saved in a file named MEMO.MAC. Memo Macros can be assigned any combination of ALT and an alphabetic key.

CREATING A MACRO

To create a macro in RapidFile, follow these four steps:

1. Enter CONTROL-K to begin the key-recording process.
2. Enter the key combination to be assigned to the macro (SHIFT-F1, ALT-B, or whatever). Use CONTROL, ALT, or SHIFT and any function key to create a Program Macro. Use ALT and any alphabetic key to create a Data File Macro or Memo Macro.
3. After you hear the high-pitched tone, enter the keystrokes that will make up the macro. If you make an error, enter CONTROL-K to halt the recording and begin again.
4. Once all keystrokes have been entered, press CONTROL-K to end the recording.

After the macro has been defined, type the assigned key combination to produce all the keystrokes stored within the macro.

For a quick example of what macros can do for you, start RapidFile (if you have not already done so) and load the database MEMBERS. Perhaps you regularly add records in a form layout, and you want to automate the process of switching to that layout and getting to the bottom of the database. If the file is not in a table layout, use the Layout menu to select "Table" layout, your starting point.

Enter CONTROL-K to begin defining the macro. You hear a tone, and the following message appears at the bottom of the screen: **Press the key combination to define as macro. When macro is complete, press Ctrl-K to end macro recording.**

Since this macro will be used only within this data file, you can define it as a Data File Macro. Enter ALT-A to assign the key combination ALT-A to the macro. The high-pitched tone indicates that RapidFile is recording your keystrokes.

Open the Layout menu with CONTROL-L, select "Choose layout type," and then select "Form." Press CONTROL-END to move to the last record in the database. Then press PGDN to move to a new, blank record.

Enter CONTROL-K to end the macro recording and you hear a low-pitched tone. All the keystrokes entered since the first CONTROL-K are now assigned to the macro, ALT-A.

To see the effects, go back to the table layout by pressing F3 and use PGUP to get to the top of the database. Assume that you have just loaded the file and that you want to add a record in form layout. Instead of pressing a half dozen keys, just enter ALT-A. All the keystrokes are entered from the macro, and you are presented with a blank form ready for data entry. To make sure that the macro is always available for use, all you need to do is save the database file in the usual manner. Data File Macros are saved whenever you save the database file.

RULES AND LIMITATIONS OF MACROS

Macros cannot contain more than 240 keystrokes. To get around this limit, if necessary, you can have one macro call another macro by making the second macro keystroke a part of the first macro.

The keystroke combination assigned to the macro cannot be made a part of the same macro. For example, if a macro is called with CONTROL-F1, you cannot use CONTROL-F1 within the macro. Such a technique would set up an anomaly known in programming as a *recursive loop*, in which the program chases its own tail. RapidFile does not let you get away with this—an error message appears if you try it.

Allowable key combinations for assigning macros are the CONTROL, SHIFT, ALT, and the function and the alphabetic keys. An attempt to use any other keys to assign a macro produces an error message.

A MORE COMPLEX EXAMPLE

Now that you have an idea of how RapidFile macros operate, consider a more complex example. Perhaps you print a report on a daily basis for your department, and you want to fully automate the report-generating process. You want to use a macro to load a database file, choose a layout, open the Print menu and start the printing, save the file, and leave the cursor at the point where you can exit RapidFile. Because the macro must operate outside a database file, it must be a Program Macro. To build the macro, perform the following steps:

1. Enter CONTROL-K to start recording the macro.
2. Enter SHIFT-F1 as the key combination to be assigned to the macro. (You hear the high-pitched tone.)
3. Enter CONTROL-F. (This combination opens the File menu if you are in another file when the macro is used.)
4. Enter R (to retrieve a file).
5. *Do not* use the arrow keys to select the file because the order could change when you add files. Instead, type

   MEMBERS

   and press RETURN.
6. Enter CONTROL-L (to open the Layout menu).
7. Enter C (for "Choose layout type").
8. Enter T (for "Table").
9. Enter CONTROL-L (to open the Layout menu).
10. Enter U (for "Use/Save layout").
11. Enter U (for "Use layout").

12. Type the word

    STAFF

    and press RETURN.
13. Enter CONTROL-P (to open the Print menu).
14. Enter D (for "Destination").
15. Enter F (for "First printer").
16. Press ESC (to close the submenu).
17. Enter B (for "Begin printing").
18. Enter CONTROL-RETURN (to save the file in the current layout).
19. Enter CONTROL-F (to open the File menu).
20. Press the DOWN ARROW key eight times.
21. Enter CONTROL-K to end the macro-recording process.

To try the effectiveness of this macro, open the File menu with CONTROL-F and retrieve any file other than the database MEMBERS. (The database BOOKS that you created in Chapter 8 should also be on your data disk or data directory.)

Once you are in the new file, press SHIFT-F1 to start the macro. All the processes represented by the keys within the macro are carried out: MEMBERS is loaded, the "Staff" layout chosen, the report printed, and the File menu is left open, ready for you to choose the option "Quit RapidFile." For now, press ESC to close the File menu.

EDITING MACROS

You may want to make changes to macros without having to re-create the entire macro. If so, you want to edit macros on the Edit Macro screen. To get to the Edit Macro screen, enter CONTROL-E. The Edit Macro screen appears as shown in Figure 17-1.

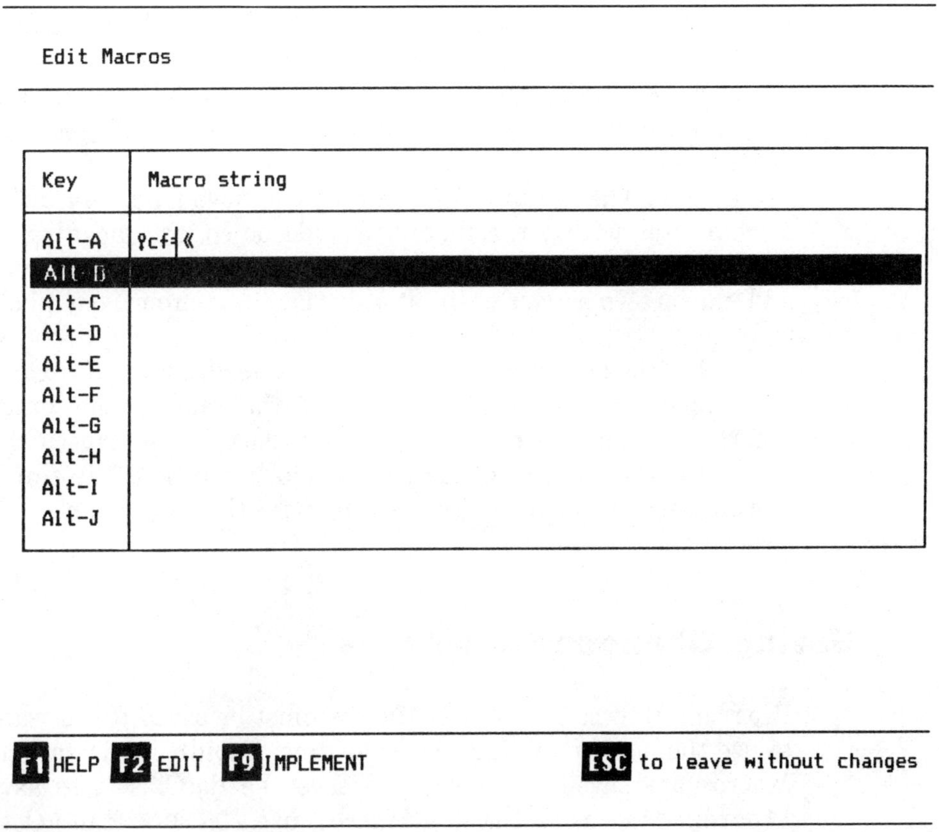

Figure 17-1. The Edit Macro screen

The Edit Macro screen displays the characters contained within all macros, beginning with the key combination ALT-A. To edit a macro, use the PGUP and PGDN keys and the UP ARROW and DOWN ARROW keys to highlight the desired macro key combination. Then press F2 (EDIT) to edit the macro.

The symbols that appear in the macro string, as shown in Figure 17-1, may not make much sense because macros are stored as a combination of alphanumeric characters and other symbols. These characters and symbols indicate various non-alphanumeric keys (such as RETURN, PGUP, ESC, and so forth).

When you edit the macro, however, those symbols are translated for your reference. As an example, highlight the macro ALT-A, which you created earlier. Press F2 and the symbols and their respective translations appear in the Edit Panel (see Figure 17-2).

Use LEFT ARROW and RIGHT ARROW to move from character to character within the macro. As you do so, the meaning of each character appears at the bottom of the screen. Delete or add characters as you wish. To add nonalphanumeric symbols (such as RETURN, PGUP, PGDN, and so forth), enter CONTROL-X. Then type the key combination you want to add. For this example, place the cursor at the end of the macro, and enter CONTROL-X. Then press DOWN ARROW once. (This causes the macro to move the cursor down one additional field.) To finish editing the macro, press RETURN to close the Edit Panel.

Saving Changes to Macros

Program Macros and Memo Macros must be saved if you want to use them after exiting and reloading RapidFile. (Data File Macros are saved whenever you save the database.) To save Program Macros and Memo Macros, use CONTROL-E to get to the Edit Macro screen, and then press F9 (IMPLEMENT). RapidFile will ask if you wish to update the macro file. Choose "Yes." The macros will be saved and you will be returned to the database layout.

ABOUT THE MACRO FILES

As mentioned earlier, different types of macros are saved in different places. Data File Macros are saved along with the database, Program Macros are saved in a file called RF.MAC, and Memo Macros are saved in a file called MEMO.MAC. If

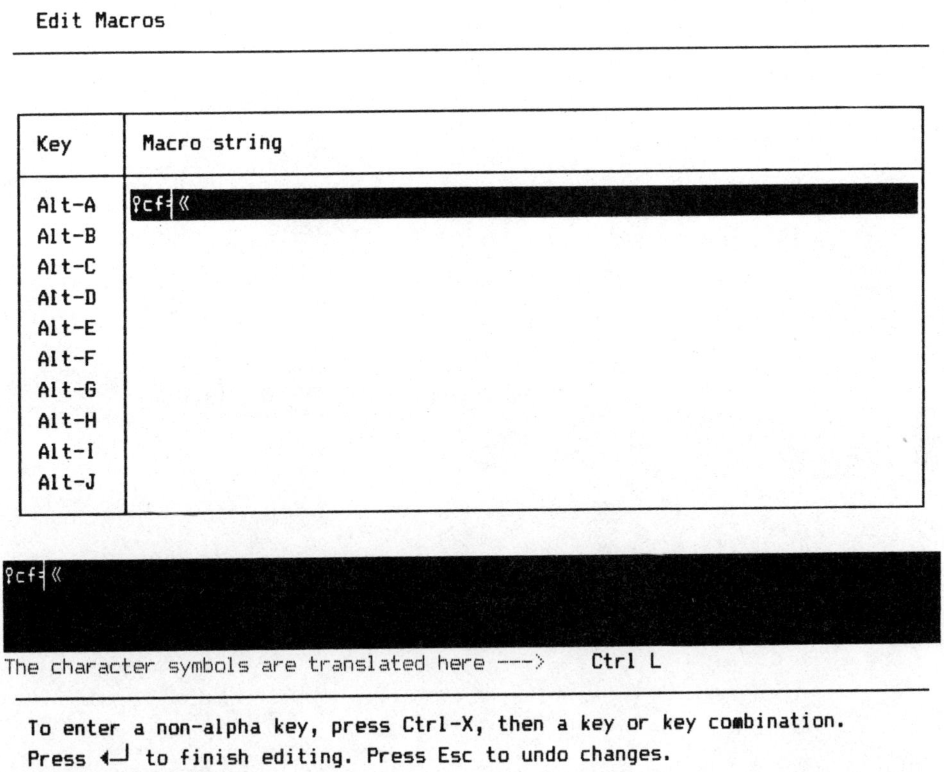

Figure 17-2. Macro symbols and corresponding translations

you are using a hard disk, the RF.MAC and MEMO.MAC files are stored in the parent directory (\RAPID), along with the rest of the program files. These files must be present for RapidFile to operate in a normal manner.

Sample Applications

Chapter 18

This chapter contains examples for designing databases and using RapidFile for specific applications in the areas of sales, personnel, and professional time management. The various examples have been chosen because they represent common areas of use that may be similar to your database management tasks and because the different areas place different demands on any database management system.

PERSONNEL TRACKING

Maintaining accurate records for the personnel at any company can be a time-consuming task. Two features of RapidFile that are of significant help in this area are the form layout and the memo writer. You can use RapidFile's ability to imitate existing paper-based forms used by the personnel department. The memo writer can produce important memos to the staff regarding vacation dates, insurance benefits, performance review schedules, and similar correspondence. Once a detailed personnel database has been built, you can sort and select records to monitor employee performance and the progress of Equal Employment Opportunity (EEO) at the company. Consider the following scenario.

Rocky Mountain Mills, a North Carolina-based garment manufacturer, uses RapidFile to track personnel records for employees at their two plants. The task of personnel tracking begins with a database structure that looks like the one in the File Structure Table in Figure 18-1.

File Structure Table

Field Settings			Preset Layout Settings		
Field name	Type	Expression	Field Format	Table size	Form size
last_name	Text		None	20	25/1
first_name	Text		None	15	25/1
soc_security	Text		None	11	25/1
address	Text		None	20	25/1
city	Text		None	15	25/1
state	Text		None	5	25/1
zip	Text		None	10	25/1
race	Text		None	10	25/1
sex	Text		None	3	25/1
date_of_birth	Date		None	8	8/1
date_hired	Date		None	8	8/1

F1 HELP F2 EDIT F9 IMPLEMENT ESC to leave without changes

Figure 18-1. Personnel File Structure Table

The Fields

One key field in any personnel database is either the employee number or the social security number. The aim of using a *key field* (a field that is unique to that record) is to provide a fast, effective way to search for one employee among hundreds or thousands. Names are not unique, and are, therefore, not as efficient a way to find a particular employee. Each record in the personnel file for Rocky Mountain Mills also contains the employee's name, complete address, date of birth, date of hire, sex, and EEO data. Also contained within the database is the date of each employee's last performance appraisal. A calculated date field, Time_Employed, shows how long (in days) an employee has been with the company. The field is calculated by subtracting the value of the Date_Hired field from Today( ), which contains the date within the PC's system clock. A form layout for the personnel database might resemble the one shown in Figure 18-2.

A personnel database can provide important views of a company's human resources by sorting and selecting the data in various ways and producing appropriate reports. An alphabetical sort on the last name and a select based on the Last_Review field greater than a given date (in this example, 04/27/86) shows all employees whose performance reviews were more than 6 months ago. These employees are past due for performance evaluations. Figure 18-3 shows the records in the database that meet this criteria.

Dozens of reports can be produced from a personnel database. The next example uses a numeric expression within a calculated field to calculate the number of weeks of vacation due an employee. The field, called Vacation, is added to the File Structure Table, and the field type is defined as calculated. The expression entered for the field calculation is IFNUM(Time_Employed > 1825,3,2). The expression translates to: If the number in the Time_Employed field is greater than 1825 days (5 years), then store a value of 3 (weeks) to the Vacation field; otherwise, store a value of 2 (weeks) to the Vacation field. A sample printout containing the results of the calculated field is shown in Figure 18-4.

```
File      Layout      Records      Write      Print                09:25 pm

* 1 *

last_name    : Lee
first_name   : Timothy
soc_security : 246-90-255

address: 1217 Pine Tree Way
city: Tarboro                    state: NC
zip: 27454

race: white                     sex: M

date_of_birth: 04/22/56
date_hired : 06/20/85

time_employed: 494               last_review  : 04/19/86

FORM: Unsaved layout  | C:PERSONNL.RPD | Selected: 8 of 8 |
```

Figure 18-2. Form layout for personnel database

Store the reports you use most often along with appropriate selection criteria within Program Macros so you can recall and print such reports with a single keystroke.

PROFESSIONAL TIME AND BILLING

Professionals know all too well the importance of the saying, "Time is money." Professionals bill their expertise to those willing to pay at an hourly rate, and if those hours are not care-

File   Layout   Records   Write   Print   09:26 pm

	last_name	first_name	soc_security	address
1	Lee	Timothy	246-90-255	1217 Pine Tree
2	Mills	Jeanette	232-11-679	195 Pinetops Ro

TABLE: Unsaved layout | C:PERSONNL.RPD | Selected: 2 of 8

Figure 18-3. Selected records in personnel database

last_name	first_name	soc_security	date_hired	vacation
Lee	Timothy	246-90-255	06/20/85	2
Mills	Jeanette	232-11-679	09/15/82	2
Johnson	Ree	675-90-235	05/08/72	3
Robinson	William	343-11-237	12/01/77	3
Morse	Marcia	453-21-670	06/01/84	2
Simpson	Charles	565-34-911	07/15/75	3
Fu	Anne Lao	343-60-703	11/01/80	3
Jackson	David	653-10-457	04/28/85	2

Figure 18-4. Printout containing vacation calculation

fully tracked, the bills are inaccurate, and the professionals wind up being short-changed when it comes to income.

Those who bill for their time—attorneys, designers, computer consultants, accountants, and members of dozens of other professional occupations—can use RapidFile to track hourly charges and to send out accurate bills on a regular basis. If you fall into this category and you have been generating bills with a calculator and a word processor, you will be pleasantly surprised to see a process that formerly took hours streamlined to a matter of minutes. The approach described in the following scenario uses a form letter to each client, which accompanies an attached itemized bill. The bill is actually a Quick Report printed after all records for a particular client have been selected.

Winnken, Blinnken, and Knod is a Los Angeles-based law firm specializing in personal law: divorce, wills, malpractice, and accident and injury cases. The area in which these professionals practice may be specialized, but the database design, shown in Figure 18-5, is readily usable by professionals in other fields because the tasks involved in billing time do not change significantly from profession to profession.

If the database, which is called TIME, seems simple, it is partly because a second database is used to store the clients' names and addresses. The design of this database appears in Figure 18-6.

Storing certain fields in separate databases avoids unnecessary duplication of information. The clients' addresses are needed only once each month, when the bills are mailed. However, the database that calculates the bill is used each day, as records are added to indicate how many hours must be billed to a client. If all the fields were in one database, personnel would find it necessary to enter the same names and addresses over and over for each record.

File Structure Table

Field Settings			Preset Layout Settings		
Field name	Type	Expression	Field Format	Table size	Form size
CLIENT_ID	Text		None	15	25/1
DATE	Date		None	8	8/1
STAFF_NAME	Text		None	15	25/1
RATE	Numeric		None	10	10/1
NO_HOURS	Numeric		None	10	10/1
TOTAL_CHARGE	Calc,N2	RATE*NO_HOU	None	10	10/1
DESCRIPTION	Text		None	15	25/1

F1 HELP F2 EDIT F9 IMPLEMENT ESC to leave without changes

Figure 18-5. File Structure Table for billing time

The Fields

The first database, TIME, contains fields for a client identification code, the date the work was performed, the name of the staff member who did the work, the billing rate, the number of

File Structure Table

Field Settings			Preset Layout Settings		
Field name	Type	Expression	Field Format	Table size	Form size
CLIENT_ID	Text		None	15	25/1
LASTNAME	Text		None	15	25/1
FIRSTNAME	Text		None	15	25/1
ASSIGNED_TO	Text		None	15	25/1
ADDRESS	Text		None	15	25/1
CITY	Text		None	15	25/1
STATE	Text		None	15	25/1
ZIP	Text		None	15	25/1
PHONE	Text		None	15	25/1
CONTACT	Text		None	15	25/1

F1 HELP F2 EDIT F9 IMPLEMENT ESC to leave without changes

Figure 18-6. File Structure Table for database CLIENT

hours worked, the total fee charged, and a description of the work.

The second database, CLIENT, contains fields for a client identification code, client name and address, the name of the staff member assigned to the client, the phone number of the client, and a contact name. The database CLIENT is used at the end of the month to generate the form letters that serve as

```
File      Layout      Records      Write      Print                 09:31 pm

* 1 *

CLIENT_ID     : ASK
LASTNAME      : Knisch
FIRSTNAME     : Alfred
ASSIGNED_TO   : Blinnken
ADDRESS       : 3 Sunset Brook Lane
CITY          : Century City
STATE         : CA
ZIP           : 90213
PHONE         : 213-555-1212
CONTACT       : Mr. Knisch




FORM: Unsaved layout  || C:CLIENT.RPD || Selected: 3 of 3 ||
```

Figure 18-7. A sample record in the database CLIENT

cover letters for the detail statement (or bill). The detail statements are Quick Reports created by selecting records for a given client within the TIME database. Each client receives a unique identification code so staff can find records for that client quickly. Being a small law practice, the firm uses a simple three-letter code that uses the initials of the particular client. A record from the database CLIENT resembles the form shown in Figure 18-7.

```
File      Layout      Records      Write      Print                    09 32 pm

* 7 *

CLIENT_ID    : SFP
DATE         : 10/15/87
STAFF_NAME   : Winnken
RATE         : 150.00
NO_HOURS     : 2
TOTAL_CHARGE : 300.00
DESCRIPTION  : Preparation, filing civil suit, slander, against
               opponent, U.S. Senate

FORM: Unsaved layout  | C:TIME.RPD  | Selected: 10 of 10 |
```

Figure 18-8. Form layout of the database TIME

The database TIME has one record added for each unit of time a professional bills to a particular client. For this purpose a form layout like the one shown in Figure 18-8 works best.

At the end of each month, the billing clerk in the accounting department sets a Select Matching Records screen to select all records for a given client where the data falls within that month. Figure 18-9 shows the Select Matching Records screen to accomplish this task for a client with the client code ASK for the month of October 1987.

Select Matching Records

Field name	Match criteria (1)	Match criteria (2)
CLIENT_ID	ASK	
DATE	> 09/31/87 .AND. < 11/01/87	
STAFF_NAME		
RATE		
NO_HOURS		
TOTAL_CHARGE		
DESCRIPTION		

F1 HELP F2 EDIT F9 IMPLEMENT ESC to leave without changes

Figure 18-9. Select settings for client ASK for October 1987

A Quick Report is produced for that particular client, and the Date field determines the sort order within the report. The report resembles the one shown in Figure 18-10.

The total for the Total_Charged field can be entered within the form letter generated from the database CLIENT. Figure 18-11 shows the result.

At the end of each month, one form letter is printed for each client, and the letters are attached to the appropriate statements (Quick Reports).

Client Activity Report for October 10/27/86

DATE	STAFF_NAME	RATE	NO_HOURS	TOTAL_CHAR	DESCRIPTION
10/02/87	Blinnken	150.00	2	300.00	Filing, preparation for appeal in U.S. Government vs. ASK
10/04/87	Knod	150.00	1	150.00	Preparation of appeal, Sarah L. Knisch vs. ASK
10/09/87	Knod	150.00	4	600.00	Research for appeal, U.S. Government vs. ASK
10/16/87	Paralegal	65.00	7.5	487.50	Westlaw, library research on IRS statutes and precedents in prior rulings
10/21/87	Blinnken	150.00	2	300.00	Met with counsel for opposing side. Exploratory settlement.
				==========	
		Total for File		1837.50	

Figure 18-10. Quick Report for client ASK

SALES TRACKING

Sales tracking is an area that, in some shape or form, is vital to every business. RapidFile's table layouts can be used to generate printouts of sales data to monitor sales on a day-by-day basis. Quick Reports can be used to show monthly and yearly sales data, and to draw comparisons between items sold. Consider the following scenario, which shows how RapidFile can assist in tracking sales figures.

```
File   Layout   Search   Typestyle   Merge   Print                    06 48 pm

                    Winnken, Blinnken & Knod
                        attorneys at law
                      2200 Sunset Boulevard
                     Los Angeles, CA 90020


10 November 1987

Alfred Knisch
3 Sunset Brook Lane
Century City, CA
CA90213

Dear Mr. Knisch

     Enclosed is our invoice for $1,837.50 for services
rendered for the month of October, 1987.  If you have any
questions regarding this invoice, please contact Mr. James
A. Paralegal in our Administration department.  We
001 ....2.......3.........4.........5.........6.........7..
         7369 Bytes left  || C:\RAPID\CLIENT.MMO          || Page 1 13/07
Record number 1
```

Figure 18-11. Form letter for client

Big D Motorcars is a Dallas, Texas, auto dealership offering various models of new and used cars. Details of each car sale are entered into a record in a RapidFile database. The file is usually sorted by sales representative or by model of auto to provide the managers with quick printouts showing which sales reps are selling above or below quota and which models are selling better than others. The design of the database, called CARSALES, looks like Figure 18-12.

File Structure Table

Field Settings			Preset Layout Settings		
Field name	Type	Expression	Field Format	Table size	Form size
Date	Date		None	8	8/1
Sales_Rep	Text		None	15	25/1
Make	Text		None	15	25/1
Model	Text		None	15	25/1
Year	Numeric		None	10	10/1
Wholesale	Numeric		None	10	10/1
Cust_Price	Numeric		None	10	10/1
Salestax	Calc,N2	.06 * cust_	None	10	10/1
Total_price	Calc,N2	Cust_price	None	10	10/1
Delivery_date	Date		None	8	8/1

F1 HELP F2 EDIT F9 IMPLEMENT ESC to leave without changes

Figure 18-12. File Structure Table for database CARSALES

Again, a form layout proves the most convenient for entry of each record. Figure 18-13 shows the form used for the database CARSALES.

The Fields

The fields used in CARSALES are fairly self-explanatory, and similar fields could be used for other types of sales activities.

```
File      Layout     Records     Write     Print                    09 45 pm

* 3 *

Date         : 10/26/86
Sales_Rep    : Robinson, L.

Make         : Oldsmobile
Model        : Delta 88
Year         : 1987


Wholesale    : 14410.00

Cust_Price   : 19890.00         Delivery_date: 10/27/86
Salestax     : 1193.40

Total_price  : 21083.40


FORM: Unsaved layout    C:CARSALES.RPD  Selected: 8 of 8
```

Figure 18-13. Data entry form for database CARSALES

Fields are provided for date of the sale; sales rep's name; make, model, and year of the auto; delivery date; and the wholesale and retail (customer) prices. A calculated field defined within the File Structure Table stores the calculation .06 * Cust_Price for the Salestax field. (The formula calculates a sales tax of 6 percent.) The field Total_Price is also a calculated field, which is based on the addition of Cust_Price and Salestax.

One Quick Report sorts the database by make (the first sort field) and model (the second sort field), and the resulting report, shown in Figure 18-14, shows what models are hot in

```
                    Report from CARSALES.RPD on 10/27/86

REC# |Date     |Sales_Rep      |Make       |Model       |Year|Delivery
-----+---------+---------------+-----------+------------+----+--------
   1 |10/22/86|Arby, G.        |Oldsmobile|Cutlass      |1987|11/05/86
   2 |10/26/86|Robinson, L.    |Oldsmobile|Delta 88     |1987|10/27/86
   3 |10/22/86|Williams, R.    |Oldsmobile|Firenza      |1987|11/05/86
   4 |11/27/86|Arby, G.        |Pontiac   |Bonneville   |1986|11/27/86
   5 |10/20/86|Williams, R.    |Pontiac   |Fiero        |1987|11/01/86
   6 |10/26/86|Williams, R.    |Pontiac   |Fiero        |1987|11/15/86
   7 |10/17/86|Williams, R.    |Pontiac   |Fiero        |1987|10/20/86
   8 |10/19/86|Robinson, L.    |Pontiac   |Grand Am     |1987|11/05/86
```

Figure 18-14. Quick Report grouped by make and model

```
REC# |Date     |Sales_Rep    |Make         |Model      |Year|Wholesale
-----+---------+-------------+-------------+-----------+----+---------
   1 |10/22/86|Arby, G.      |Oldsmobile   |Cutlass    |1987|11545.25
   2 |11/27/86|Arby, G.      |Pontiac      |Bonneville|1986|11907.55
                                                           ----------
                                       Total for Arby, G. 23452.8

   3 |10/26/86|Robinson, L.|Oldsmobile   |Delta 88   |1987|14410.00
   4 |10/19/86|Robinson, L.|Pontiac      |Grand Am   |1987|9203.66
                                                           ----------
                                   Total for Robinson, L. 23613.66

   5 |10/22/86|Williams, R.|Oldsmobile   |Firenza    |1987|7260.00
   6 |10/20/86|Williams, R.|Pontiac      |Fiero      |1987|12678.05
   7 |10/26/86|Williams, R.|Pontiac      |Fiero      |1987|12205.05
   8 |10/17/86|Williams, R.|Pontiac      |Fiero      |1987|10705.90
                                                           ----------
                                   Total for Williams, R. 42849.
                                                           ==========
                                           Total for File 89915.46
```

Figure 18-15. Quick Report grouped by sales rep's name

Dallas. The managers then slant that month's TV advertising to feature the more popular models.

To see how the sales reps are performing, another Quick Report sorts the file by the sales rep's name. Figure 18-15 shows the results.

The large number of ways sales managers want to see sales data makes sales reports another ideal application for the use of Program Macros to automate the generation of reports.

Customizing RapidFile

Chapter 19

RapidFile includes a customization program that allows you to change many settings of the program. You can change the style of menus used by RapidFile, what printer ports are used by the program, what screen colors will be displayed, and what margins will be used. These and other settings are stored in a file called CUSTOM.DAT, which is stored in the same directory as the rest of the RapidFile program. Each time RapidFile is loaded, the settings stored in the CUSTOM.DAT file are read. These settings determine the defaults for RapidFile. By using the Customize utility, you can change these settings to your own liking. The following are the four steps to customizing RapidFile:

1. From the DOS prompt, enter

   RF CUSTOM

   Once you assent to the license agreement by pressing RETURN, the first screen (or "page") of the Customize utility appears.

2. Use the PGUP and PGDN keys to move between the four pages of the Customize utility. Highlight those options you wish to change and use either the arrow keys (in the case of on/off or multiple-choice options) or the F2 (EDIT) key (when text must be entered or colors chosen) to change the option to your preferred setting.
3. When you are done changing the settings, press F9 (IMPLEMENT) to store the changes to the CUSTOM.DAT file.
4. Restart RapidFile for the changes to take effect.

In the sections that follow, you will examine each page of the customization program in detail.

PAGE 1

If you are in RapidFile, exit the program and get back to the DOS prompt. To load the Customize utility, enter

RF CUSTOM

and press RETURN. When the RapidFile registration message appears, press RETURN, and the first page of customization options appears (see Figure 19-1).

With the exception of "Default data directory," all options on this page are on/off or multiple choice, so use the LEFT ARROW and RIGHT ARROW keys to select the desired option. Use the UP ARROW and DOWN ARROW keys to move among the options. The options on page 1 of the Customize utility affect the following:

Menu style. RapidFile menus can be one of two styles—*pull-down menu* or a *horizontal menu.* Pull-down menus are those menus that have been shown throughout this text. Horizontal menus are in a horizontal line along the top of the screen. Such

Program Settings Customize: Page 1 of 4

1. Menu style	:	Pulldown • Horizontal
2. Function key help	:	On • Off
3. Status line	:	On • Off
4. Load memo writer	:	On • Off
5. Default data directory	:	
6. Directory display	:	Filtered • Expanded
7. 1st printer port	:	LPT1 • LPT2 • COM1 • COM2
8. 2nd printer port	:	LPT1 • LPT2 • COM1 • COM2
9. Sound	:	On • Off
10. Enable color	:	On • Off

F2 EDIT F9 IMPLEMENT Esc to leave without changes

Figure 19-1. Page 1 of the Customize utility

menus bear a strong resemblance to menus used in Lotus 1-2-3, Symphony, and most other spreadsheet programs. When you pick the horizontal menu option, you can use the SLASH key to cause the menus to appear, just as it is used in Lotus 1-2-3. Figure 19-2 shows a sample screen from RapidFile with the horizontal menu option turned on.

```
File     Layout     Records     Write     Print
Retrieve Save Create Modify Disk/directory Append Import Export Quit
```

Figure 19-2. Sample of a horizontal menu

Function key help. Turning on this setting causes the function key help messages to be displayed at the bottom of the screen. When using RapidFile, you can switch the help messages on and off at will with the key combination CONTROL-H.

24-hour clock. This option, which is preset to the 12-hour clock, causes time to be displayed in military format. The time is displayed in the upper-right corner of the screen.

Load memo writer. Turning on this setting causes the memo writer of the RapidFile program to be loaded into memory with the rest of the program. If you do not use the memo writer, you can reserve more space in the computer's memory to keep additional records by turning off this setting. Doing so increases RapidFile's performance with large files.

Default data directory. This setting allows you to specify which directory you want to use when loading and saving files. If you installed RapidFile for use with a hard disk, the default value (unless you changed this option) is /RAPID/RFDATA. You can change this so that another directory is used to save and retrieve files. For example, a user of dBASE III PLUS might prefer to keep RapidFile and dBASE III PLUS data files in the same directory, a directory named C:/DBASE/DATA. To change the setting, the user would highlight "Default data directory," press F2, and enter C:/DBASE/DATA as the desired directory name.

Directory display. Selecting "Filtered" for this setting causes the normal directory within RapidFile to show only RapidFile or dBASE database files when in the file manager and only memo writer files when in the memo writer. Selecting "Expanded" for the setting causes all files to be displayed. Note that when you are using RapidFile, you can switch the directory from "Filtered" to "Expanded" by pressing F3 (FLIP) whenever the directory appears on the screen.

1st printer port and *2nd printer port.* These settings permit you to assign LPT1, LPT2, COM1, or COM2 as valid ports for the options "First printer" and "Second printer," which appear in the Destination submenu when printing. Note that if you use a serial printer (COM1 or COM2), you may need to also use the DOS command MODE before RapidFile is loaded. The command configures your system to match the printer's baud rate and parity settings.

Sound. Selecting "On" causes RapidFile to beep when the user makes errors in the use of the program. Select "Off" if you find the sound annoying.

Enable color. If you are using a color monitor, selecting "On" causes RapidFile to display text, menus, and backgrounds in various colors. If you are using an amber or green monitor connected to a graphics adapter, turning on this option causes the data to be presented in varying shades. Once you have enabled color with this setting, you can use the settings on page 4 of the Customize utility to change the color.

PAGE 2

Pressing the PGDN key reveals page 2 of the Customize utility (see Figure 19-3). The settings on page 2 relate to the file manager settings and to the memo writer settings.

```
Program Settings                                    Customize:  Page 2 of 4

File Manager settings:

 1. File to load on startup     :
 2. Date input                  :  M/D/YY  * D-M-YY
 3. Currency symbol             :  Dollar  * Pound

Memo Writer settings:

 4. File to load on start-up    :
 5. Vertical ruler              :  On        * Off
 6. Carriage return markers     :  On        * Off
 7. Columns before scrolling    :  3
 8. Lines before scrolling      :  3
 9. Lines to jump PgUp/PgDn     :  20
10. Maximum memo size (linked)  :  8

F2 EDIT  F9 IMPLEMENT                        Esc to leave without changes
```

Figure 19-3. Page 2 of the Customize utility

File Manager Settings

The file manager settings on page 2 affect the following:

File to load on startup. This setting allows you to enter the name of a database file that you want to load automatically each time you start RapidFile. To change this setting, highlight it, press F2, and enter the name of the desired file.

Date input. This setting changes the format for dates entered into a RapidFile database. For the American date format (MM/DD/YY), select "M/D/YY." For the European date format (DD-MM-YY), select "D-M-YY."

Currency symbol. This setting changes the currency symbol that appears when you format a field of numbers as currency. Select either "Dollar" to display the dollar sign or "Pound" to display the symbol for the British pound.

Memo Writer Settings

The memo writer settings on page 2 affect the following:

File to load on startup. This setting allows you to enter the name of a memo writer file that you want to load automatically each time you load the memo writer. To change this setting, highlight it, press F2, and enter the name of the desired file.

Vertical ruler. Turning on this setting causes the vertical ruler to appear; turning off the setting hides the vertical ruler.

Carriage return markers. Turning on this setting causes the triangular symbol that indicates a carriage return to appear in the memo writer. Turning off this setting hides the carriage return marker.

Columns before scrolling. This setting allows you to change the point at which the screen begins to scroll horizontally. To do so, enter a numeric value to represent the number of characters from the left or right edge of the screen at which the screen begins to scroll. To change the setting, highlight it, press F2, and enter a number. For example, if you enter 10, the screen scrolls to the right when the cursor gets within ten spaces of the right margin.

Lines before scrolling. This setting allows you to change the point at which the screen begins to scroll vertically. To do so, enter a numeric value to represent the number of lines from the top or bottom edge of the screen at which the screen begins to scroll. To change the setting, highlight it, press F2, and enter a number. For example, if you enter 4, the screen scrolls when the cursor gets within four lines of the top or bottom of the screen.

Lines to jump PGUP/PGDN. This setting allows you to set the number of lines that scroll up or down on a memo writer screen when you use the PGUP and PGDN keys. To change the setting, highlight it, press F2, and enter a number.

Maximum memo size (linked). This setting allows you to vary the amount of memory available for a memo that is linked to a database record. To change the setting, highlight it, press F2, and enter a number from 1 to 64. The numbers translate to kilobytes of memory (1K to 64K). Every 2K of memory is equivalent to approximately one typed, single-spaced page of text.

To optimize performance, do not allocate more space than is necessary for linked memo files. The amount allocated must be reserved in memory while you are using the file manager, so performance can be adversely affected if you allocate a large amount of memory for linked memo files.

PAGE 3

Pressing PGDN reveals page 3 of the Customize utility (see Figure 19-4). Page 3 contains settings that affect the formatting of both the file manager and the memo writer. Each of these is changed by entering a number or character. To change any of the settings, highlight it, press F2, and enter the desired value or character.

```
Print Defaults                                          Customize:  Page 3 of 4

   File Manager                               Memo Writer

 1. Page length       66 :  66             11. Page length       66 :  66
 2. Top margin         3 :  3              12. Top margin         6 :  6
 3. Bottom margin      3 :  3              13. Bottom margin      6 :  6
 4. Record spacing     0 :  0              14. Line spacing       1 :  1
 5. Left margin        0 :  0              15. Left margin       12 :  12
 6. Right margin      80 :  80             16. Right margin      72 :  72
 7. Record numbers       :  On  •  Off     17. Left indent        5 :  5
 8. Border character   | :  |              18. Right indent       5 :  5
 9. Merge delimiter    , :  ,              19. Merge delimiter    , :  ,
10. Setup string         :                 20. Setup string         :

F2 EDIT  F9 IMPLEMENT                                Esc to leave without changes
```

Figure 19-4. Page 3 of the Customize utility

File Manager Settings

The settings on page 3 that relate to the file manager affect the following:

Page length. This setting controls the maximum number of lines that will appear on a printed page. The normal default for 11-inch-long paper is 66. For legal-sized (8 1/2 × 14-inch) paper, use a setting of 84. For other sizes of paper or custom forms, measure the length of the sheet and multiply by 6 for each inch of length.

Top margin. This setting defines the size of the top margin in terms of the number of lines.

Bottom margin. This setting defines the size of the bottom margin in terms of the number of lines.

Record spacing. This setting controls the spacing between records. The entry 1 specifies one blank line between records, 2 specifies two lines, and so on.

Left margin. This setting specifies the margin that appears at the left side of the page in terms of the number of characters.

Right margin. This setting specifies, in terms of the number of characters from the far left, the position beyond which data does not appear.

Record numbers. Turning on this setting causes record numbers to appear at the left edge when printing. Turn off the option to omit record numbers when printing.

Border character. The character specified by this setting appears as a divider between columns of data when printed (assuming that the "Borders" option is turned on during printing).

Merge delimiter. The character specified by this setting is the field delimiter you use to create delimited files for use with other software. If you are transferring data from RapidFile to another program that uses different delimiters, change the delimiters accordingly. Note that the delimiters used by both the file manager and the memo writer must be identical before form letters can be generated.

Setup string. The codes that you specify for this setting are sent to the printer prior to printing. For example, entering 15 causes Epson or Epson-compatible printers to print compressed type.

Memo Writer Setting

On page 3 of the Customize utility, the settings Page length, Top margin, Bottom margin, Line spacing, Left margin, and Right margin function just as they do in regard to the file manager. The other settings that relate to the memo writer affect the following:

Left indent. This setting specifies how far, in terms of the number of characters, the left side of the text should be indented from the left margin when you turn on the "Indent" option.

Right indent. This setting specifies how far, in terms of the number of characters, the right side of the text should be indented from the right margin when you turn on the "Indent" option.

Merge delimiter. See Merge delimiter for the file manager.

Setup string. See Setup string for the file manager.

PAGE 4

Pressing PGDN again displays page 4 of the Customize utility (Figure 19-5). Page 4 of the Customize utility is used to change the colors displayed on a color monitor. For the colors to be visible, you must also turn Enable color on page 1 of the utility to On. To change any of the color settings, highlight the desired setting, and press F2. When you do so, a color bar appears along with a prompt at the bottom of the screen (see Figure 19-6).

To select a color, simply move the cursor to the desired color by using the LEFT ARROW or RIGHT ARROW key and press RETURN. In many cases you are asked to choose both a foreground color and a background color. Foreground colors are used to display text and data. Background colors are the colors over which the text or data appears. As you make the choices,

```
Color Settings                                        Customize:  Page 4 of 4

   File Manager                                   Memo Writer

 1. Menu color         :  sample text        9. Menu color      :  sample text

 2. Table layout       :  sample text       10. Normal text     :  sample text
 3. Form layout        :  sample text       11. Bold            :  sample text
 4. Half table         :  sample text       12. Underlined      :  sample text
 5. Half form          :  sample text       13. Italic          :  sample text
 6. Label layout       :  sample text       14. Raised          :  sample text
 7. Quick report       :  sample text       15. Lowered         :  sample text
 8. Custom report      :  sample text       16. Combinations    :  sample text

F2 EDIT  F9 IMPLEMENT                        Esc to leave without changes
```

Figure 19-5. Page 4 of the Customize utility

they take effect at the locations on the screen marked "sample text." This helps you to see the effects of a color before implementing your options with F9 (IMPLEMENT). Note that for both foreground and background colors, black is a valid choice. This is not readily apparent on a color monitor because the black box blends in with the rest of the screen while you are setting the options. The black box is located immediately to the left of the other colors.

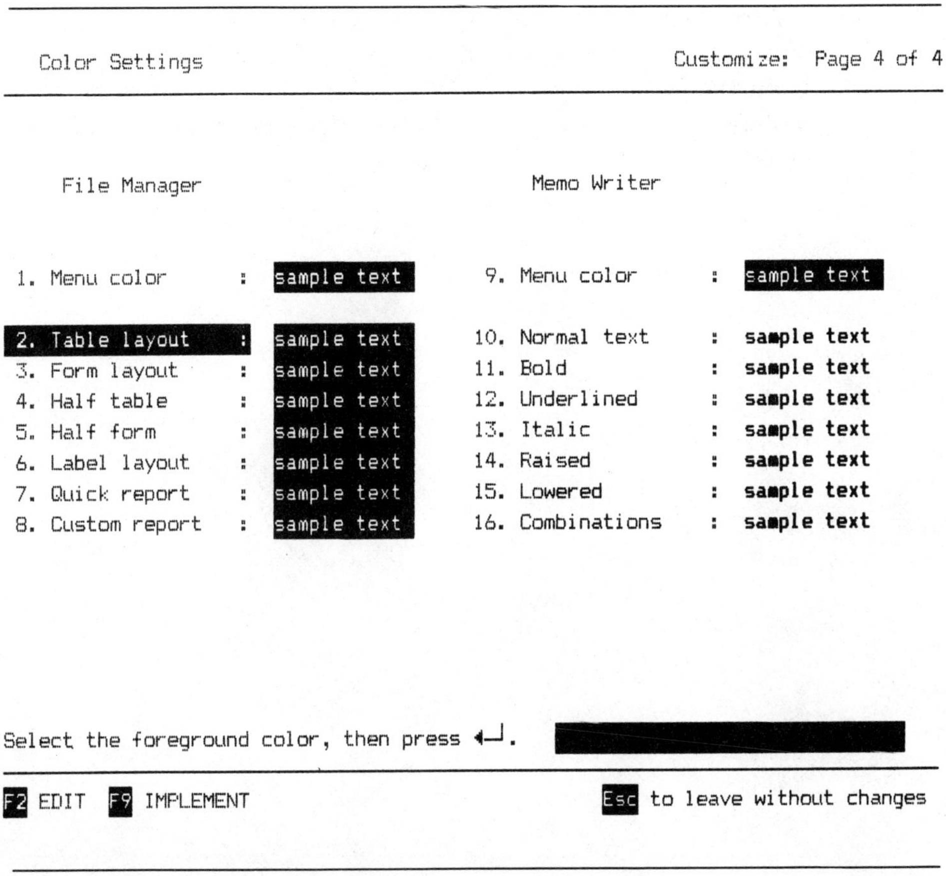

Figure 19-6. The prompt for changing colors

SAVING YOUR OPTIONS

Once you make your choices, press F9 (IMPLEMENT) to store the changes to the CUSTOM.DAT file. As an option, you can press ESC if you wish to exit the Customize utility without saving any changes.

After saving the changes restart the program, and the changes take effect. Note that if you run the Customize utility from the option "Access DOS" of RapidFile, you have to completely exit the program and restart it before the changes are evident.

Trademarks

The following names are trademarked products of the corresponding companies.

AT&T®	American Telephone and Telegraph
COMPAQ®	COMPAQ Computer Corporation
COMPAQ Deskpro™	COMPAQ Computer Corporation
dBASE II®	Ashton-Tate
dBASE III®	Ashton-Tate
dBASE III PLUS™	Ashton-Tate
Epson®	Seiko Epson Corporation
Framework®	Ashton-Tate
Framework II™	Ashton-Tate
Friday!®	Ashton-Tate
IBM®	International Business Machines Corporation
IBM Personal Computer AT®	International Business Machines Corporation
IBM Personal Computer XT™	International Business Machines Corporation

Leading Edge®	Leading Edge Products, Inc.
Lotus®	Lotus Development Corporation
MailMerge®	MicroPro International Corporation
Microsoft®	Microsoft Corporation
Microsoft File™	Microsoft Corporation
Microsoft WORD®	Microsoft Corporation
MS-DOS®	Microsoft Corporation
MultiMate®	MultiMate International Corporation, a subsidiary of Ashton-Tate
1-2-3®	Lotus Development Corporation
PC-File III™	ButtonWare Inc.
pfs®	Software Publishing Corporation
pfs:FILE™	Software Publishing Corporation
ProKey™	RoseSoft, Inc.
R:base® 4000™	Microrim Corporation
R:base® 5000™	Microrim Corporation
R:base® series V™	Microrim Corporation
Reflex®	Borland/Analytica, Inc.
SideKick®	Borland International Corporation
SuperKey®	Borland International Corporation
Symphony®	Lotus Development Corporation
Tandy® 1000™	Tandy Corporation
Tandy® 2000™	Tandy Corporation
Tandy® 3000™	Tandy Corporation
Twin®	Mosaic Software
VP Planner	Paperback Software
WordPerfect™	WordPerfect Corporation
WordStar®	MicroPro International Corporation

Index

The manuscript for this book was prepared and submitted to Osborne/McGraw-Hill in electronic form.

The acquisitions editor for this project was Nancy Carlston. The technical reviewer was Catherine Mone. Lyn Cordell was the project editor.

Text design is by Judy Wohlfrom, using Century Expanded for text and Eurostyle for display.

Cover art is by Bay Graphics Design Associates. Cover supplier is Phoenix Color Corporation. This book was printed and bound by R. R. Donnelley & Sons Company, Crawfordsville, Indiana.

Advanced dBASE III PLUS™: Programming and Techniques
by Miriam Liskin

Liskin's enormously successful *Advanced dBASE III®* has been completely revised to offer comprehensive coverage of dBASE III PLUS.™ Expand your dBASE® skills as you learn programming techniques that let you design and implement more effective dBASE III PLUS business applications. Nationally known columnist and consultant Miriam Liskin addresses the "real world" business environment so you can make the most of dBASE III PLUS modes of operation. Liskin's discussion of new features offers you greater convenience when you work with multiple files at the dot prompt. You'll learn how to write portable, hardware-independent systems and use new error-trapping capabilities so you can work with more flexible on-line help systems. You'll also find out how to benefit from file- and record-locking features that enable you to design a multiuser data base system that can be especially important in networking.

$21.95p
0-07-881249-6, 816 pp., 7³/₈ x 9¹/₄

dBASE III® Tips & Traps
by Dick Andersen, Cynthia Cooper, and Bill Demsey

Take some tips from Dick Andersen and his co-authors and you'll save computing time and avoid troublesome dBASE traps with this helpful collection of creative shortcuts. *dBASE III® Tips & Traps*, another in Andersen's *Tips & Traps* series, is written for all dBASE III® users, beginning and experienced. You'll find hundreds of tips and trap solutions for planning an application system and establishing a database, entering and updating data, ordering and retrieving data, relating databases, customizing screen displays, generating reports, interfacing with other software, and converting files from dBASE II.® All tip and trap entries are illustrated and follow a concise "how-to" format.

$17.95p
0-07-881195-3, 300 pp., 7³/₈ x 9¹/₄

Using dBASE III® PLUS™
by Edward Jones

Osborne's top-selling title, *Using dBASE III,®* by Edward Jones, has now been updated to include Ashton-Tate's new upgrade, dBASE III® PLUS.™ With Jones' expertise you'll be in full command of all the new features of this powerful database software. Learn to design, create, and display a dBASE III PLUS database, devise entry forms with the dBASE III PLUS screen painter, generate reports, use Query files, and plug into dBASE III PLUS networking. In addition, you'll find out how to install dBASE III PLUS on a hard disk, conduct data searches, and manipulate assistant pull-down menus. *Using dBASE III® PLUS™* is a thorough and practical handbook for both beginning and experienced dBASE III users.

$18.95
0-07-881252-6, 350 pp., 7³/₈ x 9¹/₄

dBASE III PLUS™: The Complete Reference
by Joseph-David Carrabis

This indispensable dBASE III PLUS™ reference will undoubtedly be the most frequently used book in your dBASE III® library. *dBASE III PLUS™: The Complete Reference* is a comprehensive resource to every dBASE III and dBASE III PLUS command, function, and feature. Each chapter covers a specific task so you can quickly pinpoint information on installing the program, designing databases, creating files, manipulating data, and many other subjects. Chapters also contain an alphabetical reference section that describes all the commands and functions you need to know and provides clear examples of each. Carrabis, author of several acclaimed dBASE books, discusses the lastest features of dBASE III PLUS, including networking capabilities; the Assistant, a menu-driven interface; and the Applications Generator, a short-cut feature for creating database files and applications without programming. *dBASE III PLUS™: The Complete Reference* also includes a glossary and handy appendixes that cover error messages, converting from dBASE II to dBASE III PLUS, and add-on utilities.

$22.95p
0-07-881012-4, 600 pp., 7³/₈ x 9¹/₄

pfs:®Software Made Easy Write, File, Report, Access, Graph
by Carl Townsend

Why pfs:®Software? Increasingly, business professionals are recognizing the value of integrated software for word processing, maintaining data files, and generating reports and graphics. *pfs:®Software Made Easy* introduces you to this series, explains its unique features, and helps you learn each program, pfs:®Write, pfs:®File, pfs:®Report, pfs:®Access, and pfs:®Graph. Invaluable tips for integrating programs and working with advanced applications make this book the ideal companion for your pfs:®Software program documentation.

$17.95p
0-07-881147-3, 250 pp.. 7³/₈ x 9¹/₄

Advanced PFS:Professional®: Write & File

by Janice M. Gessin

Use this new software to maximum advantage in the corporate environment with *Advanced PFS:Professional®: Write & File*. The PFS:Professional® series offers word processing (Write) and database (File) modules that can be used separately or integrated in various combinations on the IBM® PC. This book addresses each module in a four-part presentation that quickly proceeds from an introduction and overview of program features to useful applications and advanced techniques. Then you'll learn how to integrate PFS:Professional modules for an even greater variety of business tasks, and how to transfer data between PFS:Professional nd other software products. A helpful appendix lists similarities and differences between the original pfs:® series and the PFS:Professional series. This book has been written with the support of the developers, Software Publishing Company.

$16.95 p
0-07-881001-9, 300 pp., 7³/₈ x 9¹/₄

PC Secrets: Tips for Power Performance

by James E. Kelley

Power performance is at your command with these secrets for mastering the PC. This collection of shortcuts and solutions to frustrating and frequently encountered problems gives users of the IBM® PC and PC compatibles the inside edge. James Kelley, author of numerous books on the IBM PC, discloses his secrets for controlling hardware, peripherals, DOS, and applications software. You'll learn tips for keyboard harmonics, display enhancements, controlling fixed disks, managing the printer, and manipulating DOS routines that include batch files, directories and subdirectories, as well as system menus. You'll also find programs that help you use WordStar® and Lotus™ 1-2-3™ to greater advantage. With *PC Secrets*, you don't need to be a technical expert to become a PC power user.

$16.95 p
0-07-881210-0, 224 pp., 7³/₈ x 9¹/₄

PC-DOS Tips & Traps

by Dick Andersen, Janice M. Gessin, Fred Warren, and Jack Rodgers

Solve immediate problems and quickly perform specific business tasks on your IBM® PC or PC-compatible with *PC-DOS Tips & Traps*. Written for everyone using PC-DOS 2.1 or MS-DOS 2.11, Andersen provides an array of tips and discusses frequently encountered traps with their solutions. You'll find a broad range of helpful information from initializing your system and formatting disks, to controlling peripherals, and managing the DOS environment. Throughout the book Andersen shows you how to use the DOS Batch files to design your own commands and automate certain tasks. Tips for using DOS utilities including EDLIN for text editing and DEBUG for programming are also discussed. You'll save time and minimize the chance for error with Andersen's insights on the PC- and MS-DOS® operating systems.

$16.95 p
0-07-881194-5, 250 pp., 7³/₈ x 9¹/₄

Microsoft® Word Made Easy, Second Edition

by Paul Hoffman

Hoffman's top-selling *Microsoft® Word Made Easy* has been revised to cover Microsoft's latest version of this widely used word processing software. Both beginning and experienced users will find a clear presentation of Word's new features, "made easy" for immediate application. Hoffman covers text outlining, spelling correction, hyphenation, creating indexes and tables of contents, and laser printers. Word's new functions, style sheets, windows, and glossaries are described in depth, and you'll find extra tips for using the mail-merge function. In the tradition of Osborne's "Made Easy" series, all techniques are explained with practical hands-on examples and are illustrated with helpful screen displays.

$16.95 p
0-07-881248-8, 300 pp., 7³/₈ x 9¹/₄
AVAILABLE: 8/86

Advanced WordPerfect®: Features & Techniques

by Eric Alderman and Lawrence J. Magid

You can make this word processing software for the IBM® PC and compatibles work above and beyond the usual with *Advanced WordPerfect.®* Written by columnist and consultant Eric Alderman and Los Angeles Times syndicated columnist Lawrence Magid, *Advanced WordPerfect®* brings you application tools and concepts that greatly increase your productivity. After a brief review of basic functions, you'll learn how to apply macros to open, close, and resize windows; make document format changes; even control memo headers. You'll also find out about paragraph numbering and outlining, indexing and building tables of contents, using WordPerfect's mathematical capabilities, setting up printing formats, and integrating WordPerfect™ with other products, such as Lotus® 1-2-3,® dBASE III,® Sidekick,® and ProKey.™ *Advanced WordPerfect®* is the source for ambitious users who want information that exceeds the documentation.

$16.95 p
0-07-881239-9, 300 pp., 7³/₈ x 9¹/₄

Using Lotus® Manuscript™

by William Fletcher

Here's a complete, fast-paced user guide for Lotus® Manuscript™, the speedy, new, IBM® PC-based word processing software from the creators of Lotus® 1-2-3®. This sophisticated document processing package is designed specifically for engineers, scientists, technical writers, and business professionals who are creating lengthy reports. Fletcher quickly leads you from beginning concepts to advanced techniques. You'll learn the details of Manuscript as you follow numerous examples that demonstrate its impressive features: automatic outlining, footnoting, table of contents preparation, and text formatting and fonts for laser printers. You'll also find out how to include equations and tables in your projects, read 1-2-3 files into Manuscript, and use the unabridged dictionary to check spelling.

$18.95p

0-07-881003-5, 350 pp., 7³/₈ x 9¹/₄

Advanced MultiMate® and MultiMate® Advantage™

by Mark Brownstein

Experienced users of MultiMate®, the powerful word processing package for the IBM® PC, get two books in one with this addition to Osborne's "Advanced" series. You'll have a fast-paced tutorial to both MultiMate® and Advantage™ (versions 3.5 and 3.6). High-powered techniques are discussed and illustrated in short applications and examples. Brownstein emphasizes the new features of Advantage, including its networking capabilities; multi-column documents; the On-File™ database program, which simulates an index-card file system; and the GraphLink™ program, which transfers graphics to MultiMate from Lotus® 1-2-3®, Framework®, and other popular software packages. Brownstein, the former editor-in-chief of *Easy Home Computer* magazine, is a free-lance consultant and author.

$17.95p

0-07-881247-X, 325 pp., 7³/₈ x 9¹/₄

AVAILABLE: 9/86

Project Management Using Microcomputers

by Harvey A. Levine

Business professionals in all fields can make informed decisions about the best project management software available for their specific needs with the essential information in this guide. Levine discusses state-of-the-art project management techniques that can be applied to every business and to most computer systems. Beginning with an overview of project management, Levine considers the role of the microcomputer in this application. Various capabilities of project management software are then discussed: resource and cost planning, reporting and graphing, scheduling, and tracking. To give you a better idea of how project management software can be used, Levine divides applications into elementary, intermediate, custom designed, and mass-market categories. Every category offers project management examples, each contributed by an industry expert who discusses the reasons and methods behind the application.

$18.95p

0-07-881221-6, 350 pp., 7³/₈ x 9¹/₄

The Practical Guide to Local Area Networks

by Rowland Archer

Deciding which local area network is right for you doesn't have to be a difficult process. With *The Practical Guide to Local Area Networks,* you'll be prepared to evaluate and select the LAN that's best for your business needs. LAN specialist Rowland Archer guides you through the process of planning your LAN installation, pointing out the advantages and potential pitfalls every step of the way. Archer then applies the criteria he has developed to five of the most popular LANs available for the IBM® PC and compatible computers: 3Com Ethernet®, Corvus Omninet®, Orchid PCnet®, Novell NetWare™, and IBM® PC Network and Token Ring.

$21.95p

0-07-881190-2, 250 pp., 6¹/₂ x 9¹/₄

Micro-to-Mainframe Links

by Ronald F. Kopeck

Here's a book that sorts out all the complex issues involved in linking microcomputers to mainframes for sophisticated, high-powered applications. With *Micro-to-Mainframe Links,* data processing and communications professionals can fully understand the major considerations behind PC-to-mainframe integration. A concise, detailed text thoroughly explains the planning and evaluation process used in determining how PC-to-mainframe linking fits into your office environment. Data transfer, security, and use of existing networks are also discussed. You'll find out about link products and the real and hidden costs of linking, as well as maintenance and service. And you'll learn about monitoring, the safe ways to begin the PC-to-mainframe link by establishing and evaluating tests and measurements. Kopeck, a widely-known consultant and editor of *Micro-to-Mainframe Link News,* draws on his extensive knowledge of this field to bring you the most comprehensive coverage possible.

$18.95p
0-07-881228-3, 300 pp., 7³/₈ x 9¹/₄